MW00586142

The Confounding Island

The Confounding Island

Jamaica and the Postcolonial Predicament

Orlando Patterson

The Belknap Press of Harvard University Press

Cambridge, Massachusetts
London, England
2019

Library of Congress Cataloging-in-Publication Data

Names: Patterson, Orlando, 1940– author.
Title: The confounding island : Jamaica and the postcolonial
predicament / Orlando Patterson.
Description: Cambridge, Massachusetts : The Belknap Press of Harvard
University Press, 2019. | Includes bibliographical references and index.
Identifiers: LCCN 2019015063 | ISBN 9780674988057
Subjects: LCSH: Postcolonialism—Jamaica. | Nationalism and
sports—Jamaica. | Reggae music—Jamaica. | Urban poor—Jamaica. |
Jamaica—Social conditions. | Jamaica—Economic conditions.
Classification: LCC HN223.5 .P37 2019 | DDC 306.097292—dc23
LC record available at https://lccn.loc.gov/2019015063

For Anita
and for Kaia, Barbara, and Rhiannon

But islands can only exist
If we have loved in them.
　　　　—*Derek Walcott*

I shall return again; I shall return
To laugh and love and watch with
　　wonder-eyes
　　　　—*Claude McKay*

Contents

Contents

III. The Failures of Policy and Politicians

The Confounding Island

Introduction

There are few places on earth more confounding than Jamaica. A little island barely the size of Connecticut, it has a larger global profile than countries hundreds of times its size; at times celebrated for the spectacular performances of its stars and the worldwide impact of its cultural creations, it is often condemned for the depravity of its gangsters and racketeers and the failures of its economy. Jamaicans, all too aware and selectively proud of this record, are prone to say, "Wi lickle but wi tallawah," a creole expression meaning "We are little but so mighty."

In global comparisons Jamaica has an unnerving way of ending up within either the best or the worst group of countries. Jamaicans frequently claim that, with over sixteen hundred places of worship, the country has the greatest number of churches per square mile in the world, which suggests a truly God-fearing group of people. Whatever the accuracy of that finding—Bermuda and Malta may have more, in per capita terms—there is little doubt that Jamaicans are in serious fear of God and, even more, Satan, judging by the numbers in attendance on Sundays and Saturdays (both the prime minister and governor general belong to the large and puritanical Seventh-day Adventist denomination) and the fire and brimstone sermons of its fundamentalist preachers. It has also produced what has become a global religion, Rastafarianism, with followers all over Europe, America, and Asia and the high and soothing motto of "peace and love." Nonetheless, it is one of the most violent, reckless, and downright sinful of nations, at one time having the highest homicide rate in the world and for most of this century remaining firmly in the top ten most murderous places.

Its national music, reggae, is globally influential, with its national hero, Bob Marley, arguably one of the world's most recognizable voices, his message of love, hope, and resistance serving as inspiration to people of every faith and culture. Nonetheless, the latest version of reggae, dancehall, celebrates violence, thuggery, homophobia, and sexism to such a degree that several of its best singers have been banned from performing in Europe and the United States. Its track athletes dominate the world and have run the fastest times on record. But off the track, Jamaicans are notorious for being among the slowest people to show up for appointments. Indeed, they take pride in their tardiness, with another telling expression, used with maddening frequency, being "soon come," which can mean anything from an hour to a week.

For all its global excellence in athletics and music, which paradoxically is based not, as many may think, simply on raw talent but on careful institution building, adroit entrepreneurship, and hard work, the island's economic performance, with the exception of its booming tourist industry, has been a dismal failure. Although blessed with one of the richest deposits of bauxite in the world, extraordinary natural beauty both on its beaches and in its lush, soaring mountains, which makes it a paradise for tourists, the island has had stagnant or negative rates of growth since the 1970s. "Soon come" may have something to do with that. But even here the place confounds. To the World Bank (2004), which has expended enormous (unsuccessful) effort trying to turn its economy around, the island presents an inexplicable economic conundrum, which it described in one of its country studies as the "paradox of the 1990s." Understandable, given that throughout that decade and continuing in the twenty-first century, although its growth rate stalled or went negative, its poverty rate kept going down, falling by nearly 50 percent at the same time. This defies all economic logic, and the World Bank has all but given up trying to explain it. Equally perplexing is the fact that after several decades of economic stagnation the island's economy has suddenly come to life under a new generation of young leaders. In 2015 Bloomberg announced that Jamaica's little stock market was the best performing in the world (Fieser 2015), and *Global Banking and Finance* in 2018 called Jamaica the best place in the world to start a business.

But defying economic, social, and medical logic seems to be a specialty of the island, and it is no accident that the term *paradox* appears so often, in both expert and lay attempts to understand the place. To take another example from its demographic history, during the second third of the twentieth century, though it was an impoverished colony in a neglected part of the British Empire, the island's population went through an astonishing demographic transition from medieval-level life expectancy to one on a par with the advanced nations. The demographer James Riley (2005) entitled his work on the subject—what else—*Poverty and Life Expectancy: The Jamaica Paradox*. Life expectancy keeps going up, in spite of chronic violence (the fifth main cause of death), alcoholism (yes, there are likely more rum bars per square mile than anywhere else), and insanely reckless driving. Before she died in 2017 at 117, Violet Brown was the world's oldest living woman. Another Jamaican woman, Merlene

Ottey, was the world's oldest track star, in 2012 still competing in an international meet at the age of fifty-two.

One might think that with so much violence, such poor economic performance, so many head-scratching paradoxes, Jamaicans would be an unhappy lot. Not a chance. In the first World Happiness Report of 2012 (Helliwell, Layard, and Sachs 2012), Jamaica ranked in the top happiest quarter of the 156 countries measured. And while that organization has reported a decline since then, the Britain-based Happy Planet Index (New Economics Foundation 2016) begs to differ, finding Jamaicans, in 2016, to be one of the eleven happiest populations on earth. A Jamaican columnist (Wignall 2012) was understandably led to ask if Jamaicans are happy for the wrong reasons. "Could a mentally disturbed man (read nation) be more happy than a normally adjusted person?" he asked. The fellow had no good answer. What is clear is that Jamaicans imagine themselves to be a very laid-back people. The expression "Jamaica, No Problem," broadcast globally by the island's tourist industry, has been embraced with gusto as a national motto. That Jamaica is among the top ten marijuana-consuming countries in the world (UNODC 2014b) may have something to do with this self-perception—or self-delusion, depending on your point of view. Whatever the explanation, a positive attitude may well be best for a country with so many problems and perplexing contradictions.

As a Jamaican and a historical sociologist, I have pondered Jamaica's problems for most of my adult life. My first academic work (Patterson 1967) explored one major source of its problems: that for nearly two-thirds of the five centuries since its European discovery by Columbus in 1494, Jamaica was a slave society—all the more compelling a factor given that the 183 years of British plantation slavery (1655–1838) may possibly have been the most brutal in the abominable annals of slavery. The British spared no quarter in their extreme exploitation of the island and of the Africans imported as slaves to work the sugar plantations, coffee farms, and cattle pens. For over a century Jamaica was the most lucrative colony in the British Empire, "a Constant Mine, whence Britain draws prodigious riches," according to a contemporary (cited in Burnard 2001), its trade with Britain outstripping that of the American colonies. It was also "the most unequal place on the planet," far more so than the US slave South (Burnard, Panza, and Williamson 2017). As I note in Chapter 1, the economic and physical savagery of the British that made this vast production of wealth possible took an unspeakable toll on the slave population, which, unlike that of America, never reproduced itself. But the Jamaican slave population did not take it passively. Indeed, the level of resistance, which took many forms, was perhaps unparalleled in the history of slavery, with the mighty British colonial army at one time forced to sue for peace before agreeing in a treaty to allow the rebels to form their own state within a state on the island, with its own laws and rulers. There is no similar treaty by a slave-holding class in the history of slavery—or for that matter in the history of empire. My first major academic paper was a study of this ninety-year rebellion (Patterson 1970).

So, this is how modern history began and emerged in Jamaica; that is, after the matter of the genocidal destruction of the once-abundant indigenous Taíno population, which the Spanish accomplished in a mere thirty years. It is a past drenched in blood, like no other place on earth, marked by the swift genocide of the Taínos and the slow-motion genocide of the Africans. What happened during the colonial period, both before and after slavery, is thus critical for any understanding of the island's postcolonial history, and Chapter 1 of this work investigates that subject.

However, this first chapter, like most of the others, attempts more. The fascinating thing about Jamaica and its puzzles is that they not only are interesting in themselves but also pose problems that are of broader and deeper significance, both for the greater postcolonial and developing world and for the social sciences. Thus Chapter 1 is, first, an attempt to explain Jamaica's poor economic performance since independence by way of a close comparison with one of its sister Caribbean islands, Barbados, which has done so much better. The comparison also allows us to resolve one of the most vexing issues in the study of social and economic development: that of the relative significance of institutions and good policies in explaining development. In recent years the institutionalist approach has gained ascendancy among social scientists. However, the Jamaican economist Peter Henry (2013) has used a comparison of the two islands to argue forcefully that good policies trump institutions. In this chapter I push back against Henry in favor of the institutionalist position, especially that of Daron Acemoglu and his collaborators, but with several important qualifications that, I hope, improve it.

Chapter 2, which takes "Why Is Democratic Jamaica So Violent?" as its title, has a similar twofold purpose. It addresses one of the island's greatest problems: its abysmal level of violence. However, tackling this problem allows us to probe an equally troubling issue that is more general: the question of democracy's relation to violence. Thus the subtitle of the chapter: "Revisiting the 'Democratic Peace' Thesis." This is a vexed issue in political science. It is assumed by many that democracy inherently promotes peace—that, indeed, it is premised on the very idea that conflicts can, and should, be resolved amicably through negotiation and peaceful, participatory give and take. The dilemma Jamaica immediately poses is that it has a working democracy that has been vibrant, if more than a little turbulent.

This is not what *The Economist* once called a "phoney democracy," in reference to the growing number of illiberal electoral states (2000). Jamaican democracy is alive and well; people are thoroughly committed to it and play by the rules of the democratic game in all fundamental respects. Jamaica's turnout rate for elections puts the United States and many of the advanced democracies to shame. Furthermore, Jamaican democracy has repeatedly passed the ultimate test of genuine democracies: It has had numerous changes of government resulting from the people's vote. So the question Jamaica poses is quite simply this: Why is so genuine a democracy so utterly violent? Could the two problems be connected? Could it be that democracy, far from being inherently peaceful, is in fact inherently violent? Chapter 2 attempts to answer these questions by probing deeply into the theory of what has been called the "democratic peace thesis," and the answer we arrive at is somewhat disturbing, if not for democracy in the advanced world, most certainly for transitional democracies in postcolonial societies.

In Chapter 3 I take on yet another claim about Jamaica's unusual pattern of development. In an early work, the well-known labor economist Guy Standing argued that Jamaica was unusual, not only among postcolonial societies, but in the development of capitalism, in its male labor force remaining chronically un-proletarianized and, further, in its women being brought into the labor force and proletarianized to a far greater degree than its men. If this were indeed the case, Jamaica would have gone against a pattern of development in the sexual division of labor during the rise of capitalism that labor economists regard as something akin to an iron economic law. This is the finding that it was men who first experienced the disciplining of the capitalist labor force during a period in which women were economically marginalized as their traditional patterns of employment were disrupted, only much later re-entering the labor force as the economy entered a more mature phase of development. As it happens, I had collected a large body of data on the Jamaican postcolonial labor force during the same period that Standing had studied, the early 1970s. This chapter revisits Standing's study and largely unchallenged findings. What I found partly supports Standing's argument regarding the rapid incorporation of women into the labor force but qualifies the finding that men were under-proletarianized. More importantly, I found a far more complex postcolonial system of labor exploitation that had its roots deep in the colonial and slave past of the island.

These first three chapters, constituting Part I, are concerned primarily with the major structural forces that drove the postcolonial economy and political life of Jamaica. Part II, "Three Cultural Puzzles," shifts to a consideration of more cultural processes during the postcolonial period. As I have emphasized elsewhere (Patterson 2014), there can be no rigid separation of the cultural and the structural (read economic and political institutional structures) in the social sciences. In broad terms I mean by "the cultural" the system of schematized knowledge, norms, values, symbols, and rituals unevenly shared by networks of people at different levels of aggregation, from small groups to entire nations. Such knowledge systems never exist in isolation but are in interaction with the physical and social-structural environment acting pragmatically through the agency of individuals. There is, however, a narrower sense in which the term *culture* is used, one preferred by economists and political analysts when they do use it, namely, that which makes for distinctiveness in a given group. In this sense, someone speaking of Jamaican "culture" means that which makes Jamaica distinctive; or at the level of the company, that which makes an organization such as IBM or AT&T distinctive. I use the term in both senses in this part of the work.

Chapter 4 examines what is likely the most confounding puzzle about Jamaica to non-Jamaicans all over the world. How can a little nation of less than three million people outperform the rest of the world in sprinting? How and why, in terms of Olympic medals won, can Jamaica best countries hundreds of times its population size and wealth, including its former colonial overlord, Britain? Not only do its professional runners repeatedly beat those of mighty America, which prides itself on its long tradition of athletic excellence, but Jamaica's youngest high school runners, many hailing from impoverished rural villages, also annually outperform the best-trained Americans in the Penn Relays. The all-too-tempting answer, that Jamaicans are endowed with a gene for speed, has been shown by the most rigorous scientific studies to be without foundation. If it's not in their genes, then, the answer must be social and cultural, and I argue for just such a conjunction.

The social factor is a demographic one already mentioned, that Jamaicans are the beneficiaries of a major public health campaign that culminated in a stunningly fast health transition, the result being that, in spite of the island's poverty during the late colonial period, it was peopled by some of the healthiest young bodies anywhere. A distinctive cultural tradition of track athleticism took full advantage of this demographic resource. This is an example of "culture" in the narrower sense mentioned earlier. To elaborate, this aspect of culture may be described as a pattern of institutionalized selection bias. The way in which culture works to give a group its distinctive qualities is by creating a strong preference for particular patterns of beliefs, ideas, or behaviors. That is, it efficiently identifies, selects, and nurtures the specific behavioral or ideational trait. This trait can be anything—

mathematics, dancing, yoga, spiritualism, painting, classical music, beer drinking, whatnot. The important point is that the behavior or belief may have nothing to do with the distribution of genetic talent in the population. There is no reason to believe that European Jews had a greater proportion of genetic talent for mathematics than non-Jews, or that the German population was better endowed with genes for classical musical composition than the British, with their lackluster history in this domain. Rather, there develops a strong, sometimes obsessive bias in favor of finding and nurturing traits of a certain kind.

Much the same argument applies in explaining why Jamaica, with its population of 2.8 million, outperforms India, with its population of 1.5 billion, in sprinting. It is highly likely that India has the same proportion of talented sprinters as Jamaica, which means that the pool of sprint talent is 460 times greater in India than in Jamaica. However, when an Indian peasant sees a child running swiftly after a ball, he sees a potential messenger or maybe a cricketer; a professional sprinter is far from the first thought. When a Jamaican peasant father sees a fast-running child he immediately thinks of Usain Bolt, and the kid's fate is sealed. How such a virtuous cycle or bias comes about, and how it takes advantage of the serendipitous presence of a population of unusually healthy bodies—this is the stuff of cultural and institutional history, which I offer in this chapter.

Chapter 5, which has to do with violence at cricket matches, explores the workings of culture in the broader sense mentioned above. The puzzle here is why Jamaicans (and West Indians more broadly) engaged in a series of riots during international test matches with Britain. More particularly, why did these riots take place only during the late colonial and early postcolonial period? And why only against Britain, especially after the British had eagerly left or expressed their intention of closing up the colonial shop as expeditiously as they could. I show that these riots had less to do with the British visiting teams and more to do with the nature of the societies of Jamaica and other West Indian nations, especially the gross inequalities on the island and the ways in which these inequalities were expressed in terms of racial and color values. In the course of this analysis I introduce a concept of broader significance for cultural inquiry, what I called a "transubstantive symbol," one that stands for and actualizes itself. The cricket match, I argue, was symbolically constitutive of every tension in Jamaican society, but under normal circumstances this factor remained dormant, especially if the home team was winning a given game or—at the very least—was not being beaten too badly. At such times culture symbolically canalized or even controlled people's anxieties and resentments. All this changed whenever the home team was being whipped by the visitors, when the country's heroes were being devastated. At such times the symbolic structure of the game was totally transformed. Instead of the game symbolizing the society, the society would symbolize the game; the game would literally become the society. This is culture in action, explosive action. All the pent-up rage, humiliation, other-hatred, and self-hatred of a brutally iniquitous society, built up over three hundred years of colonial rule and six years of neocolonial mismanagement in which only the new elite, the already privileged bourgeoisie, appear to have benefited, came to a head and, like a putrid sore, burst into uncontrolled violence, becoming what Frantz Fanon (1961) once described as a "cleansing force" for the decolonizing native.

Another great puzzle that Jamaicans present to the world is the astonishing success of their popular music, especially reggae, discussed in Chapter 6. When, near the end of the last century, *Time* magazine named the album *Exodus* by Bob Marley and the Wailers the greatest album of the century, not many aficionados of popular music were very surprised. Thirty years after his death Marley is still one of the most recognizable voices and faces in the world. However, a large number of artists from the island are world famous: Desmond Dekker, Jimmy Cliff, Peter Tosh, Toots Hibbert, Sean Paul, Buju Banton. What is less understood is that, even before reggae, Jamaican music had had an outsized influence on global popular music. Thus the first album in the history of music to sell over a million copies is a collection of folk songs and folk-inspired compositions hailing not from Europe or America or Asia, but from Jamaica, featuring the mento peasant music of the island in the form of "The Banana Boat Song" (also called "Day Oh!"), sung by the Jamaican-raised Harry Belafonte.

In explaining the enormous reach of reggae, we are led, once again, to the broader problem of global cultural significance. This is the question of whether globalization is leading to a homogenization, or more specifically Westernization and Americanization, of the world's cultures. Many have expressed such fears, not least of all the celebrated German scholar Theodor Adorno and the eminent folklorist Alan Lomax. I argue strongly against this view, in line with a group of scholars who have emphasized the principle of glocalization, a mode of analysis that blends attention to both the macro (global) and micro (local) aspects of cultural artifacts, in the interactions of Western and other musical traditions around the world. Far from homogenizing the local musics of the world, the diffusion of musical traditions from one part of the world to others has generated a vast amount of musical creativity, in which indigenous traditions are hybridized with foreign elements to produce wholly new and exciting creations.

Jamaican reggae music is a near-perfect illustration of this process of glocalization. Under the impact of black American music, its musicians created a vibrant new music, ska, which soon mutated into what has become known as reggae. But reggae, in turn, was to spread abroad, especially back to the United States, where it was instrumental in generating the secondary glocalization process that culminated in hip-hop; the innovative DJ Kool Herc (Clive Campbell), a Jamaican immigrant, is acknowledged as one of its founders. Hip-hop and reggae continued to mutually influence each other and, in turn, influence other popular musics of the world in a global wave of tertiary glocalization. In addition, reggae and one of its important mutations, dancehall, continue to generate other secondary glocalizations in Britain, continental Europe, Africa, and Asia. I end this chapter by noting that this happy outcome remains mainly true of popular creations at the proletarian musical and artistic level. The same cannot be said of what happens at the bourgeois and macroeconomic levels of global contact. Here globalization often does lead to Westernization, and especially Americanization, and such premature modernizations have often proven fatal for the sustainable economic development of postcolonial societies in the Caribbean and elsewhere.

The two chapters that make up Part III, "The Failures of Policy and Politicians," focus on the politics and policy of the 1970s, generally considered the most critical and damaging period of postcolonial Jamaica. For eight years, between 1972 and 1980, I was special advisor for social policy and development to Prime Minister Michael Manley and served on the nation's Technical Advisory Council. Those were heady days. The island's first decade of postcolonial development appeared at first to have been a great success, certainly when measured in macroeconomic GDP terms, which showed a robust growth rate of 4.5 percent. But, as in many other countries at that time, the national mean income data bore little resemblance to the lived experience of the mass of the population. As discussed in Chapter 3, far from declining, there was a massive increase in the level of unemployment, accompanied by serious disruption in the agricultural sector; tremendous growth of the urban population, nearly all of it in the wretched slums that circled the shorelines of Kingston; soaring inflation rates; and an escalation in crime and violence.

Although I was involved with a range of policy programs, my work was focused on the alleviation of the problems of the urban poor. I had been engaged with the urban poor from my high school days, when I lived for over two years in the Jones Town (then known as Jones Pen) neighborhood, which bordered on the notorious Denham Town and Trench Town, the latter made famous in the lyrics of Bob Marley. Later, as an undergraduate, I did research on the sex workers of East Kingston, on unemployed youth, and on the newly emerging Rastafarian religious group, having been present at the moment of their millenarian crisis in 1959, when the ship of their god, Haile Selassie, failed to turn up to take them back to the paradise of Ethiopia, as they had fervently been led to believe. These experiences provided the materials for my first novel, *The Children of Sisyphus* (Patterson 1964), which was written largely when I was an undergraduate and which has subsequently become a required text in the high schools of the island.

As I explain in the introduction to Chapter 7, the period that I worked among the urban poor of Kingston coincided with a marked shift among economists of development and members of the international policy community toward an emphasis on the basic needs of the poor. This came from a realization that the policies of the postwar era had had little positive impact on the poor and, instead, had worsened their condition. Interestingly, a similar renewed emphasis currently animates economists of the developing world, best expressed in the "poor economics" writings of Abhijit Banerjee and Esther Duflo. The "basic needs" approach of the 1970s dovetailed perfectly with the egalitarian emphasis of Michael Manley's democratic socialist program. When I explained it in detail to Manley, he became so enthusiastic about it that he instructed me to develop a similar program for his own constituency, located in the low-income area of south-central Kingston. The centerpiece of that program was an abandonment of the previous emphasis on the building of housing estates as the way to help the urban poor—a hopeless, wasteful, and thoroughly iniquitous approach that resulted in the displacement of thousands from the neighborhoods on which they depended for mutual support in favor of a chosen few who were politically connected to the ruling party. Instead, I set about implementing an upgrading program that focused on improvements in sanitation, sewage clearance, water supply, infant day care, public health, home repairs, and aid for the destitute, especially the elderly. The result, it was made clear from the beginning, would be a neighborhood that still looked like a slum but that would be far more livable, providing the basics of human habitation and a community organization directed by local leaders.

My program failed, even with the initial support of the prime minister, who, under pressure from local leaders, eventually gave in to the demand for a housing plan. I was most surprised by the reasons for my failure and by the people who worked behind my back to undercut the program, many of them loud-mouthed advocates of the urban poor in public. Reflecting several years later on the reasons for the failure of the program, I drew several lessons, which I argue are relevant to all attempts to help the poor in the developing countries of the world to this day.

Finally, I come to what has been, and remains for me, one of the most difficult experiences to write about: my relationship with and view of Michael Manley. It is presented, indirectly, in Chapter 8, which I originally wrote as a foreword to his daughter's memoir. I first met Michael Manley, along with his father, the great and much-revered founder of the Jamaican nation, Norman Manley, when I was an undergraduate at the University of the West Indies. We stayed in touch during my graduate studies and subsequent faculty appointment at the London School of Economics. It was partly to join forces with him in opposition to the governing Jamaica Labor Party that I quit the faculty of the LSE and took up a position at the University of the West Indies in Kingston. By 1970 I despaired that the People's National Party, as Manley's party was called, would ever win, in light of the growing authoritarianism and corruption of the ruling party, which in 1968 had resorted to the expulsion of a popular lecturer (and friend of mine) named Walter Rodney from the island because of his association with the urban poor. When I was prevented—at gunpoint—from leaving the campus for my home after a demonstration on Rodney's behalf, I decided that the time for loyalty was over and that the time to exit had finally arrived. I went to Harvard as a visiting scholar in 1970 and the following year accepted its offer of a tenured professorship. Not long after my move to Harvard, however, the political tide turned, and two years later, against all expectation, Manley's party won the elections, thanks in good part to the strong support of the urban poor and the reggae musicians. Manley wanted me to return home, but the pull of scholarship and family responsibilities made that difficult. Instead, I divided my time between Harvard and his office. The program we pursued was called, perhaps too grandly, democratic socialism. It was, in fact, straightforward social democracy modeled almost in its entirety on the program of the British Labour Party and other left-of-center parties in Western Europe. That, however, was not how it appeared to the island's bourgeoisie or for that matter the American CIA, during the height of the Cold War and, soon after, the adventures of Fidel Castro.

Our failures, however, were largely self-inflicted. We tried to move too far too fast. Our problem during the first term was not a lack of funds—tall, articulate, and unusually handsome, Manley cut such a grand figure on the world stage with his rhetoric of a new world order and leadership of the Non-Aligned Movement that the enchanted social democratic leaders of Europe were willing to prop us up with all the funds we needed. (That changed in the second term, when the economy nearly collapsed under a massive balance of payments crisis.) Our problem was an inability to follow through with the numerous projects we instituted, some of them half-baked, nearly all lacking in capable leadership. The tragedy of radical change is that you can't implement it without able managers; but such reform, accompanied by reckless revolutionary rhetoric, is exactly what is guaranteed to send the bureaucrats fleeing, especially when it was a virtual mark of status among them to have a visa to (and bank account in) not-so-distant America. Monetary capital flight was swiftly followed by human capital flight.

However, the movement's biggest problem may well have been Manley himself. It was a sight to behold him, the charismatic leader par excellence, holding a crowd spellbound in rapture and adulation. On the stage, transformed by his own dazzling rhetoric, he was given to talk of demolishing capitalism brick by brick. And yet, he could be quite distant in personal interactions unless he was making an effort to charm you into adopting his point of view. He loved the people, but he was rarely at ease with ordinary people. He was at heart an intellectual; my most animated discussions with him were about ideas rather than the details of the policies I was involved with. His public life was one of utmost propriety, honesty, and integrity; unlike nearly every Third World leader of his day (and this day) he left office with less money than he had had when he entered office. Indeed, he left office nearly broke. But his private life was marked by ruthless selfishness and sexual exploitation. With the exception of two of his five wives—the beautiful third one who died young in his arms, the older fifth one in whose arms he died—he broke the heart of nearly every one of the many wives and lovers who succumbed to his irresistible charms. Alas, he was an enigma also to his daughters.

I was so perplexed by Manley that I have never been able to write directly about him. It was not until his eldest daughter, Rachel, a talented memoirist and novelist, honored me with the request to write the foreword to *Slipstream: A Daughter Remembers,* her revealing memoir of her father's dying days, that I found the will to write about him. I was able to do so only after absorbing the hauntingly beautiful prose that carried her memories of life in the ebbing "slipstream" of her father. I did not have much to add to her revelations, really, but what little I did is about all I ever wish to say about the man who so confounded us.

I

Explaining Postcolonial Failure

1

Why Has Jamaica Trailed Barbados on the Path to Sustained Growth?

The Role of Institutions, Colonialism, and Cultural Appropriation

The geographer David Lowenthal (1978) once noted that the Caribbean, somewhat like the Mediterranean, with its vast range of social and economic systems in a relatively small area of the globe, constitutes a veritable laboratory of natural experiments for the social scientist. This chapter takes advantage of one such natural experiment, a comparison of the divergent paths to development pursued by Barbados and Jamaica. The exercise has two objectives. One is the substantive aim of understanding why Jamaica has performed so badly in its effort at economic development. A close comparison with its Caribbean counterpart, Barbados, which has done so much better, offers one path to understanding this problem. The comparison also allows us to accomplish a second goal, which is resolving one of the most vexing issues in the study of social and economic development: assessing the relative significance of institutions and good policies in explaining development.

In recent years the institutionalist approach has gained ascendancy among social scientists. However, the Jamaican economist Peter Henry (2013) used a comparison of the two islands to argue forcefully that good policies trump institutions. In this chapter I push back against Henry in favor of the institutionalist position, especially that of Daron Acemoglu, Simon Johnson, and James A. Robinson, but with several important qualifications that, I hope, improve the quality of insights available to those interested in the field. Like all the other chapters in the book, then, this chapter, in untangling the confounding puzzle of Jamaica, contributes to a resolution of broader problems in the development of postcolonial societies.

Institutions versus Good Policies: Debate and Definition

Following the "perceived failure" of earlier explanations of economic growth by economists and other social scientists, several competing explanations have emerged in recent years (Engerman and Sokoloff 2008: 119). At one end of a spectrum of explanations has been a growing emphasis on institutions as the major source of growth. As the leading proponents of this position write: "Countries with better 'institutions,' more secure property rights, and less distortionary policies will invest more in physical and human capital, and will use these factors more efficiently to achieve a greater level of income" (Acemoglu, Johnson, and Robinson 2001: 1369; see also Acemoglu and Robinson 2012: 45–69; Evans 2005; Rodrik, Subramanian, and Trebbi 2004). Contesting this view, at the other end, are those who emphasize good policies, focusing on investment in physical and human capital as the key to successful development, and contending further that authoritarian regimes that pursue such policies are just as likely to achieve growth as democratic ones (Barro 1997; Przeworski et al. 2000; Glaeser et al. 2004; Henry 2013). Actually, the critical distinction between the two camps is more one of causal priority, since all agree that effective institutions and policies are both necessary for growth. However, institutionalists argue that getting the institutions right is a prerequisite for growth and, further, that historical factors are critical in explaining which countries initially got it right in the postcolonial period, whereas the policy advocates claim that successful growth, even when initiated by authoritarian regimes and regardless of the colonial past, will inevitably yield the right institutions.

Between these two ends of the spectrum are scholars who contend that "institutions matter, but they are influenced by the political and economic environment. Institutions must change as circumstances change to permit growth to be maintained" (Engerman and Sokoloff 2008). They argue, further, that different kinds of institutions may substitute for each other and that there is no compelling evidence that a particular set of institutions is required for capitalism to flourish (Przeworski et al. 2000). Most important, they emphasize the role of culture, geography, and natural endowments and argue that the interaction between these factors and institutions is complex and reciprocal (Engerman and Sokoloff 1991, 2002, 2008). This approach augments rather than detracts from the institutionalist position, especially that of Acemoglu, Johnson, and Robinson, and is in line with the sociohistorical analysis presented below.

But what exactly are institutions? Economists tend to take a narrow view of institutions, so it will be useful to begin with a brief statement of what, as a historical and comparative sociologist, I mean by the term. Institutions are durable structures of knowledge that define the rules and expectations of recurrent behavior. They range from weakly sanctioned, intermittent interactions (such as ritualized greetings) to formally sanctioned, continuous networks of rules, roles, and activities designed to achieve specific goals, such as organizations. Nearly all institutions involve formal and informal norms and are efficient to the degree that the two are smoothly coupled (Brinton and Nee 2002; North 1990; Douglas 1986). An important aspect of institutions is institutional strength. Formal institutional rules may or may not be enforced and, instead of stably taking root, are often contested, violated, and changed (Levitsky and Murillo 2009).

There are two additional features of institutions, strongly emphasized by Chang (2006). One is the importance of distinguishing form from function, which involves recognizing that the same institution may serve different ends and, conversely, that several institutions may achieve similar outcomes. While not neglecting form, Chang suggests a greater emphasis on function. Second, there can be more than one tradition in a country's culture and institutions (Chang 2006: 9). This is important to remember when dealing with heterogeneous societies such as the non-Hispanic Caribbean.

Central to the argument I will be making in this chapter are institutional learning and practice. Douglass North (1990) used the analogy of games to distinguish institutions as rules of the game from the players or organizations implementing these rules, which leads to the issue of how competently the institutional game is played. Drawing on cognitive science, he and Mantzavinos (Mantzavinos and North 2004) argued that institutions are, in external terms, "shared behavioral regularities or shared routines within a population," while internally "they are nothing more than shared mental models or shared solutions to recurrent problems of social interaction." Organizations and their members are the players of the institutional game who must learn both the formal and informal pragmatic rules of interaction in order to achieve desired goals.

A distinction from cognitive science greatly clarifies this: that between declarative and procedural knowledge (Patterson 2014). The former refers to our knowledge of facts, the latter to know-how or skills, defined as "the sequences of interrelated operations that transform, store, retrieve and make inferences based on declarative knowledge" (Smith 1994). Declarative knowledge can be learned verbally, whereas procedural knowledge is learned only through observation and practice; it is, for example, the difference between knowing what a bicycle is and does and how to ride one. As Grzegorz Kolodko has noted, "institutions are not only built, promulgated and decreed, but also understood and learnt," and "this learning process, even if very actively pursued, must be gradual and lengthy." Extrapolating from the transition experience of post-communist Eastern Europe, he adds: "To be able to follow the rules of the market game, one needs an adequate knowledge, which may not always be acquired from textbooks or from other actors, *but must be learnt by experience*" (Kolodko 2006: 11, emphasis added; see also Mantzavinos 2001: chaps. 5–9). Or, as several sociologists succinctly put it: "institutional effects unfold over time, sometimes a great deal of time and . . . these temporal effects are cumulative" (Gerring et al. 2005: 325). In addition to learning through interaction, playing the institutional game is also facilitated by their "enforcement characteristics" (79), which, along with competition, can reduce transaction costs in the economic domain. With regard to Chang's emphasis on institutional functions, I suggest that the effectiveness of institutional functioning may largely be a function of how well institutional actors have learned to play the institutional game.

Shared learning of an institution at both the declarative and procedural levels will be part and parcel of the path-dependent process that emerges at critical junctures in a society's development. Critical junctures are, as Giovanni Capoccia noted, "moments in which uncertainty as to the future of an institutional arrangement allows for political agency and choice to play a decisive causal role in setting an institution on a certain path of development, a path that then persists over a long period of time." During this period of uncertainty, different options or pathways are possible: "Antecedent conditions define the range of institutional alternatives available to decision makers but do not determine the alternative chosen; one of these options is selected; and its selection generates a long-lasting institutional legacy" (Capoccia 2015). Acemoglu and Robinson have shown that in comparing two societies over time, small differences in the antecedent conditions of otherwise quite similar societies (say, early nineteenth-century Jamaica and Barbados) may become extremely consequential for future paths of institutional development as a result of exogenous shocks which disrupt the existing socioeconomic and political balance *and* the choices made by agents to cope with the disruption (2012: 101–103). The outcomes are contingent and unpredictable, "shaped by the weight of history" (Acemoglu and Robinson 2012: 110), but once an institutional path is established it tends to become internally self-reinforcing and externally reinforced. Mantzavinos and North suggest that there are "increasing returns of an institutional framework" insofar as "once the problem solutions are learned by agents, they are unconsciously applied each time similar problems arise" (2004: 81).

The Colonial Origin of Comparative Development Argument and Its Critics

The basic argument of Acemoglu, Johnson, and Robinson, or "AJR" as they are sometimes called (2001), begins with the observation that there was wide variation in the kinds of colonial societies established by Europeans, which had important consequences for the kinds of institutions they established. At one extreme, Europeans established settlement colonies, such as the United States, Canada, and New Zealand, where they replicated the institutions of the home country; at the other, they established largely exploitative colonies in which the main goal was to extract resources to be sent to the metropolitan country. The type of colonization they pursued, and hence their institutional transmissions, depended on the feasibility of settlement, which was largely determined by the mortality rate of the early colony. In simplest terms, they hypothesized that "settler mortality affected settlements; settlements affected early institutions; and early institutions persisted and formed the basis of current institutions" (Acemoglu, Johnson, and Robinson 2001: 1373). The significance of the historical record is that it neatly gets around the problem of endogeneity that besets most attempts to explain current economic outcomes in terms of current institutional performance, since there is no easy way of figuring out what the causal direction is. What is needed is a source of exogenous variation in institutions if the current effects of those institutions are to be properly estimated. Early settler mortality, they argue, provides a powerful instrument in estimating the effects of current institutions (measured mainly by an index of government protection against expropriation); it correlates highly with current per capita income, but the relationship is mediated almost entirely by colonial institutional history. This now-seminal paper has survived nearly all attempts to poke holes in it. The analysis took account of all possible alternate factors that may have correlated with settler mortality and economic outcomes—climate, disease, the identity of the main colonizer, soil quality, ethnicity, and even legal origin (civil vs. common law)—and found that none undermined their results. Thus, others have argued that the same diseases that accounted for variation in European settlement may well continue to account today for low economic outcomes (Bloom and Sachs 1998), but this was shown not to be the case (Acemoglu, Johnson, and Robinson 2001: 1391–1393). Glaeser et al. argued that the most important thing the Europeans brought with them were "themselves, and therefore their know-how and human capital" (2004: 21). However, it is hard to imagine how this initial human capital persisted other than through durable educational institutions.

By far the most important critique of the AJR thesis is that authored by the economist Peter Henry, whose line of attack deployed the divergent postcolonial economic performance of Jamaica and Barbados, to which I now turn.

Henry's Critique of AJR Using the Barbados-Jamaica Comparison

Henry, following on an earlier study with Miller (Henry and Miller 2009), boldly claims that a comparison of the post-independence development record of Barbados and Jamaica "throws cold water on this [AJR] theory" (Henry 2013: 23). His basic argument is that, as ex-British colonies, the two islands "inherited virtually identical institutions: the English language, Westminster parliamentary democracy, constitutional protection of private property, English common law, and the Anglican Church for good measure" (Henry 2013: 23). In addition, the comparison would seem to offer a natural control for several other crucial factors: their populations are both predominantly of African ancestry; both shared a similar history of the Atlantic slave trade and plantation slavery; and both are blessed with near-perfect tourism resources—sand, sea, and sun. In addition, Jamaica is well endowed with bauxite, the ore that produces aluminum, which makes their different development trajectories even more puzzling. Henry further claims that the two islands began the independence era with similar standards of living.

However, he continues, if we fast-forward to the present, we find dramatic differences in the economic performance of the two islands, as Figure 1.1 shows.[1] Beginning in 1960 (the eve of independence for both countries: Jamaica in 1962, Barbados in 1966) with per capita incomes of $8,666 for Barbados and $4,960 for Jamaica (both in constant 2011 US dollars), Barbados by 2000 had a real per capita GDP of $22,694 compared with Jamaica's $5,819, almost four times greater. Since then, the per capita GDP of Barbados has declined in the face of harsh external shocks to its economy, especially that caused by the Great Recession of 2008, to which it was more susceptible because of its greater global exposure. Even so, its per capita GDP is still more than twice that of Jamaica. Per capita GDP, as is well known, is a limited gauge of a nation's true standard of living. But on most other major social and economic indices Barbados also stands well ahead of Jamaica and indeed ahead of nearly all of the Caribbean and Latin America. Its score on the Human Development Index (a composite of life expectancy, educational attainment, and living standards) for 2017 places it in the group of very high human development, far above Jamaica, and much the same holds for other indices: labor force participation, unemployment, literacy, and so on (see Table 1.1 and Figure 1.2). Of special note is the stark difference in homicide rate. In recent

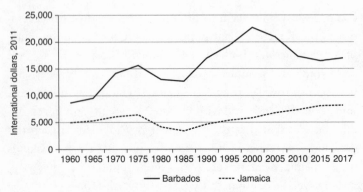

Figure 1.1. Real GDP per capita in Barbados and Jamaica, 1960–2017

Data source: Calculated from Penn World Tables 9.0 for years 1960–2010; from World Bank database for 2010–2017.

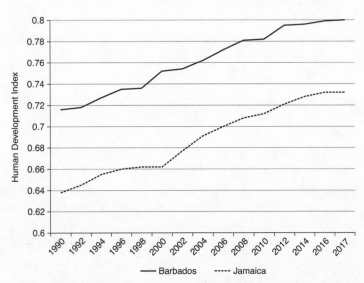

Figure 1.2. Human Development Index for Barbados and Jamaica, 1990–2017

Data source: Calculated from UNDP, Human Development Data, 1990–2017, Statistical Updates 2018.

Table 1.1. Some Social and Economic Indicators for Jamaica and Barbados, 2017

Indicator	Barbados	Jamaica	Description of Indicator
Human development score	0.80 Rank: 58 of 189 countries	0.73 Rank: 97 of 189 countries	Composite of life expectancy, education, living standard
Real GDP per capita (World Bank)	$16,978	$8,095	In constant 2011 international dollars
Public debt as % of GDP	157.3	101.0	Total internal and external government debt as a percentage of annual GDP
Unemployment rate	10.1	12.2	% of unemployed persons in labor force seeking work
Life expectancy at birth	75.9	76	Average years newborn expected to live, at birth-year mortality rate
Health expenditure per capita, 2015	$1,160	$294	Sum of public and private health expenditures as a ratio of total population
Mean years of schooling	10.6	9.8	Average completed years of schooling for those twenty-five years old and older
Literacy rate	99.7% (2008)	88.7% (2016)	Population fifteen years old and older who can read/write/understand a simple sentence on everyday life
Gender Inequality Index	0.284 Rank: 60 of 160 countries	0.412 Rank: 95 of 160 countries	Reflects inequalities in reproductive health, political empowerment, and economic activity Lower is better
Homicide rate	10.9	55	Homicides per 100,000 persons
Global Entrepreneurship Index	33.6 Rank: 55 of 137 countries	22.21 Rank: 89 of 137 countries	Identifies policies and programs promoting growth
Political Rights Index (2018)	1	2	Higher is better 1=Best on 1–7 Score
Civil Liberties Index (2018)	1	3	1=Best on 1–7 Score

Sources: World Bank, *World Development Indicators*; UNDP World Development Report 2018; IMF Country Profiles, Barbados, Jamaica; various global-index development organizations.

decades Jamaica has seen some of the worst crime rates in the world—55 per 100,000 in 2017, over five times that of Barbados, at 10.9 per 100,000—the total cost of which the World Bank estimated at 3.7 percent of GDP in 2001, with a generally disastrous effect on business and social well-being (World Bank 2004: 115–139).

Henry explained these differences primarily in terms of the economic policies pursued by the two governments, reflected especially in their different responses to the oil price shocks of 1973 and 1990. He argued that the failed democratic-socialist policies of the Manley regime in Jamaica between 1972 and 1980 delivered a severe blow to the Jamaican economy, from which it has never quite recovered (see Stephens and Stephens 1986), while Barbados not only recovered earlier from the oil shocks of the early seventies but, faced with the later oil crisis of 1990, also made "disciplined" choices involving its trade unions, government, and private sector. These "disciplined policy choices," he argued, were generally in keeping with the free-market, neoliberal policy reforms prescribed by the US Treasury, the International Monetary Fund, and the World Bank, sometimes known as the Washington Consensus for growth that came to prominence in the 1980s. I do not have the space here to get into the details of these policies. In any event, I do not dispute that policy differences play an important role in explaining different economic outcomes; no institutionalist does so. Both are essential for growth. The important questions, however, are why the Barbadian government was able to make the "disciplined" choices that it did and what role its colonial past, as well as its past and present institutional structures, played in enabling these policy choices and actions.

An important element of Henry's critique is the assumption that both islands began their postcolonial period under similar

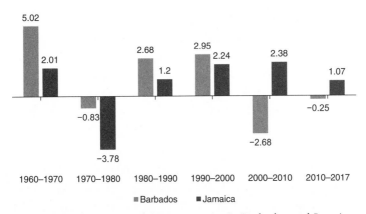

Figure 1.3. Change in real GDP per capita in Barbados and Jamaica, 1960–2017

Data source: Calculated from Penn World Tables 9.0 for years 1960–2010; from World Bank data bank for 2010–2017.

social and economic conditions. A closer look at the economic and institutional performance of the two economies since independence tells a more complex story. The Penn data I used to calculate growth rates (see Figure 1.3) shows that Barbados outperformed Jamaica in every decade up to 2000; to the degree that growth reflects better policies, this would seem to support Henry's argument.

World Bank data on the policy performance and institutional effectiveness of these two countries, however, seem to cut both ways in regard to the relative importance of institutions and policies. Figure 1.4 charts the World Bank's most recent indicators of policy effectiveness and institutional quality in the two countries in addition to Latin America and the entire Caribbean. The chart offers equally strong support for the institutional argument. Barbados's institutional strengths are truly remarkable. Not only does it far outrank Jamaica and all the other states of Latin

America and the Caribbean, but on two indicators—not shown in the figure—it outranks the major OECD countries (mainly Western Europe, North America, Japan, and Australia).

Although Henry does not take account of these data, his most likely response to them would be to cite the endogeneity problem mentioned earlier. He could easily argue that these differences are the *result* of the "disciplined policy decisions" made by Barbadian leaders since independence: good policies, after all, lead to good institutions. We are therefore forced to return to the starting point of the modern postcolonial development era and ask whether his claims of institutional similarity and an even starting point hold up.

Two important indicators that immediately raise questions about his claim of initial similarity are found at the end of the colonial period. The first is a statistic for 1960 (two years before

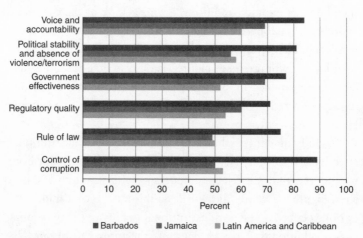

Figure 1.4. World Bank governance indicators for Barbados, Jamaica, and Latin America and the Caribbean, 2017

Data source: Worldwide Governance Indicators (2018), World Bank, available at http://info.worldbank.org/governance/wgi/#reports, accessed January 15, 2019.

Jamaica achieved independence, six years before Barbados did) already noted (see Figure 1.1). Barbados began the period of independence with a 57 percent higher per capita GDP: $8,666 purchasing power parity (PPP) in 2005 US$, compared with Jamaica's figure of $4,960. (Using the nominal income comparison favored by Henry, I calculate that the Barbadian per capita GDP was already 53 percent higher than that of Jamaica's, $3,395 US versus $2,208.) That difference of $3,706 (in 2011 US$) was considerable; it meant the difference between the poor living in shantytown hovels (then rapidly growing in Jamaica) and the tidy "chattel houses" found all over Barbados; between children going to bed hungry in Jamaica and moderately fed in Barbados; between resentful Jamaican workers feeling exploited and ready to sabotage their workplace and Barbadian workers feeling that they were at least receiving a livable wage (compare the findings of Carter 1997 and Dann 1984, to which I shall return). To be sure, initial per capita income at the start of the independence era (or any specified period, for that matter) does not necessarily predict later growth outcomes (Glaeser et al. 2004: 25). Nonetheless, it does strongly suggest that there were factors during the colonial period that led to this important GDP difference.

The second important indicator on the eve of independence, one that was later to be of enormous cumulative importance, was the striking difference in educational attainment inherited from the colonial past. As Figure 1.5 shows, the average Barbadian in 1960 already had 1.5 more years of schooling than the average Jamaican, a reflection of the fact that the Barbadian pre-independence government was spending 2.3 times more per student than was the Jamaican government in 1960. As I will show in greater detail, the nature and extent of literacy rates differed substantially in the mid-1940s, when more detailed census data on both islands first became available. Glaeser and colleagues

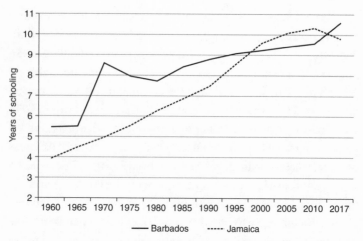

Figure 1.5. Mean years of schooling for population age fifteen and over in Barbados and Jamaica, 1960–2017

Data source: Barro-Lee Data Set for years 1960–2010 for population age fifteen and over, World Bank; UNDP data on educational attainment for year 2017.

have pointed out that "educational investment a century ago is a strong predictor of the level of economic development today" (Glaeser et al. 2004: 23). And AJR have noted that spending on education constitutes one of the most important mechanisms of institutional persistence: "If agents make irreversible investments that are complementary to a particular set of institutions, they will be more willing to support them, making these institutions persist. . . . For example, agents who have invested in human and physical capital will be in favor of spending money to enforce property rights, while those who have less to lose may not be" (Acemoglu, Johnson, and Robinson 2001: 1377; see also Acemoglu 1995: 17–33).

The striking differences in these two leading indicators are consistent with the findings of two major economic studies, conducted several years before the end of the colonial era. The Oxford economist K. H. Straw (1953: 8), in a thorough analysis of the Barbadian economy in 1951, concluded that the island's "natural resources are well-developed and there is no urgent demand for capital equipment to expand primary production" and that "Barbados cannot be compared with the underdeveloped countries of Africa or the East," as it was already so far ahead of the game. In striking contrast, a detailed study of the structure and growth of the Jamaican economy in 1952 found "a vicious circle of national poverty resulting from low productivity; low productivity resulting from (mainly) the small amount of capital available for use in combination with human effort; and this small amount of capital itself resulting from low income and, consequently, a low saving rate" (Thorne 1955: 96).

We are therefore led to ask, what does the socioeconomic history of the two islands tell us, especially with regard to colonial policy as well as institution building? Given the broad similarities in their histories, was there a critical moment when the existing differences, combined with fateful decisions in response to some external shock, initiated divergent institutional pathways that would lead to different outcomes on the eve of independence that favored greater postcolonial performance for Barbados?

Another, even more successful economy on the other side of the world urges us to take the colonial past seriously in attempting to unravel the mystery of postcolonial economic development, namely Korea. Atul Kohli has argued that "a significant component of the explanation for why countries traverse different developmental paths lies in their colonial heritage" (1999: 135). He surmises that the reason that scholars of development have failed to recognize this is because of "the tendency to homogenize the antidevelopmental nature of all colonialism." He then demonstrates how, for all its brutality, Japanese colonialism in Korea left a deep "architectonic" impact on Korea that substantially contributed to its postcolonial development, the most significant being a bureaucratic state with a high level of state capacity that segued into the developmental state of the postcolonial period with its unusual capacity to control and transform (Kohli 1999: 95, 107–123, 135–136). I entirely agree that a comparative analysis of the colonial past will illuminate much about different postcolonial developmental trajectories, and it is to just such a comparison that I now turn.

A Brief Historical Sociology of Both Islands

A proper comparison of Jamaica and Barbados aimed at teasing out the factors accounting for their differences would require an entire volume, indeed a pretty large one, given the abundance of primary and secondary data on the two countries. In what follows I present a summary of results based on my own earlier archival and later field studies as well as policy work on Jamaica, on contemporary accounts from both islands, and on the published works of others.

History and Geography

Stuart Schwartz (2015) has recently emphasized that geography is as important to Caribbean studies for understanding the region's history, culture, and institutions as it is to the Mediterranean studies of Fernand Braudel and Emmanuel Le Roy Ladurie. Two closely related geographic differences were to have major consequences for the colonial institutional history of the islands. The first is that, although in global terms Barbados and Jamaica are small islands, Jamaica is more than twenty-five times larger than Barbados in terms of area. Second, and more important,

Jamaica is an extremely mountainous island with deep, densely forested inland valleys that are difficult to reach, whereas Barbados is a flat coral island. One immediate consequence of this is that only the fertile coastal regions of Jamaica are suitable for sugar cane production, whereas the entire island of Barbados is. This geographical difference entailed different economic decisions by planters and offered very different opportunities to the mass of the population.

The geographer Bonham Richardson has pointed out that the distinction between highland and lowland regions had major socioeconomic and political consequences in the Caribbean, not least of which was the association of lowland regions with planter control, with a contrasting absence in highland regions (Richardson 1997). In Barbados, the entire island was soon under sugar cane cultivation after the introduction of the slave plantation, and planters relied on imports to feed their slaves (Ligon [1657] 2011; Menard 2006; Watts 1987). The black Barbadian population was trapped within the confines of the plantation, and because nearly every acre was under cultivation, security was tight throughout the island, all areas of which were easily accessible (Richardson 1997: 134–135; 157–158). In Jamaica, most of the land was marginal for sugar cane cultivation; where not used for coffee and cattle production, the planters made the decision to let the slaves produce their own food on their backlands instead of importing it, even giving them days off to do so. This had a major impact. The slave population was on its own for one or two days each week and used the opportunity to reproduce African horticultural practices and to sell their spare products in Sunday markets, all of which was highly reminiscent of West African markets. This, in turn, formed the nucleus of what Mintz has called a "proto-peasantry," which blossomed after slavery was abolished (Mintz 1961; Mintz and Hall 1960). As can be imagined, this encouraged a degree of independence on the part of the Jamaican slaves, although it also meant greater insecurity in their subsistence when compared with the Barbadian system of regular provisions from the slave owners. Thus, after a hurricane destroyed their provision grounds in 1787, some fifteen thousand slaves died of starvation (Patterson 1967; Higman 1976: chap. 6; Sheridan 1995: 48–67; Turner 1995: 34).

Of equal importance, however, is the fact that the mountainous interior of Jamaica offered ideal opportunities for guerrilla warfare. When combined with the high ratio of imported Africans who had been born into freedom, the result was that Jamaica arguably had the highest rate of revolt in the history of slave societies. For the first seventy years of the slave system in Jamaica, a series of brutal slave revolts took place that culminated in the British elite's decision to sue for peace and the signing of a treaty that granted the victorious Maroons state-within-a-state rights to their own political autonomy, something unheard of in the annals of world slavery (Patterson 1970). This did not stop the revolts, which continued in Jamaica right up to the eve of the passage of the abolition bill, when the greatest of all revolts took place, an island-wide conflagration led by a converted Baptist slave (Reckord 1968).

The British came to regard Jamaica as a dangerous place due to the usual group of tropical diseases that awaited them (and took a heavy mortality toll) and to the well-deserved reputation of rebelliousness on the part of the slaves. In such an environment, elites are loath to lay down institutions, which assume some permanence of residence. To the contrary, the island was viewed as a hellhole in which, if one was lucky, a fortune could be made with which to return to the mother country to set up a country residence and perhaps buy a borough in the British parliament. The result was an extremely high rate of absentee ownership of estates, which itself resulted in the harsh treatment of slaves, since overseers and managers were paid on a commission basis and had little interest in preserving the slave "stock" (Ragatz 1931, 1963; Patterson 1967).

In contrast, throughout the eighteenth century, and up to the abolition of slavery in the British Empire between 1834 and 1838, there was only one slave revolt of any note in Barbados. Although, objectively, Barbados was perhaps no less exposed to tropical diseases than Jamaica (indeed, during the seventeenth century it was regarded as a major source of the tropical diseases that spread throughout North America [Sheridan 1985: 1–41; Menard 2006: 120–121]), the island over the course of the eighteenth century came to be seen as more congenial to whites and even as a place in which to restore health (Lambert 2005: 4). Thus, one of its most famous visitors during the mid-eighteenth century was George Washington, who in 1751 spent two months there with his ailing brother in the hope that the island's climate would cure him of tuberculosis. Instead, Washington contracted a mild case of smallpox.

However, there are a couple of objectively real climatic and geological differences between Jamaica and Barbados that served to exacerbate demographic and social differences. Jamaica lies in major hurricane paths and frequently experiences devastating loss of property and life as a result. Additionally, it is located near a major earthquake fault and has experienced some of the worst earthquake disasters in modern history. Barbados lies far to the east of the Caribbean, which is much of the reason why, although it has been occasionally battered by hurricanes during the past three centuries, its hurricane risk is less than half that of Jamaica's; it is also safely remote from the major earthquake fault of the region.[2] That it is flat also means that the ocean breezes cool the island to a greater degree than is possible in mountainous

Jamaica. Thus the reputation of the island as being more congenial to Europeans, and amenable to settled life more generally, is not entirely imaginary.

The Slave Systems Compared

Like all plantation slave systems, Barbados and Jamaica were brutal regimes for blacks. Nonetheless, there were significant differences between the two islands that were to have important consequences during the critical period after the abolition of slavery. Jamaican planters had little interest in naturally reproducing the black population. They made the economic calculation that it was more profitable to buy young adult male slaves from Africa, work them as hard as possible, and then buy more when the existing workforce died off. The result was that males always substantially outnumbered women slaves in Jamaica—which itself worked against reproduction—and the African ratio of the population remained relatively high, constituting over 33 percent at abolition (Patterson 1967; Craton and Walvin 1970; Higman 1984). The Jamaican slave population never reproduced, and planters relied on imports both to replace those who died and to boost the population (Roberts 1957: 30–34). Incredibly, more African slaves were imported to this little island over the course of the slave trade than were imported to the entire continent of North and Central America (Fogel and Engerman 1974: vol. 1; Higman 1984: 72–75; Sheridan 1985: chaps. 7–9).

A team of historians (Burnard, Panza, and Williamson 2017) recently concluded that during the late eighteenth century Jamaica was "markedly different from other British colonies" and "seems to have been the most unequal place on the planet"; the ratio of the estimated income of the top 10 percent of slaveholders to the "income" owned by slaves was approximately 536, reflecting a staggering gap between masters and slaves—the comparable figure in the American South was 16. Their analysis confirmed that the island had the highest cost of living in the late eighteenth century for all places in the world for which evidence exists, and noted "the especially brutal nature of slavery on the island.... Jamaican slaves lived at the bare edge of subsistence even in good times. Slaves were worked excessively hard, and lived short lives."

Barbadian planters' economic calculation led them to a radically different policy of slave rearing, especially during the second half of the eighteenth century. To implement this policy, they bought slaves in equal sex ratios, encouraged greater fertility (albeit not very successfully), and, most important, reduced infant and child mortality through better nutrition (Kiple 1984: 104–119; Klein and Engerman 1978). The result was a demographic structure unique in the Caribbean and indeed in the entire Americas except for the US South: Women exceeded men throughout the period of slavery,[3] and the local born (creole) slave population far exceeded that of the declining African segment (Higman 1984: 307–314, 349, 373). The cultural and institutional consequences of this stood in striking contrast to the strong persistence of African influence in Jamaica. According to Beckles:

> The impact of rapid black creolisation [i.e., locally born] during the eighteenth century upon the slave community was profound. It meant that African culture in Barbados came under greater internal pressure as a result of the diminishing parentage of African recruits. That creole slaves would respond to planter stimuli in rejecting things African cannot be dismissed as unlikely. The social culture of Africans was degraded by the white community, and blacks were penalized for adhering too closely to it. (1990: 52)

Another way of expressing this is to say that black Barbadians were under strong pressure to conform to and to get to know the institutions of the white slaveholder class, in striking contrast to Jamaica, where the much greater numbers, proto-peasant time off, autonomous Maroon communities, and constant inflow of Africans made possible the emergence of a creole Jamaican culture among the blacks that was profoundly influenced by African culture either in its pure form, as in the slash-and-burn hoe cultivation, or in a syncretized form, as in the many Afro-Christian religions and folk traditions (Patterson 1967).

An additional, equally important factor was the far greater stability of the white elite in Barbados compared with its Jamaican counterpart. I have already noted the high rate of absenteeism in Jamaica. The absentee rates were much lower in Barbados, and plantation ownership showed far greater continuity. Residency in Barbados also led to greater efficiency in the management of estates by minimizing agent fees and employee fraud (Butler 1995: 57–58). Watson has argued that one of the main reasons for this is that even the largest Barbadian plantations were small compared with those in Jamaica and hence did not generate fortunes large enough to support absentee ownership (Watson 1979: 34). Far more committed to residence on the island, Barbadian whites were likelier to regard the island as their permanent home rather than to yearn for the leisurely life of an absentee landlord in Britain. As two contemporary observers wrote, Barbadian whites "have found it possible to forget that England is 'home' and . . . glory in the title of 'Barbadians.' They possess a real nationality, with characteristics, neither English, Irish, nor Scotch" (Sturge and Harvey 1838: 152). This tendency led to another striking contrast with Jamaica—indeed, arguably a unique feature of Barbados compared with all other Caribbean slave societies—the majority of white women. As early as 1715, white women outnumbered white men in Barbados and continued to do so throughout the period of slavery. In Jamaica, like most other Caribbean islands, there was always a severe shortage of white women, who constituted no more than 40 percent of the white population in 1780 (Beckles 1993: 71–72).

The institutional and broader cultural consequences for the two islands were considerable—with regard to marital rates and stability, the number of locally born whites, and religious life and the general moral tone of the society. White men were less inclined to compete with blacks for sex or to rape black women, although there is ample evidence that this happened, albeit on a much smaller scale than in Jamaica (Newton 2008: 169–172; compare Burnard 2004). Indeed, there were so many white women that it was felt necessary to discourage the destitute among them from having intimate relations with black men; the authorities did so, interestingly, not by passing anti-miscegenation laws but by denying white women suspected of "unruly sexuality" (that is, sex with blacks) access to the poor relief rolls (Jones 2007: 5). Whether or not they succeeded is hard to say, but contemporaries were generally of the view that the greater presence of white women had a stabilizing effect on the white community in Barbados. The stable tradition of marriage among whites also meant greater consolidation of British institutions; the island during the period of slavery was even known as "little England" due to "the prevalence of English comforts and refinements" (Sturge and Harvey 1838: 152). In sum, Watson is correct in his overall assessment that "the presence in Barbados of a permanent white elite contributed a great deal to the formation and shaping of the character of the island. . . . They gave, and still give, the island a conservative air which, despite negative aspects, contributed to the stability of society and institutions on the island" (Watson 1979: 41).

This contrasted sharply with Jamaica, where there was far greater institutional instability among both whites and blacks, not to mention considerably more tension between masters and slaves as a result of greater physical and sexual exploitation (Patterson 1967; Butler 1995; Beckles 1993; Burnard 2002, 2004). Burnard has argued that, in spite of the mortality risks and rebelliousness of the slave population of Jamaica, young Britons were still more eager to go there than to North America, not only because of the potential to strike it rich but also because they enjoyed the weak institutional constraints, which made possible the sexual exploitation of black and colored (mixed race) women and the perverse pleasure of dominating black male slaves. The main reason for the failure of settlement was that Jamaica and a host of other Caribbean islands were known as "killing grounds for white immigrants" (Burnard 2002: 80). Between 1719 and 1758, 36 percent of all indentured servants arriving in the island died within five years. Newly arrived Europeans died at four times the rate of newly arrived Africans of the same age. Furthermore, even native-born whites suffered high mortality, and those who attempted to establish families experienced demographically disastrous infant mortality rates, with the great majority of children dying. Even those atypical immigrants who somehow managed to establish families left no lasting legacy, since their descendants tended not to reproduce successfully (Burnard 2002: 80).

Another important difference in racial composition and relations between Barbados and Jamaica was the large number of extremely poor whites in Barbados, the "Redlegs" (previously "Red shanks"). They constituted more than half the population of whites, descendants of the indentured servants of the first decades of the colony during the seventeenth century. Later they found employment during slavery mainly as militiamen protecting the plantations but, as we will see, their condition took a severe turn for the worse during the critical period after emancipation, with important consequences for race relations in the island (Sheppard 1977; Keagy 1972).

What all this added up to was that Barbadian slave society was a brutally efficient and innovative economic system. Indeed, Simon Newman has argued that Barbados was the originator of the integrated, gang-based plantation system, developed from its earlier use of white indentured labor. As a result, Barbados was the fulcrum of the revolution in labor exploitation of both blacks and whites in the entire British American Atlantic system during the seventeenth and eighteenth centuries. "Having used and killed many thousands of bound white servants, and then discarded those who survived, the Barbados plantocracy fashioned the plantation, 'the most distinctive product of European capitalism, colonialism and maritime power in the late seventeenth and early eighteenth centuries'" (Newman 2013: 193, quoting Robin Blackburn). This plantation system was the forerunner of the modern industrial factory system.

The Critical Junctures: Post-Emancipation Developments in Jamaica (1838–1865) and Barbados (1838–1850)

The abolition of slavery in the British Empire between 1834 and 1838 constituted a massive external shock to the British Caribbean slave societies. This was followed by another external shock, almost as momentous, when the British shifted to a liberal free trade regime and removed preferences for Caribbean-grown sugar, most prominently by introducing the Sugar Duties Act of 1846 and the Sugar Equalization Act of 1854.

In addition to differences already established during slavery, significant new factors influenced developments after abolition, creating a period of great uncertainty, as is typical of critical junctures. As in other post-slavery societies, the most important of these, as Foner pointed out, were the "effort to create a dependent labor force, the ideological conflict over changing definitions of labor and property, the impact of metropolitan policies, the place of society in the larger world economy, and the uses of the state in bolstering the plantation regime" as well as "the ongoing struggle between freedmen and planters" (Foner 1983: 38). In the Caribbean, differences in land-labor ratio have generally been considered one of the most critical factors in accounting for postemancipation developments, although, as Bolland (1981) has pointed out, the dominative strategies or decisions of the ruling class were of equal significance.[4] In both respects—land availability and the effective use of state power—Jamaica and Barbados stood at the two extremes of response to the new order.

The abolition of slavery and the shift toward free trade in Britain, combined with absentee ownership, had disastrous consequences for the plantation system in Jamaica during the critical period between 1838 and 1865 (Long 1956; Eisner 1961; Curtin 1968; Hall 1959, 1978; Green 1976; Holt 1992). The new era began with an institutional void between the ex-masters and the ex-slaves, well described by the Marquis of Sligo, Jamaica's governor, who wrote during the last year of slavery:

In truth, there is no justice in the general local institutions of Jamaica; because there is no public opinion to which an appeal can be made. Slavery has divided society into two classes; to one it has given power, but to the other it has not extended protection. One of these classes is above public opinion, and the other is below it; neither are, therefore under its influence; and it is much to be feared, that owing to the want of sympathy between them, to the want of dependence and mutual confidence, to the poorer class being able to provide for necessities of life without any application to the higher, there never will be in Jamaica, or in any other slave colony, a community of feeling on which public opinion can operate beneficially. (cited in Holt 2000: 42)

Economic collapse confronted the planters at every turn. Fully 15 percent of the indemnity for their slaves that Jamaican planters received went directly to the British merchants to whom they were indebted, and a substantial part of the remainder belonged to other creditors (Butler 1995: 57). Unable to find buyers, many plantations were simply abandoned; others were sold off cheaply. By the 1850s half of all sugar plantations had been abandoned, along with two-thirds of the coffee farms (Holt 1992: 161). A major factor in their decline was the withdrawal of a substantial proportion of the ex-slaves from the labor force, at first mainly women and children, later men also. Many retreated to their former provision grounds and to abandoned estates and Crown lands or, with the aid of sympathetic nonconformist missionaries, pooled their resources and bought up plantations, which were then subdivided into peasant lots. During the first half of this critical juncture, the Jamaican ex-slaves, in gratitude for the support of the missionaries, seemingly went through a phase of massive Christianization. We should be careful, however, not to interpret the growth of the peasantry as a process of complete separation from that of the broader economy and culture. First, a substantial minority of ex-slaves made their livelihood mainly from continued work on the plantations. Second, even those who became primarily own-account peasants returned during the sugar harvest periods to work on the plantation in order to gain the cash necessary to buy dry goods, meats and fish, clothes, and implements in the money economy. Thus a majority of ex-slaves remained connected to the plantation in one form or another. The notion that they were lazy or had reverted to African "barbarism" hostile to the dictates of the wage-labor system was incorrect. Instead, what drove the development of the peasant sector were the below-sustenance wages offered by the planters, the unconscionably high rents estate owners charged for those who continued to reside on the plantation, and the ex-slaves' strong desire to achieve independence from direct white control (Holt 1992: 143–175; Knox 1977; Mintz 1987; Besson 2002).

In addition to large numbers becoming self-sufficient farmers, Jamaican ex-slaves consolidated the creolized African traditions that were inherited from slavery and formed the basis of a syncretic Afro-Jamaican culture with its own institutions of religion, marriage and family, farming, folklore, and music (Besson 2002; Warner-Lewis 2002). These African-influenced traditions were strongly reinforced by new arrivals from Africa in the form of slaves rescued by the British Navy from slave ships attempting to take them to the still-flourishing slave societies of the Spanish islands (Schuler 1980).

The planters who remained after slavery would limp along economically during most of the critical juncture of the post-slavery decades up to 1865. Their biggest problem was labor. One solution was, like their counterparts in Trinidad, Guyana, and Cuba, to turn to indentured labor from India and China. The initial effort was a failure in Jamaica. About a third of the Indians who came went back home, and the British Colonial Office was soon accusing the Jamaican planters of "gross breaches of faith" in their dealings with the indentured workers (Hall 1959: 109; Look Lai 2004). There was no structurally determined reason why it failed. The system succeeded with the same set of migrants (many coming over on the same ships) in Trinidad and Guyana. Human agency was largely at play: the hardened attitude toward labor and palpable bad faith toward the indentured workers on the part of the whites, on the one hand, and on the other hand, the agency of the black population, which clearly saw the indentured Asians as a threat to the bargaining power of the not insubstantial minority of ex-slaves who continued to work on the plantations as well as the peasants who worked part-time during the harvest, both of whom often reacted with violence toward the immigrants. Later in the century, another batch of indentured Asians was imported, with somewhat more success for the planters, to the degree that they worsened the already bleak bargaining power of laborers forced to return to the plantation due to land scarcity (Bryan 2000: 151–155).

In addition to their labor problem, they were also burdened by increasing debt, declining sugar prices, and declining fertility from the overfarmed canefields. Increasingly, the planters ratcheted up their resistance to the ex-slaves' attempt at independence by evicting them from private and Crown lands upon which they had settled and through legislative and crude police tactics. Various tenancy, vagrancy, and trespassing laws were used to this effect. In addition the white-controlled assembly increased taxes on most of the basic necessities of the ex-slaves such as clothes, utensils, and tools, including carts (Robotham 1981).

By the early 1860s, the island was in dire economic straits. The declining price of sugar on the world market and incompetent management by the planters led to a decrease in the already meager wages offered and to layoffs. At the same time, those who had turned to peasant farming had reached the limits of available land and were less and less able to eke out a living on their small, overworked plots. To make matters worse, the American Civil War led to a spike in the price of essential items such as salted fish and meats, dry goods, and raw materials, also exacerbated by high duties. In the midst of this economic depression came another contingency: a severe drought that ravaged both plantations and peasant farms. Many faced starvation and took to praedial larceny (the stealing of food from farms) as well as the theft of roadside fruits, to which the legislature responded with harsh punishments (Heuman 1981; Robotham 1981).

Following a letter from a concerned Baptist missionary leader, Edward Underhill, to the British Colonial Office detailing the impoverished condition of the population, a series of meetings were held throughout the island to assess the state of affairs. This process gave some voice to the blacks and their leaders, although the governor and white population attributed the impoverishment of the blacks to their laziness. One group of black leaders sent "an humble petition of poor people of Jamaica" to the queen begging for relief from taxation as well as for the possibility of leasing land at reasonable rates, which the governor then forwarded to the colonial office with a scathing negative commentary. The response of the colonial office on behalf of the queen has achieved notoriety in Jamaican history. The so-called "Queen's Advice," 50,000 copies of which were circulated throughout the island by the governor, informed the blacks in severe Victorian terms that they had only themselves to blame for their misery and that the solution lay in prolonged hard work to be made available whenever it was needed "and for so long as it was wanted" (Heuman 1994: 54–55). The letter, which few believed the queen had written, incited outrage and only added to the growing resentment among the masses.

On October 11, 1865, several hundred blacks, armed with sticks and machetes, marched to Morant Bay, where they attacked the police station and courthouse, which they set on fire, killing the custos of the parish and several others. Several neighboring estates were also attacked. Governor John Eyre declared martial law and after quickly restoring order in Morant Bay unleashed a reign of terror on the local population in which 439 blacks, including many women and children, were indiscriminately killed, 600 were flogged, and over a thousand homes were burned. Eyre used the emergency to charge a prominent colored member of the assembly, George Gordon, with treason and had him hanged after a kangaroo trial. The brutality of the reaction horrified many members of Britain's liberal elite; after an intense controversy engaging some the most famous intellectuals of Britain—J. S. Mill, Charles Darwin, and Thomas Henry Huxley called for Eyre's indictment for murder, while John Ruskin, Charles Dickens, and Alfred, Lord Tennyson stoutly defended him (Semmel 1962)—Eyre was stripped of his governorship and recalled to Britain in disgrace. In his defense, Eyre claimed that his action was necessary to prevent Jamaica becoming "a second Haiti," in reference to the successful slave revolt on that island and its subsequent black-ruled republic.

Before leaving Jamaica, Eyre persuaded the Jamaican House of Assembly to do something unusual in the annals of political history: The great majority of its members voted to abolish their assembly and nearly two hundred years of self-rule, calling on the colonial authorities to rule the island directly. This is a case of what the historical sociologist Ivan Ermakoff (2008) calls "constitutional abdication," which he distinguishes from political surrender, based on his study of the two most famous cases in modern times: that of the German parliament's abdication of all powers to Hitler and the French assembly's similar abdication to Pétain and the Vichy regime. Ermakoff assigns a secondary causal role to coercion, collusion, and miscalculation in the European cases, attributing it instead primarily to an alignment that comes from solidarity with peers in the face of uncertainty of what the future holds, under the comforting tutelage of a dominant figure. This was also true of the Jamaican case, although its abdication was not as complex. Outright fear of two groups and racial peer solidarity on the part of the white assemblymen largely explain the vote for political abdication. Fear of mass revolt by the blacks and the specter of another "Haiti," which seemed reasonable enough in light of Jamaica's long history of subaltern revolts, was one factor (Patterson 1967; Patterson 1970; Reckord 1968; Bakan 1990). One scholar has even suggested that Haitian immigrants were involved with the Morant Bay rebellion and that together they developed a "peasant democratic ideology" (Sheller 2001). It is certainly the case that the Haitian revolution "frequently haunted both colonial and anti-colonial discourses as a seeming moment of rupture within imperial capitalism," alarming white racists as much as it inspired black rebels (Reddy 2017: 75). But added to this was another fear of what the future held: the inevitable takeover, by legitimate means, of the legislature by the more prosperous of the colored leaders, whose increasing wealth gave them access to the wealth- and tax-based franchise. In 1859 an increased poll tax and new qualification for salaried workers had drastically reduced the voting rolls and the already limited number of colored and black voters, shifting control back to the planters, but this had not been enough to allay the fears of the white planters that the colored group would inevitably gain control of the government.

These twin fears led the whites both to racial solidarity and to the eager embrace of Eyre's fear-mongering and openly racist leadership as well as the comforting prospect of imperial protection. Ironically, a majority of the colored assemblymen also voted in favor of the bill to abdicate, preferring imperial rule to that of the resurgent planters, although a degree of collusion by some of the more conservative of them with the whites, out of their own racial ambivalence and fear of the black lower class, were also important factors (Campbell 1976: 367–368). Alarmed at the desperate economic situation in Jamaica; the obvious restiveness of the masses; the incompetence of the venal, unrepresentative, and corrupt Jamaican political elite; and the embarrassingly brutal repression by Governor Eyre, the British colonial authorities acceded to their wishes (Holt 1992: 215–309; Heuman 1981: 153–196). On top of everything else was the increasing racist conviction in England that the black and brown peoples of the empire were incapable of civilization and not fit for self-rule. Significantly, this accession came about only after requiring the Jamaican assembly to surrender its powers to the queen, stating that the body could not constitutionally terminate itself, which the Jamaicans obediently did.

In 1866 Britain imposed Crown colony government or direct rule over the island, along with its other Caribbean possessions— with the notable exception of Barbados. The governor and a nominated council ruled with authoritarian powers, answerable only to the colonial office. This marked the end of the critical juncture in Jamaica. The island was fortunate in getting a governor of unusual competence and integrity, Sir John Peter Grant, who governed from 1866 to 1874 using a remarkably successful form of benevolent dictatorship, which one slightly disgruntled white journalist called "paternal despotism" (cited in Marsala 1967). He streamlined the government; cut away unnecessary expenditure; levied new taxes that were efficiently collected by a revamped revenue department; reorganized the police force and legal system, introducing for the first time a semblance of the rule of law for all; repaired and greatly increased the island's infrastructure; overhauled the educational system, which now provided elementary education for a substantially increased number of poor children (albeit still a small minority); established island-wide medical facilities; and, not least, disestablished the reactionary Anglican church, which had until then been a bastion of the white oligarchy (Marsala 1967).

Between the end of this critical period and the start of the de-colonization movement in the 1930s emerged what may be viewed as the classic period of stable colonial rule in the island. Following the social, infrastructural, and legal reforms of Grant were two key economic developments. Many estate lands were consolidated and sold to foreign owners, and a shift in economic priority was effected toward banana production, mainly by what eventually became the United Fruit Company, whose owner be-came a resident of Jamaica and directed the expansion of the en-terprise into one of America's early multinationals from the is-land. Later in the century the sugar estates were also modernized, partly under foreign ownership, and went through a major re-vival, reaching a peak during the First World War, when sugar prices soared (Satchell 1990; Cumper 1954a).

With the seemingly more enlightened approach to the peas-antry and small farming in colonial policy following Irish land reform in the late nineteenth century, Crown land was leased in moderate-sized plots in Jamaica, leading to the modest growth of a more prosperous group of small farmers during the last de-cades of the nineteenth century, although this would attenuate by the late 1880s (Holt 1992; Satchell 1990). They grew crops such as cane, coffee, pimento, coconuts, limes, and bananas, constituting just under 40 percent of the island's cash crop (Eisner 1961: 80). Not only were the peasants contributing sub-stantially to the island economy by the late nineteenth century but, as Marshall has pointed out, they also were major "eco-nomic innovators in the economic life of the community," in introducing new crops and diversifying the system (Marshall 1993: 103). It is important to note that in purely material terms the Jamaican peasants were actually better off than their Barbadian counterparts from the late nineteenth century up to late 1930s. For all their greater literacy and efficiency, Barbadian plantation workers were paid significantly less than their Jamaican and other West Indian counterparts and consumed substantially less than Jamaican peasants, resulting in greater rates of crude, infant, and maternal mortality and susceptibility to epidemics.[5]

Accompanying the modestly improved economic situation of the peasantry was the consolidation of their syncretic rural culture, best exemplified by the free village of Martha Brae, in which emerged an innovative land tenure system that combined European private ownership with a distinctively Jamaican family-land pattern of collective ownership available, at least in principle, to all cognatic kinsmen. Such land was the symbolic embodiment of freedom from slavery and, if need be, proletarianization, powerfully reinforced by the presence of the tombs of ancestors (Besson 2002). Within this economic framework emerged distinctive familial, linguistic, musical, and religious forms that blended the remnants of African culture that survived slavery and the turmoil of the early post-emancipation period with elements of British lower-class culture, especially Celtic culture, and wholly local innovations (Austin-Broos 1997: chaps. 2–6; Warner-Lewis 2002; Moore and Johnson 2002). Of special significance in welding these developments into a dynamic, wholly Jamaican cultural system were the various creole religions that syncretized nonconformist Christian doctrine with spirit beliefs, revival feasting, and ancestral worship evocative of the funeral rituals that had emotionally and spiritually sustained their slave ancestors in life and in the hope of after-death return to Africa and had also fortified its worshipers to revolt, both during slavery and before the Morant Bay rebellion (Schuler 1980; Gordon 1998; Hutton 2009).

The planters who remained on the island, their descendants, and urban whites, as well as the colored group and Jews, formed the second sociocultural complex of what the historian Philip Curtin (1968) called "two Jamaicas": an Anglo-Jamaican middle-class and an elite group with a culture focused on a creolized version of British institutions and customs. The whites, though a small minority, nonetheless continued to control most of the land and "maintained their position by the habit of power and by the power of habit" under the protective arm of the colonial power (Bryan 2000: 68). During the late nineteenth century they were joined by banana magnates derived partly from the local merchant class and from America and Britain (Bryan 2000: 67–76). An important element of the Anglo-Jamaican cultural segment was the colored middle class, which had emerged during slavery from the progeny of white planters and their black concubines (Hall 1959; Campbell 1976; Holt 1992; Bryan 2000). While not large by Latin American standards, they had become an important buffer in a slave system in which black slaves outnumbered their white masters twelve to one. They were able to leverage their position into the attainment of full civil liberties (achieved at the same time as the small Jewish population) before the end of the period of slavery; the wealthier among them owned a significant amount of property. Obsessed with skin color, they strove hard to express their loyalty to the white elite, not only in their tradition of successful men marrying "up" (including marriage to white women, since the island never had any laws against intermarriage) but also in their zealous pursuit of British culture. As we have already seen, most of them had voted for political abdication, partly out of the same fears the white assemblymen had (Henriques 1953: 33–63; Bryan 2000: 80–81).

At the bottom of this group were the more dark-complexioned (though usually with a bit of white ancestry) petty bourgeois who peopled the lower end of the island's bureaucracy and its teaching and nursing professions and made up many of the island's policemen, mid-sized farmers, and skilled craftspeople. Their culture was also solidly Anglo-Jamaican, focused on the Anglican, Methodist, and Baptist churches. This lower-middle-class group constituted the backbone of stable life in rural Jamaica outside of the peasantry and was the main intermediary between the peasantry and plantation working class, on the one hand, and the colored and white elite on the other. To the degree that Anglo-Jamaican culture and the declarative knowledge of its institutions penetrated the peasantry and plantation working class, it was via this group in their roles as teachers, parochial counselors, nurses, and civil servants (Heuman 1981; Bryan 2000: 67–91). The Anglo-Jamaican sector constituted no more than 22 percent of the total population during the nineteenth century, of whom the whites were a declining fraction, from 4 percent in 1834 to 1.7 percent in 1921.

Paton's study of nineteenth-century penal developments illustrates the often-agonistic engagement of the Jamaican peasants with the bourgeois high culture. While acknowledging that the state and its courts favored the rich and the white, and that they had their own folk system for resolving disputes, they nonetheless participated in the formal judicial system. They frequently sued each other, often over private quarrels, packed the courts when in session (and cheered the decisions of judges they considered just), and even turned over escaped convicts. At the same time, they were willing to attack unjust decisions and freed prisoners they considered unfairly imprisoned as well as punishing those they thought had been mistakenly freed (Paton 2004: 156–158). Clearly, the ex-slaves of Jamaica were active agents during this period of the island's development. They knew what they wanted. They treasured the freedom they had fought and suffered so much to achieve. The essence of that freedom was the independence that land ownership (if only via the symbolic means of family land) and self-sufficient farming offered. Contrary to imperial and local elite racist propaganda, they were extremely hard-working when farming their own or leased lands, or working as artisans. What they did not care for was laboring for others, not only because it was too often materially exploitative but also because it meant being under the control and authority of another, which was then, as it is now, the ultimate experience of unfreedom.

However, by the second decade of the twentieth century, plantation labor is what increasing numbers of the rural population were obliged to accept. With a growing population and increasing land concentration in the hands of American and British corporations, the peasants reached the limits of their available resources. At the same time, mainly under the more efficient management of external companies, there was a revival of the sugar industry in the early twentieth century, boosted by the First World War and the curtailment of competition from European sugar beet production. The Jamaican rural population was increasingly re-proletarianized, reluctantly drawn back into what Mintz (1979) called the "corporate land-and-factory-combine" of the modernized plantation, with its socially and economically destabilizing seasonality of labor (Clarke 1957; Cumper 1958) and, even more resentfully, into the banana plantations of the United Fruit Company, which swallowed up the small banana farms that had once been the foundation of their economic security, pride, and sense of freedom and independence (Post 1981; Bakan 1990; Cumper 1954a; Holt 1992: chaps. 9–10). This re-proletarianization into the plantation belt had a corrosive impact on gender and familial relations and undercut the male role as father and main provider, leading such workers to rely primarily on male peer group socialization, away from women and children, as their primary source of masculine status confirmation (Clarke 1957; Cumper 1958; Patterson 1982; Couacaud 2012).

Crown colony government, even though it restored some order to the island and paved the way for the stabilization of the economy, was to be the major factor in the eventual postcolonial unpreparedness and mismanagement of the island. Essentially, it led to the removal of Jamaicans, except for a sprinkling of local whites and near white "coloreds," from all the commanding heights of the country's economy, political life, and administration. British colonial officers now dictated its political life, not only at the top but also at all the important lower levels of the government, bureaucracy, and judiciary. The security services were also under the control of Britons, even as far down as the positions of superintendents and inspectors in the police force and sergeants in the military (Bryan 2000: 82). Nearly all of the plantations and large farms were owned and managed by foreign corporations, again, right down to middle management. The commercial sector was increasingly taken over by white ethnic minorities from the Middle East in addition to the small resident Jewish population, all highly endogamous. Even the mom-and-pop groceries serving the smallest villages in the peasant interior and country towns were, by the 1930s, monopolized by former Chinese indentured laborers and their immigrant spouses, who would eventually come to dominate the wholesale commercial sector, drawing on their ancient Hakka informal institutions of rotating savings and credit schemes and transient trading skills (Patterson 1975: 305–349). Banking and finance were completely white, right down to the job of the teller. "Colored" (or mixed race) individuals and the sprinkling of blacks who had emerged quickly after slavery into important leadership positions were largely confined to the less lucrative professions—barristers (rather than the higher-paid solicitors), civil servants, teachers, field officers, lower-level bureaucrats, clerks, and attendants. They rose just enough to learn the declarative knowledge of the institutions in which they served, but they received little or no practical training in their operation, much less the critical know-how or procedural knowledge of their management (Bryan 2000: 216–236).

The mass of black Jamaicans faced complete institutional exclusion. As Bryan observes: "The paternal imperialists and the employers of labour had one thing in common—a profound belief that the coloured population was destined to be, for the foreseeable future, the cheap manual labor force." Furthermore, the fact that the mass of workers were a race apart "strengthened the ability of the ruling class to maneuver racial symbolism in order to achieve greater social control" (Bryan 2000: 156–157; see also Holt 1992: 340).

*   *   *

Developments in Barbados during the critical post-emancipation juncture could not have been more dissimilar. As Engerman has noted, "Barbados was regarded as the major success of emancipation, as it maintained a plantation system, had productive labor, and increased output immediately upon emancipation and continued to do so into the twentieth century" (2007: 51). It did so in good part through the elite's strategic use of state power, being one of the best exemplifications of Eric Foner's generalization that "how effectively the power of the state was mobilized in the interest of the planter class after abolition often determined the nature of the adjustment to emancipation" (1983: 10). What is most striking about the post-emancipation development of Barbados is the pitiless, unyielding, unified, and ultimately successful effort of the white elite to maintain as much as possible of the old order without crossing the line of re-enslaving the black population. Working strongly in their favor was that nearly every acre of cultivable land in the island was in sugar cane cultivation under the control of the planters. In the 1830s, 69 percent of the slave population worked on the sugar plantations, which generated 98 percent of the island's exports (Butler 1995: 16). Learning from what they observed in Jamaica, the Barbadian elite acted as a single body to prevent the abandonment or breaking up of plantations and subsequent sale to the ex-slaves. Preventing the emergence of a peasantry was the explicit goal. When a planter faced financial distress, others prevented him from selling to the blacks by buying up his property and keeping it intact (Butler 1995: 74–91, 109–120). Thus the vast mass of the ex-slave population had no choice but to work on the plantations, the urban area of Bridgetown offering only limited and precarious employment.

Reinforcing this was the notorious Masters and Servants Act, better known as the Contract Law, passed by the legislature immediately after the end of slavery in 1838. Workers were allowed to live on plantations and occupy cottages owned by the planter. Notice was required for termination of employment, at which point the workers had to leave their homes, including the garden plots that they cultivated to supplement their meager incomes. Workers could be imprisoned for insubordination or disorderly behavior, and many plantations employed a private police force to apply the law. Outside the plantation a well-trained, publicly funded police force vigilantly maintained law and order, including discretionary arrests on the charge of vagrancy for anyone found idly wandering the streets with no good reason. While the harsher aspects of the law were modified by the imperial authorities (the rule against vagrancy was disallowed by the colonial office, and notice of intent to quit by the laborer was reduced from a year to one month), the Contract Law succeeded in reducing the Barbadian worker to a condition of tenantry, strongly reinforced by the threat of starvation for anyone who was summarily dismissed by the plantation owners. The rapid growth of the black population after slavery, making Barbados one of the most densely populated countries in the world by about the middle of the nineteenth century, strengthened the planters' hand all the more. The law was not repealed until 1937, a century after its passage (Beckles 1990: 103–135). It is significant that similar such masters and servants laws did exist on the books in other islands, including Jamaica, where it was largely a dead letter, given that the mass withdrawal of labor to the peasant sector initially gave workers the upper hand in their relations with the planters (Hall 1959: 19–20). The more aggressive behavior of those Jamaicans who did offer their labor and the existence of large areas of the island without a public police force made any attempt to apply the law futile, if not outright dangerous.

So confident was the Barbadian elite of its control of the working class that Barbados was the only Caribbean island not to abolish its system of elite representative government in the latter half of the nineteenth century in favor of direct Crown colony rule from Britain out of fear of being taken over by the increasingly educated colored groups. The Barbadian Assembly remained in place until the 1950s, which contributed to securing a three-hundred-year history of legislative continuity. Another remarkable expression of the elite's self-confidence appeared much earlier, as the island's police force was composed entirely of Afro-Barbadians by 1842, a mere four years after the final abolition of slavery (Newton 2008: 184–185, 197).

A distinctive feature of post-emancipation Barbadian society, especially in contrast with Jamaica, was the existence of a large group of extremely poor whites. In 1834 there were 8,000 of them, constituting well over half of the white population of 12,797 (Jones 2007: 16). After abolition a crisis emerged as to what to do with them. Deeply racially prejudiced, they refused to work on the plantations alongside the blacks. One seemingly obvious role for them was the occupation of policemen in the security force, founded in 1835, to which they were initially hired, but remarkably, the white elite soon rejected them in favor of freed blacks, who were held to be more competent. There was also no place for them in other skilled occupations or small businesses, since these were monopolized by blacks and mixed-race individuals soon after emancipation (Newton 2008: 154). After this, the group moved to the rural areas, where they scratched out a living on garden plots, occasionally on the dole, and as paupers, often begging and stealing from their black neighbors. They came to constitute the lowest level of Barbadian society, viewed with contempt by the white elite as well as the blacks, who, according to two contemporary observers, outcompeted them in "almost every field where free laborers were wont to exercise their skill and industry." These same observers added that "from their idle and dissolute habits they are more degraded than the negros but are proud of their caste as whites" (Sturge and Harvey 1838: 133). The Barbadian white elite eventually came to view them as "a class of degenerates who had fallen from white grace" and were indifferent to occasional attempts to "rewhiten" them (Jones 2007: 20). Attempts to export them from the island largely failed.

This racial situation was unique throughout the British Caribbean and the United States, and indeed throughout the imperial world. In the other British and French Caribbean islands, being white offered special opportunities for mobility, and every effort was made to prevent the "tarnishing" of the white brand by having too many of them below the status of blacks: "privilege was a function of whiteness or gradations of whiteness" (Keagy 1972: 27). In the United States, where there was a large poor white population, the white elite deliberately played whites off against blacks by emphasizing the racial superiority of all whites, no matter how poor, thereby building a bond of solidarity that would provide the foundation of the *Herrenvolk* democracy of the antebellum and Jim Crow South (Morgan 1975; Roediger 2007). The Barbadian white elite felt no need to socially or psychologically elevate the poor white majority or to pay them what Du Bois (2007), in reference to US poor whites, called a "psychological wage" in order to maintain their own elite colonial democracy. Neither did they feel their own sense of racial superiority in any way threatened by the presence of the poor whites: "The class structure of Barbados evolved more directly from equating economic standing with social rank. . . . If a poor white in Barbados enjoyed less economic success than a man of color, he was axiomatically beneath him socially" (Keagy 1972: 27). To be sure, there were pockets of poor whites on other islands, including Jamaica, but these small and isolated communities were destined to die out or be absorbed in the broader community over the course of the twentieth century. Only in Barbados did a large, majority segment of the white population constitute, in the view of both elite whites and all blacks, the very bottom of the social order, both in class and cultural terms "despised, pitied, economically deprived, conspicuous, introverted and isolated" (Keagy 1972: 42).

As might be imagined, this unusual situation strongly influenced black Barbadian views of race, class, and culture. It clearly signaled that, however economically oppressive and racially exclusive members of the white elite were, economic interests and institutional efficiency trumped race in their dealings with all members of society. The lesson Barbadian blacks learned from the condition and status of the despised "Redlegs" was that with the acquisition of the right knowledge, it was possible to out-perform them and move up the social ladder, even if only to a modest degree. To a lesser extent, this was reinforced by the fact that, unlike in the United States, there were no anti-miscegenation or segregation laws. Upwardly mobile colored or black men who chose to marry or cohabit with white women were free to do so, although such white women could certainly expect total ostra-cism from the white group. And, of course, anti-segregation laws were pointless, since the poor whites lived cheek by jowl with the black plantation workers.

With that, the period of critical juncture in Barbados ended, hardly a decade after emancipation. The planter class had skill-fully negotiated both the shock of the emancipation of its labor force and the loss of the imperial preferences that came with the free trade acts. Their efficient management of their estates al-lowed them to compete with the expanding sugar plantation system of the Hispanic Caribbean, in stark contrast with their Jamaican counterparts. The ex-slave population remained firmly in place on the plantations, their disciplined labor the envy of planters in the other islands, so much so that the Barbadian planters sometimes found it necessary to take measures to pre-vent other planters from poaching their laborers. Remarkably, Jamaican planters during the late nineteenth century even tried to import Barbadian workers, offering them wages, housing, and medical facilities substantially better than what Jamaican workers received (Bryan 2000: 155). The free colored group was a fawning cadre of urban petty bourgeois supporters. That the po-lice force was mainly black and seriously disciplinarian also clearly signaled to the blacks and coloreds that the elite was ut-terly secure in its leadership and control of the island and had

no fear of their overwhelming demographic majority. This astonishing expression of racial and class dominance awed not only
all the other white elites of the Caribbean but the imperial authorities as well. As noted earlier, when the colonial office made
the major shift toward Crown colony government in 1866, the
Barbadian assemblymen politely let it be known that they had
no need of protection. Concurring, the colonial office allowed
the Barbadian elite to continue with its exclusive elite democratic
rule for nearly another century.

Faced with this repressive situation and total elite solidarity,
Barbadian workers were limited to three options: remain on the
plantation and work as efficiently as they could so as not to run
the risk of homelessness and starvation; acquire an education so
as to be able to pursue one of the limited number of occupations
in the urban areas or the skilled work required by the plantation; or migrate. These were not mutually exclusive—indeed, education was seen not only as the means toward attaining one of
the limited number of skilled jobs but also, and more importantly,
as a facilitator of migration. Thus, soon after the end of slavery
there developed what Beckles called "a cult of education among
the older generation who insisted upon their children's acquisition of literate skills" (1990: 105). The desire for their children to
gain an education strongly motivated the older ex-slaves to work
hard on the plantations in order to earn the extra income
needed to pay for school fees. Responding to this educational
demand were the free people of color, for whom "popular education was among the most significant areas of civic involvement" during the apprenticeship period and after slavery
(Newton 2008: 159).

The educational practices of the whites also enhanced the
prestige of education among the blacks. Unlike in Jamaica, the
planter elite had developed a moderately well-functioning edu-

cational system for themselves; in 1834 there were already 213 schools in the island, which with a white population of 15,000 meant that there were more such institutions per capita (1 school for every 70 whites) than anywhere else in the Caribbean and perhaps in the entire New World except New England. These schools were, of course, highly segregated because, like planters everywhere, the Barbadians felt strongly that education would alienate the blacks from their assigned role of workers. That the leaders of the sole slave revolt in the island in 1816 were literate simply reinforced this prejudice.

Nonetheless, while limiting educational opportunities, the planters did grudgingly approve some funds for elementary education, partly under pressure from the imperial authorities but also out of recognition that a modicum of the right kind of education would make for more efficient workers. This was supplemented by the work of the churches. By some miracle, this patchwork of barely supported educational structures worked—certainly more efficiently than on the other islands. In 1844, only six years after the end of slavery, there were fifty-six church-organized schools, mainly Anglican, and 149 private schools, with a total enrollment of 7,452 students. In addition, adult education was offered in Saturday, Sunday, and evening schools (Planning Research and Development Unit 2000). By the middle of the nineteenth century, blacks from Barbados were the most literate in the Caribbean. When educational opportunities were substantially increased by the imperial authorities in the last third of the nineteenth century, Barbadians were in a better position to take advantage of them than any other group. A report from 1933 stated that the Barbadian educational system (along with that of Trinidad) was "a class apart" from the other islands of the eastern Caribbean (Mayhew 1968). MacMillan, writing in the mid-1930s, observed of Barbados that "the self-respect and industry of its coloured people are testimony to the efficacy of education in making economic existence possible in difficult conditions, and to the desire of the Negroes to use the opportunities afforded them" (1936: 132). MacMillan's observation was confirmed by the 1946 census of Barbados, the first in which a literacy question was asked: 91 percent of the population over ten years of age was able to both read and write, with a total illiteracy rate of only 7 percent (the difference made up by the semi-literate, those who could read but not write); the white rate was 98 percent, with mixed race or coloreds and blacks attaining 94 percent and 90 percent, respectively (*Census of the Colony of Barbados 1946*: 27, table 38). By contrast, the census of Jamaica of 1943 shows that only 74 percent of the population ten years and older could both read and write (*Eighth Census of Jamaica and Its Dependencies, 1943*: 120, table 63). The racial breakdown in the Jamaican census was given only for the population seven years of age and over; it shows that only 72 percent of the black population was literate, compared with 86 percent of coloreds and 97 percent of whites (*Eighth Census of Jamaica and Its Dependencies, 1943*: 108, table 54). What stands out in these figures is not only the substantially higher proportion of the population that was literate in Barbados, but the much smaller gap between the different ethnoracial groups: there was only an eight-point difference between blacks and whites in Barbados, compared with a twenty-five-point difference between the two groups in Jamaica, and a fourteen-point difference between blacks and the mixed-race group.

A third striking difference in the educational profile of the two colonies in this period concerns the gender gap. Males were more literate than females in Barbados, while the opposite was the case in Jamaica: in Barbados, 5.97 percent of males were illiterate, compared with 8.3 percent of females (*Census of the Colony of*

Barbados 1946: 27, table 38), while in Jamaica 28 percent of males were illiterate, compared with 23 percent of females (*Eighth Census of Jamaica and Its Dependencies, 1943*: 108, table 54). Furthermore, the gender gap was greatest in the black population: 31 percent of Jamaican black males over the age of seven were illiterate, compared with 25 percent of Jamaican black females over the age of seven. One likely reason for both the higher rate of illiteracy as well as the nature and extent of the gender gap in Jamaica was the high proportion of the population in the peasant sector, nearly all of whom were black. It was long reported that a substantial number of Jamaican peasant children were either kept out of school one or two days each week to help on the farm and to prepare for market day (Saturday) or were entirely removed from school prematurely. In this regard, boys were considered more valuable for their labor and hence removed at greater rates than girls, which explains both the nature and extent of the gender gap in literacy (Bryan 2000: 116–121). The absence of a significant peasant sector in Barbados meant that this incentive for disproportionately removing boys from schools did not exist. To the contrary, education, as I have already noted, was seen as the only path to both physical and social mobility for the working classes, and parents made little distinction between boys and girls in encouraging their children to get an education.

The strong commitment to education among all classes has persisted and grown in modern times. When Sidney Greenfield conducted his anthropological research in Barbados in the mid-1950s, he found that even among cane-cutters "the first major responsibility of a father to his children is to see that they receive a school education" (1966: 104). This contrasts sharply with the disorganized familial patterns of the Jamaican sugar regions, where mothers and children are often abandoned by their partners/fathers (Clarke 1957; Cumper 1954b: 156). Further-more, the pattern of peasant parents withdrawing their male children from school has persisted, although to a lesser degree, after independence.

One of the many positive consequences of the higher rate of education in colonial Barbados was the much greater labor force participation rate of both genders, a pattern that has persisted to this day. As Table 1.1 shows, the total participation rate is higher in Barbados, and most of the difference in rates between the two islands is explained by the substantially lower partici-pation of women in the Jamaican labor force, even though women continue to be more educated than men on the island. Already far behind Barbados in its overall level of literacy, Jamaica further fails to utilize the more educated half of its population—its women. Not surprisingly it ranks far below Bar-bados in the United Nations Gender Inequality Index (Table 1.1). These differences, far from being the product of present policies, are all deeply rooted in the colonial histories of the two islands; from as early as the 1860s Barbados had one of the highest female participation rates in the world. In fact, between 1860 and 1921 women substantially outnumbered men in the agri-cultural labor force, with a sex ratio of 895 in 1851 (that is, 895 men per 1,000 women), which fell to a low of 669 in 1921, perhaps the highest relative female participation rate ever re-corded by any society during peacetime (Roberts 1955: 279). The reason for this unusual labor force gender pattern was the other main means of survival for Barbadians: emigration.

Outmigration proved to be the primary means by which Bar-badians escaped entrapment on plantations after slavery. As Mel-anie Newton notes, migration had always been "an expression of freedom," and "post-1834 migration patterns echoed those of the slavery era, when they were a defining characteristic of

freedom for 'masterless people' such as free Afro-Barbadians"
(2008: 10–11). Both pull and push factors worked in their favor.
By the 1860s "flight from Barbados to avoid starvation was the
predominant feature of the decade" (Beckles 2003: 108). At the
same time, by the middle of the nineteenth century Barbadian
workers had acquired a reputation for being the most educated,
disciplined, and hard-working in the region, even though they
were paid the lowest at home; by the second half of the century
their "propensity to emigrate was well known" (Richardson
1997: 162). It was not long before employers in other regions
came to recruit them. As G. W. Roberts pointed out, between
1860 and 1921 there was an outward movement of nearly
150,000 individuals, resulting in a net outmigration of 103,000:
"But for emigration on a relatively large scale, Barbados, already
very densely settled in 1844 (with 740 persons per square mile),
might by now [1955] have reached a disastrous state of over-
crowding, relief from which would have been possible only by
widespread starvation, disease and death" (1955: 246). Outmigration not only reduced the rate of growth of the population; it
even led to a decline. With their usual ruthlessness, the planters
tried to restrict the laborers' movement but were prevented by
the imperial authorities, who actively promoted emigration. Attempts to ban labor recruiters were only marginally successful
(Richardson 1985: 100–104). Thousands of Barbadians spread
out over the region, and the building of the Panama Canal
brought a major new opportunity for mobility through outmigration. Migration to Panama and the "Panama money" remittances sent back home came at the same time that the Barbadian
sugar industry faced a major economic crisis at the turn of the
nineteenth century. For the first time, a significant number of
planters were forced to sell off their plantations or face bank-
ruptcy. Returning migrants as well as those in receipt of their

remittances avidly grasped the opportunity to become freehold landowners (Richardson 1985: 170–232). It is significant, also, that the land bought by black Barbadians was not used to create a subsistence economy but rather to produce cane, which had the effect of integrating the newly prosperous blacks even more into the formal money economy (Richardson 1985: 194–196). It was from this newly emerged class of relatively prosperous freeholders and more progressive members of the colored middle class that the nationalist leaders of the second third of the twentieth century were to emerge (Beckles 1990: chaps. 7–8).

There was one other important respect in which late nineteenth- and early twentieth-century Barbados was unusual in terms of learning British institutional procedures. Rarely mentioned in traditional histories of the island is the application of what has been called the "Gurkha syndrome" (Enloe 1980: 26–27) to Barbadian blacks by the British imperial authorities: the practice of identifying certain colonial groups as naturally well endowed in qualities the British considered useful for both the maintenance and expansion of the empire (Enloe 1980; Caplan 1995). The British applied this imperial tactic primarily to one group outside of Asia: black Barbadians. To be sure, thousands of African-born slaves were recruited and trained as soldiers to man the lower ranks of the British West India Regiments throughout the Caribbean during the period of slavery, but there was no conception of these Africans as a superior category of blacks; to the contrary, the alien and "uncivilized" background of the recruits was the quality most prized in them, and free blacks could not be induced to join these regiments because of the low status of the soldiers (Buckley 1979).

The approach was entirely different toward the Barbadians recruited to imperial service during the post-emancipation period. From early in the nineteenth century, British colonial authorities became convinced that West Indians were immune to the illnesses that plagued the white troops in Africa and had begun to consider using them as "low level imperial agents in Africa" (Newton 2008: 200). While other West Indians, including Jamaicans, were already so employed, a shift toward Barbadians began to occur. The Barbadians themselves, it is important to note, were active agents in this imperial venture. Indeed, as early as the 1840s, long before the British began to focus on them, elite Afro-Barbadians "saw themselves as the defenders of Africa in the British Empire and as the potential vanguard of British 'civilization' on the African continent" (Newton 2008: 196). What emerged by midcentury was a peculiarly "Afro-Barbadian racial consciousness [that] combined imperial nationalism with a discourse of imperial civilizationalism" (Newton 2008: 197). Initially, the Barbadians had boldly decided to bend British imperial power and culture toward their own ideological ends of liberating Africa from slavery and "backwardness." In 1847, a group of 103 Barbadian blacks founded the Barbadian Colonization Society and informed the colonial office that they were ready to emigrate to Africa in order to help the British suppress the slave trade there and "civilize" the masses (Newton 2008: 274). Later, their more immediate goal was to escape the unwavering power of the white elite, especially the elite's reluctance to broaden the property qualifications for the franchise.

Seeing how impressed employers on the other islands were by the disciplined work ethic, education, and lack of rebelliousness of Barbadians, the British imperial authorities by the latter half of the nineteenth century, deciding that Barbadians were the "smart" and loyal blacks, proceeded to train and use them in their imperial expansion and consolidation in Africa, the Caribbean, and Central America as they had done with groups such as the Sikhs and Gurkhas. In discussing the British imposition of order in the Bahamas during the 1890s, two historians of British imperialism remarked: "The men eventually recruited for the constabulary [in the Bahamas, 1891] were Barbadians—the West Indian counterpart of the 'martial races' of India—who similarly served in the police forces of the colonies in the eastern Caribbean and in mainland British Honduras" (Anderson and Killingray 1991: 78). Descriptions of young recruits in 1892 by the British inspector reflected the imperial bias: they were "young, intelligent, and of good character, presenting favourable material"; another report described them as "literate, as might be expected of the superior class from which they [were] drawn" (quoted in Tinker 2011: 39). Although resented by black Bahamians, the Barbadians were greatly favored by the white oligarchy, and before long they came to dominate the black professional classes and were a "key catalyst for educational reform in the Bahamas, especially from the 1920s through the 1960s" (Tinker 2011: 39).

Barbadian troops were also used in the conquest of what would later be called Ghana in the scramble for Africa at the end of the nineteenth century, manning the ranks in the fiercely fought Anglo-Ashanti wars (Ellis 1885). Barbadians were used not only as advance troops but also as missionaries and schoolmasters all over the Caribbean and in the pacification and Christianization of West Africa. As early as 1850 a black Barbadian became the main organizer of an Anglican mission to what is now Gambia, followed five years later by another mission, under the auspices of the Anglican Church, to Rio Pongas in the same region, which lasted for over a century. The geographer David Lowenthal was simply reporting a long-established fact when he wrote in the 1950s that "in many respects Barbados is a model territory, proud of her peaceful and progressive population and her unbroken connection with Britain; and she has a special place in the affection of the mother country" (1957: 497).

Barbadians were also recruited as artisans and middlemen in South America. During the Amazon rubber boom years of the early twentieth century, they played an important role as skilled workers and middlemen for North American engineers and British railroad managers in the construction of one of the earliest railroads into the Amazon and in the building of the camp town of Porto Velho. They also founded the residential construction industry of the town, one section of which came to be known as Bajan Hill. Among both expatriate managers and local Brazilians, Barbadians were regarded as efficient, educated, skilled employees; indeed, they were so dominant that all foreign blacks became known as "Barbadianos" (Greenfield 1983). Less glorious was their role in the rubber boom of Peru at that time. Recruited by the notorious British-registered Peruvian Amazon Company, they were used as "muchachos" or gangmasters in charge of the Putumayo Indian slaves and were sometimes ordered to commit atrocities against them. Eventually Roger Casement, whom the British Foreign Office had sent to investigate the horrible conditions, evacuated them (Gatehouse 2012; Asprey 2002).

The reputation of Barbadians as dependable and efficient workers carried over into modern late-imperial practice. Thus, during the postwar economic boom in Europe, thousands of West Indians and people from the Indian subcontinent migrated to Britain to fill unmet labor needs. With the exception of one group, the migrants all arrived on their own initiative, to increasingly unwelcoming hosts. The one exception was Barbadian migrants. London Transport, one of the largest employers of labor in Britain, actually sent representatives to Barbados to actively recruit laborers there to work in the London transportation system.

One major consequence of the distinctive colonial history in Barbados was that a single cultural system emerged. To be sure, it was marked by sharp class variants and racial segregation. Nonetheless, there was nothing approaching the bicultural segmentary creolization that developed in Jamaica. An ethnographic study undertaken near the end of the twentieth century found that rural Barbadians "imitated the design elements that they observed in plantation homes on a smaller scale in their own village or tenantry homes"; within those homes, especially those of older black Barbadians, walls were decorated with photographs of the British royal family side by side with plaques displaying religious sayings such as "God is my copilot" (Gmelch and Gmelch 1997: 14–15). An earlier ethnographic study of family life in Barbados by Sidney Greenfield found that the matrifocal family that predominated among the lower classes did not originate in the conditions of slavery (as was true of Jamaica) but was a "variant of English culture," specifically the ancient British institution of trothplight, brought to the island by whites in the seventeenth century, which permitted cohabitation that could only culminate in marriage with the ownership of property (Greenfield 1966: 163–165). Greenfield concluded his now-classic ethnography of the island as follows:

> Barbados, though inhabited by the descendants of Africans, is English in culture. The Barbadian family, then, as a cultural phenomenon, is to be traced to and understood within the English frame of reference. Neither Africa nor the institution of slavery can account for the forms of the family to be observed in Barbados. The English influence ties the island and its institutions to another cultural tradition. Within that tradition, Barbados and the behavior of its inhabitants are both explicable and understandable. (1966: 174)

Decolonization and the Institutionalization of Democracy

I have emphasized throughout this chapter the distinction between the declarative and procedural knowledge of institutions. In other words, simply knowing the institutional rules of the game is distinct from knowing how to work or play the game. I now briefly discuss one other area where this distinction was, and remains, of greatest import when comparing Jamaica and Barbados.

Outwardly, the decolonization movements of the two islands were strikingly similar. Beginning with labor riots on the plantations as a result of the Depression of the 1930s, when the price of sugar plunged to record lows, leading to massive unemployment and unacceptably low wages, a nationalist movement emerged in both islands led mainly by moderate members of the colored middle classes (Post 1978; Munroe 1972; Chamberlain 2010). After an initial phase of riots, both islands became models of gradualist transfer of power from Britain, moving seamlessly from parliamentary systems dominated by the white elites, to self-government with increasing growth of the electorate, to final independence. When the British flag was withdrawn in the 1960s, all that remained to be done was to transfer the last remnant of power held by the governor over foreign affairs.

Both islands entered independence with two-party parliamentary systems scrupulously modeled on the British system, with constitutions that codified thinly localized versions of British law. Indeed, most laws remained on the books exactly as they had been written by the colonial government and stayed in place even after Britain had changed its own versions of them. From very early on, however, the way Jamaicans played the institutional game of parliamentary democracy differed radically from the

Barbadian performance. The leaders of the two main political parties in Jamaica, in order to ensure perpetual election to their constituency, developed a pattern of political clientelism in the urban areas focused on the provision of apartments in housing projects and jobs in, or for, government. The system was iniquitous in conception in that large numbers of people were removed from their shantytown dwellings and replaced by loyal constituency leaders who made sure that residents voted for the constituency representative. This became known as the garrison system, which I discuss in Chapter 2. Thus election periods became seasons of violence, albeit confined mainly to the urban areas (Stone 1973, 1983). To make matters worse, Jamaica became a major waystation in the international illicit drug trade between South America and the United States. As we will see in Chapter 2, this development was disastrous not only in the inevitable escalation of violence that came with the vast sums of money that poured into the island's underground economy but also in its effects on the democratic system. Most of the drug gangs were originally political gangs. Now that the gangs were flush with cash, they turned the tables on the politicians, who went from patrons to clients and tools of the drug dons, as they came to be called. With their piles of drug money, the dons became the virtual government leaders of the slum areas they controlled, providing welfare services and enforcing rough justice to protect what were now their constituencies. The politicians of these urban lower-class constituencies became dependent on these dons to deliver votes (Sives 2010; Gunst 1995).

In spite of this distortion of the urban democratic process, it would be going too far to claim that the Jamaican state lacks legitimacy. Students of state legitimacy have long observed that voters distinguish between the state and its government (Gilley 2006), and this is certainly the case in Jamaica, where strong disdain for the politicians of opposition parties is not reflected in the delegitimization of the state. Not only do people vote in numbers that surpass turnout rates in the United States, but state functions such as the independence week celebrations elicit mass participation, with thousands of Jamaicans returning home for the event. Jamaicans are also fervently nationalistic. Furthermore, Jamaica has a vibrant civil sphere and an extremely competitive and free press. It is noteworthy that there has been a marked decline in electoral violence in the island since the early 1990s, brought about in large part by civil society activists who successfully instituted electoral reforms to protect the democratic process, as well as by the political parties themselves (Sives 2010: 118–142). Jamaica is more like India than its West Indian sister states; a rambunctious and slightly tattered though genuine democracy thrives there, and the state has mass support and legitimacy.

Turning to Barbados, the contrast could not be greater. The last decades of transition to independence in Barbados provide a model of gradualism in both its economic and political institutions. The strong and highly effective state structure that the colonial elite had built over the centuries was gradually taken over by the emerging nonwhite leaders, who substantially increased expenditure on infrastructural growth, especially in education, housing, and health, and also supported new facilities favoring tourism (Howard 1989: 24–27). While the extent of expenditure, especially on social infrastructure, was new, it is important to note that the capacity of the decolonizing and postcolonial Barbadian state was something inherited from the colonial past, with its strong tradition of colonial autonomy and self-rule by the plantocratic merchant elite. By the late nineteenth century the British Colonial Office had opted for a hands-off policy when dealing with Barbados. As Howard correctly

described it, by the 1930s Barbados was "not a colonial government but a national autocracy which at times challenged colonial authority" (1989: 2). Unlike the colonial and postcolonial
autocracies of Latin America, it was an autocracy that ruled with
hard-nosed, indeed sometimes callous efficiency in preserving the
plantocratic and later planter-merchant capitalist system in ways
that promoted the shared objectives of the elite. In striking contrast with the Jamaican colonial elite, the Barbadians very early
solved the collective action problem of free riders (Olson 1965)
in the provision of public goods that benefited the system and
their class. We already saw this in the rigorously pursued policy
of preventing distressed planters from selling land to ex-slaves
so as to prevent the emergence of a peasantry, which they correctly saw as a threat to the plantocratic system. We find another
indicator of this in the late colonial period, when the tax rates
of the islands are compared. Starting with the introduction of the
income tax in 1921, Barbados had a higher tax rate than Jamaica
and nearly all of the other colonies of the region. By 1956 its tax
rate was 18.7 percent, compared with 12.6 percent in Jamaica
and 13.4 percent in Trinidad; in 1964, two years before independence but two years after Jamaica became independent, the Barbadian tax rate stood at 23.1 percent, compared with Jamaica's
17.3 percent (Howard 1989: 118).

Thus, what the decolonizing black and colored leaders inherited was a strong state with the institutional capacity to exercise a remarkable degree of control over the "disposition of
purchasing power in the economy" (Howard 1989: 118). Decolonization was simply a matter of taking control of this institutional structure and utilizing it toward the new end of bene-
fiting the greater Barbadian population, emulating its previous
managers in the art of effectively running the system. Howard
writes:

The period 1953–1964 was an era of rapid growth, where capital expenditure grew at a compounded annual rate of 15.8% and current expenditure at a rate of 9.1%. This period was characterized by a deepening of the economic infrastructure as well as a rapid expansion in the cost of maintaining the colonial administration. Toward the end of the period new initiatives were taken in areas of housing, education, road building and the provision of social amenities during the transition to political independence. (1989: 120)

In like fashion, Barbadians exhibited remarkable competence in the smooth takeover and management of the political system. To use the terminology of Gerring et al. (2005), the "accumulated stock of democracy" was long and deep in Barbados, albeit one that was of the *Herrenvolk* kind, confined to the elite. The centuries-old parliamentary system—one of the longest-lasting in the history of parliamentary governments—fiercely defended, nurtured, and fortified by the white elite in the exclusive service of that class, was adopted in its entirety by the decolonizing leadership, with the crucial difference that now the electorate was expanded to the entire adult population and its leaders derived from the formerly excluded classes. The new leaders preserved everything of value in the system they inherited, right down to its rituals, building on the stock to create one of the world's most admired democracies. Barbados, as a result, has become a global model of parliamentary democracy. Freedom House regularly ranks it among the top democratic nations, very often above several of the major West European nations and occasionally even higher than the United States. Unlike Japan and other near-one-party democracies, governments have changed hands regularly over this period. Debates in the Barbadian parliament vie with those of the British House of Commons for their caustic wit and civility. To the best of my knowledge there has not been a single fatality in Barbadian politics during the more than half century of its post-independence existence.

What is true of its parliamentary system holds also for all the major institutions of government. "Government's approach to development planning," Downes (2001) has written, "was (and has remained) largely indicative, that is, offering fiscal and other incentives to the private sector in order to promote investment and growth. The government saw its role as providing the institutional, physical and policy framework within which economic activity would take place." In light of the institutional and sociocultural history just reviewed, we can better interpret the World Bank indicators of quality of governance shown in Figure 1.4. Barbados ranks between the 70th and 90th percentile of countries in voice and accountability, political stability, government effectiveness, regulatory quality, rule of law, and control of corruption. On all these measures except voice and accountability, Jamaica ranks just about the 50th percentile, passable in global terms but far below Barbados.

Barbados's Social Partnership System: An Unusual Solution to the Collective Action Problem

All societies face a collective action problem, but this is especially true of developing countries that inherit traditions of exploitation and distrust between their major groups. Cooperation between major groups is essential for full institutional functioning and socioeconomic growth, but free riding and the pursuit of interests that are good for certain groups (usually the elite) often work against the interests of others and of the society as a whole in the provision of essential public goods (Olson 1965). Barbados has solved this problem in a remarkable way, which indicates its capacity not only to effectively execute the procedural rules of inherited institutions but also to create its own institutional structures. This is demonstrated by its social partnership system.

The social partnership system emerged out of the crisis of 1991–1993, sparked partly by the oil shock of 1990 and increasing US interest rates, which led to the Barbadian economy facing growing budget deficits, high wage growth, increasing foreign debt payments, and rapid depletion of the nation's foreign reserves. When the International Monetary Fund (IMF) proposed its usual set of financial stabilization and structural adjustment policies, the government, trade unions, and the business sector united in opposition to its draconian demands, especially the call to devalue the currency and reduce government subsidies (Fashoyin 2001: chap. 1). In an unprecedented act of social unity, employers from the Barbadian private sector actually joined trade unionists and civil society groups in a huge street rally against the proposed policies (Fashoyin 2001: 20–21). I know of no other instance in the history of the developing world in which the leaders of the capitalist ruling class locked arms with trade unionists and civil servants in opposition to a common external economic threat. The solidarity of the Barbadian ruling class in taking this action harks back to its remarkable class solidarity during the critical post-emancipation juncture, only now it was acting in conjunction with, rather than against, the working class.

In 1993, the three groups negotiated the first of seven protocols aimed at sustained economic growth. In the *Protocol for the Implementation of a Prices and Income Policy 1993–1995*, the employer group, union leaders, and government leaders, in defiance of the IMF, committed to preservation of the Barbadian exchange rate of 2 Barbadian dollars to one US dollar; a wage freeze in both the private and public sectors in exchange for workers' employment security; an agreement not to increase prices except those deriving from imported inflation; the indexing of future wage increases to cost of living changes; and a pledge by the government to use its tax policies in support of this agreement (Ministry of Labour 2018). There were subsequently five other such protocols, agreed to every three years, each reaffirming the principles of a stable industrial relations climate, reduction of inequalities through increased employment, and "the consolidation of social dialogue through tripartite consultation." These objectives were called a "social compact" in order to "emphasise the broad scope of the agreement but also to emphasise the social partnership as an all-inclusive one in which all segments of society were to be taken into account in policy formulation and implementation." The third protocol also explicitly stated that economic and social progress depended "to a considerable extent upon an ongoing individual and collective commitment to a philosophy of governance which was characterized by participatory democracy and the subjugation of sectoral interests to the national good" (Ministry of Labour 2018).

The institutionalization process carried the principle of social dialogue from the national to the lower levels of Barbadian society: the hotel industry, industrial companies, and health and occupational safety organizations. A former prime minister of Barbados, Owen Arthur, described the social partnership system as "the most momentous and creative piece of public policy engineering in the history of Barbados, both symbolically and substantively. For it has taken the practice of democracy to its highest form" (Arthur 2015: 4). This unusual partnership arrangement, along with its counterparts in Ireland and Botswana, was hailed as a global model for developing countries since it allowed these countries during the 1990s to "achieve levels of development and stability that other states yearn to attain" (Minto-Coy 2011; see also Charles-Soverall and Khan 2004). To be sure, the program experienced difficulties after the 2008 financial crisis, and the sixth protocol was not formally renewed after its official expiration in March 2013. (There have been similar difficulties in Ireland.) Industrial strife followed the withdrawal of one of the trade unions after layoffs in the private and public sectors. However, it has long been widely acknowledged that the partnership is a "work-in-progress" (Charles-Soverall and Khan 2004: 23–24) that has evolved in significant ways as it adapts to changing external pressures. As the newly elected prime minister, Mia Mottley, put it, "This . . . is a marathon, not a sprint." One of her first acts on becoming prime minister was to meet with the social partnership leaders and in subsequent months restore the social partnership system to its former prominence with the promise that the burden of recovery would be shared equally by all parties, as would the bounties of the promised recovery (Mottley 2018). There are early signs that her efforts have already yielded some success in restoring the Barbadian economy (Cari-CRIS 2019).

Nowhere is the institutional contrast with Jamaica greater than in this area. Jamaica made several attempts to emulate the Barbadian model, but until six years ago, all had failed badly. The previous Jamaican failure well illustrates a point made earlier: that it is one thing to know and learn the declarative knowledge of an institution but quite another to learn the procedural knowledge or know-how to practice it successfully. As Tayo Fashoyin points out, the Jamaican government and private sector leaders developed and signed an elaborate draft partnership agreement in 1996; however, it not only was too complicated for an initial protocol but also lacked the necessary commitment of all stakeholders. There was chronic lack of consensus, both within and between the various stakeholders, one of which, the trade unions, never formally signed up. In explaining why attempts at social partnership failed in Jamaica as well as the three other Caribbean societies that tried to emulate the Barbadian model, Fashoyin (2001) found that "a minimum level of national consensus or understanding is required within and between the parties on the nature of the issues for joint resolution, on the desirability of a strategic alliance for a collective response to globalization and trade liberalization, and on the impact of these on social and economic development." For such a consensus to emerge, "effective leadership as characterised by trust, openness, accountability, transparency and the sharing of information among partners in society is critical in creating the requisite paradigm shift" (Caribbean Leadership Project 2013). Jamaica simply lacked these essential elements.

However, Fashoyin (2001: 50–62) concluded that Barbadian success in instituting such a partnership relates to factors peculiar to Barbadian history, society, and culture, which dovetails with the argument presented here. He identified six such distinctive factors: first, the absence of a history of major conflicts; second, the ability of the island's major stakeholders—employers, unions, and the government and public workers—to act in a cohesive fashion, both internally and with each other; third, the strikingly homogenous nature of Barbadian society, partly facilitated by its small size;[6] fourth, the country's remarkably stable and pluralistic democracy; fifth, strong family ties; sixth, the powerful role of civil society, especially the churches, which played a critical role in the development of the social dialogue, intervening when communication seemed on the verge of breaking down, building a "spirit of give and take" that "helped to focus attention on the national interest and promote understanding among contending parties." For these mainly sociocultural reasons, Fashoyin came to the pessimistic conclusion that attempts to export the Barbadian model "may not be a promising path to follow" (2001: 62).

Happily, it turns out that such pessimism was unfounded. While the distinctive features of Barbadian society certainly account for its precocity and success in creating the social partnership system, the implementation of this system elsewhere, especially in Ireland and Botswana, indicates that given the right level of commitment, the institution is transferable to other countries. That is exactly what has happened over the past six years in Jamaica. In 2013, facing economic collapse, a younger generation of leaders from the private and public sectors and civil society successfully revived the moribund social partnership system into a new organization called the Economic Programme Oversight Committee (EPOC). Cochaired by the governor of the Bank of Jamaica and the CEO of one of the island's largest financial organizations, the eleven-person committee meets regularly to monitor and analyze reports from the Jamaican government on its progress in meeting the Precautionary Stand-By Arrangement signed with the IMF in 2016; these reports are then released to the public (EPOC n.d., 2019). It has been a remarkable exercise in transparency and cooperation involving all major stakeholders in the society and has been, as the minister of finance pointed out (Clarke 2019), a major factor in the recent successful turn in Jamaica's economic performance.

How Do the Off-Shore Financial Centers in Barbados Affect the Argument?

At this point, I must consider one possible objection to my argument: the role of offshore financial centers (OFCs). The presence of OFCs in Barbados and their absence in Jamaica raises two questions. First, what has been the impact of the OFCs on the economic growth and relative success of Barbados? If the effect is substantial, this would largely invalidate my analysis, since a wholly exogenous, post-independence factor, having nothing to do with differing institutions, cultures, or histories will have been the primary, or at least a major, cause of the difference between the two islands. Second, even if its OFC sector does not contribute in an all-determining way to Barbadian success (as is clearly the case in places like the Cayman Islands) but is nonetheless an important factor, this would also bolster the argument that policies trump institutions, because the presence of the OFC sector is the result of such policies.

First established in the Bahamas in 1936, these centers are typically found in small economies, many located in the Caribbean; some are sovereign states, others dependencies of the former imperial powers. Their main legitimate goals are to provide international banking and other financial services to nonresidents, who are exempted from income and other taxes and enjoy minimal regulation and no currency controls. Regulatory standards and transparency vary widely in these countries, and their role as tax havens has come under increasing scrutiny in recent years, especially from the United States (Brei 2013). Although several large countries, including the United States, provide such services, the IMF has proposed that a defining feature of such countries or jurisdictions is that they provide "financial services to nonresidents on a scale that is incommensurate with the size and functioning of [their] domestic economy" (Zoromé 2007: 7).

Brei estimates that a total of $4.6 trillion of international funds flow in a "round-tripping" process to and from the metropolitan centers, especially the United States, primarily to reduce income tax payments (2013: 4). The IMF estimates assets and liabilities at US$2.7 trillion and US$3.2 trillion, respectively, constituting 8 percent of the world's cross-border holdings in 2009 (Schipke 2011: slide 5). Remarkably, 60 percent of these funds reside in the broader Caribbean region (Schipke 2011; Brei 2013: 4). The nations of the non-sovereign Caribbean, which remain dependencies of the former imperial powers, Britain and the Netherlands in particular, hold most of the Caribbean funds. Of the sovereign Caribbean states that have OFCs, Barbados and the Bahamas are the most important. Significantly, Jamaica does not have an OFC worth speaking of.

At first sight, it appears as if there is a high correlation between the presence of OFCs and better macroeconomic indicators (see Brei 2013: table 3). Caribbean countries with OFCs have, on average, substantially greater GDP per capita income than those without this sector—$21,362 versus $3,950. They also have somewhat lower external debt/GDP ratios and inflation rates. Quite apart from the fact that correlations do not indicate causal relations, however, a closer examination of the comparative macroeconomic data presented by Brei calls into question Brei's own view that Caribbean countries with OFCs are doing better. Bermuda's per capita income of $84,460 (considerably higher than the US figure of $51,748 as well as that of all the advanced European countries) and the Cayman Islands' figure of $43,717 are largely meaningless, reflecting the tax haven status of these countries and the wealth of a tiny fraction of their nonresident populations. In fact, it is best to remove them from the comparison since they are not independent economies but extensions of the United Kingdom, which controls their financial sector and regulatory systems and, in the case of the Cayman Islands and the Turks and Caicos Islands, their police forces. If there was any doubt about this, it was made startlingly clear on December 11, 2012, when the Royal Cayman Police Service unceremoniously arrested the country's prime minister, Mc-Keeva Bush, on charges of corruption and theft three days after former Turks and Caicos Islands premier Michael Misick, who had been on the run, was arrested by Brazilian authorities on an extradition order by the British government relating to corruption charges filed three years earlier (*Miami Herald,* December 11, 2012).

If we confine our analysis to the sovereign states, only Barbados and the Bahamas truly stand out. On most other measures, the OFC countries have worse indicators. Overall, I disagree with Brei's conclusion from his own data that the spillover effects of OFCs are generally positive. Significantly, the real growth rates of the non-OFC countries reported by Brei are substantially better than their OFC counterparts, even including the Cayman Islands and Bermuda; excluding these islands, the non-OFC countries are way ahead, with the Dominican Republic and Trinidad and Tobago the stellar performers of the region. This interpretation is consistent with the findings of Leo-Rey Gordon (2008) of the Jamaican Development Bank, who found that the presence of OFCs in the Caribbean "has not had a positive impact on key financial indicators such as private sector credit to GDP, loan-to-deposit interest rate spread, net interest income and capital to assets ratio," the main reason being that the international companies in the OFC countries are not allowed to do business with local residents or make loans to local banks. Gordon's study was in tune with an earlier IMF country report on the eastern Caribbean, which concluded that the tax incentives offered by these economies had no impact on the level of foreign direct investment (IMF 2005).

In spite of the unimpressive performance of the other OFC states, it may nonetheless remain the case that the exceptionalism of Barbados (along with that of the Bahamas) can be attributed to the management of its offshore industry and the contribution of this sector to the other sectors of its economy. So exactly what effects have its OFC had on its broader economy? Answering this question is difficult, which is hardly surprising given the secretive nature of OFC transactions. In 1999, the Central Bank of Barbados attempted to assess the contribution of the offshore sector (including both the manufacturing and OFC subsectors) to the island's economy. In spite of the already billion-dollar magnitude of its offshore industry, the bank was only able "to explore threats to the future viability of the sector," due to "the severe data constraints encountered" (Doyle and Johnson 1999: 96).

Data availability has improved sufficiently in recent years, allowing the IMF and other researchers to make a better assessment of the impact of OFCs on the domestic economy. It was found that the main effects are derived from income from direct employment by OFCs; spillover benefits to the domestic service sector, especially tourism and restaurants; infrastructure, especially telecommunication and transportation; and income from taxes and fees (Schipke 2011; on the nature of these financial services and fees, see Zoromé 2007: 7). In addition, the domestic economy also benefits from an increased number of specialists such as fund managers, accountants, and high-level specialists in finance (Brei 2013).

For 2008, the IMF study (Schipke 2011) found that in Barbados there were total assets of US$50 billion, constituting 1,300 percent of the island's GDP, and that 11 percent of government revenues were derived from the sector, amounting to 4 percent of GDP (Table 1.2). A total of 3,500 people were employed in the sector, constituting 2.5 percent of the labor force. The total contribution of the sector to the country's GDP (taking account of private sector contributions) was 7.8 percent, which

Table 1.2. Caribbean Countries: Selected Indicators of Economic Contribution of OFC sector, 2008

	Antigua & Barbuda	Bahamas	Barbados	St. Kitts & Nevis
Total assets (billions US$)	2	800	50	—
as percent of GDP	64	105	1,300	—
Government revenue from sector				
as percent of total revenue	0.2	0.05	11	2.1
as percent of total labor force	0.05	0.1	4	0.8
Employment in the sector	271	1,163	3,500	—
as percent of banking sector employment	—	23	—	—
as percent of total labor force	—	—	2.5	—
Average salary in sector (US$)	9,630	74,200	—	—
ratio with domestic sector	—	1.7	—	—
Contribution of sector to GDP (in percent)[1]	1	7.4–9.2	7.8	—

1. IMF Staff estimates based on contribution of this sector to revenue flows, employment, and services.

Source: Schipke 2011.

is in line with the sector's contribution to the GDP of the Bahamas (estimated at 7.4 to 9.2%).

This is certainly a nontrivial contribution, and it may even have been important in buffering Barbados during the rocky economic period it has experienced since the start of the 2008 global recession. However, given the vast sums involved, the OFC's effect on the Barbadian economy is modest at best. It certainly cannot be said that the relative success of Barbados is due primarily to this exogenous, post-independence sector, and as such, it in no way invalidates my comparison.

This brings us to the second question: Is the presence and modest contribution of the OFC to the Barbadian economy another indication of the priority of good policies over institutions, especially in light of the absence of an OFC in Jamaica? The answer is an emphatic no. The comparative data on OFCs quickly make it clear that their presence has little to do with the policy effectiveness or even the level of corruption in the host country. Looking first at the Caribbean region, we find, on the one hand, that better-run economies with well-established reputations and relatively low corruption such as the Dominican Republic and Trinidad and Tobago do not have, or have not encouraged, OFCs, while, on the other hand, the Cayman Islands, the Bahamas, the Turks and Caicos Islands, and Antigua and Barbuda, which do have OFCs, have all had thoroughly corrupt leaders. It is noteworthy that the arrest of the Cayman Islands' prime minister did not make the slightest dent in the US$1.76 trillion of international claims in the territory (6% of total international claims) (Brei 2013: 10). The same holds for Panama, another very corrupt country beloved by OFCs, whose Corruption Perception Index dropped from 73rd to 102nd rank between 2010 and 2013 even as its OFCs soared (Gibney 2014). When we broaden our scope to consider all OFCs globally, the weight of the evidence strongly indicates that good domestic policies in the host countries have little to do with their presence. To the contrary, it has been shown in a well-modeled and thoroughly documented paper by Rose and Spiegel that two bad "institutional features" account for OFCs: "Being either a tax haven or a money launderer has an economically and statistically strong effect in raising the probability of being an OFC," confirming the findings of earlier results that "sinful countries are strongly associated with offshore financial centres" (2007: 1318).[7] To be sure, Barbados falls at the good, non-corrupt, and collaborative end of the range of countries with OFCs, and it is a reasonable assumption that Jamaica's reputation as a violent place with a history of radical politics would discourage an inflow of OFC funds, should its government ever attempt to attract such funds, but both of these reputations, as we have already seen, are deeply rooted in the islands' colonial past.

Are the IMF and Neoliberalism to Blame for Jamaica's Economic Troubles?

It has become commonplace to blame the IMF and the neoliberal turn that occurred in the 1980s for Jamaica's catastrophic debt crisis and attendant maladies—zero to negative growth, an unsustainable fiscal mess, a reduction in social welfare spending, increased unemployment, and growing inequality and violence (Levitt 1996; Manley 1987; Watson 2000; Weis 2005). However, while I am very critical of IMF policies and the dogmatic faith in neoliberalism as the only pathway to development, this "explanation" is inconsistent with the facts of Jamaica's postcolonial economic failures. These economic problems began with the import-substitution / modernization approach of the 1960s, rightly mocked as "screwdriver industrialization" by Caribbean social scientists, in which GDP growth merely reflected initial low value-added import substitution and fixed investments in mining, infrastructural works, and hotel building (Girvan 1971; Jefferson 1972; Brown 1981: 7–15).

The problems of mass unemployment, rapid urbanization, sprawling slums, agricultural decline, and growing inequality were already evident by the mid-1960s. This grim state of affairs is what led me to title my first book on Jamaica *The Children of Sisyphus*; the book was based on my observations of the abysmal conditions endured by the slum dwellers of West Kingston. The oil crisis of the early 1970s exposed the unsustainability of this early modernization period and immediately thrust the island into its first major debt crisis. The social democratic policies of the Manley regime (which I served as an advisor) initially allevi- ated this situation largely through an increase in the levy on bauxite mining, and certainly did something to help the rural and urban poor.[8] However, the hostile environment of the Cold War, rash socialist rhetoric by the noisy left wing of the ruling party (which scared the professional and capitalist classes into capital and personal flight), possible destabilization action by the CIA (Covert Action Publications 1980; Levi 1989: 128–154, 167–179; Smith 2016: 177–178, 183–187, 191–198), and the institutional incompetence of the civil service—as well as those charged with implementing the many new programs—led to a decrease in GDP as well as a foreign exchange crisis, prompting the Manley regime to seek help from the IMF (Stephens and Stephens 1986; Brown 1981: 15–21; Smith 2016: 214–227). As Adlith Brown pointed out: "The greater leverage which the IMF had as a lender of last resort was reinforced by the lack of a coherent and consistent set of government proposals, the government's weak- ened financial position and a lack of political cohesion. At the same time, IMF policies were incapable of maintaining invest- ment and the merchandise account of the balance of payments was improved at the cost of output growth and structural change" (1981: 7).

Between 1977 and 1979 Jamaica entered into three agree- ments with the IMF, which, however, were canceled because the Manley regime refused to meet the severe conditions of the loan. The ensuing hardship in 1980 led to political and social turmoil and the victory of the conservative Jamaica Labour Party (JLP), which made a radical ideological shift toward neoliberal policies and the emerging Washington Consensus, a shift that found strong support from all classes of Jamaicans, who had grown weary of hard times (Henke 1999: 11–16; Smith 2016: 255–279). The Reagan administration was very well disposed toward the JLP regime, which was led by Prime Minister Edward Seaga, and Jamaica had a high-profile role in the Reagan administration's Caribbean Basin Initiative of 1983, which was reinforced by Jamaica's support of the US invasion of Grenada. Three waivers were granted to the Seaga government between 1981 and 1988 following breaches of IMF program-target conditions. Reinforcing IMF financial stabilization were several World Bank structural adjustment programs. Conditions improved slightly with liberalization during the early 1980s, but the Jamaican business community promptly squandered the opportunity by bickering among themselves, with the "screwdriver" import-substitution manufacturers dependent on tariffs and tax holidays at constant odds with the newly energized free-market "comprador" exporters (Henke 1999: 18–21). The middle class further weakened the Jamaican farming sector by indulging in an import binge of luxury goods and subsidized American foods. More importantly, devaluation, inflation, and draconian cuts in social spending and subsidies worsened the already desperate condition of the poor and severely undermined the island's health programs (Anderson and Witter 1994). Unsurprisingly, the Seaga government remained desperately short of foreign capital throughout its tenure, at one time engaging in fraudulent transactions with the US Bank of Commerce and Credit (Henke 1999: 23–24).

In the end, despite strong support from the Reagan administration, the neoliberal policy of the Seaga regime failed, due in good part to the institutional inadequacies of the country and the incompetence of its businesspeople. As Henke notes, "Despite the negative experiences of the 1980s, in the long run liberalization of the economy has to be considered an important element for the attraction of much needed foreign direct investment" (1999: 28). In the 1980s Taiwan was successfully pursuing export-oriented neoliberal policies very similar to those attempted in Jamaica, the difference being an adroit and effective developmental state, fast-learning entrepreneurs who reinvested their profits instead of eating into them with lavish consumption, and a middle class that did not ruin the balance of payments by over-spending or fleeing with their capital (Tsai 2001).

After the return to power of the People's National Party (PNP) in 1989, programs with the IMF were completed in 1990, 1991, 1992, and 1995. Relations with the IMF would not resume again until 2010. Neither the IMF nor the World Bank nor mysterious consumer winds blowing in from the global economy coerced Jamaicans to start buying luxury cars and expensive wines and clothes or to consume imported delicacies. Converted to the free market approach, with the enthusiastic endorsement of a changed Manley, the PNP government relaxed the restraints on imports and the financial sector, leading to a reckless increase in risky endeavors exacerbated by managerial incompetence in the insurance and banking industries, insider trading, crony capitalism, an overheated real estate industry, and overt corruption (Daley, Matthews, and Whitfield 2008; Kirkpatrick and Tennant 2002). This was exacerbated by a laudable but poorly managed effort to promote black and brown Jamaicans into the higher sectors of commerce, from which they were still largely excluded three decades after independence (Robotham 2000). In 1996 the financial system was on the verge of a meltdown, to which the government responded by rescuing it at enormous public expense and with almost no legal consequences to those who had caused the crisis (Kirkpatrick and Tennant 2002). In addition, the government also repeatedly bailed out and eventually socialized several major companies that were losing millions of dollars annually, most notably the incompetently run National Water Commission and the national carrier, Air Jamaica, a vanity enterprise that had operated at a loss in all but two of its forty-plus years of existence, with an accumulated deficit of US$1.54 billion dollars in 2010, a substantial proportion of the nation's debt that had nothing to do with the IMF, the World Bank, or global neoliberalism (International Finance Corporation 2011).

In 1995 the debt-to-GDP ratio was a sustainable 69 percent; after the crash it soared, reaching 123 percent by 2003, making Jamaica one of the most indebted countries in the world. As Owen Arthur, former prime minister of Barbados, pointed out: "The evidence suggests that the conditions for sustainable macroeconomic stability had been established in Jamaica immediately prior to the financial crisis. The resulting deployment of billions of dollars, largely to protect depositors and directors of institutions against losses, have compromised Jamaica's capacity to underwrite the restructuring of its economy that coincides more with its long term strategic interests" (2000: 19). By 2008 the public debt of a trillion Jamaican dollars represented more than three years of government revenue (King and Kiddoe 2010), with half of all revenues going toward paying the interest, leaving precious little for social welfare, infrastructure, and other investments. This all happened during the fifteen-year period in which Jamaicans had no relations with the IMF. In other words, the rescue of the collapsed banking sector, which led to an unsustainable debt burden, was an entirely internal affair. By 2009–2010 an unprecedented 66 percent of government revenues were consumed by interest payments, the highest in the world (King and Kiddoe 2010). It was only then, in the throes of its largely self-inflicted and catastrophic fiscal crisis, that the government reestablished contact with the IMF, which responded with the usual package of conditionalities. While it rescued the economy

from near-certain collapse, its harsh requirements further worsened the condition of the poor and have had no effect on growth,
which is typical of IMF effects. Yet Jamaica has been such a model
client of the IMF that that organization has repeatedly praised
the government for meeting its conditions (IMF 2014b, 2018a).

While the IMF deserves every criticism for its disregard of the
often harmful social consequences of its loan "conditionalities"
and for what the economist Joseph Stiglitz calls the "neoliberal
fantasy that unfettered markets will deliver prosperity to everyone"
(2019), it makes no sense to blame it for Jamaica's economic
problems and general failure to grow. It is ironic that Peter Henry
(inaccurately) attributes the success of Barbados to the very same
neoliberal policies. Apart from its insistence on maintaining parity
with the US dollar, the policies of Barbados have been no different
from those of Jamaica for the past thirty-eight years; it has similarly sought relief from the IMF in times of fiscal crisis, as it is in
the midst of doing in 2019 (IMF 2014a, 2019). It is clearly implau-
sible to explain the divergent paths of these two nations in terms
of their policies, which have been largely similar. The divergent
outcomes of Barbados and Jamaica, even as they pursue similar
policies with identical small island economic exposure to a globalized world, illustrate the fallacy of what Acemoglu and Robinson
call "the ignorance hypothesis," which maintains that "poor
countries are poor because they have a lot of market failures and
because economists and policymakers do not know how to get
rid of them and have heeded the wrong advice in the past"
(2012: 64). Like Acemoglu and Robinson (2012: 67–68), I am
not saying that policies do not matter; there are numerous cases
of bad policies leading to disaster, such as Jamaica's bailout of its
banks. But in general, what matters far more are effective institutions (that are also well managed) and good politics by political
leaders who learn from their mistakes and make institutionally

appropriate choices that lead to better outcomes. It is this more than any other factor that explains the far better postcolonial economic performance of Barbados. As former prime minister Arthur, one of the people most responsible for the country's postcolonial successes, explained, Barbados was able to "go beyond the Washington Consensus for the substance and direction of our macroeconomic management and development strategies" by adopting "a carefully balanced and properly sequenced approach to the implementation of schemes for liberalization" (2000: 19).

A recent study of Jamaica's failed development notes that, historically, there has been "a serious implementation deficit" of government policies and that this is largely due to a failure to "engage in policy learning" and limited institutional flexibility: "It is limited on the one hand by the political culture among elected officials and, on the other, by some bureaucratic traditions and practices found in the public sector that resist new policy learning and processes. Research is done, repeated consultations are held, and reports are written, but the resulting learning opportunities inconsistently affect the routines and the body of knowledge on which policies are based" (Bertelsmann Stiftung 2016: 28, 29–30).

Since 2016 there has been a remarkable improvement in Jamaica's debt crisis, under the guidance of a new generation of young leaders, most of them born after independence. The debt-to-GDP ratio has been reduced to 96 percent from a high of 147 percent and is forecast to decline to 60 percent by 2025–2026, which would represent a feat of fiscal recovery not achieved by any other country without a bailout or reneging on its debts. Jamaica is almost out of the fiscal woods after decades of high deficits (IMF 2018b; Clarke 2019). This change came about not as much from changes in policy as from more astute political practices leading to more capable implementation of policies and better management and adaptation of existing institutions. In the Epilogue, I will return to a brief consideration of this promising turnaround.

As for the IMF, it is like an emergency room doctor whose treatment saves the patient from dying but has such painful side effects that life hardly seems worth living. Recent studies of the real effects of the IMF on the countries with which it has engaged have arrived at similar conclusions, if in less figurative language. IMF intervention, one study found, does tend to reduce the chances of a crisis but has only mixed effects where a crisis is already in progress, and the amount it lends and the degree of compliance with the conditions it imposes have been found to have little effect (Dreher and Walter 2010). I agree with Stiglitz (2019) that the unbridled commitment to neoliberalism "should be put to rest."

Conclusion

This comparative institutional and broader sociocultural history of Jamaica and Barbados, far from undermining the institutionalist position, actually strengthens it. There is no way to explain the dramatic differences in economic outcomes in the two islands solely, or even primarily, in terms of different postcolonial policies. It is not my argument, to repeat, that policies do not matter. However, we need an explanation of why often similar policies work so well in Barbados and not in Jamaica given that, apart from the 1970s, their economic strategies have not been all that different. Furthermore, as noted above, over the past six years, very similar policies as those that had been pursued in Jamaica over previous decades, with negligible or negative consequences for GDP growth, are now yielding large reductions in the debt-to-GDP ratio, lower unemployment, and a return to per capita GDP growth.

We have seen that the attempt to undermine the institutionalist argument by claiming that Barbados and Jamaica began their independence era with similar institutions and economic assets collapses in the face of the sociohistorical record. The assumption of similar levels of development based on equally well-functioning institutions at the end of the colonial era turns out to be false. The Barbadian economy was already well ahead of its Jamaican counterpart at the start of the independence era by every measure, including per capita GDP, the result of more efficient management as well as a highly disciplined elite and a population with far greater human capital, which was educationally, psychologically, and culturally appropriate for the construction of a modern capitalist economy. The Barbadians also inherited a colonial state with over three hundred years of continuous parliamentary rule by a local elite focused entirely on local issues with deeply instituted formal and informal norms and an efficient, highly educated bureaucracy, giving the nation extraordinary levels of state capacity. In these respects, its political inheritance was even more pre-adapted to a high-functioning developmental state than was that of South Korea as a result of its Japanese colonial past. As the American economist William Knowles, who studied Jamaica at the end of the colonial era, observed: "Jamaica is European in culture by reason of its government, law, language, religion, education, tradition, and history; but because of the particular configuration which historical accident took, these European values failed to take root and did not lead to economic development" (1956: 62).

Jamaica, I hasten to add, was rich in other forms of human capital at the end of the colonial era, resulting from its vibrant cultural system. Scholars such as Dawson (2013) misinterpret the economic and cultural situation in the island when they claim that the two main creole cultures—or three, if one distinguishes between the rural and urban Afro-Jamaican creole cultures—are separate and hostile to each other. The island's peasant and small farming economy was engaged with the broader economy (Newman and Le Franc 1994: 119; Foner 1973: x) and even took the initiative in introducing new crops. Indeed, with its more diversified farming, the Jamaican lower class was less susceptible to shocks from the world economy and was materially better off than its Barbadian counterpart. In fact, what has emerged, especially in the postcolonial period, is a remarkably creative tension and interpenetration between the island's traditional cultures, ethnicities, and classes (Thomas 2004: 29–91; Chevannes 2000).

In sharp contrast with Barbados, Jamaica's elite and middle classes are among the most diverse in the region, composed of blacks, whites, mixed-race groups, Chinese, Lebanese, Syrians, and East Indians (Robotham 2000). There is also far greater ethnoracial diversity at the middle and upper levels of society. It is striking, too, that in spite of the frequent expression of racial pride in the Afro-Jamaican past and current culture, race has never acted as a barrier to political leadership. Indeed, one of the island's founding fathers, Alexander Bustamante, was phenotypically white, though culturally more Afro-Creole; additionally, the longtime leader of one of the two main parties and the island's prime minister for many years, Edward Seaga, was a white Jamaican of Lebanese ancestry. For all its deep celebration of Africa (mainly Ethiopia), the Afro-Jamaican peasant past, and the black "ragamuffin" urban street culture of its shantytowns, there is very little active racial separation in Jamaican public life. Though they worship a black god and consider Ethiopia heaven, the followers of the Jamaican-constructed Rastafarian religion have nonetheless made room for Twelfth Tribe persons (in other words, whites) to join them. The religion has long diffused transnationally with branches as far away as Japan (Chevannes 1994). The traditional Afro-Jamaican syncretic creeds of the nineteenth century have also gone through major transformations, and there has been a massive infusion and adaptation of American Pentecostal Christianity as well (Austin-Broos 1997).

The beneficial consequence of this more complex cultural matrix is that Jamaica has become a major player in the international community in cultural affairs, especially sports (see Chapter 4) and popular music (see Chapter 6). The country also has a highly developed civil society and press and, for all its problems, a life expectancy level that places it among the top third of nations, out of all relation to its per capita GDP (see Chapter 4). Unfortunately, apart from its tourist industry, this abundance of cultural capital and creativity seems not to play as well in the generation of an efficient capitalist economy, although it certainly gives expression to the island's problems.

The more unified cultural system of Barbados is accompanied, ironically, by a far less diverse and more racially segregated social order. The island is still largely made up of the two major racial groups that have been entwined with each other for over three and a half centuries. After a long history of one group dominating the other, a more complex class system has emerged in which elite whites continue to dominate the economy (though no longer exclusively), while blacks and mixed-race groups control the nation's political, administrative, educational, and artistic sectors; beneath both groups is the anomalous population of Redlegs, over 40 percent of whites, who constitute a kind of white underclass (Sheppard 1977). The two racial groups maintain a respectful distance from each other, meeting where necessary to conduct the nation's business but voluntarily living apart

(Layne 1979). Nonetheless, as we have seen, the society has effectively solved its collective action problem via its social partnership system.

Most blacks from other Caribbean islands, however much they may admire the economic and political success of Barbados, find this social arrangement distasteful and suffocating; this is especially true of Jamaicans, who love to point out that the only claim to international success in sports Barbados can make is in the once very British game of cricket.[9] However, British elite whites, and increasingly upper-class white Americans, find the Barbadian social system extremely congenial, and this has partly accounted for the growth of a flourishing offshore banking sector and expatriate white community, a trend enabled by nimble legislative maneuvering.

This chapter, while broadly supporting the AJR thesis and, more generally, the new institutionalist position, strongly suggests four modifications. The first is that the distinction between declarative and procedural institutional knowledge and practice is crucial. Barbados has outperformed Jamaica because it acquired from its colonial institutional and broader cultural history not just the declarative knowledge of British institutions but also the procedural knowledge of how to play the institutional game. Cognitive scientists have demonstrated that procedural proficiency in one domain usually has strong carry-over effects to others (Forster and Liberman 2007: 215). Having learned to play the institutional games of British colonial culture so well (as disciplined, productive workers; lower and mid-level colonial administrators; soldiers; policemen; artisans and other skilled workers; Anglicans; diligent pupils; schoolmasters; missionaries; lawyers and other professionals; and, not least, cricketers), it was natural for Barbadians to carry over these procedural skills to running the institutions they finally inherited with independence as well as implementing policy in an effective way.

Once one takes account of the declarative-procedural distinction, several otherwise puzzling cases of institutional similarity with sharply different economic outcomes between the two countries are easily explained. While Jamaicans have, and declaratively know, all the institutions that Barbadians also inherited, they have simply not mastered the skills needed to run them efficiently. There is a "serious implementation deficit" (Bertelsmann Stiftung 2016). Perhaps the best indicator of this is the explanation of what two authors from the Bank of Jamaica have called Jamaica's growth puzzle (Thomas and Serju 2009). The island, it turns out, has no shortage of investment capital. Indeed, in the first decade of this century, Jamaica had one of the highest rates of investment as a proportion of GDP in the Caribbean and Latin America—averaging 28.8 percent and as high as 34.8 percent in 2005, significantly higher than the Barbadian rate of 18.8 percent during the same period—yet registered a marginal growth of only 1.3 percent between 1990 and 2005 and has not attained even that in the years since then. Thomas and Serju (2009) explain the puzzle by pointing to the "poor quality of labor inputs, capital efficiency, (self-induced) adverse shocks, low capacity utilization and debt." Thus, over 70 percent of the labor force had no training and had never passed any kind of examination. This, however, is not a failure of policy. Indeed, the World Bank has even praised the Jamaican government for its *successful focus on education policy* and a strong household demand for education" reflected in high and increasing public spending on education, which went from 3.4 percent of GDP in 1992–1993 to 6.1 percent in 2001–2002, well above the Latin American and Caribbean average of 4.5 percent (World Bank 2004: 102, emphasis added). The country knows what path to take, as made clear in the detailed specification of problems and national strategy for reform in the Planning Institute's Vision 2030 national plan (2019: 57–76), and it has the educational institutional structure and the funds to implement these well-articulated policies. It has simply bungled the execution, lacking the procedural knowledge of how to make its educational institutions work. In its recently introduced Human Capital Index, the World Bank (2018) found that, while Jamaican children can expect 11.7 years of schooling, this is equivalent to only 7.2 years when quality of learning is taken into account. Some 30 to 40 percent of grade 6 leavers are functionally illiterate, and the national secondary school pass rate is worse than that of all the other Anglophone Caribbean islands (World Bank 2004: 99, 109; Robotham 2018) and far below that of Barbados, which by 2002 boasted one of the highest literacy rates in the world (99.7%), higher even than those of the United States and the United Kingdom (CIA World Factbook, 2014).[10]

However, the problem of poor procedural knowledge lies not only with inept government administrators and teachers. Nearly as incompetent have been the island's entrepreneurs in their management of the country's private sector institutions, with the notable exception of the tourist industry. Comparing Jamaica with Barbados and the Dominican Republic, Thomas and Serju (2009) concluded that Jamaica "was not an efficient user of capital."[11] The failure to take advantage of the opportunities offered by the very sympathetic Reagan administration during the early 1980s, when Jamaica was among the top five highest per capita recipients of American economic aid in the world, and the catastrophic collapse of the island's banking system and of several major companies during the mid-1990s, are extreme examples of this entrepreneurial and managerial incompetence.

The second conclusion is that formally similar institutions may perform very different functions (as emphasized by Chang 2006). In Jamaica, the plantation was a largely destructive force. It corroded familial and other social relations among workers and created a tradition of deep hostility between managers and workers, resulting in a strong distrust of authority on the part of workers from the plantation belt (Beckford and Witter 1982; Carter 1997: 24). These attitudes, when transferred to the urban areas and the modern factory, have proven to be extremely problematic, as Kenneth Carter documented in his study of Jamaican worker attitudes: "Because of defective objective authority structures and a consuming urge to 'get even' with the system, work organizations are saturated with workers leaning on the doom of their organizations. Over 67 percent of workers interviewed . . . stated emphatically that they know that they are underproducing, but that they do not intend to produce any more, for, given present circumstances, they are already overproducing" (1997: 23–24).

In striking contrast, the plantation system in Barbados turned out to have been an effective institution for enculturating the Barbadian work force to capitalist work norms, although at a high price in terms of material security (hence, all Barbadians from post-emancipation times were eager to see their children move up and away from the sugar estates). Sir Courtney Blackman, a black Barbadian who became the first head of the nation's central bank, reflecting on his life growing up in the shadow of Staple Grove plantation, made a remark that would be unthinkable coming from a Jamaican: "I found those white plantation men to be good men" (quoted in Gercine Carter 2013). At about the same time that Kenneth Carter conducted his survey among Jamaican workers (between 1974 and 1988), Graham Dann studied the quality of life among Barbadian workers in the full range of occupations (1980–1981) and found extremely high job satisfaction among them (comparable to that of British workers) as well as the widespread sentiment that "a person's job is reckoned to be a salient domain in the overall quality of life" (Dann 1984: 120–121).

My third conclusion, already hinted at, is that geography matters. Thus, we have seen that although Barbados and Jamaica share the same tropical climate, the more rugged and mountainous terrain of Jamaica, with its variety of tropical microclimates (in sharp contrast with the terrain of Barbados), offered different combinations of opportunity sets to the elites and masses in the two societies. As we have seen, this had major sociocultural and institutional consequences. I noted further, that the subjective perception of geography also mattered. Initial endowment, as Engerman and Sokoloff (1991) have argued, did make a difference. However, that difference worked its way almost entirely through the institutional structures of the plantation systems that emerged in these two colonial societies (on which see Beckford 1972). Furthermore, as the cases of Belize and the colonies in southern Africa indicate, a ruling class with sufficient ruthlessness and institutional manipulation can circumvent geographic factors, such as a low ratio of people to land, that would seem to favor labor (Bolland 1981; Foner 1983: 30–38).

In fairness to AJR, I should point out that while they may have underplayed geographical factors in their 2001 paper in order to foreground the importance of early institutions for later outcomes, in other works they have clearly indicated the importance of geography, most notably in their study of the rise of western Europe, where they identified location on the Atlantic coast and access to its sea lanes as critical variables (Acemoglu, Johnson, and Robinson 2005). Their position is that geography is important but that its effects are always mediated through institutional processes (Acemoglu, pers. comm.), a position with which I fully agree.

Finally, my comparison suggests a refinement of AJR's classification of colonies. In addition to extractive and settlement colonies, I suggest a third category of what may be called colonial settler elite democracies. These are systems in which western Europeans established permanent settlements and fully transferred the institutions of private property, parliamentary democracy, the rule of law, and functioning judiciaries while differing from other settler colonies in two crucial respects: The settlers constituted a racial minority, and they applied the benefits of the institutions mainly to themselves, with the exception of relatively small co-opted groups of natives, immigrants, and mixed-race people (see Van den Berghe 1972: 18; Vickery 1974; Fredrickson 1982). The extreme instance of this type of society is South Africa, but included in the category are the other southern African colonial states of Southern Rhodesia (Zimbabwe) and Northern Rhodesia (Zambia) and the British Caribbean colonies.

The distinctive feature of this category of colonies is that the existence of fully functioning western European institutions, lasting in some cases for centuries, as in Barbados and South Africa, had, at the very least, a demonstration effect for the mass of the excluded population. People acquired some declarative knowledge of these institutions and, more importantly, saw how effective they were for the ruling minority in administering economic, legal, and political affairs. Because people usually desire what the elites possess, especially when the thing desired is ruthlessly denied to the mass of people, these Western imperial institutions became highly desired. Thus, in spite of Jamaica's long tradition of lower-class agitation, an attitude survey of Jamaicans at the end of the colonial era found that the "typical lower class attitude was . . . one of emulation or aspiration to the standards of life and behavior exhibited by the privileged classes" (Mau 1968: 103). This, in turn, meant that upon independence the new native rulers already had in place the institutions critical for development as well as a strong preference for them. However, what they often did not have, and what was to become a source of variation within such postcolonial states, was the procedural knowledge of running these institutions. The postcolonial success of such states was largely determined by the degree of precolonial institutional learning among segments of the non-white classes. The near-collapse of these institutions in Zimbabwe and Zambia represents one postcolonial extreme. In South Africa, the colored, Asian, and educated African groups, as well as the substantial if declining white population, have provided a sufficiently large body of people with the procedural knowledge of these institutions to ensure continuity of the capitalist system and democratic institutions, although the transition has not been without its problems. In the Anglophone Caribbean we find a similar variation, although the degree of institutional learning in the region has been far greater among a larger segment of the population than in any of the African cases. Barbados, I have argued, may well present the most unusual case in this category of settler elite colonial democracies in that the procedural knowledge of the metropolitan institutional culture was assimilated to an unusual degree by the non-white population.

Coda: The Neglected Strategy of Counter-Hegemonic Appropriation

The Barbadian experience may at first sight seem like a standard case of Gramscian cultural hegemony (Gramsci 1971: 12–14, 181–182; see Williams 1977: 108–114)—the "'spontaneous' consent given by the great masses of the population to the general direction imposed on social life by the dominant fundamental group"—especially when compared with Jamaica's relatively successful peasantry (up until the late 1930s), subversive working class, and muscular, globally influential popular culture (Cooper [1993] 1995, 2012; Hope 2006). However, my analysis suggests that something more complex was at play in the institutional and broader cultural interactions between the white elite and the colored and black classes of the island—what may more properly be called a counterhegemonic strategy of subaltern cultural appropriation. The Caribbean region is unusual in the degree of subaltern resistance to the political and cultural hegemony of the white ruling classes: There were more slave and post-emancipation revolts in this region than in any other comparable area of the world, including the only case of a successful slave revolt in world history, as well as a large number of creole cultures and languages that explicitly rejected, or syncretically transformed, the cultures of the elites (Craton 1982; Dubois 2005, 2012; Rodriguez 2006; Patterson 1970; Mintz 1974).

The Barbadian subaltern classes appeared to have arrived at the conclusion, not long after the failed Bussa slave revolt of 1816, that the best response to oppression was not to get angry or withdraw but to culturally and institutionally appropriate—sometimes moderately, at other times radically, as the situation allowed. By the middle of the nineteenth century we find them fully committed to the acquisition of literacy and the broader Euro-Barbadian cultural traditions of the elite and especially of the imperial overlord. Not long after emancipation, all segments of the Afro-Barbadian leadership came to the conclusion that there could be no better model of a successful group than one that was on the way to conquering half the world, and no system more worthy of emulation than its institutions. "People of color," writes Melanie Newton, "both former slaves and pre-emancipation free people, venerated British law" and were convinced of its role as "the impartial arbiter between white and non-white Barbadians" (2008: 209–210). They were also, she found, fully committed to the classical economic liberalism of the day, especially free trade and private property. In line with this, they shared the elite view that a strong and buoyant sugar industry was the only path to prosperity in the island.

Remarkably, this view appears to have been shared by the mass of the Barbadian working classes. We also find a clear recognition among them that, in their small and overpopulated island, subsistence peasant cultivation of the sort pursued in Jamaica and Haiti would be a disaster, even were it possible, and capitalism and its institutions were the only ways of surviving beyond starvation levels. As we have seen, when, at the turn of the twentieth century, the more prosperous among them had the resources and the opportunity to buy land, they rejected peasant farming in favor of producing for the plantation economy. In addition, from the early post-emancipation period, black working-class Barbadians began to outcompete the mass of poor whites as workers, as artisans, and as low- and mid-level clerks, to such a degree that the poor whites were reduced to a condition of economic irrelevance and chronic penury. Colored Barbadians also rapidly acquired competency in the professions, especially the all-important institution of law, to such an extent that by the late nineteenth century the white elite, on its own initiative, appointed a colored lawyer, Conrad Reeves, to be chief justice of the island—so clearly had he outclassed the white competition, even as they persisted in their domination of the island's polity and economy (Beckles 1990: 126–127).

Barbadians of all classes recognized, further, that appropriating the institutions of the ruling class also meant assimilating the myths, sports, ceremonies, and other informal norms and practices that invisibly sustained them (see Meyer and Rowan 1977). Mastering the game of cricket, literally beating the British at their own game and becoming world leaders at it, was not just a powerful act of symbolic appropriation but also involved the acculturation of all the deeply embedded accoutrements that went with the game, which rapidly became "a national institution, surpassing all else in importance as recreation, spectator sport, social activity and natural competition" (Carrington et al. 2003: 58; see also Sandiford 1998: 7). Like the white cricket clubs, those patronized by blacks and coloreds "believed that the principles of the cricketing culture were admirable guidelines for social behavior and held these up as standards to be emulated by an oppressed and mostly landless working class.... Combermere, the school of the black middle classes, did not question these values, but mimicked them in a manner which suggested profound acceptance" (Beckles 1990: 150; see also Sandiford 1998: 106–145; on cricket and violence in Jamaica, see Chapter 5). Cricket to the Barbadian is more than a metaphor, as C. L. R. James (1963) has famously argued. It is, in the words of a black Barbadian scholar, "the mirror of the society's soul. It reflects the society's ethos, aspirations, dreams and mores in a way in which no other single activity does or can do" (Sandiford 1998: 153).

There was nothing subservient about the Barbadian appropriation of the institutions and broader cultural systems of the ruling class. Nearly all commentators on the character of black and colored Barbadians were struck by their dignified, transparent, and upright bearing. A widely traveled British woman's first impression of black Barbadians near the close of the nineteenth century was typical: "On landing at Barbados, the bold bearing, the gay-hearted insouciance, and the air of insolent independence of the native Barbadians strike at once. The women walk erect, clad in spotless white dresses and colored turbans, and with swinging gait and statuesque pose, they carry all burdens on their heads. They look you straight in the face out of their bold black eyes, as if to say, 'I am black, but I am as good as you any day, if not better'" (Hart 1900: 331; see also Newton 2008: 174–195). A half century later, the Oxford economist K. H. Straw wrote that the Barbadian working class "compared with most of the rest of the Caribbean territories, is of a high standard, the people being proud, dour, steady and not easily excited" (1953: 8). When pushed to extremes, of course, the Barbadian masses showed themselves quite capable of political resistance (Beckles 1984, 1989, 2003), especially by the very effective method of arson: Burning the canefields just prior to harvest was a canny and largely risk-free form of protest that registered forcefully with the plantocratic class (Beckles 2003: 76). But these physical methods were always a last resort for Barbadians, who saw clearly that with the superior military might of the ruling class, backed up by the imperial power of Britain, the odds were too heavily stacked against them for any reasonable chance of success, not to mention the loss of institutional and cultural capacity in the event of a political conflagration à la Haiti or Morant Bay.

This is a very different view of counterhegemony from that of Gramsci and his followers (for a modern restatement of which, see Frank 2007). Barbadians refused to accept existing relations as the natural order of things, but they rejected any notion of a "revolutionary consciousness" that called for the replacement of the institutional and broader cultural weapons of the ruling class with something radically different, such as the black proletarian consciousness that emerged among the lumpenproletariat of Jamaica (Stone 1973; Brown 1979; Thomas 2004). Instead, Barbadians, especially after emancipation, came to realize that in an extremely asymmetrical contest, the only effective strategy for the weaker party was to appropriate and use the power of the stronger party to their own ends. This, in essence, was the strategy of subaltern cultural appropriation. The strategy was facilitated by the peculiar status of the poor white, or Redleg, population of the island, which led black Barbadians to the view that race was not the all-determining factor explaining their condition; rather, it was their lack of institutional and cultural knowledge and know-how. While fully recognizing the presence of racism, they saw that, in non-intimate affairs, the white elite judged performance by the coldblooded standards of a capitalist system in which institutional competence, private property, the dictates of the market, and the efficiency principle were paramount. Barbadians thus avidly seized every opportunity to exploit what Raymond Williams (1977: 114) called the "authentic breaks" in the hegemonic system, without being confounded by soothing ideologies of compensatory ethnoracial consciousness. It is a form of counterhegemony that went way beyond, and was ultimately far more effective than, the "everyday forms of peasant resistance" documented by James Scott in his *Weapons of the Weak* (1985). And it is in sharp contrast with Jamaica, where a long-established peasantry and large, angry, and culturally creative proletariat take pride in rejecting the institutional and cultural practices of the elite.

The radical Jamaican economist Norman Girvan (1989) once pointed out that "Barbados' success, in juxtaposition to the dismal economic performance of Guyana and Manley's Jamaica, has occasioned as much discomfort to Caribbean radicals as it has delighted conservatives." Among fellow radicals discomfited by this comparison is the eminent Guyanese economist Clive Thomas, who, echoing Gramsci, lamented that "the broad mass of the [Barbadian] population appears to believe that progress is being made and to accept the cultural forms that go with it. Resistance is still isolated despite the formation of a Marxist party." He adds, hopefully, "It is my opinion that this development [i.e., resistance] will occur irrespective of the actual course of economic events" (Thomas 1988: 277, 279, cited in Girvan 1989). Girvan, however, was skeptical of his fellow West Indian's entire line of "radical" reasoning and speculation, contending that "this begs the question . . . of what is objectively in the interests of the Barbadian masses. Who is to decide that Thomas is right and the Barbadian masses are wrong, or at least misguided, and will one day wake up to their 'dominated' condition?" Obviously, only the Barbadian people, who, as citizens of one of the world's most democratic polities, have the means of doing so and have emphatically chosen not to. Furthermore, contrary to the view that the Barbadian people are culturally and institutionally "dominated," I argue that their strategy of counterhegemonic cultural and institutional appropriation is itself a special form of radical resistance similar to the cultural appropriation of Christianity by black Americans in their "quest for hope and freedom" and successful civil rights revolution. "The human cry for help," Cornel West has written, "and the mortal effort to find a way out of one's predicament always bear the mark of one's cultural, political and economic contexts" (2002: 7, 131–148).

Not by physical force, nor by foreign ideological compensations, but by capturing, mastering, refashioning, and deploying to their own ends the institutional knowledge and know-how of the ruling class and the broader cultural, political, and economic context within which they were embedded, would Barbadians ultimately triumph. And it is their remarkable success at this cunning counterhegemonic strategy that explains why Barbados has so greatly outperformed Jamaica in the postcolonial struggle for economic prosperity and growth.

2

Why Is Democratic Jamaica So Violent?

Revisiting the "Democratic Peace" Thesis

This chapter is motivated by a paradox at the heart of Jamaican society. On the one hand, there is the all-too-familiar fact that Jamaica is one of the most violent places in the world, measured in terms of its overall crime rate and, more specifically, its homicide rate. In 2005, its murder rate of 58 per 100,000 persons made it the most homicidal nation in the world. It has lost that unenviable distinction since then, but as Figure 2.1 shows, it has remained among the ten most murderous societies. There was a decline in the rate between 2010 and 2014, but since 2015 it has begun to increase again, reaching a new peak of 60 killings per 100,000 in 2017, which places it among the top five. This level of violence is not only a source of great human suffering within the society but also a major factor explaining the country's slow to stagnant economic growth.

On the other hand, in spite of this horrific problem, the island has a genuinely democratic system of government. It is flawed and still transitional, to be sure, but it is a genuine democracy nonetheless. This is no mean achievement. Jamaica is

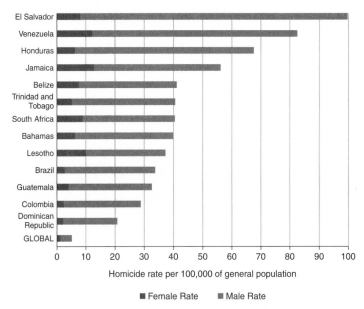

Figure 2.1. Homicide rate per 100,000 persons in Latin America and the Caribbean and selected African countries, 2016

Data source: Small Arms Survey Data Base, 2017 (Geneva: Graduate Institute of International & Development Studies).

not what *The Economist* magazine once called a "phoney democracy," and it is also not an "illiberal democracy," a label for countries that have the form but not the substance of democracy, with elections that are either rigged or meaningless because there is no true choice available, or "elected" executives who act as dictators, as in Russia and Hungary. Nor is it what has been called a "guided democracy," in which elected leaders claim to speak for one general will of an organic undifferentiated whole. Instead, Jamaica has what political and sociological students of the state recognize as the constituent features of all authentic democracies: competitive and highly contested elections, particularly for the legislature and chief executive, through a multiparty system; a high turnout rate; a free, vigorous, and competitive press; and basic civil and political liberties. Jamaica also has other features considered essential by many analysts: a thriving civil society, an independent if overburdened judiciary, and a moderately noncorrupt civil service. It is a democracy that has been repeatedly tested in the one critical area where it matters most, namely, political succession; since independence there have been repeated changes of government after fiercely fought, some may say ferociously fought, elections.

Freedom House has ranked Jamaica a "free state" with a robust electoral democracy every year since the beginning of its rankings in 1972. This long-term consistency is more important than the ranking for any given year and, at least in this regard, places Jamaica firmly among the small group of institutionalized democracies outside of the advanced Western states. This steadfast commitment to democracy persists in a world which has seen a disturbing decline in freedom after the promising rise in global freedom during the last decades of the twentieth century. In its 2017 report, Freedom House found that in 2016 only 45 percent of nations could be rated free. In more specific terms, on a scale of 1 to 7 (with 1 being the most free and 7 the least) Jamaica has had an average ranking of 2 on both civil and political liberties (Freedom House 2018). Freedom House notes, in addition, that "the constitutional right to free expression is generally respected" (the island has the highest per capita number of radios in the Caribbean), as are the right to freedom of religion and the right to freedom of association and assembly, and "none of the major political parties identify on religious, ethnic, or cultural grounds" (Freedom House 2016: 341, 340). An earlier report (Freedom House 2007) noted that "Jamaica has a robust civil society, though the most influential nongovernmental actors tend to emanate from business interests," and "Labor unions are politically influential and have the right to strike." Both of these remain true. Indeed, there has been a vigorous growth of civil society groups and activities since 2007. In 2018, Jamaica's press was ranked the fifth freest in the world, far above that of the United States (Reporters without Borders 2018).

However, the 2017 Freedom House report also highlighted the nation's problem with violence, which I address in this chapter as a serious threat to its democracy. Although institutionalized, Jamaica is not yet a mature democracy. It is still in the transition to a full, mature democracy, and that, as we will see, can be a dangerous stage. The Jamaican government's own report states the problem with unflinching candor: "Crime, corruption and violence, along with the various social problems that exacerbate them and are perpetuated by them, are the Tier 1 threats to Jamaica. They result in so many deaths and injuries that Jamaica now has one of the highest homicide rates in the world and, largely as a result, has also suffered from four decades of low growth. They are the foremost threats to the security of Jamaica, to the integrity of the State, to the economy, and to the lives of the people" (Clayton 2012: 5). The most disturbing aspect of Jamaica's chronic crime problem is that its citizens may have become inured to it. One observer noted some years ago that a process of normalization has developed, especially toward street and election-related crime (Harriott 2003: 4–5).

The question then is this: How can a country with so thriving a democracy, robust civil society, and enviably free press have such a violent record? The reason why this is a problematic, some may say paradoxical, state of affairs is that many major students and theorists of democracy associate the system with peace and tranquility. Indeed, this assumption goes by the name of "the democratic peace" (see Mansfield and Snyder 2007: 21–33,

71–72; Ray 1998). The Anglo-Australian political theorist John Keane has provided the most eloquent statement of the democratic peace thesis:

> Violence is the greatest enemy of democracy as we know it. Violence is anathema to its spirit and substance. This follows, almost by definition, because democracy, considered as a set of institutions and as a way of life, is a non-violent means of equally apportioning and publicly monitoring power within and among overlapping communities of people who live according to a wide variety of morals. . . . In principle democracy enables everybody to act at a distance from its power centers by means of a functioning civil society that is independent of publicly accountable governmental institutions; together, elected, responsible government and the dispersal of power within civil society provide organized protection from the fear or fact of injury or loss of life. (2004: 1)

We have just seen that Jamaica meets all the conditions of democracy specified by Keane. Yet it fails terribly in what he claims to be the major consequence of such a system: "protection from the fear or fact of injury or loss of life." How do we explain this?

There are at least four answers that one may tentatively offer as a starting point in exploring this conundrum. The first is that Jamaica is simply an extreme outlier, an exception to the general rule, which holds for all but a few odd cases due to peculiar historical, sociocultural, and other idiosyncratic factors. Indeed, it has been argued that the claim that Jamaica is a genuine democracy must be "revised" because of its high levels of violence (Gray 2004: 4–5), which skirts the problem by definitional fiat: Democracy is nonviolent by definition; Jamaica is violent; therefore Jamaica is not a democracy. This move, we will see, is inconsistent with the realities of democratic history and practice. I fully share the view of one of the leading observers of Jamaican politics, Carl Stone (1986), that for all its combative clientelism and violence, the island does have a genuine parliamentary system.

The second is that the internal version of the democratic peace thesis, the idea that peace and democracy are inherently and constitutively associated, is simply false—in other words, that there is really no such inherent relationship. Democracies vary in their degree of violence, and this variation must be explained in terms of other factors—history, culture, economic factors, distinctive institutions, and so on. That is, there is really no paradox and Jamaica is not necessarily peculiar in this association of violence and democracy. The third response is that the democratic peace thesis has been too broadly defined: Reconceived in more precise terms, the thesis may well be valid, but it may be valid in a way that does not apply to Jamaica and other democratic societies experiencing its level of violence. The fourth possible explanation is that there is indeed a strong relationship between democracy and violence but that it is the very opposite of that claimed by the democratic peace thesis. This disturbing argument would run that there is an inherent relationship between democracy and violence. Far from being an outlier, Jamaica may well be a typical example of the constitutive association between violence and democracy. In other words, Jamaica is violent, not in perverse opposition to the inherent trend and not in spite of democracy's inherent tendency, but in keeping with the inherent tendency of democracies to be violent, especially democracies at an intermediary stage of development.

These arguments are not all mutually exclusive (for a recent review of the democratic peace thesis literature, see Reiter 2018). In fact, I will argue that there is something to the third response and that it is quite consistent with my main argument: that contrary to Keane's and other democratic peace theorists' view of the matter, one source of the problem may be the very nature of democracy itself.

There are really two versions of the democratic peace thesis. One is the strictly external claim that democracies are far less likely to engage in warfare; the second is the internal claim that democracies are far less prone to domestic violence. I focus mainly on the second claim, since this is what is most pertinent to Jamaica. The two versions, however, are not unrelated. One of the earliest and most vigorous explanations of why democracies are less likely to go to war with each other rests on the internal cultural argument that the norms—both cultural and legal—of democracies foster a propensity to peacefully settle differences via courts and civil discourse. Indeed, it has been claimed that this was the argument of Immanuel Kant ([1795] 1986) in, pre-sumably, the very first statement of the democratic peace thesis (Doyle 1983a, b), although it has been strongly contested that this is a misrepresentation of Kant's argument (Cavallar 2001). Owen (1994) attributes the propensity toward inter-state peace on the part of democracies directly to the internal workings of democracy. However, a more recent statement of the internal sources of the external version of the democratic peace thesis is Mousseau's (2009) argument that it is less democracy, per se, and more the cultural emphasis on respect for contracts and the rule of law that explains the tendency of democracies to settle their differences by nonviolent means. But nondemocratic states can also exhibit such qualities. Once one controls for this in-ternal "contractualism," he argues, the international correla-tion between peace and democracy is reduced to insignificance.

For completeness' sake, let me briefly comment on the ex-ternal aspect of the democratic peace thesis. In the broadest terms, this claim is that democracies are simply less prone to go to war. (For the standard modern view, see Rummel 1983.)

Many studies seriously question this finding in its unqualified version (Weede 1984; Mansfield and Snyder 2007). Thus, Melvin Small and David Singer (1976) have shown convincingly that between 1816 and 1965, 58 percent of inter-state wars were provoked by democracies.[1] Those who live in the Western Hemisphere, and especially in the Caribbean, can only view the broad claim as a bad joke. Between the late nineteenth century and the third quarter of the twentieth century, the United States, the leader of the free world and one of its great democracies, invaded other countries in the region at least twenty-six times. More recently, America helped to undermine one of Latin America's most robust democracies, Chile, and invaded another country on the other side of the world, Iraq, for what turned out to be the wrong reasons, then later justified the invasion as an attempt to impose democracy on the Iraqis at the point of a gun. The record of the imperial democracies of Europe is hardly better (see Russett and Oneal 2001). Mansfield and Snyder (2007) have argued that it is young democracies during the transitional stage that are most prone to go to war. This is largely correct, but the record of presumably mature democratic regimes such as the United States, in its invasions of Latin America and the Caribbean, as well as France and the United Kingdom, in their Middle East interventions, indicates that there are major exceptions.

There is, however, a narrower version of the external democratic peace thesis that would seem to stand the empirical test: namely, that democracies almost never go to war against other democracies. This is sometimes called the dyadic version of the external thesis, as opposed to the monadic version—that democracies are less prone to invade nondemocratic countries, which is empirically groundless. The dyadic version of the external thesis seems, at first sight, to be true for the entire course of the twentieth century, leading Levy (2013) to declare it a law of politics. But even this limited version of the argument has been challenged (Mousseau and Shi 1999). Mansfield and Snyder cite numerous cases of transitional democracies going to war, with the risk of warfare among them rising by a factor of four to fifteen (2007: 95–138).

Happily, these are not Jamaica's problem. No one loses sleep over the possibility that Jamaica might be invaded by another country. Its problem, rather, is the island's horrendous internal violence, and the question to which I now turn is the degree to which its buoyant transitional democracy is itself implicated in this crisis.

Violence as an Inherent Feature of Democracy

There are several arguments in favor of the view that violence is endemic to democracy. Consider, first, the democratic renewal thesis of Thomas Jefferson. Historically, it is perhaps not an accident that democracy, in both the ancient and the modern worlds, emerged in violent ways and in the context of tremendous class and ethnic conflict. It was in ancient Greece that formal, fully institutionalized Western democracy was invented. And it has been noted by many scholars, including myself, that it was no accident that this first democracy emerged in the institutionalized violence of large-scale slavery (Finley 1960; Patterson 1991). Another ominous feature of this first democracy was that at its height, during the second half of the fifth century B.C.E., Athens was riddled with internal strife and also instigated violent imperial wars, as recorded in great detail by Thucydides in his *History of the Peloponnesian War*.

Fast forward twenty-two hundred years, and we find one of the most remarkable cases of history repeating itself. The first instance of what may be called a genuine democracy in the modern world emerged in Virginia, itself a large-scale slave society in which, as Edmund Morgan (1975) has shown, democracy among the white demos emerged on the backs of, and in contradistinction with, the violent enslavement of the black population. "We the people" meant we who were free, white, and male, defined in sharp contrast with those who were unfree and black and female.

It is no wonder, then, that the most celebrated advocate of what has been called the "democratic renewal" argument was the Virginian slaveholder who wrote America's *Declaration of Independence* and who saw no contradiction between his glowing advocacy of liberty and democracy and his practice of slavery. In what has become known as his "Liberty Tree" letter, Jefferson (1787) wrote to William Stevens Smith: "What country ever existed a century and a half without a rebellion? And what country can preserve its liberties, if its rulers are not warned from time to time, that this people preserve the spirit of resistance? Let them take arms. What signify a few lives lost in a century or two? The tree of liberty must be refreshed from time to time with the blood of patriots and tyrants. It is a natural manure."

Was Jefferson right? Does democracy require periodic violence for its renewal? The political scientist Victor Le Vine (2000) has noted that if Jefferson was right we have yet another paradox, since democracy, in the first place, "predicates the creation and maintenance of institutional mechanisms for non-violent resolution of conflict." Le Vine strongly questions Jefferson's democratic renewal thesis even while conceding that there may be positive consequences for some limited violence in democracies. A democracy must always be wary of those who would abuse its privileges to undermine it and hence must be willing to rise up in resistance to such threats. The problem, of course, is what constitutes a legitimate threat. One person's opportunity may be another's loss; freedom for the mongoose is death for the chicken. Nonetheless, Le Vine concludes that democracies "do not thrive on a diet of political violence, that in the long run violence begins to generate more violence to the point where a tradition of violence may emerge which ultimately leads to democratic breakdown." We will return to this matter shortly and leave the Jefferson thesis open. I suspect that both Jefferson and Le Vine may be right. Democracy does require periodic bouts of violence to keep liberty alive against the forces of tyranny that thrive on the development of inertia and a tendency to take freedom too much for granted. At the same time, too great an alertness to the loss of liberty and too great a tendency to resort to violence against such threats can lead to a pattern of violence that ultimately threatens democracy. It is a delicate balance that every democracy must learn to deal with.

Is this Jamaica's problem? I doubt it. To be sure, many Jamaicans are concerned about the threat to civil liberties posed by a police force that seems too often to be out of control and also the more subtle threats posed by political corruption (Jamaica currently scores below the international average in Transparency International's annual ranking of nations by their level of corruption). However, it is not those people who feel threatened who have resorted to violence. Rather, the violence comes from criminal elements and police overreaction as well as electoral violence. There is a sustained pattern of violence in Jamaica, but it is certainly not due to any kind of effort at Jeffersonian political renewal.

The Democratic Transition Argument

The second important way in which democracy might have an inherent tendency toward violence is the democratic transition process. The argument here is that countries in the transition to democracy or countries that are not fully democratic but are trying to become so, so-called intermediary democracies, are the most prone to civil and foreign wars and other forms of domestic violence (Mansfield and Snyder 2007). The empirical evidence is unambiguous on this matter: Well-established or mature democracies, as well as established authoritarian states, tend to have lower levels of violence and very few civil wars, while intermediary regimes have had far more such violence over the course of the past two centuries.

In other words, there is a danger zone for all young democracies. Scholars have suggested an inverted U-shaped curve between democracy and civil wars. As countries become more democratic they become more prone to internal violence, sometimes leading to civil war; then, as democracy consolidates, they become less prone to such violence, eventually settling down to the stage of mature democracy where, once again, we find a very low likelihood of domestic violence. As Hegre and his collaborators (2001) note: "The road to democracy is complicated and can be marked by internal violence and even collapse of the state. Autocratic countries do not become mature democracies overnight. They usually go through a rocky transition, in which mass politics mixes with authoritarian elite politics in a volatile way. Political change deconsolidates political institutions and heightens the risk of civil war." Mansfield and Snyder (2007) argue that it is the absence of strong institutions such as the rule of law, a free press, and established political parties that explain this propensity to violence, but the Jamaican case rather complicates this general-ization, as we will see.

The big question here is whether this greater tendency toward violence and civil wars is due more to the transitional nature of the economies of such regimes or to the fact that they are not fully mature democracies. Is democracy the problem, or is it their socioeconomic condition? Hegre and colleagues (2001) are of the view that the greater tendency toward civil unrest definitely has to do with something about transitional democracies themselves. Thus the bad news is that in the short run, "a democratizing country will have to live through an unsettling period of change." How far must a country move toward the state of full, mature democracy before violence abates? Sadly, the answer seems to be the whole way; there are no half or even three-quarter measures. As even Eric Neumayer (2003), who strongly believes that good policies can lead to violence reduction, admits: "the transition from autocracy to democracy is likely to be accompanied by a rising homicide rate . . . until *full* democracy has been achieved" (see also Mansfield and Snyder 2007; Snyder 2000; Ward and Gleditsch 1998).

When we turn from civil wars and threats to the vulnerability of the state to the more specific problem of ordinary violence, especially homicide, we also find clear evidence of an inverted U-shaped relationship between levels of violence and the degree of transition to mature democracy. In a longitudinal study of homicide trends in forty-four countries between 1950 and 2000, LaFree and Tseloni found strong support for the hypothesis that "violent crime rates will be curvilinear, with the highest rates in countries transitioning between autocracy and democracy" (2006: 32). Homicide rates in transitional regimes were found to be 54.4 percent higher than in autocratic ones. Rates were also substantially lower in fully democratic regimes, with no consistent cross-national variation among them. A more recent study by Fox and Hoelscher (2012) arrived at similar conclusions, with what they call "hybrid" political orders, especially those with weak institutions, experiencing higher rates of violence than autocratic or fully democratic regimes (but see Lin 2007).

What do these findings mean for Jamaica? Like nearly all its Commonwealth Caribbean sister states, Jamaica, although still in a transitional period, has already passed the halfway mark toward mature democracy and is beyond the point of vulnerability to civil war. However, it remains highly vulnerable to criminal violence. It is significant that the five cases of moderately serious civil unrest that Jamaica faced all took place during the first transitional decade of its democracy. There was, first, the Ronald Henry rebellion of 1959–1960, in which Henry's Rastafarian group of about a hundred militants conspired with the First Africa Corps, a militant group in New York, to overthrow the government (Meeks 2000: chap. 1; Hibbert 2013). The second was the Coral Gardens incident in 1963, when a gang of Rastafarians attacked a Shell gas station in Coral Gardens, resulting in the death of eight people. Some think that this was more a criminal act than an attack on the state, although, as Terry Lacey notes, "the full weight of state power was mobilized against four men whose motives and proposed actions were unknown" (1977). Deborah Thomas, in her more probing study, argues that there are deeper meanings to be drawn from the events concerning the nature of citizenship in mid-twentieth century Jamaica, the question of who was considered to be included within the Jamaican body politic, and "how those who have suffered as a result of their exclusion envision redress" (2011: 175). Third, there were the anti-Chinese riots of 1965, in which mobs of up to three hundred burned and looted Chinese property in Kingston, paralyzing commercial life and transportation services in Kingston for a day. In 1966–1967, political warfare between armed gangs culminated in the declaration of a state of emergency. And finally there were the Rodney riots of 1968, in which youth mobs attacked property with a special focus on foreign-owned property, following the expulsion of Guyanese lecturer Walter Rodney from the island. Rodney had established links with intellectuals at the University of the West Indies, radical Rastafarians, and youth gangs during the six months of his lectureship in 1968, but it is doubtful that any serious plots were afoot.[2] The government certainly overreacted when it sent troops to Mona, where the main campus of UWI is located. None of these riots were really serious threats to the government. More importantly, there has been little violence against the state since that time.

However, the island well fits the model of a transitional democracy plagued by violent crime. The question is why. It is interesting that few of the comparative studies showing a strong tendency toward violence among transitional democracies offer a persuasive explanation for the association. LaFree and Tseloni (2006) argue that the Durkheimian social strain is the mediating variable accounting for violence, but they are conflating the democratic transition with another factor, economic change. There is nothing in the nature of democracy, per se, that should induce Durkheimian value strain. To the contrary, democracy, as a participative process based on party loyalty, induces just the kind of organic solidarity that is eroded by economic change, to which I shall return. Alas, the organic solidarity of democracy is more akin to the tribalism of traditional societies that are prone to chronic inter-tribal conflicts. The violence that we find in transitional democracies is inherent in democracy itself and is most likely to be found in those transitional systems that are well on the way toward full democracy. It is to these inherent forces that I now turn.

The Problem of Elections: Bullets and Ballots

Perhaps the most serious inherent threat of violence posed by democracy is the crisis endemic to elections. David Rapoport and Leonard Weinberg have rightly upbraided social scientists for neglecting this problem because of their reluctance to consider the possibility that it is democratic processes themselves that encourage violence (2012: 1–14). They cite the view of Bingham Power that democracy is "a gamble that discontent can be channeled through legitimate electoral channels" (3–4) and then note that the gamble often does not pay off. Their study shows that there is a "double link" between elections and violence, between ballots and bullets. Ballots are often the substitute for bullets in solving revolutionary violence—this was true in Nicaragua in 1990, El Salvador in 1991, Guatemala in 1995–1996, and South Africa in 1994. But sadly, there is no shortage of cases of ballots leading to bullets: Greece in 1967, when the army took over to prevent Papandreou's party from winning office; Sri Lanka in 1988–1989, when fourteen candidates and 300 party workers were killed; Indonesia in 1997, when 253 people were killed; and Algeria in 1992, when the army intervened to prevent the militant Islamists from winning office, resulting in the deaths of over 100,000 people. The Algerian case is an especially acute one for democracy. What does a democracy do when a party has a platform for the destruction of democracy and intends to replace it with either a theocracy or a communist or fascist regime?

In this regard Jamaica has a unique and unenviable reputation. Nearly all scholars who study the dangers of elections point to Jamaica as the most extreme case: in per capita terms Jamaica leads the world in the violence of its elections and the number of deaths resulting from them—the 844 persons killed in the

October election of 1980 (following 162 murdered in the previous election of 1976) being perhaps the worst in the history of democracies on a per capita basis. The question is whether this violence is an extreme case of electoral democracy, or the result of other socioeconomic developmental factors shared with several other countries, or a reflection of factors peculiar to the political culture of the island.

I submit that it is all three. There are distinctive features of Jamaica's economic condition and culture that exacerbate the problem, as we shall see, but the historical evidence indicates that nearly all democracies experience violence on their path to maturity. This was true of Europe and the United States throughout the nineteenth and early twentieth centuries. Indeed, America's founding fathers, especially Madison, were only too aware of this possibility, based on their readings of the fate of ancient democracies (Federalist Papers 10).

Their fears have been fully demonstrated by the later history of democracies, including their own. This tends to be most evident when the stakes of election results are very high for those participating. In clientelistic democratic polities with scarce resources, such as Jamaica, where elected officials are expected to deliver after elections, violence is almost inevitable during and after elections as people living on the margins fight to protect their jobs, shelter, and whatever scant physical security they have. Carl Stone amply documented how this happened in Jamaica (1983: 111–122). One of the two main parties, the Jamaica Labour Party (JLP),

> set the pace in the transition towards clientelistic, pork-barrel, machine politics. It de-emphasized formal organizational structure, relying mainly on clientelistic networks of personal support for its political bosses and particularly on the dema-

gogic crowd appeal of the flamboyant [Alexander] Bustamante. Its message to the masses was the delivery of short-run material benefits and inducements in exchange for support. It reinforced patronage politics with the cement of Bustamante's charisma and symbolic image of champion of the poor and the downtrodden.

Although the other major party, the People's National Party (PNP), under its own highly principled leader, Normal Manley, tried its best to model itself on the British Labour Party with an emphasis on inclusive nationalism and left-leaning ideology, it was soon overtaken by the imperatives of electoral politics: "The pressure to gain votes and the primacy of electoral advantages over political consciousness converted the party over time into an electoral apparatus controlled by party bosses promising to dispense patronage" (Stone 1983).

Inevitably, this led to more violence, which, as recent studies by Sives (2010) and Williams (2011) have shown, began almost with the birth and consolidation of the two-party system and electoral politics in the early 1940s. Both note that violence with the use of sticks, stones, and machetes during the 1940s and 1950s took a fatal turn to guns and more extreme forms of violence soon after independence in 1962, when government-sponsored housing schemes became heavily armed political garrisons defended by gangs whose role was to deliver votes at elections. The basic argument of Williams's thesis, that "politically motivated violence has not been incidental to Jamaican politics; rather it has been endemic to the political system," holds true for the great majority of early and intermediary democracies and remains true even of advanced ones, such as the world's largest democracy, India, to which I briefly return below. Indeed, in her nuanced political history of violence and democracy in Jamaica, Amanda Sives has argued that "not only has violence been part of the political identity construction, but it has assisted in its continuation," and further, that while the Westminster two-party system has undoubtedly brought stability to Jamaican politics, "it has been achieved through the incorporation of low level violence" (Sives 2010: 180). In other words, the democratic process both enables and is enabled by violence.

The Un-Sweet Spot: Democracy, Violence, and Economic Transition

There is yet another transition that partly explains the greater tendency of democratic regimes to violence: economic change. This should not be confused with the democratic transition. There are poor countries that are either stagnant or in the early stages of transition that are very democratic, such as India during the first three decades after independence, and there are countries in the throes of economic transition that are authoritarian, such as China and the East Asian "Tigers" before their democratic transition. Economic change, per se, also induces violence. Transitional democratic societies, however, because they are more responsive to the needs of their citizens, are more prone to pursue too-rapid, sometimes radical economic change, and this combined with associated violence can negatively affect economic growth, even though in the long run mature democracies are positively associated with economic growth (Papaioannou and Siourounis 2007). Thus they find themselves caught in the throes of two transitions, the political and the economic, each of which independently induces violence but which together reinforce it even more.

The extent to which development influences crimes of violence and the reasons for this influence are surprisingly complicated. A recent UN study of global violence finds that there is a consensus that "lethal violence is often rooted in contexts of paucity and deprivation, inequality and injustice, social marginalization, low levels of education and a weak rule of law" (UNODC 2011). There is no doubt that these factors are interconnected, as numerous studies have shown, but there is less consensus about their causal relations and direction of influence. In broad terms, there is agreement that higher degrees of homicide are related to lower levels of development, though not the lowest levels (Haiti, for example, the poorest state in the Western Hemisphere, has a homicide rate that is among the lowest in the region). The most examined developmental factor is inequality. A study by World Bank economists arrived at the position that there is a positive association between crime rate and degree of inequality both within and between countries and, further, that the relation is causal and robust (Fajnzylber, Lederman, and Loayza 2002; see also Messner 1980). The UNODC (United Nations Office on Drugs and Crime) reports that "inequality is also a driver of high levels of homicide" (UNODC 2011: 30). The UN study further found that higher values of the Human Development Index are associated with lower levels of crime.

However, not only is this more common view contested by several scholars, but there is also little agreement about the reasons for the association between inequality and violence. Several scholars explain the relation in partly macro-cultural Durkheimian, partly social-psychological terms. Economic change and the inequality that it brings, they argue, generate a breakdown of social bonds and solidarity, the anomic disintegration of shared social norms, relative deprivation, severe strain, a sense of unfairness, and general anomie, which are the mediating factors causing crime (Messner 1980; LaFree and Tseloni 2006; Krahn, Hartnagel, and Gartrell 1986). Chamlin and Cochran (2005) argue that it is the extent to which inequality is perceived to be ascribed rather than (fairly) achieved that induces crime, although this holds mainly for more advanced modern societies. However, in a later study they found, somewhat puzzlingly, that while the degree of economic and political illegitimacy felt by citizens was positively associated with homicide rate, it did not mediate the effect of inequality on crime (Chamlin and Cochran 2006).

Several scholars have questioned these findings. Richard Bennett (1991) criticized the methodology of previous studies using cross-sectional data to assess the effects of change. Using pooled time series data, he found that development level did not affect the homicide rate, but that growth rate did—in an unexpected direction. Nations with low growth rates had higher levels of homicide than those with higher rates, which he claimed, somewhat hastily, refutes the Durkheimian culture strain explanation. A more recent study (Pridemore 2011) has also soundly criticized previous works claiming a positive association between inequality and homicide on the grounds that they failed to control for poverty, even though poverty is the main predictor of crime in the United States and other advanced societies. When Pridemore replicated two previous studies showing a strong association between inequality and homicide, he found that the inclusion of a poverty variable in the same models revealed a strong poverty–homicide association while reducing to nonsignificance the inequality–homicide association. His findings accord with those of Neumayer (2003), who stated flatly that equity improvement had no lowering effect on violence and that the association between inequality and violence reported in previous work was spurious. It would be rash to dismiss the numerous studies showing a strong association between inequality and homicide rate, but I agree with Pridemore that a reassessment may be overdue; I also find it odd that poverty, per se, has not been found to have a direct effect on homicide in the developing world in light of its well-established link in the United States. The most plausible connection would seem to be that found by Hsieh and Pugh (1993) in their meta-analysis of thirty-four aggregate data studies on the links connecting poverty, inequality, and violent crime—namely that, in global terms, poverty and income inequality are each associated with violent crime (homicide more so than rape and robbery), with a great deal of variation in the estimated size of the association.

Two additional variables associated with development, population growth rate and urbanization, have also been found to be important. Higher population growth rates usually result in the youth cohort (between fifteen and twenty-nine) constituting a larger segment of the total population. Since this group commits crime at a much higher rate, their greater demographic presence is positively associated with greater national homicide rates (United Nations 2014: 9; Krahn, Hartnagel, and Gartrell 1986; Lee 2001). Rapid urbanization and the growth of cities, especially large central cities with surrounding shantytowns, have been shown to increase violent crime (Alda 2011), partly through the growth in heterogeneity and the decline in communal solidarity and shared norms (Hansmann and Quigley 1982; Gaviria and Pagés 2002), but also due to higher returns to criminal activity, a lower probability of detection, and the growth of single-parent households resulting in less parental control and socialization of children (Glaeser and Sacerdote 1999).

On every one of these factors found to be associated with high crime rates, Jamaica stands as a near-perfect example. It is the classic case of an economy stalled midway between traditional backwardness and self-sustained growth (see Chapter 1). Several studies by economists have explored the relation between developmental processes and violence in the island (Ellis 1991; Francis and Campbell 2001; World Bank 2004; UNODC and World Bank 2007; Gilbert and Sookram 2010). Not surprisingly, they claim to find significant associations between socioeconomic patterns and the Jamaican crime rate. However, their claims are qualified, and a closer look at their regression results indicates that these findings are decidedly mixed. Ellis reported deterrent effects for increases in GDP and a positive effect of the unemployment rate and the size of the youth cohort, and Francis and Campbell appeared to agree. However, in a more recent study, Gilbert and Sookram found virtually no impact of social expenditure as a proportion of GDP or any of the standard economic variables. The World Bank (2004) also found no significant effect of GDP or the youth unemployment rate on the homicide or robbery rates although, revealingly, they found the youth unemployment rate to significantly increase the rate of rape and carnal abuse as well as of shooting incidents. Unemployed young men take out their frustration over their failure to find meaningful work on young women by abusing and sometimes killing them, it would seem (Jamaica, in 2018, had the highest rate of female homicide in the world). Inequality was also found not to have any significant effect on crime in Jamaica (UNODC and World Bank 2007).

The failure to find robust associations between the unemployment rate or GDP growth and homicide, while counterintuitive, is consistent with work done elsewhere (Chatterjee and Ray 2009). In regard to unemployment, this might be due to the coarseness of the measures used by these studies. A recent study of the effect of unemployment on crime in the United States (Kleck and Jackson 2016) found important differences in the effects of this variable depending on the kind of employment being considered. Thus unemployed people actively seeking work, as well as the underemployed, are no more likely to commit serious crimes than the fully employed. However, people who have withdrawn from the labor force for no good or "acceptable" reasons are far more likely to commit crime, especially youth between eighteen and twenty-nine (the so-called disconnected). Even so, other (unexamined) factors may well be at play in explaining the higher rate of crime among this group. The link, they admit, is "complicated." Those who work on the Caribbean are well advised to consider these complications. (I examine some of the complexities of defining employment, under-employment, and work-force participation in Chapter 3.)

All in all, with regard to the likely effects of development on violence, what the works on economic and demographic factors suggest is that there are strong links connecting poverty, the cost of food, population density, the degree of urbanization, the size of the youth cohort, and possibly, the extent of certain kinds of male youth unemployment, but only in the long run and only to a limited degree (Francis and Campbell 2001). The share of employee compensation (higher income shares for labor), while having no impact on the homicide rate, has a significant deterrent effect on rape and carnal abuse, robbery, and shootings (World Bank 2004: 163–167).

However, the causal link between development and violence is bidirectional (World Bank 2004: 112). Crime, as several reports have documented, has had a devastating effect on the Jamaican economy through health costs resulting from injuries and death; lost productivity due to premature death and injuries as well as greater levels of imprisonment; expenditure for increased security; effects on business and the general investment climate; and losses due to the decline in human and social capital such as the increased rate of migration (Francis et al. 2009; World Bank 2004; UNODC and World Bank 2007; Ward, Brown, and Butchart 2009; Clayton 2012; Jaitman 2017). Most of these studies estimate the cost of crime at between 3.7 and 4 percent of GDP, with Jamaica currently ranking fourth in the Western Hemisphere behind Honduras, El Salvador, and the Bahamas in such losses. The UNODC and World Bank study (2007) estimated that were Jamaica to reduce its homicide rate to the level of Costa Rica, it would experience an annual 5.4 percent increase in its growth rate. These are conservative estimates; some analysts claim that the annual cost may be as high as 7.1 percent of GDP when the full health costs are considered (Ward, Brown, and Butchart 2009; Clayton 2012). The Jamaican government study argues, reasonably, that the full cost of crime should take account of the cumulative cost of four decades of lost productivity due to violence.

Jamaica, then, seems to be caught at the vicious intersection of two transitional inverted U curves: that of a country slowed on the way toward full democracy by violent forces inherent to the democratization process, and that of a transitional economy stalled on the way toward self-sustained growth. It suffers all the troubles associated with these two transitions, the most grievous of which is a high rate of violence. Jamaica's flawed democracy, especially its clientelistic, garrison-based politics, has independently generated a great deal of violence and laid the foundation for the current high rate of urban gang violence (Gray 2004: 194–222, 329–330). At the same time, the island's economic stagnation at the middle level of development has independently generated a great deal of violence resulting from over-urbanization and the massive spread of smoldering slums, poverty, youth unemployment, precarious adult employment and income, and poor education. These two sources of violence intersect and reinforce each other. Economic insecurity and unfulfilled expectations make politics explosive as people turn to political leaders to fulfill needs they can only superficially and inequitably meet through handouts to partisan supporters in garrisoned constituencies. By doing so they worsen the crime situation, which, in turn, increases the cost of doing business, creates an environment that discourages investment, and encourages the outmigration of human and physical capital, further undermining economic growth.

The analysis thus far is grim enough, but other forces, sad to say, further contribute to Jamaica's tragic experience of chronic violence.

Vulnerability of Democracies to Other Sources of Violence

Beyond all the above factors, democracies enable or are vulnerable to other sources of violence. It has been found that all except the most mature democracies are especially vulnerable to tensions associated with multiethnic communities, to organized crime, to terrorism, and last but not least, to the growth of a self-perpetuating pattern of crime and violence.

The vulnerability of democracies to ethnic violence is well known (Dahl 1971: 114–118; Rabushka and Shepsle 1972; Diamond and Plattner 1994; Snyder 2000; for opposing views, see Fish and Kroenig 2006; Beissinger 2008). Violent outcomes are by no means inevitable, as the consociational democracies of Europe demonstrate (Lijphart 1977). Nonetheless, more often than not, multiethnic democracies are prone to violence. Among the worst cases are India, Sri Lanka, and postcommunist Eastern Europe. The rules of the democratic game, especially the tendency of leaders to use ethnic communities as a basis for political mobilization and the constant temptation to form secession states on the basis of ethnic identities, are a spur to chronic violence.

Even democracies that have long passed the midpoint of the transition to democracy face grave crises in this regard. In his study of democracy and violence in India and Sri Lanka, Dennis Austin (1994) observes that "the somber fact that both countries carry the scars of communal and political violence through almost fifty years of parliamentary democracy is a strong counter to current assumptions that democracy will tilt the balance against oppression throughout the world." In multiethnic democracies, he finds, "Democracy itself is a spur to violence. When societies are divided democracy adds depth to the sense of division." The problem of democracy, he notes further, is that it "lives by recruiting. It enlists voters and whets the appetite of many previously unaware of their power. To use a homely metaphor, democracy stirs the political pot, adds new ingredients and draws them together." Hundreds of thousands have lost their lives as a result of this devastating stirring of the pot of democracy and communal identities.

Caribbean societies present both positive and negative cases of the association between ethnic violence and democracy. Indian–black violence in Guyana and persisting viciousness toward people of Haitian ancestry in the Dominican Republic are at their worst during election seasons. On the other hand, Trinidad, though a violent and multiethnic country, may have been made less violent by its democracy (see Patterson 2003–2004).

On this matter Jamaicans can take some small pride, because, apart from the brief Chinese riots of the 1960s, attempts at using democracy to stir racial hatred and achieve political gain have never succeeded. For all their violence, the two major political parties have refrained from mobilizing voters on racial or ethnic terms, in spite of the high level of racial consciousness. It is striking that on an island that is over 80 percent black, one of its two founding fathers, Alexander Bustamante, was phenotypically white; another of its prime ministers, Edward Seaga, was white and of Lebanese ancestry; and Michael Manley, its most popular charismatic leader for many years, was the son of a mulatto father and a white mother and in appearance was also phenotypically white. Another prime minister, Donald Sangster, was also light-complexioned enough to pass for a southern European. Jamaicans are quite conscious of race and color differences; as we saw in Chapter 1, one component of the decolonization process was the vigorous promotion of the island's African heritage—in reggae music, dancehall culture, literature, and theater—in a successful devaluation of the British colonial cultural and racial heritage (on the complexities of this process, see Stone 1973; Thomas 2004: chaps. 1–2; Robotham 2000; Gray 1991: 82; Gray 2004: 4–59). Thus it is even more remarkable that Jamaicans have avoided playing the race card in their democratic wars. It's another of the island's many enigmas.

Democracies, as the world now knows, are especially vulnerable to terrorist threats. Terrorists notoriously exploit the freedoms that democracies allow their citizens. They can enter more easily, move around without being watched, have access to numerous targets, take advantage of free markets to launder money and buy weapons, make full use of the internet to communicate among themselves and spread their ideas, and are shielded by legal systems that assume innocence until guilt is proven (Schmid 1992; Eubank and Weinberg 1994, 1998). A more nuanced claim is that mature democracies are less likely to experience terrorism because the price of nonviolent political behavior and expression is low, while newer and less mature democracies are significantly more vulnerable (Eyerman 1998). It should be pointed out, though, that recent developments in Europe and the United States undermine this claim. With the exception of Trinidad, Jamaica and the other Caribbean societies have so far not fallen victim to this democratic vulnerability.

We come closer to home when we take account of another of democracy's vulnerabilities: organized crime. Jamaica is a prime example of this threat, along with several of its sister Caribbean democracies. Organized crime, including illicit drug production and trading, is a threat to democracies worldwide, however, and the mature democracies of Europe are no exception. A recent white paper from the Council of Europe notes that, with some 3,600 groups active on the continent, organized crime has become endemic not only in eastern and central Europe but also in several of the major Western democracies, most notably Belgium and the Netherlands. It notes further that transnational organized crime

> contributes significantly to undermining the rule of law and compromising the integrity of democratic institutions. . . . The negative impact on national economies cannot be overstated. Significant amounts of money are lost through tax evasion, money laundering and illegal economic markets, not to mention the indirect economic harm caused by organised crime as a criminal activity that can undermine the credibility and competitiveness of a state's financial and commercial sectors. (Council of Europe 2014: 9)

Paradoxically, organized crime groups, though authoritarian and violent in nature, need a democratic environment and its freedoms in which to establish themselves and thrive, according to Allum and Siebert: "to protect their illegal as well as their legal businesses organized gangs increasingly penetrate and seek to influence the legal, judicial and security systems" (2008: 5). Jamaica is among the list of countries they single out as being especially vulnerable (see also Harriott 2008).

Many Caribbean societies, including Puerto Rico, the Dominican Republic, Antigua, and even little St. Kitts, are attractive to organized crime, especially the drug cartels, because of their geographic location and democratic though relatively weak states. A joint study by the UNODC and the World Bank (2007) concluded that the narcotics trade was the major cause of the exceptional level of crime and violence in the region, the street value of the drugs coursing through its small economies exceeding the value of the entire legal economy (see also Solis and Aravena 2009: 23). Writing of Jamaica, Central America, and Brazil, Manwaring contends that their organized crime gangs have evolved into "internationalized commercial-political organizations" constituting a new kind of civil war in which national sovereignty is being invaded street by street, neighborhood by neighborhood in a "clash of controlling values between liberal democracy and criminal anarchy" (2007: 1–12).

Jamaica offered special attractions to the international drug cartels (Harriott 2008). These included the preexisting urban political and criminal gangs, the long-established ganja (marijuana) drug culture hailing back to the late nineteenth century, and, more generally, a greater cultural tendency toward violent and underground economic activities enabled by the island's huge informal economic sector. As a major recent study of crime in the island reports, "Gangs and organized crime are major engines of violence in Jamaica, particularly homicides" and "Organized crime is a prime source of corruption in the state and polity" (Harriott and Jones 2016: 38; see also Gray 2004: 27–29, 74–76, 238–240). In 2013 there were 238 gangs on the island, concentrated in the urban areas, especially western Kingston, accounting for 79 percent of all homicides.

How extensive is the illicit drug trade in Jamaica when compared with other countries of Latin America and the Caribbean, and what are its possible effects on the homicide rate? One measure of drug involvement is the amount of drugs seized annually by the authorities. I have used UNODC data on seizures of all illicit drugs in the region between 2010 and 2014 to construct a simple index of seizures per 100,000 persons. For each country, I have used a single year, that in which there was the highest amount of seized drugs; in the case of Jamaica, that year is 2013. Note that this was not by any means the highest amount of seized contraband ever in the island—only for the 2010–2014 period, when the island's involvement with the trade was actually in decline due to vigorous interdiction activity by the US government in collaboration with the Jamaican authorities. Figure 2.2 presents my findings. Jamaica, as we can see, is by far the country with the highest rate of drug seizures per 100,000 persons in the region and very likely in the world. The index for the island in 2013 was 59,950 kilograms of illicit drugs seized per 100,000 persons, far above Belize and Trinidad/Tobago, the countries with the second- and third-highest seizure rates, 37,661 and 35,785 kilograms respectively. Remarkably, the Jamaican seizure rate was 18.4 times that of Colombia (3,252 kilos per 100,000) and 76 times that of Mexico (790 kilos per 100,000), the dominant drug-exporting countries of the hemisphere in absolute economic and demographic terms. As Figure 2.2 indicates, the seizure rate moderately predicts the homicide rate ($R^2 = 0.3655$).

There is an additional role of organized crime that is especially pertinent to Jamaica and other democracies with failed or stagnant economies: in some cases, transnational crime organizations act as an alternative state providing what the economic system fails to do for many in its poorest areas—jobs, protection, security, goods, and services (Gray 2004: 286–302; Fahim 2010; Thomas 2011: 42–43). In reference to this "democratization of

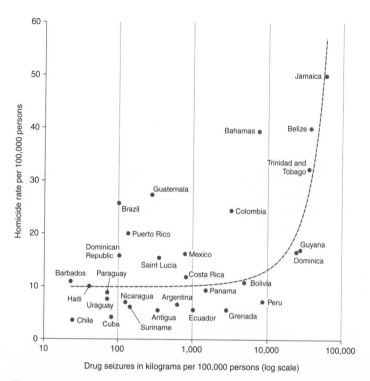

Figure 2.2. Homicide rate by highest annual drug seizures per 100,000 persons in Latin America and the Caribbean, 2010–2014

Data source: Annual Seizures 2010–2014, UNODC Statistics.

violence" in the Dominican Republic, the sociologist Lilian Bobea writes: "In such settings, state power is co-opted, ceded or shared with non-state, sometimes criminal and violent, actors. Rather than a lack of institutional presence in the strict sense of the term, these societies are characterized by the emergence of alternative authorities, actors and arbiters that renegotiate power, both public and private, formal and informal, licit and illicit" (2011: 6; see also Allum and Siebert 2008).

This pattern emerged in spectacular fashion in Jamaica after the 1980 election, when the more entrepreneurial and violent members of the various political gangs became increasingly involved with the international drug cartels and migrated to America, where they cut deep into the United States illicit drug trade, leaving a wave of brutal murders in their wake (Gunst 1995; Manwaring 2007: 33–40). Establishing an illicit transnational community between Jamaica and the United States, they were soon far wealthier than their previous Jamaican political patrons. They turned the tables on them by becoming dons or overlords in the political constituencies to whom the politicians had to turn for support during and after election periods (Gray 2004: 251–316; Blake 2012; Sives 2010: 133–142; Harriott 2003: 89–112; Figueroa and Sives 2003: 63–87). These dons spent lavishly in their garrisons and other domains and offered in brutal fashion the security, partial peace, and basic economic benefits that the state had failed to deliver (Blake 2013).

The most famous of these international dons was Christopher "Dudus" Coke, a second-generation druglord who headed the transnational gang called the Shower Posse that shipped huge quantities of marijuana and cocaine to the United States. When the US government in 2010 demanded his extradition to America, it created a crisis for the reigning Jamaica Labour Party because Coke's domain was the notorious garrison community of Tivoli Gardens, which was the heart of an important constituency for the previous as well as the current prime minister. When, under pressure from the Obama administration, the government sent in the military to dislodge Coke, a civil war nearly erupted in the West Kingston area that was under Coke's control. The impoverished residents in his domain lionized him as a Jamaican Robin Hood who provided schoolbooks to children, furnished loans and gifts to the needy, hunted down and executed people guilty of crimes such as rape and theft (though many dons themselves demanded the sexual submission of young girls), and promoted wildly popular biannual reggae concerts, with one of Jamaica's most revered reggae singers, Bunny Wailer (formerly of Bob Marley and the Wailers), even recording a song in his honor. Over seventy civilians, gunmen, and outraged ghetto residents (including a soldier and two police officers) died in the chaos, and some five hundred were arrested. Among the placards posted by resisters in Coke's defense was one that read "Jesus died for us, we will die for Dudus" (see Grillo 2014; Schwartz 2015). The reduction in the homicide rate after the arrest and extradition of Dudus Coke left no doubt that international organized crime is a major contributor to this problem.

The homicide rate has nonetheless recently begun to increase again. Although the Jamaican government, working closely with US authorities, has cut down greatly on the transshipment of illicit drugs through Jamaica, this has had a perverse effect on homicides, as Peter Phillips, formerly the minister of justice, explained to me when I interviewed him several years ago. When the illicit trade was thriving and vast sums of money were flowing through the island's underground economy, people were killed for real or perceived transgressions involving relatively large sums of money. A pilfered or unaccounted-for thousand dollars here or there was not worth the bother of drawing the attention of the authorities or hiring a hitman. However, as this abundant flow of cash dried up, more and more players found themselves fighting for a declining pool of illicit funds, resulting in a rapid increase in the rate of homicide.[3]

The Cultural Dimension of Jamaica's Violence

Various studies, including the UNODC study of global violence (UNODC 2014a), have noted that the Caribbean and Latin American regions exhibit levels of violence far above the rest of the world, in ways that cannot be fully explained in terms of the socioeconomic and political factors examined above. Several authors have argued that distinctive aspects of the history and culture of the region must be at play in accounting for this excessive level of violence. What Jerome Neapolitan (2003) wrote of Latin America holds with even greater force for Jamaica and most of the other Caribbean islands: that there is "a strong cultural component to the high homicide rate" that "evolved out of the history of colonization and subjection that is shared by these nations."

Before proceeding, it ought to be noted that in certain sections of the social science community there is strong intellectual aversion to most "cultural" explanations. This aversion goes back to the mid-twentieth-century deterministic and teleological views of Parsonian and modernization theory, the culture of poverty thesis championed by Oscar Lewis as far back as the 1960s, and later uses of the culture concept by conservatives as a way of blaming the poor for their condition. There is also a racial dimension originating in reaction to the 1965 Moynihan Report, which attributed black disadvantage, in part, to the single-parent black family. This is not the place to engage at any length with these issues, except to say that modern cultural sociologists have long moved beyond them (Small, Harding, and Lamont 2010; Patterson 2014, 2015); any remaining debate now amounts to both flogging a dead horse and throwing the baby of cultural processes and causality out with the bath water. I have discussed these issues at length elsewhere (Patterson 2014).

There is no such thing as *the* culture of poverty. Poor people are as varied in their cultural processes and behaviors as middle-class and rich people. Nonetheless, cultural practice is a defining feature of the human condition, and cultural processes do matter in any full account of social outcomes. The question is how. I define cultural processes as any shared and valorized set of schematized knowledge and beliefs among given networks of persons and their pragmatic expressions (Patterson 2014). Such networks can exist at any level of generality, from gangs, organizations, and communities to nations and civilizations. Further, people are not confined to a single cultural network. In our modern complex world we share several sociocultural configurations (a term I prefer; see Patterson 2014: 20–22), some overlapping, others not, in much the same way that we have multiple identities. As a Jamaican professor at Harvard with homes, and networks of different classes, in both countries, I share multiple cultural configurations and multiple identities. Shared cultural schemas are predispositional but not deterministic. They are deep preferences, habits, *hexis* (body posture and style), what Bourdieu (1990) called *habitus,* derived from "status-linked home environments driven both by the child's exposure to parental practices keyed to instruction and socialization, and by her active, bodily interaction with material objects and built environments, as well as her exposure to specific sensory experiences" (Lizardo 2010). Cultural processes are contextual and always operate interactively and situationally with the socioeconomic environment. Our decision to activate particular cultural schemas is a function of our situation and available resources (Patterson 2014: 19–20). And Wacquant, Bourdieu's collaborator, recently made clear that "habitus is never the replica of a single social structure but a dynamic, multiscalar, and multilayered set of schemata subject to 'permanent revision' in practice" (2016).

There can be no doubt that the distinctive features of Jamaica's past have much to do with the cultural schemas and practices of violence that preexisted and enabled modern socioeconomic and political factors to contribute to its high homicide rate. Slavery was an institutionalized form of naked violence. Violence was also ritualized and publicly represented in many ghastly ways, such as male slaves being forced to eat the feces of their fellow slaves, whippings, masks, gags, severed heads impaled on roadside posts, amputations, brandings, disfigurings, quarterings, garrotings, hangings, and endless scenes and rituals of death (Burnard 2004; Vincent Brown 2010; Patterson 1967). The belief that all forms of discipline and persuasion ultimately rest on force had nearly two centuries to develop and become ingrained in the emerging creole cultures, to be perpetuated during the post-emancipation era by extreme retaliation against riots and the regular use of the cat-o'-nine-tails as a supplement to imprisonment for often minor crimes, practices that persisted until as late as the 1990s. Tragically, this valorization of corporal punishment was also culturally perpetuated in child-rearing practices as well as in interpersonal and employer–employee relations. It is not by accident that the great majority of post-slavery societies exhibit much higher rates of homicide, among the descendants of slave owners and slaves alike. With good reason, states in the US South, especially those that had the highest levels of slavery in the nineteenth century, by and large have the highest homicide rates in America (Wyatt-Brown 1986; Nisbett and Cohen 1996). To be sure, slavery was not all-determining. As we have seen, Barbados has a relatively low rate of homicide, its slave past notwithstanding. But Jamaica's slave system was especially brutal, and its post-emancipation history was also unusually violent.

While the subject is complex, let me highlight three cultural processes in Jamaica that are critical in explaining its unusual level of violence, reinforcing the political and socioeconomic factors discussed above. First is the fact that the vast majority of the nation's children, some 86 percent, are being brought up without the psychological or financial support of a father and by mothers who, while desiring the best for their children as mothers everywhere do, are often too overworked, underemployed, or underpaid (and overstressed) to devote sufficient care, beyond meeting basic needs, to their children. Emotional neglect resulting from maternal exhaustion and anxiety is a major consequence. Jamaican urban low-income children, and even some middle-class ones, told researchers that their parents had little time for their emotional concerns and that attempts to raise such matters were generally futile. Indeed, for several of them "discussing their feelings with their parents seemed a strange concept" (Brown and Johnson 2008: 35). It is therefore hardly surprising that a recent econometric study of crime and development (UNODC and World Bank 2007) found, at both the household and communal/provincial levels in Jamaica, a significant positive relation between the homicide rate and the proportion of single-parent households, the size of the cohort of young men, and the educational level. Interestingly, these associations were not significant for the Dominican Republic and Haiti. As Mackey notes, a causal link is yet to be proven, but what seems clear is that the "continuous presence of a social and biological father does reduce the level of violent crime within a community" (2004: 70).

Second is the closely related but distinctive fact of tension-ridden and abusive relationships between men and women (Harriott and Jones 2016: 25–28, 31–33; Arscott-Mills 2001; Le Franc et al. 2008). Jamaica stands out globally in this regard. Researchers have established that the values of patriarchy and the sexual exploitation of women are "deeply embedded in Jamaica's gender system" (Ishida, Stupp, and McDonald 2011: 6), leading

to high-risk sexual behavior, multiple partners, and the marginalization of (and violence toward) women, starting from adolescence (see also Eggleston, Jackson, and Hardee 1999; Waszak
Geary et al. 2006; Baumgartner et al. 2009). This was startlingly
evident to me from my ethnographic fieldwork in a low-income
central Kingston community during the early 1970s. A disturbing
feature of Jamaica's homicide rate is the fact that a significant
proportion of murders are domestic killings (nearly 10% in
2012), often involving fights between men and women (Harriott
and Jones 2016: figure 2.19). A 2006 report by Amnesty International, aptly titled "Sexual Violence against Women and Girls in
Jamaica: 'Just a Little Sex,'" found that harassment and assault
by strangers, relatives, friends, and acquaintances were at near-
epidemic levels on the island, creating not only a brutalizing environment for women but also severe health risks for them and for
the nation at large, sexual assault being the second most common
cause of injury to women, after fights. One horrendous aspect of
the control of poor neighborhoods by criminal dons is their expectation of sex from young girls under threat of death to the
girls or members of their families. A thirteen-year-old girl told
AIDS researchers that "some of the Dons. . . . when they call for
you, you have to go. And they don't use condoms . . . but if you
don't go to them they will shoot you or your family. So you get
AIDS and die later, or you refuse [to have sex with them] and
they shoot you now" (Hutchinson et al. 2007: 44).

A major problem is that the authorities, including the Jamaican state, do not take gender violence seriously. According
to the report, "violence against women in Jamaica persists
because the state is failing to tackle discrimination against
women, allowing social and cultural attitudes which encourage
discrimination and violence." Indeed, the report found that "discrimination is entrenched and often exacerbated in the police

and criminal justice system. Women and adolescent girls are rarely believed by the police, so have little confidence in reporting crimes against them" (Hutchinson et al. 2007). Other studies have replicated these findings (Lazarus-Black 2008). One consequence of all this is that in 2016 Jamaica had the highest homicide rate for women and girls in the world: 25.6 per 100,000 of the female population (McEvoy and Hideg 2017: 12, 67).

Also related is the third factor: childhood abuse and violence-inducing child-rearing practices. Too many Jamaicans confuse bringing up a child with physical punishment, to a degree that would land them in jail in most Western societies (Smith and Mosby 2003; Samms-Vaughn, Williams, and Brown 2005; Harriott and Jones 2016: 28–30). A World Bank study on urban poverty and violence in Jamaica reported appalling testimony from Jamaicans about the brutalization of children (Moser and Holland 1997). One interviewed woman, for example, called the problem a disease in her community that, she said, was "perpetuated particularly by women, and particularly when times are hard and money in short supply." She told the authors of the report that as a result, children fled their homes and became delinquent; she described children being subjected to verbal abuse, harsh flogging and kicking, and even the burning of their body parts. One deeply moving, if horrifying, personal testimony to the punishment meted out to children by their parents or caregivers in Jamaica is the recent autobiography of Yvonne Shorter Brown (2010), who grew up in the same small country town as I did (May Pen). Her descriptions of the frequent "murderations" (the creole term many Jamaican parents use for specially harsh lashing of their children) she endured were distressingly familiar.

As indicated earlier, these three cultural processes are closely interrelated. Men abuse women and abandon their baby mothers. Overburdened, the mothers often take out their frustration and anger on their children, especially on their boys, until they are too old to handle them. The boys, in turn, grow up to be abusive lovers and fathers; as is well known, child abuse is the best predictor of adult violence. Violence within the family then breeds violence toward others outside the family. This is universally the case, as Anderson and Richards point out: "Domestic abuse and neglect as well as sexual predation have repercussions beyond the family, violating the social fabric of the entire community, leaving everyone ripped up emotionally and ill at ease, permanently, with other vulnerable individuals becoming fearful as well" (2004: 4). These negative consequences are even greater if the environment offers little beyond unemployment, frustration, the underground economy of drugs, and, as Gayle (2009) documents, participation in tribal political violence.

This tragic bundle of interrelated factors also generates high-risk behavior that extends beyond sexual relations. It is related to the relatively high rate of HIV on the island (Hutchinson et al. 2007; Figueroa et al. 2008) as well as the high rate of murder of women and of other men in sexual revenge and competitive killings (a correlation found in other parts of the world; see Minkov 2009); and a greater propensity to engage in illicit activities such as domestic and international drug dealing and lottery phone scamming (Eldemire 2018) which are, in turn, major contributors to homicide.

What Can Be Done to Reduce Jamaica's Level of Violence?

How to reduce the catastrophic rate of violence in Jamaica has long preoccupied its government and people. There is no shortage of data, studies, and proposed policies for solving the problem.

Indeed, compared with other countries at its level of development, the island stands out for the number of governmental and nongovernmental studies, policy statements, and organizations devoted to the alleviation of violence. Jamaica's National Security Policy strategy (Clayton 2012) is a model of evidence-based, well-considered anticrime proposals focusing on six sensible reforms: making crime unprofitable; reforming the overburdened justice system; reforming the police force with an emphasis on eliminating corruption, increasing educational levels, training officers, and emphasizing the consent of citizens; adopting a coherent anti-gang strategy grounded in the best available research on the subject; focusing on hot spots, such as at-risk individuals and communities; and strengthening government agencies concerned with crime. Equally impressive is the more recent "five pillar strategy" (Ministry of National Security 2017). Complementing these are numerous reports by other government agencies such as the Jamaica Constabulary Force (2011). In addition, there are excellent reports by academics, domestic NGOs, and international organizations such as the work sponsored by the Inter-American Development Bank (IDB) and authored by Harriott and Jones (2016) and the report by the UNODC and World Bank (2007).

These reports have generated numerous regional, national, and local organizations devoted to both the immediate problem of crime reduction and the longer-term problem of crime prevention. The British, Canadian, and American governments have provided the island with substantial monetary and technical aid in addressing the problem of violence, especially in the reform of its police force (see World Bank 2015a). The IDB has made a major investment in the Citizen Security and Justice Program, which aims at enhancing institutional capacity in the government's anticrime organizations and coordinates with the work of nongovermental organizations on community development programs that provide economic opportunities for disconnected youth as a means of reducing crime. A table listing all these programs, projects, and initiatives runs to fourteen small-print pages (Harriott and Jones 2016: 90–104, table 4.1). They include programs aimed at police reform and accountability, justice reform, youth rehabilitation, behavior modification, gender justice, child and sexual abuse, women's resource and outreach, community renewal and empowerment, neighborhood crime watch, rehabilitation and reintegration of offenders, restorative justice, safe schools, and cultural re-socialization interventions.

Notwithstanding all these studies, policy agendas, and public and private initiatives, Jamaica's level of violence stubbornly remains among the worst in the world. After a promising decline in the five years between 2010 and 2014, the crime rate has begun to soar again, seemingly indifferent to the substantial network of institutional structures and programs aimed at reducing it. A major issue is the persistence of police corruption and inefficiency, in spite of numerous studies and recommendations to reform the system. The police not only continue to protect criminal dons in exchange for bribes but also participate in the illicit drug trade and supply arms to criminals from seized stockpiles. Extrajudicial police killings continue. Between 2000 and 2010 there were 2,200 killings by police, carried out with near impunity. The force's inefficiency is appalling: On average, arrests are made in only 44 percent of cases (World Bank 2015a). In striking contrast, the Barbadian police force solved 85.7 percent of its homicide cases in 2012 (World Bank 2015b). In such a police environment, the government's top-ranked policy goal of making crime unprofitable seems a bad joke. Not only is crime very profitable in Jamaica, but the risks taken in committing it are nearly negligible.

The factors that hinder the fight against crime and violence seem distressingly similar to those accounting for Jamaica's stagnant economy, discussed in Chapter 1—not the absence of institutions or good policies but the absence of institutional learning, know-how, and organizational competence. Even more important is the lack of political will to implement the many available recommendations, as the Wolfe Report emphasized over twenty years ago (Wolfe 1993). The problem of crime and violence in Jamaica is, in good part, a political one, enabled and reinforced by economic, cultural, and illicit international factors, and hence its solution has to begin with political reform. At the very least such reform must involve an end to the patronage-based, clientelistic method of gaining votes. How this is to be done is now well known. What is needed is the political will of both parties to implement a jointly agreed upon plan of action.

For one thing, the garrison communities must go. This will be difficult, since several leading politicians in both parties have their constituencies in these sociopolitical cesspools of violence. At the very least, the apartment complexes that house the political henchmen and their families—including the notorious Tivoli Gardens—should be cleared of violent political supporters or else torn down and their residents resettled elsewhere. The government should get out of the business of building and housing citizens and instead concentrate on upgrading existing low-income communities by bringing in basic services such as indoor plumbing, garbage collection, electricity, health services, preschools, and programs aimed at strengthening communities. This is a well-tried approach, one that I attempted many years ago. (For a discussion of the political problems of implementing such programs, see Chapter 8.)

One way or the other, a solution has to be found to the plague of criminal gang violence. These gangs, heavily involved in the narcotics trade, were started by the two main political parties, and they have now become independent or quasi-independent monsters biting the hands that originally fed them. Simply removing the dons will not, however, solve the problem. Indeed, after a brief decline in crime when attempts are made to remove them, the rate tends to rise again to even greater levels largely because a power vacuum is created in which many lesser thugs begin to complete for control of the area using even more reckless means of violence. Recall that the dons gained their position mainly by filling the socioeconomic and security vacuum left by the state in their areas. Unless the state follows up by providing these services, they will be filled by others or, worse, by indiscriminate violence.

The use of special emergency forces to temporarily occupy high crime areas is another short-term solution that eventually makes matters worse. These "zones of special operation" (ZOSO), in which police and soldiers occupy a designated area, bring peace while they are there but, as the case of Denham Town in 2017 and 2018 shows, once these security personnel leave, the violence that returns is even greater. Residents have a clear-eyed view of what is needed. One terrified woman told a *Gleaner* reporter: "This is bigger than police and soldiers. They can't stop this. Only politicians can stop this because here is a garrison." Another pointed to the only lasting solution: "The people of Denham Town are crying out for help. The governor general, the prime minister, MP, we need them to come down to this constituency and help us. The people dem need some help" (Robinson 2018).

Both parties will have to agree to a set of anticorruption rules for politicians and administrators in all branches of government. Transparency International and the World Bank have issued detailed guidelines and best practices about how to proceed in this area, and there is no need to repeat them here, since they are readily accessible (Transparency International 2013; Hunja 2015). One that I consider essential for Jamaica is asset declaration in exact values (rather than a range of values), before and immediately after leaving office and also periodically while in office. An essential component of any such system is an independent monitoring agency with the power to verify declarations, publish discrepancies, and investigate and prosecute violators where necessary (Transparency International 2016).

Structural changes in Jamaica's economy, inequality, political practices, and criminal justice system are fundamental for any meaningful and sustained improvement in the level of violence. The problem must also be addressed, however, at the microcultural and microsociological levels, through badly needed changes in interpersonal, gender, and child-rearing beliefs and practices. This includes the island's horrendous homophobia and violence toward LGBTQ individuals, especially gay men (Charles 2011). It is significant that the UNODC (2014a), in its global report on crime prevention, now places primary emphasis on sociocultural change in its recommendations for reform. The strategies recognized as most effective from its recent study of 133 countries are the following, which I cite in full because they are so very appropriate for Jamaica:

1. Developing safe, stable, and nurturing relationships between children and their parents and caregivers;
2. Developing life skills in children and adolescents;
3. Reducing the availability and harmful use of alcohol;
4. Reducing access to guns and knives;
5. Promoting gender equality to prevent violence against women;

6. Changing cultural and social norms that support violence;
7. Implementing victim identification, care, and support programs.

The Jamaican authorities are quite aware of the social and cultural roots of the problem of violence in the island, given the number of excellent studies published in recent years on the subject. They have also established programs to address some of them, listed in Harriott and Jones (2016). However, what the UNODC survey found with regard to implementation applies with special force to Jamaica: "While countries are investing in prevention programmes representative of these strategies, it is not on a level commensurate with the scale and severity of the problem" (UNODC 2014a: ix, 27–32). It is now widely recognized that Jamaican children are being badly abused, both physically and sexually. Yet parents continue to defend harsh corporal punishment, and the practice continues with impunity in schools, from kindergarten all the way up to high school. Indeed, the minister of youth and culture recently declared that the ministry was still not ready to ban the practice, in spite of appeals from the United Nations Committee for the Rights of the Child (*Gleaner,* May 11, 2015).

The problem of violence against women must also be treated as one of utmost urgency, given the island's terrible position as the country with the highest rate of female homicide. At the very least, the police should take domestic violence seriously, which they currently do not, and establish special units to deal with the problem. The emphasis, however, should be on prevention, for instance through the use of training programs on gender equity and respectful gender relations. The good news here is that the government recently indicated its recognition of the problem by launching a "10-Year Action Plan to Eliminate Gender-Based Violence" (Permanent Mission of Jamaica to the UN 2017; see also Bureau of Gender Affairs 2016). The bad news is that bureaus of gender affairs are government administrative units where high-sounding gender policies go to die. It does not inspire confidence that the bureau is tucked away in the Ministry of Culture, Gender, Entertainment and Sport. Given the scale of the problem, it should be in the prime minister's office or possibly the Ministry of Education.

The area where the government can be most effective in making these essential behavioral and cultural changes is in the educational system, which is badly in need of reform. The problem is less the expenditure of funds than the apportionment of funds in the different sectors of the system, the institutional competence of its managers, and the quality of the teachers and the curriculum (Planning Institute of Jamaica 2009: 60–66). Jamaica currently spends more per student than Barbados, with vastly different results. Currently, a disproportionate amount of government expenditure goes to the tertiary sector, and this should change in favor of the pre-primary, primary, and secondary levels of the system. This is critical in light of the fact that Jamaican tertiary-level graduates leave the country at one of the highest rates of skilled migration in the world, more than 75 percent by one estimate (Parkins 2010: 9) and even as high as 85 percent, according to the World Bank (2004). At the same time, the secondary sector is failing badly, with high rates of dropouts as well as functional illiteracy and a lack of skills among a large proportion of those who do graduate. This directly contributes to the scourge of violent gangs, since many youth leaving the system see no other alternative but to join in order to ensure a livelihood and sheer physical survival. Indeed, the problem begins even within schools, many of which have a serious problem

of violence and criminal gang activity (Planning Institute of Jamaica 2009: 62)

Educational funds should be shifted toward the improvement
of preschool, primary, and secondary education with an emphasis
on working skills. The national Human Employment and Resource Training Trust/National Training Agency, or HEART
Trust, has successfully trained thousands of unemployed and unattached youth in useful job skills, both in its own institutions
and on job sites; this is the one bright spot in the educational
system, which should be greatly enlarged. Vocational and technical training within the formal primary and secondary sectors,
however, has fared poorly. In keeping with the sound advice of
the UN, the curriculum of all schools from kindergarten to secondary school should include training in life skills, including
child-rearing skills, gender equality, respect for human life and
basic human rights including the rights of the child, civics (especially the norms of electoral politics), and norms and values that
deemphasize violence. It cannot be emphasized too strongly that
the barbaric practice of corporal punishment should be abolished
at all levels of the educational system and also made illegal for
parents and all others who care for children. There is a straight
pipeline from the "murderation" of children by their parents to
the murder of others by those very same children before they
even become adults.

Conclusion

This chapter has emphasized the relationship between democracy and Jamaica's high rate of violence. However, nothing I have
written should be taken to imply the need for any compromises
in the practice of democracy or, more broadly, of political freedom

on the island. Other factors, I have argued, are as important as Jamaica's transitional democracy in explaining its violence. However flawed, Jamaica's democracy is genuine and thoroughly ingrained in the country's way of life. There is near-universal commitment to it, even among the lawless. It has passed the ultimate test of true democracies: repeated changes of government between major political parties in unrigged, fair, and transparent elections, however violent the process. A flawed democracy, whatever the price, is always to be preferred to an authoritarian system, however benign. The false view that it is easier to develop economically under authoritarian regimes should be resisted. The few economic successes of such regimes are far outnumbered by the failures all over Africa, Asia, and Latin America. I am inclined to agree with those who argue that after a volatile transitional period democracies tend to be associated with greater prosperity, a view forcefully articulated by Friedrich Hayek when he wrote: "It is in its dynamic, rather than in its static, aspects that the value of democracy proves itself. As is true of liberty, the benefits of democracy will show themselves only in the long run, while its more immediate achievements may well be inferior to those of other forms of government" (Hayek 1960: 109, cited in Papaioannou and Siourounis 2007: 2).

I identified the role of democracy in the island's problem of violence not to justify abandoning democracy, but in order to improve it and hasten it on the path to maturity. Churchill famously quoted an unknown source to the effect that "democracy is the worst form of government except for all those other forms that have been tried from time to time." Even in its current turbulent, transitional phase, democratic Jamaica is greatly to be preferred to its authoritarian neighbors in Latin America and elsewhere, past and present. What greater Hobbesian nightmare could there be than life today in Honduras, El Salvador, and Guatemala or, not so long ago, Duvalier's Haiti, Trujillo's Dominican Republic, Pinochet's Chile, or Argentina and Brazil under the generals? What the Polish activist intellectual Adam Michnik wrote shortly after the fall of communism in his own society is worth remembering, not only by Jamaicans but also by Poles as their country veers back toward neofascist authoritarianism: "As a rule, dictatorships guarantee safe streets and the terror of the doorbell. In democracy the streets may be unsafe after dark, but the most likely visitor in the early hours will be the milkman" (Michnik 1998).

3

Were Female Workers Preferred in Jamaica's Early Economic Development?

Employment, Urbanization, and Gender among the Postcolonial Proletariat

During the development of capitalism, both in the West and in East Asian nations, the accompanying rise of urbanization tended to facilitate the emergence of two patterns that were closely linked to the structure of employment. One of these was the successful proletarianization of the labor force. Workers were alienated from the land and other means of subsistence and were hence forced to adapt to the regimen of the factory; this discipline was further enhanced by the educational system and other control mechanisms as well as by the incentive of new commercial needs (Durand 1975). Closely related to this development was the growing sexual division of labor. Women, following the decline of traditional production patterns in which they were economically integrated, were soon relegated either to the home or to a secondary labor market, where they acted as a kind of latent reserve in the potential labor force (Boserup 1970; Goldin 1990). In general, it was men who initially experienced the full disciplining of the capitalist labor force, while women were largely marginalized, their return to the formal labor force taking place only in the more mature stage of economic development. Scholars of economic development refer to this U-shaped process as the feminization U-hypothesis (Tam 2011).

While this pattern of labor force development has been reproduced in many parts of the developing world, a significant subset of developing countries, mainly in the Caribbean Basin, depart sharply from it. Jamaica is an extreme case in point. In a study conducted in the 1970s, the economist Guy Standing, with the ILO (International Labour Organization of the UN), found that the highly dependent nature of Jamaica's "industrialization by invitation" program, along with widespread poverty, unemployment and underemployment, urbanization, the educational system, and the modes of labor recruitment, created an environment in which the male labor force was chronically unproletarianized, with low levels of commitment to work, reflected in intermittent entry into the work force, high levels of absenteeism, a serious mismatch between expected and actual income, and the familiar trinity of alienation, frustration, and hostility (Standing 1981b). These same forces propelled women into the workforce to a degree greater than in most other areas of the world; women were proletarianized in much the same way that male workers in Europe, America, and East Asia had been during those regions' periods of development. In other words, not only was there no sexual dualism of the workforce, but the disciplining of labor was directed at women rather than men, with employers systematically preferring female to male labor (see also Maunder 1962).

Standing's findings are so extraordinary that they deserve reconsideration. In my capacity as special advisor for social policy to Prime Minister Michael Manley in the 1970s, I conducted several major surveys of the same urban population (Kingston) at about the same time that Standing executed his study, accompanied by a long-term ethnographic study of the urban poor. This chapter draws upon these data in an attempt to assess and replicate Standing's findings. In the concluding section I evaluate the extent to which the condition of the urban poor has improved over the more than half century of economic change since I conducted the study.

Conceptual Problems in the Comparative Study of Employment and Unemployment

Before proceeding, let us take account of some fundamental problems pertaining to any consideration of employment and unemployment in the developing world. Unlike the situation in advanced industrial countries, analysts of developing societies must first address some basic questions of the meaning and measurement of these categories. It is not at all clear just what employment and unemployment mean in these societies; more precisely, there is such variation in the definition of these terms that comparisons are often problematic. Four basic terms are at issue: the economically active population, the employed, the unemployed, and the underemployed. A great deal of effort has been expended in attempting to clarify these terms, especially by the International Labour Office, upon whose work I draw on here (Hussmanns, Mehran, and Verma 1990; ILO 2011; Standing 1981a).

The most basic problem lies in defining and measuring the labor force, that is, the economically active population. The most authoritative source on the subject, the ILO Manual, asserts that "according to international standards, the economically active population comprises all persons of either sex who furnish the supply of labour for the production of goods and services . . . during a specified time-reference period" (Hussmanns, Mehran, and Verma 1990: 11). Problems arise as soon as we come to consider what categories of persons are to be included, as well as what kinds of economic activities, leading to enormous variation from one country to another. The most important source of this variation relates to the economic role of women; to complicate matters, there is an objective and a subjective aspect of the problem. In objective economic terms, countries vary in the degree to which women are economically active in the production of goods and services, especially in the formal economic sector. However, the subjective issues are more critical. In the first place, there is disagreement from one country to the next as to whether the kinds of activities usually performed by women in traditional societies should be included in any definition of goods and services. And in the second place, religious and ideological factors greatly influence the nature of the data gathered. In many societies, for example, women who are clearly producing goods and services by the ILO definition are not counted for religious and other cultural reasons. Beyond these problems is the equally thorny question of how to define meaningful work. Deciding whether an activity is work "for pay, profit, or family gain; work for money or share of output; work in a job, business or farm; work as employee or self-employed" (Hussmanns, Mehran, and Verma 1990: 26) is a conceptually difficult challenge that has the potential to lead to distortions in labor force surveys.

These questions lead directly to the problem of defining employment. According to the international standards set by the ILO, the employed are those members of the labor force in "paid employment (1) 'at work': persons who, during the reference period, performed some work for wage or salary, in cash or kind;

(2) 'with a job but not at work': persons who, having already worked at their present job, were temporarily not at work during the reference period but had a formal attachment to their job" (ILO 1983: ix–xv). The employed also include the self-employed: those who are "(1) 'at work': persons who, during the reference period, performed some work for profit or family gain, in cash or kind; (2) 'with an enterprise but not at work': persons with an enterprise, which may be a business enterprise, a farm or service undertaking, who were temporarily not at work during the reference period for some specific reason."

We hardly need to spell out the difficulties of applying this formula with any consistency, even in the same country from one period to another, much less between one country and another. How many hours constitute "some work"? What does "formal attachment to their job" mean? What if the employer refuses to recognize any such attachment? Even more problematic are the self-employed. Using the above definition, almost all forms of human activity could be classified as employment, which partly explains the extreme variations between countries or within the same country over time. The problems become acute for those who are not in the formal market economy or who are working in the underground economy. Are beggars, hustlers, and the like "employed"? And what about those in illegal activities, such as the sale of illicit drugs? This is a major source of income for many lower-class Jamaicans, as is true of many other developing societies. What about artists and entertainers, another large category in Jamaica, with its lively reggae music culture, who often work only sporadically? The ILO is, of course, fully aware of these problems. Nonetheless, the publication of "international standards" has not done much to resolve any of them.

The unemployment rate complements the employment rate. The ILO officially defines the two categories so that they are mutually exclusive. Hence the unemployed include members of the economically active population who are "(a) without work, i.e. were not in paid employment or self-employment . . . (b) currently available for work, i.e. were available for paid employment or self-employment . . . and (c) seeking work, i.e. had taken specific steps in a specified recent period to seek paid employment" (Hussmanns, Mehran, and Verma 1990: 97).

The problems with this definition are similar to those with the definition of employment. There is a fundamental difference between advanced societies, with nearly full employment, and those in which unemployment is chronic—in many poor countries the unemployment rate ranges from 25 percent to about 60 percent. Indeed, some have seriously questioned whether it makes sense at all to speak of an unemployment problem in certain very poor and undeveloped societies where the notion of being "currently available for work" may be irrelevant, there being no meaningful formal economic activity, as defined by the ILO, anywhere on the horizon for most of the adult population (Weeks 1973: 61–65; Streeten 1973: 55–60). These considerations have led to the use of the "underemployment" concept, one rarely referred to in the advanced industrial economies. A resolution at the 1966 International Conference of Labour Statisticians stated that there is underemployment "when a person's employment is inadequate, in relation to specified norms of alternative employment, account being taken of his occupational skill (training and working experience)" (cited in Hussmanns, Mehran, and Verma 1990: 212). And an ILO manual from this period adds: "Two principal forms of underemployment are distinguished: visible underemployment, reflecting an insufficiency in the volume of employment; and invisible underemployment, characterized by low income, underutilization of skill, low productivity and other factors" (Hussmanns, Mehran, and Verma 1990: 212).

The problem of underemployment is of special relevance to developing countries with a high proportion of the labor force in agriculture and in the urban informal sector. Indeed, it may be said with no exaggeration that the majority of people in most of these societies are underemployed. And since most of them are "invisibly" underemployed, the problem of measurement is obviously acute. I know of no accurate measurement of this category of labor. It is likely that no such measurement is possible, since all criteria are likely to be either impossibly vague or too influenced by subjective factors. As the ILO manual itself notes, the criterion of "low income" is frequently meaningless as an indicator of disguised or invisible underemployment because of price fluctuations, institutional practices, and irregular patterns of earnings (see also ILO 2015).

In light of these problems, it must be seriously questioned whether the use of these concepts takes us very far in our understanding of Third World societies. My response is that they are relevant in some cases but not in others. In this regard, we may distinguish three kinds of developing economies: the traditional, the dualistic, and the newly industrialized. By "traditional," I refer to the most undeveloped economies, in which the vast majority of the population, both in rural and urban areas, do not participate in a formal labor market; that is, they do not sell their labor on any regular basis. This is true of most of sub-Saharan Africa, Haiti, and many peasant-based societies in Asia. In these societies, employment is *tradition-driven,* by which I mean that employment is defined and determined not by capital resources and effective demand but by institutional and cultural practices. People work to meet basic needs as well as kinship and other non-economic obligations; according to rhythms not set by man-made operations or organizations; and at intensities of effort having little relation to what is actually produced. Thus, a man may spend as much time producing a carving representing his dead ancestor as he does on his harvest; a woman may spend far more time selling goods in the public market, for social reasons, than can be justified by any criterion of efficiency; and patron-client obligations may dictate work effort and earnings in kind or money far more than any existing labor market. It is doubtful whether even the well-known backward-sloping supply curve of labor applies to many of the poorer of these economies, for there may be no supply curve at all, or the supply curve may be an inverted S-shape (Dessing 2002)—that is to say, the assumption that if jobs were provided there would be takers, even takers with a strong propensity to substitute leisure for money income, may be wholly unfounded.

I use the term "dualistic" economies in full awareness of its ambiguities. I mean by it, following A. W. Lewis (1960) and others (see Meier 1989), simply those societies that have a well-developed modern sector combined with a non-modern, largely informal sector. Many of these economies fall in the middle to lower-middle range of developing countries, as defined by the World Bank (1994). In these economies, employment is *supply-driven.*[1] I do not assume, however, as Lewis did, that there is an unlimited supply of labor in the non-modern sector. Nor do I assume that the non-modern sector is necessarily either traditional or rural. Indeed, a dynamic conception of these economies assumes that the construction of the modern sector—usually the urban industrial, commercial farm, and mining sectors—entails the disruption of the previous traditional sector and the emergence of an urban and rural non-traditional, non-modern sector, often described as informal, although this term has come under attack in recent years.[2] With these caveats in mind, I am suggesting that it is precisely in this set of developing societies that the concepts of unemployment, employment, and underemployment are most meaningful. Many, often most, people are unemployed or underemployed in such economies, and meaningfully so, since in both sectors people are aware of, and desire, work for wages. I place Jamaica and most of the Caribbean and Central America in this category of societies. Indeed, Lewis originally developed his theory of dualistic economies with precisely these Caribbean societies in mind. Analyzing such societies without taking account of the non-modern sector can create serious puzzles, as the World Bank discovered in its 2004 country study of Jamaica when confronted with the contradiction of several years of negative growth accompanied by decreasing poverty rates.

The third category, that of the "newly industrialized" countries (NICs), is straightforward. These are successfully developing economies in which the labor market is fully developed, often functions at capacity levels, and applies to the entire economy. As in the advanced economies, employment and unemployment are *demand-driven;* fluctuations are usually structural, and it can be assumed that an increase in effective demand, combined with increased productive capacity, will be enough to absorb additional labor. There is usually not a major unemployment problem in these societies. The East Asian economies (before their recent elevation to the advanced level of development) are included in this category. Included also is Malaysia, and few isolated cases in the Caribbean, such as Barbados and the Bahamas.

Strictly speaking, then, outside of the advanced economies, only in the dualistic economies can we speak of a serious problem of unemployment and employment creation. It is here that we find the problems of chronic long-term unemployment, labor underutilization, and labor commitment, and Jamaica is a classic case in point.

Before launching into the case study, I should mention a characteristic feature of these supply-driven, dualistic economies. It is what may be called the employment paradox in their pattern of development (or mis-development). The paradox is simply that development, which is often pursued by these governments with the primary aim of reducing unemployment, nearly always results in an increased unemployment rate. If one looks, for example, at the first four decades of development in societies such as Puerto Rico, Jamaica, Trinidad, and Mexico, one finds that, in spite of sometimes rapid economic growth—especially during the 1950s and 1960s—the rate of unemployment during the growth period, as well as today, is invariably higher than the rate during the "backward" period of the 1940s. This occurred in spite of considerable job creation. Indeed—and here is the paradox—the generation of higher unemployment rates in these societies is, in good part, the direct result of the creation of new jobs in the modern sector.

Puerto Rico is the classic case in point. In 1950, the unemployment rate in Puerto Rico was 14.6 percent; in 1983, after thirty-three years of massive growth through industrialization that earned it the title of "economic miracle," Puerto Rico's unemployment rate stood at 24 percent. It oscillated in a downward trend to a low of 9.7 percent in the early 2000s, then shot back up to almost 17 percent in 2010, then down to its 2016 rate of 12 percent. What Carlos E. Santiago wrote during the 1990s holds equally true of the other Caribbean societies in this category of development: "It seems paradoxical that despite rapid economic growth and substantial migration, Puerto Rico continues to experience a severe unemployment problem" (1992: 25).[3]

The paradox is explained in several ways. First, there is Michael Lipton's (1977) "urban bias" factor at work. The neglect or deliberate discouragement of agriculture in favor of urban modern-sector industrial development meant the reduction of the sector that generated the most jobs in favor of a new sector that tended to create fewer jobs for given expenditures of capital. Second, these economies are often victims of their own limited success. Increased government revenues from the modern sector are usually spent in successful public health programs, which, in turn, lead to a rapid increase in population. This usually means that the size of the labor force grows at a greater rate than the number of new jobs. Another important demographic development that directly affects the size of the labor force is the changing demographic composition of these populations. A growing youth population, a function of rapid overall growth, increases the sector of the population in search of work. A further complicating factor is the U-shaped nature of female labor force participation, itself an outgrowth of changing per capita income and changing attitudes. What this all adds up to, as the ILO has repeatedly shown, is that labor force participation is "more compulsive" and supply-driven in developing countries than in advanced ones and therefore "difficult to read as a target or an outcome indicator" (ILO 2014: 36).

Urbanization in all these societies is both the cause and the result of the disruption of the agricultural sectors, but it also brings in its wake another important demographic shift: that of women out of the traditional sector, where they may or may not have been in the labor force as formally defined, into the formal modern labor force. This is less the case in the Afro-Caribbean societies, where women have always worked in relatively high numbers; it is more typical of Central American societies. Nonetheless, the decline of the proportion of female workers in agriculture was substantially greater than that for males in Jamaica: In 2013 the female figure stood at 8 percent, compared with 26 percent for men (World Bank 2016).

Finally, the provision of greater education (and with it rising expectations of wage-paying jobs in the formal sector) and of higher income, combined with the inability to meet these expectations—which invariably rise at a faster pace than the creation of jobs in the modern sector—all account for both an increase in the labor force (especially among women, who disproportionally benefit from public education) and higher unemployment. A corollary of all the above, as the ILO notes, is that "unemployment in DCs [developing countries] is not an adequate measure of the state of the labour market" (2014: 33).

Jamaica is typical of this kind of economy, and I now turn to a closer examination of it, paying special attention to the problem of female labor force participation and of labor commitment, for reasons mentioned in the first section.

The Jamaican National Labor Force

As in all the other Caribbean economies and many of those in Central and South America, the process of modernization in Jamaica has had little or no positive impact on the overall rate of employment even though it has had major effects on the composition of the labor force and the quality of labor.

Table 3.1 and Figures 3.1 and 3.2 summarize the structure of the national labor force in 1972, the year before the survey data were collected. Table 3.1 confirms that the labor force participation rate of women was high by world standards: 60 percent of women over age fourteen were in the labor force, compared with 87.5 percent of men. At the same time, the employment rate for men was substantially higher, which immediately calls into question Standing's findings as far as the Jamaican population as a whole was concerned. The same is true if we look at the national data on unemployment rate by age and by industry group. In

Table 3.1. The Jamaican Labor Force, 1972

Item	Total	Male	Female
Total population	1,949,600	993,600	1,006,000
Pop. over 14 yrs.	1,104,300	521,800	582,400
Over 14 as % of total	56.6	55.3	57.9
Labor force	808,300	456,700	351,600
Labor force as % of total	41.5	48.4	34.9
Labor force as % over 14	73.2	87.5	60.3
Employed	626,500	394,700	231,800
Employment rate (%)	77.5	86.4	65.9
Unemployed	181,800	62,000	119,800
Unemployment rate (%)	22.5	13.9	34.6
% Labor force	100	57	43

Source: The Jamaican Department of Statistics, *The Labor Force, 1972,*
tables 1–3.

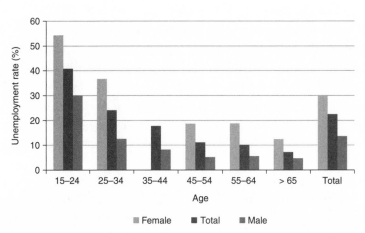

Figure 3.1. National unemployment rate in Jamaica by age and
gender

Data source: Jamaica Department of Statistics, *The Labor Force, 1972.*

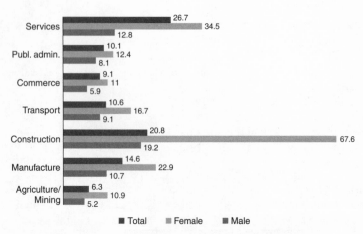

Figure 3.2. National unemployment rate by industry and gender
Data source: Jamaica Department of Statistics, *The Labor Force, 1972,* table 11.

comparative terms, the Jamaican figures, while higher than average for women, were not that much out of line with the middle-income range of developing countries.

We should, however, bear two things in mind. One is that the national statistics must be taken with a grain of salt. A different story emerges from the detailed survey data separately collected and analyzed by both Standing and myself. (It should also be noted that the participation rates for men and women in 2014 reported by the World Bank [2016] using ILO data and its more precise definitions were 71 percent and 56 percent, respectively, which suggests either that there was a decline in participation or that the Jamaican Statistics Department estimates for 1972 may have been too high.) Second, what held on the national level in 1972 was not the same for the low-income urban population. It is to a consideration of the growth of this low-income population and the structure of employment and unemployment within it that I now turn.

The 1972–1973 Survey of the Urban Poor

The data analyzed here were collected between 1972 and 1973. For two reasons, this has turned out to be a most opportune moment for the collection of materials of this kind on the island. First, while I did not know it at the time, 1972–1973 was the crucial turning point in Jamaica's postcolonial economic development. It was in that year that the economy reached its growth rate peak, in macroeconomic terms. Immediately afterward, the external shocks of the oil crisis and, with it, the escalating price of all imports and the sudden increase in the rate of interest on foreign funds, reflected in a surging balance of payments deficit and a mounting external debt, together exposed all of the contradictions and vulnerabilities of the "industrialization by invitation" model of growth pursued from the 1950s to the early 1970s (Jefferson 1972). Second, it was at around this same time period that Standing also collected his data, from which he made his generalizations about the problem of proletarianization. Thus, as a replication study the data I am using are ideal.

The survey data were collected from five research sites in the urban lower- and working-class areas of Kingston. The sites were selected to reflect not only regional variations but also basic differences in the living arrangements and economic opportunities of the low-income population (Table 3.2). Salt Lane was a classic settlement slum in an old part of the central city that was made up of subdivided buildings; McIntyre Lands was a more stable working-class area consisting of well-constructed small houses around a new housing scheme; Wareika was a lower-class area strongly influenced by the Rastafarian religion on the eastern outskirts of the city; and Seaward and Duesland were typical shantytowns, of the sort now found all over the Third World—the

Table 3.2. Characteristics of Sample Areas

	Duesland	Salt Lane	Wareika	McIntyre Lands	Seaward
Population	420	550	600	582	504
Mean age	19	26	21.6	44	21
Male/female ratio	46/54	39/61	56/44	40/60	52/48
% Rural origin	83	54	44	45	30
No. of households	96	137	97	122	105
Household size	4.38	4.32	5.12	5.1	4.8
% Married	13	4	32	28	17
% Common law	63	43	44	35	47
% Single/friending	24	53	23	36	34.8
Water availability					
% Piped in home	0	8.5	20	16	0
% Yard standpipe/private	23	92.5	30	82	22
% Public standpipe/other	77	0	46	2	78
% Toilet in home	2	68	43	55	0
% Pit toilet	80	19	39	45	78
% No toilet	18	13	17	0	21
Persons per room	3.5	3.6	3.5	3.0	3.5
% Electricity available	13.5	34	54	77	12

Mean years schooling	7	7.4	7.5	8	7
% Both read and write	54	9	72	75	38
% Employed (wage/self)	42.7 (17.7/25)	42(15/27)	70(43/27)	62(45/17)	44(25/19)
% Unemployed	16	18	12	12	16.8
% Other	41.3	39.5	18	36	39.2
Mean individual income[1]	$8.47	$6.70	$16.18	$18.44	$8.50
Household income[1]	$13	$10.30	$21.44	$24.50	$15.20
Rent as % household Income	0 (squatters)	15	16	13	0 (squatters)

Source: Author's data from study of low-income population in Kingston Metropolitan Area, 1972–1975.

1. In 1972 Jamaican dollars.

habitations being flimsy shacks hurriedly built on captured government and private lands.[4]

Characteristics of the Rural- and Urban-Born Population

Of the population surveyed, 45 percent were brought up in the country, 50 percent in the Kingston Metropolitan Area (KMA), and 5 percent in both the country and the KMA (Table 3.3). There are several striking features of the male–female distribution of migrants and urban-born residents of the KMA during this period. First is that women constituted the majority, 55 percent, of urban residents in the surveyed areas. This in itself is not particularly striking until we notice that, of the urban-born residents of the KMA, men actually outnumbered women to a considerable degree: 54 percent of urban-born residents were men, compared with 47 percent of women. That women outnumbered men in the urban population, therefore, was due entirely to the fact that women constituted a greater proportion of the rural migrant population (65% vs. 35%). Thus over half (53%) of all women in the city were migrants from the country, compared with only 35 percent of all men.

These figures raise some interesting questions. First, where were the urban-born women? Why did so many more women than men migrate from the rural areas to the city? What is the significance of the fact that almost half of the KMA population was made up of rural migrants? And fourth, what were the consequences of the fact that the male lower-class population of the city was overwhelmingly urban in origin (62%), while the female population was predominantly rural (52%)?

There are several possible explanations for the smaller number of women among the urban-born population in these areas. As

Table 3.3. Area Where Brought Up (to the Age of 15) by Various Attributes and Gender

	Country: Rural		Country: Town		KMA[1]: Outside Study Area		KMA: Within Study Area		KMA & Country		All	
	M	F	M	F	M	F	M	F	M	F	M	F
All	67 (30%)	125 (46%)	10 (4%)	18 (6%)	86 (39%)	70 (26%)	46 (21%)	46 (17%)	11 (5%)	12 (4%)	220 (100%)[2]	271 (100%)
Household size	4.2	5.0	3.4	5.0	4.2	5.2	4.5	5.0	4.6	5.5	4.27	5.12
Years in school	7.1	7.0	6.0	7.2	7.6	6.6	7.8	9.2	7.8	9.2	3.8	6.6
% Both read and write	53.3	49	40	48	57.6	57	61	69.6	8.3	46	54	54
Mean weekly income[3]	19.2	6.2	24.5	14.2	15.6	6.1	18.3	6.5	12.2	5.0	16.78	6.69

Source: Author's data from study of low-income population in Kingston Metropolitan Area, 1972–1975.

1. KMA = Kingston Metropolitan Area.

2. Percentages may not add up to 100 because of rounding.

3. In 1972 Jamaican dollars. In 1972 the exchange rate of 1 US dollar was 0.77 Jamaican dollars.

Table 3.3 shows, an equal number of men and women (N=46) born in the study areas were living there. However, far more men born outside the Kingston Metro region were living in the study areas (86 vs. 70). One possible explanation is that lower-class urban women were more upwardly mobile than their male counterparts. According to Derek Gordon, early economic development mainly expanded the number of low-paying white collar jobs into which qualified low-income women moved; at the same time, men continued to be one and a half times more likely to inherit middle- and upper-class positions (Gordon 1987, 1996). My data show nearly the same percentage of men and women in the clerical and sales category of occupations (4.3% and 4.1%, respectively), but a higher percentage of men (6.8%) than women (4.3%) *employed* in this category (Table 3.6). However, this is not inconsistent with what Gordon found, since the successful women would have been excluded from my sample. Another factor is that women dominated the domestic servant employment category, and a not insignificant number of these jobs required maids to live in their employers' homes.

Why were there so many more rural women than men in these low-income areas, even allowing for the fact that there was an overall female bias in urbanization during the late colonial and early postcolonial period? One explanation is that urban-born women, with their better knowledge of the city and its unskilled job opportunities, were able to find more favorable areas in which to live, whereas rural female migrants ended up with what was most available, namely the worst-off slums.

There are several interesting possible implications of the fact that women in the low-income areas of the city were of largely rural origin. The most important is that since women were (and still are) usually the exclusive parent involved in raising children in the city, this meant a carryover of rural methods of child-rearing to the city. Of these methods the most important was the harsh, punitive method of disciplining children, a pattern that persists to this day with disastrous consequences for the level of violence in the society, as I discussed in Chapter 2 (Brown and Johnson 2008; Evans 1989; Grantham-McGregor, Landmann, and Desai 1983). It is important to bear in mind that rural-to-urban migration in Jamaica resulted as much in the ruralization of the city as it did in the urbanization of the country folk.

Let us now move on to examine some other characteristics of the city population with regard to its area of origin. The migrant population was significantly older than the urban-born population (38.4 vs. 36.9 years); the difference was due entirely to the older age of rural men, who averaged 39.5 years compared with 35.4 for urban-born men. Women, on average, migrated from the country at an older age than men; the mean age at which men left the country was 17.7 years; that for women was 18.8 years (Figure 3.3). The overall trend was toward people migrating at younger and younger ages, with women generally migrating slightly older than men other than the youngest and the 40–49 age groups.

The migrant population was more successful than the urban-born population on most counts. Male migrants earned substantially more than the urban-born; the same held for women coming from the country, although rural women earned about the same as those born in the city (Table 3.3). The older age of men from the country may partly explain the income difference among men, though not by much; it was not relevant to women, all categories of whom were about the same age, on average.

Why did people leave the rural areas? Eight categories were coded in response to this question. The single major reason

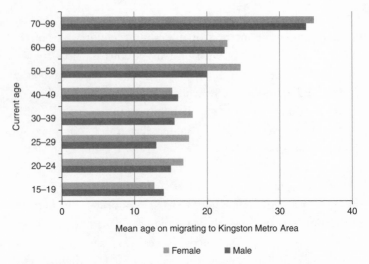

Figure 3.3. Mean age on migrating to Kingston Metropolitan Area for people of different age ranges

Data source: Author's data from study of low-income population in Kingston Metropolitan Area, 1972–1975.

offered was that they moved with, or were sent for, by a guardian or relative (32%), women more so than men (Table 3.4). The second most frequently given reason was a job offer in Kingston, women two and a half times more so than men, mainly to work as domestics. Fifteen percent left because they could not get work in the countryside, and 10 percent because they heard that conditions were better in Kingston. It is worth noting that less than 1 percent gave as their reason the fact that they did not like their work in the countryside and less than 2 percent because wages were too low, the main reason being that so many of the migrants were unemployed when they left. What all this suggests is that women were pulled to the city by two major factors (relatives and job offers), while men were pushed by a variety of factors,

Table 3.4. Reasons for Leaving Countryside by Gender

Reason for Leaving Countryside	Male *Count* *Percent*	Female *Count* *Percent*	Total *Count* *Percent*
Couldn't get work	15 16%	23 15%	38 15%
Did not like work	1 1%	0	1 0.4%
Wages too low	3 3%	1 1%	4 2%
Job offer in Kingston	9 10%	39 25%	48 19%
Heard Kingston was better	15 16%	10 6%	25 10%
Wanted change	7 8%	7 4%	14 6%
Moved in with relative	24 26%	54 35%	78 32%
Other	18 20%	21 14%	39 16%

Source: Author's data from study of low-income population in Kingston Metropolitan Area, 1972–1975.

chief of which were rural unemployment (30%), desire for a change (7.6%), and a cluster of highly idiosyncratic reasons (19.5%), which sound very much like rationalizations after the fact.

I found that an overwhelming majority of migrants (84%) preferred the city; only 7 percent claimed to prefer the countryside, and 9 percent liked both about the same. There was no significant difference in the responses of men and women. Apart from purely idiosyncratic reasons (31%), the main reasons that people preferred the city were that more employment was available (28%) and that life was generally better (11.5%).

Women had more idiosyncratic reasons than men; the employ-ment factor was as important to them, and they were more inclined to feel that life in Kingston was better (13%). Very few migrants felt that the countryside offered any meaningful agri-cultural opportunities.

Turning now to a closer examination of the data on em-ployment, income, and occupation, I found that that 53 percent of the population were employed, 37 percent were unem-ployed, and 10 percent were not in the work force. The situa-tion was much worse for women than for men: 63 percent of the men were employed, 30 percent unemployed, and 7 percent not in the work force, compared with 45 percent of the women employed, 42 percent unemployed, and 12 percent not in the work force.

Table 3.5 gives a more detailed breakdown of the employment situation among men and women. Of special note is that 30 percent of the population were working for compensation, compared with 23 percent who were self-employed. This was in sharp contrast with the Jamaican population as a whole, among whom only 3.5 percent were recorded as self-employed in 1972. Of the nonemployed, 34 percent were no longer seeking work. This might suggest a high rate of withdrawal from the labor force, but it is really nothing of the sort. The thirty-six people in the sample no longer seeking work constituted only 6 percent of the total labor force surveyed. This hardly indicates a highly discour-aged or uncommitted labor force. Indeed, given the low proba-bility of getting a job, the wonder is that there was not a higher rate of withdrawal from the labor force among the urban poor of Kingston at that time.

There is a close and significant relationship between age and employment status (Figure 3.4). For women in general, the older the age group, the higher the employment rate and the lower the

Table 3.5. Employment Status by Gender

Employment Status	Male Count Percent	Female Count Percent	Total Count Percent
Working for compensation	97	71	168
	37%	23%	30%
Self-employed	63	66	129
	24%	21.5%	23%
Vacationing	3	2	5
	1%	1%	1%
Sick	9	11	20
	3%	4%	4%
Caring for household member	1	13	14
	0.4%	4%	2%
Laid-off (temporary)	15	8	23
	6%	3%	4%
Unemployed, seeking work	32	38	70
	12%	12%	12%
Unemployed, not seeking work	13	23	36
	5%	7.5%	6%
Casual worker	11	5	16
	4%	2%	3%
Keeping house (own)	0	50	50
	0%	16%	9%
Student	0	1	1
	0%	0.3%	0.3%
Retired or disabled	8	4	12
	3%	1%	2%
Other	8	14	22
	3%	5%	4%

Source: Author's data from study of low-income population in Kingston Metropolitan Area, 1972–1975.

unemployment rate, starting with the desperate situation of female dropouts (15–19), who had an unemployment rate of 79 percent and an employment rate of 7 percent, and progressing to the age category 70–99, among whom 75 percent were employed and 25 percent unemployed. The one departure from the linear trend is the age category 60–69. Jamaica is reputed to have one of the highest rates of female labor force participation in the world, and these figures, for what they are worth, sustain this reputation. Note that nearly 100 percent of women over age 70 were still in the labor force.

The situation is far more complex for men, among whom the "other" category (those who were either not in the work force or were casual laborers working sporadically) was more important than for women (Figure 3.4). Although there was considerable variation around the non-work-force mean, it hardly affected the female employment and unemployment rates; these fluctuations had considerable impact, however, on the male rates. The youngest male age category (15–19) showed a surprisingly high employment rate (68%). In fact, it was the third-highest of all the age categories. The employment rate then plummeted to 56 percent for the 20–24 age category, although the unemployment rate remained the same. Clearly, this decrease resulted from dissatisfaction with the low income earned during the first five years of working, reflected in a substantial number of men dropping out of the regular work force to become casual workers or "scufflers" (hustlers); some may also have joined the growing numbers of "rude boys," who survived through the underground economy of drug pushing and petty crime. By the 25–29 age group, however, almost all the men had returned to the work force, no doubt sobered by their experiences in the hustling life and the harsh discipline of the justice system, but the effort to find jobs was only partially successful; thus the

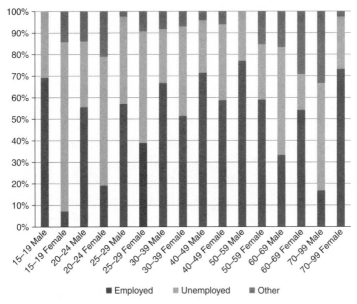

Figure 3.4. Age and employment status by gender in Kingston Metropolitan Area

Data source: Author's data from study of low-income population in Kingston Metropolitan Area, 1972–1975.

employment rate increased to 57 percent (up two percentage points), but the unemployment rate also escalated to its highest point among men under sixty, at 40.5 percent. The rates leveled off in the 30–39 range, as men took on growing responsibilities. It was at its highest, and the unemployment rate at its lowest, in the 50–59 age group. Thereafter, the employment rate dropped steeply, but this was due only partially to retirement, for the unemployment rate reached its peak at this time. Only a third of the men in the 70–99 age group had removed themselves from the work force; half of them were still seeking work and not finding it.

Information on number of weeks employed was gathered for McIntyre Lands only. For the year ending August 1972, the average resident of McIntyre Lands had been employed 36.3 weeks. Men were employed for an average of 41.3 weeks, women for 31.8 weeks. Twenty-six percent of the population experienced some unemployment during the year. This included a minority of those currently employed: 18 percent of employed men and women had experienced at least twelve weeks of unemployment the previous year. However, most of the currently employed had stable employment. A majority of the unemployed were chronically so. In conclusion, then, employed men and women worked about the same number of weeks per year. If anything, employed women worked more steadily than men. However, while 40 percent of the unemployed men had a shot at a job for some period of time during the previous year, only 17 percent of the women had such opportunities. In other words, chronic unemployment was greater among women. One caveat is that we should be careful not to generalize these results to the entire low-income population sampled, since McIntyre Lands was on several counts the least depressed area studied.

Table 3.6 reports findings on the occupational and employment structure of the low-income population studied. There were almost four times as many skilled and semi-skilled men as women, which deserves commentary only because of the relatively better education of women. As one would expect, women were disproportionately represented in the services and as higgler-hawkers (itinerant sellers of small items of food and dry goods). The most striking thing about the men is that those who were skilled or semi-skilled showed the highest rates of unemployment, higher even than men who were manual laborers. This was due to the extremely high income expectation of skilled or semi-skilled workers, many of whom preferred not to work

Table 3.6. Employment by Occupation and Gender

Occupation	Employed		Unemployed		Other		Total	
	M	F	M	F	M	F	M	F
Manual	21.6% 35	5.1% 7	29.5% 23	9.2% 11	22.2% 4	0.0% 0	24.0% 62	6.1% 18
Service	8.0% 13	24.4% 35	2.6% 2	19.3% 23	0.0% 0	10.8% 4	5.8% 15	21.1% 62
Higgler/hawker	8.0% 13	28.3% 39	2.6% 2	7.6% 9	5.6% 1	18.9% 7	5.8% 16	18.7% 55
Skilled or semi-skilled	45.7% 74	14.5% 20	30.8% 24	3.4% 4	11.1% 2	13.5% 5	38.8% 100	9.9% 29
Clerical and sales	6.8% 11	4.3% 6	0.0% 0	2.5% 4	0.0% 0	8.1% 5	4.3% 11	4.1% 12
Supervisory	1.2% 2	0.7% 1	1.3% 1	0.0% 0	5.6% 1	0.0% 0	1.6% 4	0.3% 1
Other	8.6% 14	21.7% 30	33.3% 26	40.5% 69	55.6% 10	48.6% 18	19.4% 50	39.8% 117
Percent Total	62.8% 162	46.9% 138	30.2% 78	40.5% 119	7.0% 18	12.6% 37	100.0% 258	100% 294

Source: Author's data from study of low-income population in Kingston Metropolitan Area, 1972–1975.

rather than to work for wages below what they desired. Many skilled workers were of the opinion that they could earn enough when they did work to tide them over through periods of unemployment. To their way of thinking, it was better to work for short periods of time at a higher rate than for long periods at a lower rate. This way they had more leisure time.

Guy Standing found a similar employment pattern among the skilled workers he surveyed and attributed much significance to it. Did this suggest low work commitment? At first sight it may seem so, but on closer examination I found certain important institutional constraints on skilled workers that Standing did not take into account. The problem was partly due to the employment context and legal qualifications relating to many areas of skilled work. Let me take the case of one of my informants. Trevor was a competent electrician, thirty-two years old, who had learned his trade on the job. Because he had had no formal training and saw little need for it, he could not legally practice as an electrician. It was difficult to disregard the law, since government approval was required before the electric company would connect a home to its lines. To get around the problem, Trevor had two alternatives: One was to get a qualified electrician to cover for him by signing his name on the worksheet required by the government, for which Trevor had to pay an exorbitant share of his earnings; the other was to work for a firm as an apprentice, which Trevor found even more exploitative, in view of the low salary he received relative to what he could earn on his own. Trevor therefore took his chances on the occasional job of his own, which had to be covered by a friend. He remained unemployed for over six months each year, and it is doubtful whether his annual income would have been greater if he had worked steadily for an electrical company. He had tried doing this twice before but simply could not accept the low wages and the loss of independence. He disliked working under the supervision of another person. It should be noted, further, that Trevor was not exactly "unemployed" when not working for compensation in the formal sector (which for him was the only recognized form of employment, a fact that confounds employment data). In fact, he worked sporadically in the informal sector, doing odd and often illegal electrical jobs for friends, relatives, and people who could not afford the high professional fees of the licensed electrician. This was not trivial work. Anyone observing the shantytowns at night would have seen that they were all lit up with electric lights, hardly any of them wired by licensed electricians. Much of this electricity was illegally obtained by attaching wires to the main electrical lines. Jamaica, then as now, has an extremely high rate of electrical theft, resulting in major loss of revenue to the island's monopoly utility, the Jamaica Public Service Company Ltd.

Skilled women did not have the same problem. They formed a much smaller proportion of the female work force than did skilled men in the male work force, but their unemployment rate was only 17 percent (Table 3.6). Higglers and hawkers formed the largest category of the female employed; the unemployment rate among them (16%) was higher than the male rate (12.5%). This category, it should be noted, included a high rate of underemployed people, a situation that would grow worse during the crisis years of the 1980s with the inflow of cheap Asian goods resulting from the neoliberal policies of the conservative Seaga administration (Portes and Rumbaut 1990). Higglers and hawkers earned the highest mean income among women, higher even than those who claimed to be skilled or semi-skilled, and it was the only occupation in which employed women earned more than men ($12.27 vs. $12.00). F. N. Le Franc contended that higglers suffered low status occupationally and earned only modest incomes. However, she rejected the view that the marginalized nature of higglering was due to female dominance of the occupation, given the progress that women had made in higher levels of the postcolonial Jamaican economy. Instead, she attributed their low income to their clientele's poverty and demand for only small quantities of products. Nonetheless, this occupation remained an important "cushion for the unemployed" (Le Franc 1996: 119–121, 129). My data suggest that it was the best cushion available, since higglers earned more than women in clerical and sales or, as noted above, in skilled work.

Finally, let us take a closer look at income (Table 3.3). For the entire population surveyed, the mean weekly income in 1972 was $11.43 Jamaican dollars, or US$14.84. However, men earned two and a half times what women earned: $16.78 versus $6.69. This weekly income was certainly low, but it should be considered in light of inflation. In 1972 one US dollar was worth 77 Jamaican cents. As of May 19, 2016, the exchange rate was one US dollar for 125 Jamaican dollars. One 1972 US dollar is worth $5.75 in 2016 US dollars. Thus the mean weekly income of the population was US$85.20 or $10,650.69 in May 2016 Jamaican dollars. The weekly income for men was US$125.30, or $15,663.15 in 2016 Jamaican dollars, and for women, US$49.95, or $6,245 in 2016 Jamaican dollars. Low as they may appear, these incomes were substantially higher than the income of the urban poor in Jamaica today.

The remarkable difference between male and female weekly incomes speaks to the highly feminized nature of poverty in Jamaica (then as now). There was no difference, overall, in the subjective levels of literacy between men and women: 54 percent claimed to be able to both read and write, while 46 percent were functionally illiterate, with 36 percent of both genders saying they could read and write only a little. However, among men there was a significant relationship between level of literacy and employment status. (Because of the wide variation in the quality of education across the island, I consider respondents' own assessment of their ability to read and write to be a more reliable indicator of their level of literacy than their reported years of schooling.) Men who claimed to be able to read and write properly had almost three times the employment rate as those who could not. However, there was no relationship between literacy and female employment status. There was little difference in mean income between women who claimed to be fully literate and those who admitted to being fully illiterate; for men, however, the difference was large, the mean income of literate men being two and a half times that of the illiterate (Figure 3.5). Re-

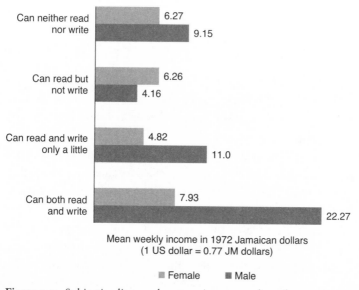

Figure 3.5. Subjective literacy by mean income and gender

Data source: Author's data from study of low-income population in Kingston Metropolitan Area, 1972–1975.

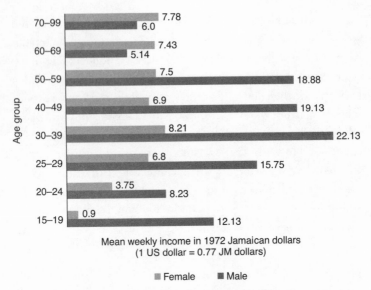

Figure 3.6. Age by mean weekly income and gender

Data source: Author's data from study of low-income population in Kingston Metropolitan Area, 1972–1975.

markably, fully illiterate men had a mean income 15 percent greater than fully literate women. The rate of return to women of their education was close to zero.

Among both men and women, age was associated with income, though the relationship was curvilinear (Figure 3.6). Young male dropouts earned a mean income of $12.13 per week. This declined during what we may call the "post-adolescent slump"—the age category of 20–24 when men dropped out of the labor force because of their failure to find jobs paying a living wage and resorted to scuffling (hustling) and "rude boy" delinquency; the price they paid for their partly enforced leisure was lower income. Income picked up again after age twenty-five and up to age forty, when it began to decrease to the last two age categories (60–99); these older men earned a mean weekly income of about $6.60. For women, the association remained linear and positive right up to the very oldest age group, with one slight deviation in the 60–69 age category.

How do the unemployed and those with very low (or zero) income survive? There is no longer any mystery to this question, which has been answered by a large number of studies on the urban poor of the less developed world (see especially Bromley and Gerry 1979; Banerjee and Duflo 2011). In addition to the survey data, I also draw upon three years of ethnographic work among the urban poor to answer this question. In brief, people support each other in a multitude of ways. In economic terms, those who earn an income redistribute it within the low-income population, first, by supporting unemployed people living in their households. It has long been established by students of the Caribbean household and family that the higher the average household income, the larger the size of the household, because more economically secure households attract less secure relatives and dependents (Clarke 1957; Smith 1971). My data bear this out. Second, people outside the household, often within the same compound or yard, were helped through loans (only sometimes repaid), gifts, and in-kind help such as babysitting. The urban slum was, in short, an elaborate loan and gift exchange system where the income of those who worked was redistributed among the dependent, unemployed, and underemployed population.

Conclusion

The profile of the low-income population of the Kingston Metropolitan Area at the end of the first phase of postcolonial economic development presented in this chapter does accord with several of Guy Standing's findings, but his claim of a large-scale problem of work commitment among Jamaican men must be qualified. A distinction must be made between different segments of the urban poor: the lumpenproletariat and the working poor. The lumpenproletariat are those who were not working in the formal sector and not seeking work, and who survived in a variety of ways such as "scuffling" (hustling) in the informal sector, relying on relatives and friends, or engaging in petty crime, the underground drug system, or political and criminal gangsterism. Many came to be known in the 1960s and 1970s as "rude boys," reflecting the fact that they tended to be youth mainly in their twenties and lived by the norms of a street culture of honorific violence, or what Obika Gray, in a penetrating study, called "badness honor" (2004: 14–15, 120–151). My data show that the majority of the 20–24 age group were unemployed or not in the work force; this held more for women than men (see Figure 3.4). Among men, some 45 percent either were not in the work force or were unemployed. Those who claimed to be working would in all likelihood have had precarious employment only marginally connected to the formal economy.

For the other broad category of the low-income population, the working poor, my evidence—both quantitative and ethnographic—indicates that men, under the right conditions, were willing to work and were no less committed than women, although the latter, being the primary and often the only caregivers and support for children, were under greater obligation to do so.

Jamaicans went through nearly two centuries of brutal proletarianization during the period of slavery, followed by a post-slavery plantation regime with a harshly capitalistic labor system and a peasant economy that required long hours of labor for basic survival. The main legacy of this experience for men was

not so much a lack of commitment to work as a strong preference for working on their own and a deep suspicion of authority
in the workplace. This distrust was well founded. It was based
on the continued plantation overseer mentality of the managers
in Jamaica, who were still reluctant to use the incentive of a living
wage to achieve higher levels of work commitment (Bryan 2000:
148) and who treated workers in a very patronizing and often
insulting manner, leading to high levels of resentment and distrust (see Gordon, Anderson, and Robotham 1997; Carter 1997).
To a degree, these managerial attitudes were exacerbated by ethnic
and color differences, factors that Standing did not consider.
Nearly all workers came from the 80 percent of the population of
African ancestry. The vast majority of managers at this time came
from the light-skinned, white, or Chinese minorities. Persistent
racial and color prejudice—although greatly reduced in recent
years, especially after the sociocultural dislocations of the Manley
regime—still partly explains the contempt with which managers
typically treated workers, and the refusal to consider higher wages
as a profitable means of increasing labor commitment and productivity (Stone 1973, 1992; Nettleford 1972).[5]

The highly developed tradition of trade unionism and of a clientelistic and violently participative democracy among the
urban masses simply intensified the mismatch between worker
expectations and managerial attitudes and practices. Jamaican
postcolonial workers had a keen interest in the nature of the
economy and its inequities as well as "a potent sense of their capacity to challenge the state" for its failure to protect their interests and alleviate their condition (Gray 2004: 13). They were
willing to work for a living wage but were reluctant to work hard
whenever they felt they were being exploited or disrespected
(Stone 1986). This situation was complicated by the fact that,
all things considered, Jamaican men much preferred working for

themselves, as reflected historically in the vigorous peasantry and, with urbanization, in the highly developed informal sector in the low-income urban areas. The American economist William Knowles, who studied labor unions and work during the last decade of colonialism, observed that when paid a livable wage with job tenure Jamaicans' "attitude toward work undergoes a complete change . . . they become ambitious, thrifty, sober, prompt, efficient, and fairly honest workers" (1956: 139).

With regard to women, the questions of their proletarianization and their incorporation into the emerging postcolonial economy must also be understood in light of the island's labor history. As with men, three centuries of exploitative gender-neutral labor on the slave and post-emancipation plantations and on the peasant farms of the island had produced a thoroughly incorporated female work force in the colonial economy. Indeed, to the degree that women dominated the sale of goods produced on the peasant farms in the rural and urban markets and as itinerant traders (higglers), they were well engaged at the fringes of the colonial capitalist economy. The tendency of many economists and others to view the Jamaican domestic marketing system as informal and completely apart from the capitalist "formal economy" must be qualified, as the Jamaican sociologist Patricia Anderson (1987) has persuasively argued. As we saw in Chapter 1, Jamaican peasants, both male and female, were incorporated in the plantation economy both as workers during the harvest season and as producers of cane for the plantation sugar mills and of bananas and citrus for the export market. Later, they were incorporated in the postcolonial capitalist economy in the food-processing export businesses, off-shore garment assembly, and other sectors, although typically in highly exploitative ways characterized by pervasive levels of justifiable distrust (Gordon, Anderson, and Robotham 1997: 210–220; Gray 2004).

What seems clear is that, in spite of their equal rates of literacy and readiness to participate in the more advanced sectors of the postcolonial capitalist economy, women continued to suffer from gender bias on the part of employers in nearly all of the higher levels of the private sector of the emerging socioeconomic order. The main exceptions were the more sex-segregated levels of the public and private sectors such as nursing, teaching, and clerical and lower-level office work. In the working-class levels, we have seen that, apart from the sex-segregated jobs of domestic service and higgling, women earned substantially less than men and gained no benefit from their education, with illiterate men earning substantially more than fully literate women. (Not considered here is sex work; see Wedderburn et al. 2011.)

Gender bias was not, however, the only or even the main reason for the failure of women to gain much from their education. Rather, it was that, beyond simple literacy, the educational institutions had failed to train the working class in the skills needed for a modern economy. Until the 1960s, primary education was badly underfunded and hopelessly inadequate for even the provision of basic literacy. The secondary school system, while better funded, was not much better—overcrowded and staffed by underpaid teachers who had no training in the teaching of skills that would prepare students for meaningful participation in the emerging economy. The result was, and remains, a high dropout rate and a high level of either complete or functional illiteracy among the youth population. As we have seen, only 54 percent of respondents claimed to have been fully literate; the remaining 46 percent were either functionally illiterate (37%) or completely so (9%).

Sadly, the situation has not changed much since my 1973 study. In 2004, 30 to 40 percent of students were "functionally illiterate at the end of primary education" (World Bank 2004: 28), and the situation remained just as bad in 2018 (World Bank 2018). Note that these studies refer to all classes of Jamaicans; for the low-income urban classes they would be worse, meaning that the situation was at least similar to what I found in 1973. Gender inequality persists, generally, but especially among the poor. As another World Bank study found: "Not only is the poverty rate higher for female-headed households than for male-headed households but it also rose more sharply—to 19.7 in 2010 compared to 13.3 percent in 2008—during the period. . . . While the [2008 global financial] crisis affected both men and women employment strongly, unemployment rates have traditionally been higher for women across all age groups (and in particular for young women). In addition, Jamaica's Gender Inequality Index (GII) suggests that women have less access to human development opportunities compared to men" (2014: 6).

Over half a century of postcolonial development has had little or no impact on the dismal condition of the Jamaican poor, especially its women. These wretched of the earth (Fanon 1961), whom I once called the Children of Sisyphus (Patterson 1964), still toil without hope on the urban dunghills of their country.

II

Three Cultural Puzzles

4

Why Are Jamaicans the Fastest Runners in the World?

The Institutionalization of Athletic Prowess

Among the most enigmatic features of Jamaican society is the nation's astonishing supremacy in sprinting. Currently, the world's fastest man and female Olympic 100-meter champion are Jamaicans. The achievement is not due only to a few superstars. Jamaica's dominance of the world's fast runners is broad and deep, manifests in both the male and female ranks, and, what's more, began to emerge more than half a century ago. In the 1948 Olympics the small island began to turn heads by winning a gold medal and two silvers. Four years later, in the Helsinki Olympics of 1952, curiosity turned to amazement when the island finished thirteenth in medals won among the nations of the world, ahead of its colonial power, Great Britain, as well as countries hundreds of times its population size, such as India and Japan. In the 2008 Beijing Olympics Jamaica established its complete dominance in sprinting with the triple gold feat of Usain Bolt—now the reigning superstar of track and field—who broke world records in the 100 and 200 meters. The small country also achieved a clean sweep of the women's 100 meters by Shelly-Ann Fraser, Kerron Stewart, and Sherone Simpson, the first and still only time that a country has done so. Jamaica ended up winning five of the six available golds in sprint and a total haul of six golds, three silvers, and two bronzes, ranking thirteenth in overall medal wins, an incredible achievement for a tiny island not quite as large as Connecticut, with a population of only 2.8 million. This near-complete dominance continued in the London 2012 Olympics, with Jamaica winning four golds, four silvers, and four bronzes and placing eighteenth among the world's nations in absolute terms. In the 2016 Olympics the little nation ranked sixteenth, with six golds, three silvers, and two bronzes, again dominating the male and female sprint events.

In per capita terms, Jamaica far outpaces all other nations in number of medals won per Olympiad. Its overall performance is more than 3.75 times greater than that of the second best performing country, Russia, seven times better than the United States, and 249 times better than its main ancestral country, Nigeria (Figure 4.1).

All over the world, sports fans and experts alike ask the same questions. How does Jamaica do it? How is it possible for so small a nation to so thoroughly dominate the world in fast running? The achievement is all the more remarkable in view of the fact that running is perhaps the most widely performed and accessible of sports. All healthy human beings are capable of running. Thus the potential competitive pool runs in the thousands of millions, as distinct from other Olympic sports such as swimming or dressage, which require access to an Olympic-sized pool or trained horses, respectively, either of which costs thousands of dollars.

Let us begin by dismissing one tempting, oft-cited explanation: that Jamaicans are somehow genetically predisposed

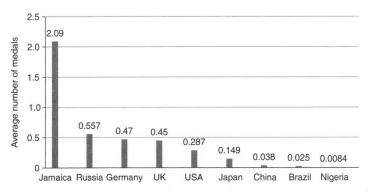

Figure 4.1. Average number of medals won in each Olympiad, per million persons, for selected countries

Data source: "Summer Olympic medallists 1896 to 2008," available at https://docs .google.com/spreadsheet/ccc?key=0AonYZs4MzlZbdHlfdoF1QlAxYjgtOW53ZXN OZoJzNVE#gid=4, accessed April 29, 2019.

toward running. Many have noticed that whenever a black population excels in a given area of sports, genetics soon rears its ugly head. Not hard work or character, not carefully nurtured institutional processes, not social or cultural factors, but instinct and genes are inevitably the answer, though most studies do not support a genetic explanation (Irving and Charlton 2010; Irving 2010; Epstein 2013). Such explanations pop up from time to time to explain black American excellence in sports such as basketball, sprinting, and football (Entine 2001; Bosch et al. 1990). Ironically, genetic factors have also been suggested as the reason why blacks did not excel in certain sports such as golf and tennis until, that is, they began to excel in golf and tennis. Sadly, even some Jamaican academics and athletes, such as Michael Johnson, have expressed support for genetic explanations (Morrison and Cooper 2006; Beck 2012). The vast majority of Jamaicans are of West African ancestry, mainly from the areas that are now southeastern Nigeria and Ghana, but a moment's examination of the Olympic and international competitive athletic records quickly dismisses the idea that mere West African ancestry explains Jamaica's athletic supremacy: West Africans are conspicuous for the near-total absence of their runners from the winning lists of such events. Although Nigeria has been competing in the Olympics since 1952, no Nigerian male runner has ever won an individual medal in running at these events.[1]

Some have suggested that selective factors are at play that make Jamaicans genetically superior to their African cousins: Only the fittest of Africans survived the horrors of the Middle Passage, followed by the sustained nightmare of 170 years of especially harsh British slavery and colonialism. The selection argument is sometimes bolstered by the hybrid vigor view, that the admixture of brutally selected Africans with Europeans explains the running gene (Beck 2012; Brooks 2014; Dawes 2016).

There are several problems with these arguments. First, they cannot explain why Jamaicans thoroughly outcompete other Caribbean blacks and black Americans who are from the same regions of West Africa and experienced an identical selection and hybridizing process, whatever it might have been. A comparison with Brazil perhaps best undermines the genetic and slave trade selection argument. Brazil has the largest population of blacks, mainly of western and southwestern African ancestry, outside of Africa: 43 percent of its 200 million people are self-identified as being of mixed African ancestry, and another 8 percent identify as unmixed Africans. That's 16 million unmixed Africans and 94 million Afro-European hybrids, many of whose ancestors went through the selective gauntlet of the Middle Passage and an equally harsh plantation and urban slavery system lasting even longer than that of Jamaica (slavery ended in Brazil in 1888, half a century later than in Jamaica). One could hardly ask for a better test of these arguments than an examination of the athletic record of these one hundred million Brazilians. If there is anything to the genetic argument, Brazil should be an athletic superpower, especially when it is considered that Brazilians are unusually committed to sports, their obsession with soccer being legendary. In fact, Brazil has been conspicuously uncompetitive in athletics, especially track and field, given its size and relative wealth. With a population 71 times that of Jamaica, it ranked 23rd in total medals in Beijing, compared with Jamaica's rank of 13th; and 22nd in London in 2012, compared with Jamaica's 18th. Although it had a twenty-eight year lead on Jamaica in Olympic competitions (a total of five Olympiads from 1920 to 1948, when Jamaica first entered) it has won only four golds in athletics, compared with seventeen won by Jamaica. It has also been thoroughly outcompeted by various much smaller West European countries.

The decisive critique of genetic explanations, however, comes from genetic studies. For over ten years, the renowned sports scientist Yannis Pitsiladis and his associates systematically collected DNA samples of athletes from Europe, Jamaica, West Africa, and East Africa, especially among the famous running tribes of Kenya and Ethiopia. Pitsiladis actually began with the strong presumption that genetic factors would explain the track successes of Jamaicans and East Africans: "I thought it was going to be a confirmatory analysis," he later told *The Scotsman* newspaper (March 23, 2010). However, his data largely undermined the genetic explanation of superior athletic performance: "There is no genetic evidence to date to suggest that this is the case," he was forced to conclude (Pitsiladis et al. 2010). Indeed, the data on East African athletes highlighted not their unique genetic constitution but their genetic diversity. Studies of the success of African and Jamaican athletes, he and his colleagues concluded, "predominantly implicate environmental factors." Other work, more focused on Jamaican and US sprinters, also found no difference between them and a control group of non-athletes in regard to certain genotype distributions that others had claimed distinguished superior athletes (Scott et al. 2010).

To understand Jamaica's preeminence in athletics we must turn to the dynamic interaction of history, culture, institutions, public health, and socioeconomics. Also important is location, primarily the island's proximity to the United States. Foremost in any explanation is the existence of a distinctive institutional system. It is now universally agreed that the single most important factor explaining the nation's athletic prowess is the institution of the annual Inter-Scholastic Athletic Championship, popularly called Champs. Champs is a five-day meet including athletes from ten years of age to eighteen, which is attended by over thirty thousand fans of all ages. Jamaica's equivalent of the Super Bowl in the United States, it is itself embedded in the broader institutional framework of athletic sports throughout the island's educational and extra-educational sports system of youth clubs and periodic special events (Robinson 2009).

When I went to high school during the 1950s, Champs was already the preeminent national sporting event, and great athletes such as Arthur Wint, Herb McKenley, and George Rhoden were by far my most adored personal heroes. All students were expected to engage in track and field, unlike cricket and soccer, which were elective, and the high point of the school year was Sports Day, when family members of all ages turned out to cheer us and our Houses (as the intramural divisions of the high schools were called, each with its own name and insignia) in the intramural contests. (I was a third-rate miler.) Devoted teachers doubled up as coaches to make all this possible. One of the most revered was Noel A. White, who, with G. C. Foster, coached my high school, Kingston College, to a Champs victory in 1957, ushering in a fourteen-year period of powerhouse victories between 1962 and 1975. White went on to found the Hotspur Athletic Club, one of the first groups focused on the training of professional female athletes.[2]

Champs, and the system of athletics of which it is the apex, is no doubt key to any explanation of Jamaica's sprint dominance. Usain Bolt was basically correct in his reply to a *Financial Times* reporter (Murad 2016) when asked to explain his supremacy in sprinting: "It's just that we have a good system. Boys and Girls Champs keep producing more and more athletes." The question, however, is how to account for this development and especially the reasons why Jamaica became such an extreme outlier in its national commitment to track and field and the cultivation of sprinting talent. The island's performance contradicts nearly all explanations of why nations succeed at the Olympics, the two most important explanatory factors usually offered being per capita national income and population size (Reiche 2016: part 1; Pfau 2006). An understanding of the island's success requires a historical sociology of the path-dependent process by which its track and field culture emerged.

Organized and informal athletic sports were introduced to Jamaica and the other British possessions by the British colonial power during the nineteenth century. This development dovetailed with British imperial culture of the late nineteenth and early twentieth centuries. The schoolmasters who led the elite British public schools "forged the link securely between sports and Empire. . . . They believed in the value of these games for the development of ethical behavior and the formation of sound social attitudes. They were loud and forceful advocates of athleticism. They held that games were the heart of the educational process. . . . And as equally convinced imperialists, they had a view of education that was not only national but also imperial"

(Mangan 1998: 42–43). By the late nineteenth century the local elite had "embraced organised sports as a means of establishing themselves as arbiters and agents of British culture and imperial philosophy" (Bertram 2012). And by the early twentieth century, all the leading schools had not only made cricket and track and field an integral part of their curriculum but had also imitated the British custom of interscholastic competition. Like the British, they tried to restrict this competition to only the most elite schools. In doing so, they simply made competitive sports more desirable to all of the other high schools on the island. In Jamaica, pressure was soon exerted to open the system up to a larger number of schools, much more so than in islands such as Barbados, which Sandiford described accurately as "grotesquely racist and snobbish" in its sports culture as in other areas of life (1998: 7). By 1910 members of the colored (mainly mulatto and light-complexioned) middle classes were attending and participating in the early annual championship events.

Jamaica differed in two other respects from the other islands. By the end of the second decade of the twentieth century, cricket had far surpassed other sports in the eastern Caribbean islands (Sandiford 1998: 6–14), whereas track and field continued to hold its own as an important, if still secondary, sport in Jamaica. A second distinction was that several important role models devoted to track and field had begun to emerge in Jamaica. This was a largely serendipitous development, as is so often the case in the emergence of cultural and institutional path-dependent processes. Role models influence later institutional developments in various ways. Some do so solely by virtue of their unusual achievements in a particular field, which lend prestige to the activity among groups who feel a special connection to, and pride in, the role model. Others, in addition, actively promote the activity as teachers and facilitators for emerging players. And still others do so by virtue of their achievement in additional fields of endeavor, which not only enhances, by association, the prestige of the activity but also allows the model to exercise influence in its promotion. Jamaica was fortunate in having all three types of modelers from very early on.

The most remarkable of the first type was Alfred Downer (1873–1912), who was born to white Jamaican parents with deep family roots on the island going back to the mid-eighteenth century. Downer was brought up in Scotland and eventually became the most acclaimed runner in Victorian England. Although he left the island as a child and never competed in Jamaica, Downer was apparently quite happy about his Jamaican background, spoke of it proudly, and made a highly celebrated visit to the island. The British public took notice of both Downer's prowess and his Jamaican background, and thus began the branding of Jamaica as a producer of athletes (Bertram 2013: 20–23). More importantly, it was fortunate for the future of athletics on the island that it first achieved international renown as a sports cradle in running (never mind that it had little to do with Downer's success; this, remember, was the era in which pedigree and ancestry mattered). That Downer was white also mattered. The mass of the brown and black population, especially the former, would have been greatly impressed by the fact that a member of the white elite had excelled at a sport that, unlike cricket, tennis, and golf, had no economic barriers to entry. I suspect that this accounts for the rapid decline of running as a competitive sport among elite circles, when compared with cricket, in the other British Caribbean islands. In Barbados, cricket occupied the same venerated cultural status as track and field eventually did in Jamaica. "It has been a craze," writes Sandiford, "some would say it has been a religion," and track and field was reduced to the lowly secondary role of simply making boys "better prepared for bowling, fielding and running between the wickets" (1998: 146). Barbados has produced some of the world's greatest cricketers, but it has had only one track athlete of note, Jim Wedderburn. While cricket was the dominant spectator sport in Jamaica at the end of the nineteenth and early twentieth centuries, track and field was also very popular and engaged more participants, especially in the popular informal meets and garden parties where there were "menagerie races, mule races, three-legged races, obstacle races, cricket matches" and an assortment of other late Victorian amusements (Bryan 2000: 196).

Beginning early in the twentieth century a number of outstanding locally born and reared track athletes emerged on the island, the most celebrated of whom was G. K. Foster, a world-class athlete who was prevented from participating in the 1908 Olympics because Jamaica was not considered a nation. Starting in 1930, Foster went on to search out, coach, and mentor athletes mainly in the nation's high schools (Bertram 2013: 20–28, 47–48, 113–114). Many of his trainees and other prominent figures, such as S. I. Foggy Burrows (who also coached at my high school when I was a student there), followed this same pattern upon completion of their training and usually brief athletic careers, thus creating a virtuous institutional circle. The institutional process, by then well established, was reinforced by the erection in 1980, with Cuban aid, of a college for coaches and physical education that was named in Foster's honor.

Jamaica is also unique among nations in that its founding father, Norman Manley, was an outstanding student athlete; his Champs record in the 100 yards, set in 1911, stood for forty-four years, and his 1912 hurdles record for half a century. Consider the effect on track's prestige in the United States had George Washington been a track star! As a revered national leader—

founding father, head of government from 1955 to 1962, and so on—Manley tirelessly promoted track and field as part of his decolonizing and nationalist agenda. Before becoming head of state, he played a leading role in the revival of the Jamaica Amateur Athletic Association during the 1930s and laid the foundation for a nationwide community development program in 1937 when he founded Jamaica Welfare Limited (later the Social Development Commission), which not only aided the small banana farmers and other peasants but also promoted literacy, folk culture, and skills training for unemployed youth (Levy 1995; see also the SDC website). The building of community centers included athletics facilities. Being deeply steeped in the British conviction that sports were an integral part of any educational system, Manley used his influence and prestige to promote athletics in Jamaica's school at all levels (in addition to his legendary athletic past, Manley was also a Rhodes scholar and the nation's preeminent lawyer).[3] His crowning contribution to athletics was his central role, when he was premier of Jamaica, in the building of the nation's national stadium in 1962. He did so in the face of strong opposition by critics who complained that the nation could ill afford it (Franklyn 2009: 216–217). Significantly, the stadium was built to accommodate track athletics and soccer (the working-class sports) rather than cricket, to the dismay of many middle-class cricket fans.

The role-modeling process eventually became self-sustaining. Thus in 2012, Usain Bolt told CNN on the *Aiming for Gold* program that he was inspired by Don Quarrie, who won the gold for the 200 meters in Montreal in 1976 as well as six gold medals in the Commonwealth Games: "For me Don Quarrie was somebody to watch and to be amazed by. That's why I love the 200 meters so much, because I've seen Don Quarrie and I said, 'I can be that good.' Quarrie, (Herb) McKenley, these are the guys that

I looked up to" (Gittings 2012). The same modeling took place with female stars in Jamaica. Campbell Brown went to the same high school, Vere Technical, as her much older female compatriot and mentor Merlene Ottey, who won fourteen world championship records, and speaks with reverence about her: "She is a very positive person, very strong, very hard-working, very passionate, and she is a friend" (*Caribbean360*, August 1, 2012).

Dedicated role models, coaches, and institutional groundwork, however important, are not sufficient to explain Jamaica's phenomenal rise to global track supremacy. After all, many advanced nations, especially the neighboring superpower, the United States, have these in far greater abundance. The success of the sport's institution builders was made possible by the availability of something nearly unique to Jamaica: an unusually healthy and vigorous youth population eager and hungry for something meaningful to make of their lives in a poor country. Not genetics, then, but healthy bodies in the context of poverty and high unemployment. To be sure, we find an apparently similar conjunction accounting for the success of certain groups in other parts of the world in various sports—most notably, poor black Americans in basketball and football, Dominicans in baseball, and working-class British youth in soccer. But Jamaica possesses two extra elements: First, Jamaican Third World poverty is of an entirely different order than that of the poor and working class in the advanced countries. And second, the sport of choice to escape poverty in Jamaica is track and field, which is unheard of anywhere else in the world. Individuals with the extraordinary athletic abilities of Herb McKenley, Arthur Wint, George Rhoden, Donald Quarrie, Asafa Powell, and Usain Bolt would almost all have ended up in basketball or football (in the United States) or soccer (in Europe) or baseball (in the Dominican Republic). If they had been born in Barbados, cricket would have claimed them. We can be certain of this in the case of Usain Bolt, whose passion as a child and early youth was, indeed, cricket. What emerged in Jamaica was a powerful cultural trajectory toward running and track athletics in the island's sports environment.

It is remarkable how early this cultural bias emerged. A story a Jamaican living in the United States told me about his father illustrates the point (C. Phillips, pers. comm., 2016). In the 1930s a medical practitioner in Kingston, Dr. C. B. Phillips, heard through the grapevine that a friend and fellow doctor who lived and practiced deep in the Jamaican countryside had a son who was a very fast runner. Dr. Phillips, on one of his swings through the countryside on business, went out of his way to visit his friend and requested a demonstration of the son's running prowess, which was promptly arranged by having the boy race and beat others down the country road. Impressed, Dr. Phillips pointed out to the boy's father that he had to go to high school in Kingston, where he could be properly trained, and offered on the spot to be the boy's guardian. The father agreed, and Dr. Phillips arranged for the boy to attend Calabar High School, which had already emerged as one of the leading schools at track and field and was a frequent winner at Champs. The rest is history. The boy in question was Herb McKenley, who went on to become one of Jamaica's iconic track stars and coaches, the only runner in history to produce the world's best times in the 100 meters, the 200 meters, and the 400 meters (in 1947) and a star at the Helsinki Olympics (with Arthur Wint, George Rhoden, and Leslie Laing), an event that established Jamaica as a major track nation and decisively tilted its sports culture toward track athletics. What is remarkable about this story is that Jamaicans were already so enamored of running during the 1930s that one father could make and follow through on such an unusual offer to another.

But this still leaves unexplained why there were so many un-usually healthy young people in a country as poor as Jamaica, especially during the late colonial period when athletics was first embraced. The answer is something no one has noticed: the phenomenal success of a public health program coincided with the rise of track athletics and Manley's community devel-opment program. Initiated in the 1920s as a public health ex-periment (beginning in the little country town of May Pen, where I was brought up) and later applied elsewhere, the program em-phasized simple hygiene education, clean water, effective fecal and mosquito control, and the strong involvement of the target populations and their local community leaders (Riley 2005: 189). The program greatly appealed to Jamaicans, especially because of the respect shown toward ordinary people, who were treated as intelligent agents capable of learning and passing on the goals and public health methods to others. This was un-heard of in the relations between British colonial public health officials and lower-class Jamaicans; indeed, the British colonial authorities at first belittled the program when broached by the Rockefeller officials, asserting that black Jamaicans were too "willful and disobedient" for it to work. But it was precisely this willfulness and self-reliance that the program mobilized in its successful implementation. The result was what the histor-ical demographer James Riley (2005) calls the Jamaican par-adox. This is the fact that Jamaica provides one of the rare ex-amples of a poor country with the life expectancy of an advanced society, a demographic transition that began in the 1920s and improved at one of the fastest rates on record, breaking through the life expectancy threshold of seventy by 1970. The countries that had previously made the fastest transitions from the begin-ning of improvement in life survivorship (following the pre-vious long period of unchanging low life expectancy at birth) to the seventy-year life-expectancy mark were mainly those in northwest Europe and Canada. Thus it took Canada 111 years (from the 1840s to 1956), England 151 years (from ca. 1800 to 1956), and France 165 years (from ca. 1790 to 1960) to reach the seventy-year mark. By contrast it took Jamaica only fifty-seven years to make this transition—from 1920, when the life expectancy was about thirty-six years, to 1977, when it passed seventy for the first time (Riley 2005: 21–29). Significantly, most of the gains in life expectancy took place between 1925 and 1940, before the availability of antibiotics and modern medicines and with the near absence of affordable doctors and health facilities.

What explains this success? According to Riley, "the factors that lead in explaining the Jamaican paradox emerged in the 1920s and 1930s from the alliance between self-reliant action by the people with effective leadership from public health authorities, including outsiders, in selecting useful and effective steps that people could take for themselves" (2005: 189). Norman Manley's Jamaica Welfare program, with its emphasis on self-help, community councils, cooperatives, good health, and athletics, all part of Manley's wider program of nation-building and eventual political independence, played a key role in the success of this program (Riley 2005: 125). The Social Development Commission (SDC), the successor organization to Jamaica Welfare Limited, points out in its history of the program that by the late 1930s there was "a shift in focus—to community associations. These were organized with full participation of community members and activities focused on community life. Cooperative development was an important component and was combined with a 'Study-Save-Work' Plan. Training in home economics and agriculture were introduced in the communities and general use of indigenous materials was encouraged. The Food for Family

Fitness (3F) Campaign was born out of this initiative" (Social Development Commission 1974).

The 3F campaign made substantial improvements in the food habits of rural Jamaicans (Francis 1969). By about the 1930s, a time of great economic and political turmoil (Post 1978), Jamaicans had arrived at a nutritional sweet spot: they were not so poor as to experience malnutrition, as had been true in the late nineteenth and early twentieth centuries (Bryan 2000: 176), but they were too poor to afford modern foods laden with empty calories and saturated fats or to avoid the body-building physical labor required to survive on quarter-acre farms, pushing heavy handcarts, walking long distances, cutting sugar cane, or harvesting bananas. Speaking personally, while growing up in the Jamaican countryside I always had just about enough to eat: never hungry, never quite full, always active—the best balance if doctors were not an option. The old mantras "healthy bodies, healthy minds" and "cleanliness is next to godliness" took hold in the nation's communities and primary schools, whose teachers were also recruited in the public health campaign. Some have argued that specific foods in the Jamaican diet, notably yams and boiled green bananas, partly explain Jamaica's sprinting success, but the evidence is slight and unpersuasive (Asemota 2010). A better case can be made for the general traditional diet of Jamaicans—both the moderate quantities as well as the different kinds of healthy foods regularly eaten: "Oranges, ripe bananas, chicken, rice, yellow yam and green bananas" are still "among the most commonly consumed foods, while rice and peas, brown stewed or fried chicken, porridges and soups were among the most commonly prepared dishes, overall" (Samuda et al. 1998).[4] It is striking that, in spite of its economic problems and the negative effects of the neoliberal, structural adjustment programs of the 1980s on the island's agriculture, the Food and Agriculture

Organization of the United Nations, in a recent country report on Jamaica, found the following: "Jamaica has greater resilience and potential for food security than most other Caribbean Small Island Developing States (SIDS) as local substitutes for imported staples are widely produced and farmers have implemented successful coping and adaptation mechanisms at the farm-level through damage reducing strategies" (FAO 2015: 4).

Jamaica was exceptionally successful not only in its public health program but also in the community development system that enabled it, initiated by Norman Manley and his sociology assistant, Thom Girvan; indeed, Jamaica was viewed as a pioneer and world leader in such programs, so much so that the British colonial government used it as a model for social development in its other Caribbean colonies, and UNESCO sent its community development officers to observe and be trained on the island during the 1950s (Francis 1969).[5] This world-leading system of community development, focused in part on youth, was another critical element in identifying available athletic talent from even the remotest parts of the countryside.

Running, as the cheapest sport, was the natural beneficiary of these remarkable public health and communal movements. It is striking that young Bolt received his initial training at a remote, poorly equipped rural grade school, where a teacher persuaded him to change to track from his first love, cricket, by bribing him with his favorite food (Moore 2015: 44) and then arranged to have him commute to a high school with a good track program in the distant parish capital. It is also no accident that the oldest individual medalist in Olympic track history is a Jamaican woman, Merlene Ottey, who was still sprinting in international meets at age fifty-two.

Somewhat related to this argument is the view, held by many, that Jamaica's mountainous geography and large distances between school and home contribute to its sprinting supremacy. A disproportionate number of the island's superior runners seem to hail from a single very mountainous parish, Trelawny: Usain Bolt, Veronica Campbell-Brown, Omar Brown, Warren Weir, Steven Mullings, Warren Weir, and Debbie-Ann Parris, to list only the best known. Furthermore, two other track superstars, Yohan Blake and Merlene Ottey, come from neighboring parishes with similar geography. Long distances between home and school, negotiated by foot, it is argued, lead to well-developed muscles ideal for sprinting. The argument seems to find support in Yannis Pitsiladis's findings that the distinctive geography of the East African rift valley, combined with the cultural practice of running long distances from early childhood, account for the dominance of athletes from this region in long-distance running (Pitsiladis et al. 2010: 256). This geocultural hypothesis has been tested recently for Jamaicans (Irving et al. 2013). No support was found for the hypothesis that place of birth, mode of travel to school (by foot, bicycle, or motor vehicle) or distance traveled to school explains high performance in sprinting. Jamaican sprinters had similar environmental and ethnic backgrounds, as well as distance and mode of walking to school during youth, as a control group of ordinary Jamaicans. There was some support for Pitsiladis's hypothesis regarding the role of geography and cultural practices in explaining successful long-distance running: High-performing middle-distance Jamaican runners were brought up in the more mountainous regions of Jamaica to a greater degree than ordinary Jamaicans. Such runners have yet to prove their mettle in international contests, however.

Three other factors reinforced these developments. A characteristic feature of Jamaican society is the combative individualism of many of its people, especially among the working class and the underclass, the dark side of which is the nation's chronic violence. The same high-risk behavior accounting for the island's unusual level of violence is linked to the psychocultural disposition favoring track athletics. The positive side of this is extreme self-reliance, which was a major factor explaining the nation's public health system and resulting life-expectancy paradox. Jamaicans were notorious among the British colonialists as a people who were "willful" and difficult to rule. Not long after the Morant Bay Rebellion, the Church Missionary Society abandoned its work in the island, declaring that Jamaicans were incapable of education and moral development. In the late nineteenth century, the limited education provided to the working classes was explicitly designed to inculcate "the habit of obedience, order punctuality, honesty and the like" (King n.d.; Bryan 2000: 116–121). It failed. In her classic study of peasant and rural working-class Jamaicans during the late 1940s, Madeline Kerr observed: "When a group of people get together to make a decision or to take some action there are as many opinions as to how it should be done as there are people present. A group going on a picnic in a truck will nearly always start about an hour late owing to differences of opinion, individuals insisting on doing some odd job first" (1963: 170–171). Kerr attributes this to the deep conflict between cultural traditions in Jamaica, the frustrations of constantly struggling to overcome socioeconomic deprivation, and the aggressive rejection of "the more unpleasing insignia of [British colonial and Anglo-Jamaican] dominance." Drawing on a battery of projective tests and her field and interview data, she found that "the man who wishes to integrate his personality must initiate the process from within himself . . . has to work out his own individuation" (Kerr 1963: 205). About the same time that Kerr published her findings, Thom Girvan, a noted Jamaican sociologist and community organizer, bemoaned the decline of the spirit of cooperation that had previously existed among the peasantry and the rise of "dog-eat-dog-ism" among many segments of the rural and emerging urban working classes (Girvan 1993). In broader terms, the economist William H. Knowles attributed what he called the "nihilistic individualism" and general disdain for authority among working-class Jamaicans to "a feeling of not belonging" in a society where "the government belonged to the colonial administrators" (1956: 143).

Not much has changed for working-class Jamaicans since those late colonial times; if anything, class divisions have grown deeper, and the combative expressions of Afro-Jamaican cultural pride stronger—in reggae music, the dancehall subculture, the Rastafarian religion, and sports. It is also expressed in highly conflicted relations between workers and their supervisors, often culminating in industrial sabotage (Carter 1997). A recent study by mental health specialists found that "conflict is endemic in almost every aspect of Jamaican society with such behaviour reflecting a significant prevalence of personality disorders," which they estimated to exist in "a broad one-third swathe of the Jamaican population" (Hickling and Walcott 2013). Less grim in its findings is the Hofstede Insight Network, a group that studies national and organizational cultures based on the work of the Dutch social psychologist Geert Hofstede (Hofstede Insights 2019). They find that Jamaicans are reluctant to accept unequal power and are characterized by independence, "hierarchy for convenience only," an emphasis on equal rights, a dislike of control, and a preference for direct and participative communication. They like "in groups" in which "loyalty is paramount, overriding most other societal rules and regulations."[6] Jamaicans score high on male dominance, assertiveness, and performance orientation and are "driven by competition, achievement and success, with success being defined by the winner/best in field," and "performance and conflicts are resolved by fighting them out" (Hofstede Insights 2019). Finally, Jamaicans scored very low on uncertainty avoidance, meaning that "deviance from the norm is more easily tolerated. . . . Schedules are flexible, hard work is undertaken when necessary but not for its own sake, precision and punctuality do not come naturally, innovation is not seen as threatening." This sounds remarkably like a formal description of the "soon come" mentality that nearly all Jamaicans acknowledge and bemoan.

This combative individualism is found in its starkest form in dancehall reggae's competitive dance and sound clashes, which, Carolyn Cooper (2004) argues, reflect the broader divisions and conflicts in Jamaican society. However it also dovetails well with running, especially sprinting, in which performance is entirely up to the athlete. One major psychological study has found that athletes who engage in individual sports tend to be more egoistic (de Man and Blais 1982: 12). The Jamaican writer Delano Franklyn attributes the sprinting success of his countrymen in part to their extreme "assertiveness":

> This belief that we are able to do anything others have been able to do typifies our athletes. They are not afraid to take on the opposition. They believe that they can outrun and outpace any opponent. This typical Jamaican culture works in our favour when it is properly organized, properly directed and properly channeled. On the other hand, if not properly controlled and properly directed . . . it can easily degenerate into indiscipline and anti-social behavior. (2009: 201–202)

This cultural disposition can be fatal in team sports, where one has to pass the ball and coordinate. As de Man and Blais observed: "Team sports, as compared to one-on-one and individual sports, require close cooperation within the team, and a willingness of the individual player to place himself in a subordinate position"

(1982: 12). Jamaican soccer players are notorious for being talented (in 2015 they beat the US national team in the semifinal game for the gold cup of the Concacaf [Confederation of North, Central American and Caribbean Association Football]) but stubbornly resistant to harmonizing with other players to produce consistently victorious team outcomes.[7] It might be objected that Jamaican runners are also preeminent in relay events. However, Jamaicans hardly consider the relay a team event. Maurice Wilson, the technical director of the Jamaican Olympic team, made this clear when he told Oliver Brown (2016) of the *Daily Telegraph* that the relay is "about four different people. It's not as if they become one. Four people going down different roads, living different lifestyles, mentored by different coaches."

The old British ethic of winning with grace has long vanished, if it was ever embraced by Jamaicans. Warren Weir, a bronze medalist at the London Olympics and alumnus of Calabar High School, one of the dominant schools at Champs, told the writer Richard Moore (2015) the evening before a Champs event: "One thing we go out there for, and that's to win. To win. To win. To win. To win. To dominate. To crush them!" The world got a startling display of this combative habitus at the Beijing Olympics when Bolt, instants away from winning the 100 meters in record time, slowed down at the 80th meter mark, thumped his chest, and spread his arms in a taunting, triumphant gesture at the men panting behind him, two of them his Jamaican teammates. "We are a confident people," he later told the BBC. Few who know Jamaicans and their cocky self-confidence would disagree. More interestingly, a review of psychological studies of high-performing Olympic athletes found a high level of self-confidence to be one of their primary characteristics (Williams and Krane 2001). A later study added that "the ability to cope with and control anxiety" and "mental toughness," the basic components of which were "resilience, perseverance and the ability to successfully deal with adversity," were among the main psychological traits of peak performing athletes (Gould et al. 2002: 199). Jamaica's unusually harsh and conflicted past has certainly contributed to the development of these traits as essential survival mechanisms in its working classes. As Gould and colleagues further note, the psychological skills and characteristics of top athletes develop "over long time periods" and are influenced by institutions such as the school, community, and family as well as "non-sport personnel, the individual himself or herself, sport environment/personnel, and the sport process" (2002: 199, 202).

The combative habitus can also lead to reckless behavior in athletic competition. Although Bolt has a clean slate, several Jamaican athletes have tested positive for prohibited substances (Franklyn 2009: 163–185). Some are no doubt guilty, and the disclosure in 2016, not long before the Rio Olympics, that Nesta Carter had tested positive for a banned substance caused consternation in Jamaica, since stripping him of his gold in the relays of the two past Olympics entailed withdrawing the gold medal from all members of both teams, including Bolt. However, it is striking that the Swiss-based Court for Arbitration in Sports (CAS) has repeatedly overturned or drastically reduced the penalties imposed on Jamaicans by the anti-doping agencies on the grounds that there were "credible, non-doping explanations" or, in Shelly-Ann Fraser-Pryce's case, that the substance involved did not have performance-enhancing effects. Jamaica has a long peasant tradition of using herbal supplements to promote good health; I personally have bitter childhood memories of these "tonics." It's likely that some of the offending athletes may have been innocently following this folk tradition. Methylhexanamine, the drug found in the re-test of two of Carter's samples, is another of those open to "credible, non-doping explanations"; it is legally and widely sold in the United States as an energy-boosting dietary supplement and was sold by Eli Lilly as a nasal decongestant up to 1983.

Jamaica has also creatively exploited its proximity to North America and the large transnational space it shares with the mainland where almost a million people of Jamaica ancestry live. Until the early years of this century, many of the most successful athletes went on athletic scholarships to America and other advanced countries. Some stayed and competed for the United States (for example, Debbie Dunn, who won three golds for the United States at the 2009 and 2010 World Championships), as many have also done for Britain (for example, the 100 meters Olympic gold medalist Linford Christie and Javelin Olympic gold medalist Tessa Sanderson) and for Canada, where migrants of Jamaican ancestry have dominated high-performance sprinting since the 1980s, most notably the Olympic gold medalists Donovan Bailey and Robert Esmie, not to mention the Commonwealth gold medalist Angella Taylor-Issajenko (for a list of Jamaicans who have represented the United States, the United Kingdom, and Canada, see Ince 2012: 230). The United States, however, was the main country to which Jamaicans went to study and train, and the influence of its sport culture has had the greatest impact. Several Jamaicans became coaches in American colleges. However, a critical number of them not only ran for Jamaica but, like former Jamaican national coaches Dennis Johnson and Herb McKenley, came back to train generations of new stars. From the 1960s on, Jamaican student athletes have also been facing the challenges of international competition at American meets such as the Penn Relays, where they have excelled.

A major new development began seventeen years ago with the establishment of the first of several for-profit track and field clubs, which have transferred to the island American sports entrepreneurship as well as advanced training techniques, especially those of the legendary San Jose State College athletics coach Bud Winter, who had earlier coached the influential former world record holder Dennis Johnson (Moore 2015: 91–101). Now nearly all the island's major track stars are being trained locally at the two leading clubs, MVP Track and Field Club, founded by Johnson in conjunction with the University of Technology (the first academic institution to establish an American-style athletic system) and Racers Track Club, led by Glen Mills, Bolt's trainer, located at the University of the West Indies. These remarkably successful clubs have greatly reduced the previous athletic talent drain while shifting the focus to adult runners, increasing their career span, and, with their greater local visibility and wealth, intensifying the island's passion for the sport. As Colin Jackson, the director of sports at the University of the West Indies told *The Guardian* (McRae 2010): "It's been a tremendous benefit. We now have Usain training at the University of the West Indies here in Kingston, and that's a real carrot for youngsters. And we have cooked the carrot a little more by bringing his coach, Glen Mills, to the campus. So we're giving all these top athletes at Champs a real incentive. They can stay here alongside Usain and Asafa. And let's not forget the women. In Beijing, Jamaica won 11 medals. Three went to [the men] and the rest were won by the women."

Somewhat related to the development of professional clubs has been the parallel rapid growth of what the sportswriter Dean

Hardman (2014) calls a "quiet revolution" in Jamaica: mass recreational running to such an extent that he estimates that Jamaica may now have more recreational and semi-competitive middle- and long-distance runners per capita than any other country in the world. Inspired by their sprinting heroes and, being Jamaicans, not content to enjoy their beloved sport simply as spectators, Jamaicans have taken to recreational running in a big way. The popularity of long-distance running in a land of sprinters is not really surprising, since sprinting is not an event for amateurs mainly interested in having a good time or staying in shape. The 2017 road race calendar put out by Running Events Jamaica featured eighteen national events with a break only in August. The biggest of these, the annual reggae marathon held in December—with a half marathon and 10k course—attracts some twenty thousand local and international runners. Another, the Digicel Imagine 5K, attracts over seven thousand runners (and another seven thousand spectators). Facilitating this passion for running are commercial enterprises such as Jamdammers and Running Events Ltd. as well as a large number of business sponsors, government athletic and health organizations, and nongovernmental organizations. Needless to say, this has only reinforced the culture's powerful bias toward running, ensuring that no one with talent in this sport will be missed by the social mechanisms of identification, selection, motivation, and training.

Thus there is now in Jamaica a fully institutionalized "virtuous cycle of sport" focusing on competitive running. According to Grix and Carmichael, this cycle "holds that elite success on the international stage leads to prestige, and elite sport contributes to a collective sense of identity; this, then, boosts a greater mass sport participation, leading to a healthier populace; this, in turn, provides a bigger 'pool' of talent from which to choose the elite stars of the future and which ensures elite success. The process then starts over again" (2012: 76–77). Although skeptical about whether this applies to Britain, as British sport officials claim, there can be no doubt that this virtuous cycle, set in motion from the early part of the twentieth century, is now fully at play in Jamaica.

Contrary to the claims of some studies that larger populations favor the cultivation of athletic prowess (Reiche 2016: chap. 5), Jamaica's small population and geographic size may well be a factor in intensifying this path-dependent virtuous cycle, inexorably culminating in maximal efficiency in the selection and production of its available running talent. In the sociocultural as in the biological world, it is generally true that larger populations tend to have greater flexibility, diversity, and adaptive potential. However, once initial challenges have been overcome and a path-dependent process gets underway, a smaller population concentrated in a smaller geographic area can sometimes more easily maximize the trajectory of a desired trait (for instance, watchmaking and banking in Switzerland; hydraulic science in Holland; diamond cutting among Hasidic Jews). The identification of the trait or skill and the transmission of knowledge about it spreads more rapidly, its cultural salience is more quickly established, and training in it becomes more readily accessible. The early discovery and training of Herb McKenley's and Bolt's running genius illustrate this process. Conversely, a large population (say, India, China, Brazil, even Canada), spread over a huge area, with the same proportion of talented individuals, can easily fail to transmit knowledge of and enthusiasm for the trait throughout the country, even when locally identified, or provide accessible training resources; and it is more difficult for a given trait or process to dominate the population.

Even if these disadvantages are overcome in larger populations (as they often are in the long run), there is also the possibility that, in the short and medium run, in the more variegated adaptive landscape of the larger country, development of a beneficial trait or practice may become trapped in local fitness zones (both literally and in the more metaphoric evolutionary sense), with the mobility of talent reinforcing these regional differences rather than reducing them—the initial situating of the movie industry in Hollywood and the auto industry in Detroit and general industrial production in the Northeast being cases in point (Krugman 1991). In a small country, on the other hand, such regional specialization of talent is not likely to happen. The whole country very soon gets engaged in the path-dependent process and the identification, selection, motivation, and training of every available talented individual are maximized, from infancy through adulthood, and from every nook and cranny of the country, even in such obscure mountainous rural corners such as Coxheath, located on the far side of the deeply rural village of Sherwood Content, where Usain Bolt grew up. Of course, small size and the same feedback that reinforces traits like the combative habitus can lead to the institutionalization of vicious cycles as well, such as a culture of feuding gangs and violence.

Conclusion

To summarize, Jamaica's global supremacy in running is due not to any single cause but to a unique conjunction of historical, sociocultural, coaching, public health, and locational factors. A colonial athletic tradition—interscholastic games—came under the powerful influence of unusually dedicated and revered role models and athletic coaches, among whom was the nation's founding father. Their work was facilitated by an unusual talent pool of poor, under- and unemployed, but extremely healthy and combatively competitive youth, the result of a harsh and contested colonial history and economy and of an unusually successful public health program that was reinforced by the nation's schools and community development system. Concurrent with this development was the nation's nationalist movement, also led by Norman Manley, who, as a former star athlete and Rhodes scholar, saw track athletics as an integral part of nation-building. Early international success greatly fostered nascent national pride, especially after the national team not only beat the British imperial overlords in the number of gold trophies, but also made an impressive showing in the overall ranking of nations at the 1952 Helsinki Olympics.[8]

The result was the island-wide, all-age institutionalization of track athletics, the apex of which was the transformation of Champs into a spectacular mass-supported cultural institution. A virtuous sociocultural circle was thus fashioned, in which the extreme cultural bias toward track athletics generated an optimal selection into running of nearly all available athletic talent, starting from kindergarten. Reinforcing these developments were educational and athletic scholarships in the United States (and to a lesser extent Canada and the United Kingdom), whose training techniques and sports culture were transferred to the island, first by returning graduates working as coaches in the nation's schools, then later via highly successful commercial coaching enterprises that stemmed the previous flow of talent from the island. The success, wealth, and local presence of these clubs' internationally celebrated stars further reinforces the motivation for, and choice of, running, over all other sports, among the nation's athletic talent pool. This conjunction of causes, amounting to the institutionalization of a virtuous cycle of sprint athleticism, sufficiently explains the island's global supremacy in running.

5

Why Did Jamaicans Riot at a Cricket Match against England?

The Ritual of Cricket in West Indian Societies

In the 1953–1954 test series between England and the West Indies, a riot broke out on the Bourda Grounds in Georgetown, Guyana. England went on to win the match by nine wickets.

In the 1959–1960 series between the same two sides another riot erupted at Queens Park Oval, Port of Spain, Trinidad. England won the match—and as a result, the series—by fifty-six runs.

On Monday, February 12, 1968, six years after Jamaica had achieved independence from Britain, a riot broke out on the third day of the second test match being played at Sabina Park, Kingston, between the West Indian team and the visiting Britons.[1]

In accounting for these riots (especially the events in Jamaica, on which I focus primarily in this chapter), one must go beyond the superficial explanations offered by sports commentators: the weather, the fact that the home side was losing, just plain lack of discipline, and so on. These simply beg the question: Why should a home team become so terribly involved in a game that the dismissal of one batsman sparks off a full-scale riot? If, as a few of the English sportswriters claimed, the West Indian masses are so ill disciplined and barbaric, why have they not revolted against economic conditions that are infinitely more frustrating than the simple dismissal of a batsman?

A closer look at the record of these riots raises further interesting issues. For one thing, although Jamaica has hosted Australian, Indian, and Pakistani touring teams that have routed the home side before large audiences, it is only against the English teams that riots have taken place.

A second interesting fact is that cricket, outside of test matches, is rapidly losing ground both as a participant and a spectator sport in the West Indies, the one exception being Barbados. In the three areas where riots have broken out, local first-class cricket matches attract relatively small audiences.

We must begin to answer the questions posed here by first observing that in the West Indies the test match is not so much a game as a collective ritual, a social drama in which almost all of the basic tensions and conflicts within these societies are played out symbolically. Furthermore, at certain moments the symbolic content of this ritual acquires a special quality—what I shall call transubstantive—that not only reinforces its potency but in so doing creates a situation that can only be resolved in violence. Finally, in a society remarkably devoid of social dramas of this kind, cricket, precisely because it is the only such ritual, becomes extremely important for the expression and channeling of certain deeply rooted grievances and tensions within the society. It is, in short, the only institution (with the possible exception of lower-class religious cults) performing certain basic cleansing or cathartic functions. As Frantz Fanon wrote in *The Wretched of the Earth*, "Violence is a cleansing force. It frees the native from his inferiority complex and from his despair and inaction: it makes him fearless and restores his self-respect."

What is it then about West Indian society that transforms cricket, a normally staid and complicated game which at first sight would seem peculiarly devoid of any deep cleansing value, into such an intense ritual? Almost everything, one is tempted to answer, but space permits me to make only three basic points about the society.

First there is the cultural dualism peculiar to all West Indian societies. If we take the case of Jamaica, we find not one cultural core shared by all members of the society with regional and class variations in lifestyle, but really a dominant culture and another more subordinate system, partly conflicting in their value systems, partly supplementary. On the one hand, there is the culture of the elite group, essentially British in orientation, the creolized version of the culture of the former colonial overlords. On the other hand, there is the culture of the masses, which, in its traditional form, is a tenuous syncretism of the fragments of African culture that survived slavery and local adjustments to the demands of the plantation system and broader colonial economy.

As one would expect, the relationship between these two cultures is one of subordination and super-ordination. The British colonial rulers defined their culture, their values, as superior, and such was their economic and political power that what was originally only ideologically defined soon became socially real. The slaves and their descendants had little real choice in the matter. They lived their way of life largely by default. The "superior" culture of the white master was accepted with all its implications of lowly conception of all things black and Afro-Jamaican. The way one looked, the way one spoke, the way one behaved were all negatively evaluated. Outside of the peasant sector, black lower-class Jamaicans accepted this and sometimes despised themselves for having to accept it. While accepting the superiority of British culture, the Jamaicans also hated it for what it had made of their own culture and of themselves. It was, in short, a deep-seated love-hate relationship, expressed in an unusual level of violence against other blacks and peculiar cultural contradictions.

The second important feature of the society is its rigid class division. A report from 1958 indicated that, of countries with available data, Jamaica had one of the most unequal distributions of income in the world (Ahiram 1964). Much has been said, although little done, about the increasing gulf between the haves and the have-nots in this society, and there is little need to elaborate here.

Color, although of decreasing significance as an active determinant of status (that is, there has been a marked decline in job discrimination on the basis of color) still largely coincides with class. While color discrimination has decreased, color prejudice is still rife. To the black, lower-class Jamaican, however, all of this, understandably, appears to be simply splitting hairs. The combined effect of the persistence of color prejudice and the correlation of light shade with high status simply reinforces his own prejudice that racial discrimination is still rampant (a prejudice, incidentally, that also serves the added psychological function of excusing his own low status). For these reasons, then, the society has not benefited in terms of racial stability as much as it should have done from the significant reduction in racial discrimination in recent years. Indeed, urbanization, improved educational facilities, and generally rising expectations have led to a growing sense of racial exploitation.

The final feature of the society we must take note of is partly implied in what has been said above—that is, the fact that there is little shared behavior among the different groups that make up the society. The Jamaican rarely experiences any sense of social solidarity either with the total society or with any sizable groups within the wider context of the nation state. It would be no exaggeration to say that the society is literally bursting at the seams with conflict. Cultural, color, and class conflicts I have already mentioned, but there are other sources of conflict within the system—conflicting political allegiances, rural–urban conflicts, sexual conflicts—all fraught with a degree of animosity unheard of in more stable social orders. The masses, then, are as much in conflict with themselves as they are with the elite. It would be the height of left-wing romanticism to imagine that the great gulf separating the elite from the masses has led to any kind of group consciousness or sense of solidarity among the latter. In the daily struggle to survive it is every man for himself.

Consider now, the situation at Sabina Park on that dramatic Monday afternoon in 1968. Both the setting and the game constituted a microcosm of Jamaican society. The differing qualities of the spectators in the various stands reflected to an almost absurd degree the differences within the society. It is difficult to resist the temptation to pun on the German word *Stand* (meaning "status group") by remarking that the stands were literally *Stands*. To the western end of the grounds was the pavilion, its members over 90 percent white or very light in color, rich and upper class. The sprinkling of browns and blacks were typical of those who had made it in this group: the governor-general—black, resplendently attired—his wife a little way down amidst a group of patronizing white ladies, cheerful, chubby, and well dressed, looking for all the world like a black version of the British Queen Mother. There were a few ministers of government, the odd uppity civil servant, the occasional black businessman. Five to ten percent. More than that and the Sabina Park pavilion would not be the place it used to be. Opposite the pavilion, at the eastern end of the grounds were the bleachers—the hard wooden benches beneath the hot sun, every inch of which exploded with people. Here were the masses, securely fenced off from the rest of the grounds with chicken wire. Their faces were nearly all black. If one scanned diligently enough the odd white or high brown face may have been spotted, but these, as often as not, belonged to some too-earnest resident of Mona, the site of the University of the West Indies.

Then to the northern end of the grounds were the covered stands with concrete seats. The spectators here were better clad, their color, on average, a cooler shade of black. There were fences here too. But not as high as the ones in front of the bleachers. Here it was possible to move about more freely. With the naked eye one could just about scan the (social) cream on the pavilion.

Finally, there were the southern and grand stands: clean, shaded, comfortable, the view excellent, the spectators orderly and well dressed. These shared with the pavilion the privilege of having no fences. Occasionally there was an exchange of greetings between a spectator from the grand stand with one from the pavilion—always polite, always cordial but somehow not without a lingering flavor of awkwardness, if not embarrassment.

And now the game. Its meaning. Its ritual significance. Need one spell it out? Cricket is the Englishman's game par excellence. The very term *cricket* has become a byword for all that is most English in the British way of life. The vocabulary of cricket is a standard pool of stock images for Tory statesmen. No better symbol of English culture could be found. Yet, this is the game that West Indians have usurped, have come to master. What the former colonial subject has done is to literally beat the colonizer at his own game. More important, he has beaten him symbolically. Here all the ambivalence of the black lower-class West Indian toward English culture can be played out. Cricket is the game "we" love, for it is the only game we can play well, the only activity that gives us some international prestige. But it is the game, deep down, that we must hate—the game of the colonizer. Hence it becomes on the symbolic level the English culture we have been forced to love, for it is the only *real* one we have, but the culture we must despise for what it has done to us, for what it has made of Afro-Jamaican lower-class culture. How better to express our pent-up rage, our agonizing self-contradiction than to acquire and master this culture, and then to use it to beat the group that forced us into acquiring it? This is precisely what cricket has done for the West Indian. This is why victory—victory against the Englishman—is a matter of such great moment.

But the game does more than this. It resolves internal conflicts in that it functions symbolically in expressing strong class hostility. Hence it is not only the means by which the ex-colonial gets back at the culture of his former master but a means whereby the masses express their rage against their "betters," the carriers of the dominant English culture in the local society. Hence it is significant that the West Indian team was almost entirely dark brown or black and of lower-class origin. Further, it is no accident that during the bad old days when the team was dominated by whites, no riots ever took place. It is also significant that the really popular members of the team were not Sobers and Kanhai but Hall and Griffith. Sobers, for example, was respected, revered, awed: As one spectator was heard to say when he once again saved the team from defeat, "'Im not no cricketer—'Im is God!'" But it is in the nature of deities that they are removed from the immediate obsessions and problems of mortals. Not so the response of the crowd to Hall and Griffith. The feeling here came straight from the gut. One reason perhaps is that, as pacemen, they performed the most aggressive roles on the team. No one who had seen Hall making his long, muscular run-up to the wicket could fail to be impressed by the beautiful, sweet violence of the act—the slow, menacing beginning, the gathering pace, the sudden climactic explosion of energy on delivery, the dashing follow-through, the plight of the lonely batsman at the other end. In this cathartic moment of truth, it was "us" versus "them." "Us" constitutes the black masses. "Them" is everything else—the privileged, the oppressor, the alien, dominant culture.

This brings us to the third symbolic function of cricket. The test match is one of the few occasions on which the lower classes experience any kind of group solidarity. The self-destructive atomism created by poverty, conflicting values, deprivation, and charismatic, clientelistic politics loses its disintegrative power in the presence of the game. Here at last, via the medium of genuine heroes—the only heroes in a land barren of heroes or a heroic tradition—the masses respond as one, share a common experience, bite their nails in a common war of nerves against a common enemy—"them." But if cricket demystifies, there is a sense in which it also enhances mystification in that it facilitates not only proletarian solidarity but bourgeois nationalism. As such, it fully evokes the ambivalence of the masses toward the elite. For "them" over there also claim to be against the British touring team. On the one hand "we" would like to deny "them" the right to feel that they are allies with "us" against the common foe, but on the other hand, it is difficult not to succumb to the temptations of bourgeois nationalist sentimentality. The elite, after all, are paying homage to "our" heroes too. "We" hate the bastards but "we" must admit a little feeling of pleasure at their submission. As long as the game follows its natural course and as long as the home team, the heroes, are winning we are prepared to be generous: "We" shall allow "them" to share some of the glory with "us."

Is this perhaps a collective projection? Do "we" somehow in this moment of triumph fool "ourselves" into thinking that it is possible to share some little of their particular glory? It is a fool's paradise. But a beautiful one while it lasts. Tomorrow the sports commentators will say how proud "we" all are, how well "we" played.

However, the demystifying function of cricket is only possible when the game is going the right way. It is a different matter when the heroes are losing, when they are being humiliated by the English team before the very eyes of the masses, as they were on that fateful Monday.

And it is at this point that the symbolism acquires a new dimension, one far more telling. Let us look briefly at the series of incidents sparking off this symbolic escalation.

The test began on Thursday, February 8. Cowdrey, the English captain, won the toss and from the first ball it was clear that this would be no ordinary test match. The West Indian bowlers toiled all day with little reward. The crowd left disappointed, worried. The next day the innings continued. Already the wicket had begun to crack up. England were all out in the late afternoon for 376 runs. By now the wicket was like a jigsaw puzzle with several enormous chasms, one of the worst ever witnessed in the history of test matches. As the West Indian batsmen came in, the tension rose. It was in no way relieved by the surprise of seeing Murray, the young wicket-keeper and normally the no. 7 batsman, opening. Clearly, even the great Sobers was worried. It was a gamble that did not come off, for before the end of play that day, disaster struck twice, as the opening pair was dismissed with the total number of runs too humiliating to mention. The next day, Saturday, the West Indian side was routed for a miserable 143. The follow-on was forced, and it was during the fightback on the following Monday that Basil Butcher was brilliantly caught by Parks behind the wicket off the bowling of Basil D'Olivera. Sang Hue, the Jamaican Chinese umpire, had no hesitation in giving him out.

But the crowd could not believe it. Did not wish to believe it. As Holford came in to join Sobers the bottles began to pop over the fence separating the bleachers from the field. Slowly at first, then as Cowdrey, the president of the Jamaica Cricket Association and later, Sobers, appealed to them, the bottles poured down even more profusely. The police then came on the scene. It was a classic display of police mismanagement. After failing to make any impact by shouting at the crowd from the playing field side of the fence, the riot squad was called in. This had precisely the opposite effect of that intended. Dressed in gas masks and carrying tear-gas guns they appeared somehow both frightening and absurd. There was something quite unreal about them for, hidden behind their masks, they appeared more like actors in a Pirandello drama of tyranny than real policemen. The police unwittingly placed themselves in the role of playing themselves. As such they became simply an extension of the drama that was already being played out.

The crowd paused for a moment and watched them. This new scene. These new actors. These strange messengers of postcolonial terror. Then the actors acted. They began to throw the tear-gas bombs into the crowd. Suddenly the ritual took a new crucial turn. As the vile fumes burned the eyes and turned over the stomachs of the masses, the drama became real. Everything was transformed—the actors lived their roles, the symbol became the thing symbolized. This was no longer a game, no longer a vivid metaphor. This was Jamaican society in all its stark, brutal reality. Now it seemed as vulnerable, its brutality so transparent. The opportunity had to be seized. It must be destroyed. And so the masses rioted.

So far I have largely attempted to explain how the ritual of cricket functions as a symbolic expression of certain basic conflicts in West Indian society. I have yet to explain the reasons for the riot itself. Indeed what I have said would seem more to indicate why a riot should not take place rather than why it should. An understanding of why the riot occurs requires an appreciation of two things. One concerns the nature of cricket itself. The other relates to the nature of symbolism.

The most striking thing about cricket, as a game, is its emphasis on order. All games, it is true, involve some acceptance of rules and cease to exist when such rules are neglected. But cricket is exceptional both for its complexity and for its almost consciously articulated ideology of obedience and authority, the latter being symbolized in the person of the umpire. Nor is it an accident that cricket is one of the few games that requires two umpires.

It is because of this internal quality, this emphasis on obeying the rules, of unquestioning acceptance of the decision of the umpire, that cricket is able to perform another vital, if negative, symbolic function. Namely, that of disobeying the rule, of refusing to accept the decision of the umpire, which in terms of its symbolic identity with the society that I have outlined above, amounts to a denial, a threat to the very existence of the society.

The ritual of cricket then belongs to that category of symbols that is potentially self-destructive in that it is most potent where it denies its reality as symbol and in the act of so doing becomes qualitatively transformed. I have called this category of symbols transubstantive. A substantive symbol must, by definition, remain a sign, that is, an object or act that mediates the meaning of some referent to a subject or group of people. However, in the case of a transubstantive symbol there is an inherent tension derived from the impulse to acquire the substance of the meaning that originally the symbol was meant only to mediate. The symbol, in short, ceases to be something meaningless in itself, ceases to be simply a mediator and becomes inherently meaningful, be-

comes the thing being mediated. It no longer stands for something else. It *is* the something else.[2]

A further point worth noting is the fact that a transubstantive symbol rarely, if ever, exists as an independent type. Instead,
it remains vested in ordinary substantive symbols as a latent or
postponed possibility—a possibility that, in certain rare moments
of deep involvement with the ritual, is realized by the subject.

Cricket, as an ordinary substantive symbol, mediates and symbolically resolves certain basic conflicts within Jamaican society.
It is also, however, a transubstantive symbol and acquires that
quality when it ceases to mediate and canalize social conflicts and
instead becomes identified with such conflicts. Such an identification is likely to occur at moments when the believers' (the spectators of the game) devotion and identity with their heroes are
in a state of crisis. And just such a moment occurred at the point
in the game when Butcher was dismissed. Like certain devout
Christians for whom the ritual of communion is one in which
the wine and the bread are actually the blood and flesh of Jesus,
so to the Jamaican lower-class spectator in that moment, the
game became the society, symbolized partly in the entire game
but more concretely in the person of the umpire, who in this case
was Chinese (as was also the case in the Guyanese riot), a racial
type inevitably associated with the dominant capitalist class in
the West Indies. And when the society literally entered the drama
through the medium of the fearsome police who then proceeded
to play themselves, the experience could only be consummated
by the expression of the most basic wish of the lower-class spectators. The wish to destroy the society, the system which was the
source of their poverty, their humiliation, and their oppression.

If my interpretation is correct, the wonder is not that so many
riots have taken place in test matches between England and the
West Indies, but that so few have occurred.

6

Why Does Globalization Not Produce Cultural Homogenization?

The Example of Jamaican Reggae Music

The modern process of global cultural interaction has repeatedly been subjected to two criticisms. The first is that it threatens the diversity and particularism of the world's cultures, resulting in a deadening homogenization of the human cultural experience. The other is that this growing global uniformity results from the dominance of Western and especially American culture—that, in effect, global culture is nothing more than American cultural imperialism. Theodor Adorno's (1990) (in)famous diatribe against the "standardization" of popular culture, and especially nonclassical music, is the locus classicus of such views, extended more recently by theorists such as George Ritzer and Michael Ryan (2002). The view is widespread; the Many Musics program of the International Music Council, for example, contends that five major international record companies based in Europe, Japan, and the United States "carry an international pop music across the globe, altering and homogenising musical preferences of audiences in most countries. This is the most obvious and most resented face of globalisation in music" (Letts 2003). In this chapter I join those who reject these claims (see Robertson 1995; Hopper 2007: chap. 5) through an examination of the origins and development of one of the less-developed world's most vibrant and globally influential cultural creations: Jamaican reggae music (Bilby 1995: 143).

In a nutshell, the argument that globalization is resulting in the cultural homogenization of the world ignores the increased vitality of local cultures and ethnicities in recent times and the complexity of global cultural diffusion and exchanges, in particular the extent to which so-called peripheral regions are increasingly contributing to American popular culture and to the world cultural scene.

The Diffusion of Global Culture

Industrialization and modernization both led to the spread of common sets of behaviors and attitudes within the context of economic change. However, the globalization of culture also takes place independent of whatever economic changes are occurring in a particular region or society. Traditionally, the transmission of culture across societies was facilitated by two main means: migration and literacy. People learned about other cultures either through their own travels—whether voluntary or forced—or from travelers, or they had new ways forced upon them by imperial powers. They could also acquire other cultural patterns through reading, although, until the twentieth century, such transmission was confined mainly to elites. Until the end of the modern colonial era, this process was largely a diffusion from the West to the rest of the world. I say "largely" because, as recent studies have emphasized, the colonial experience did culturally influence Western colonizers and their "self-constructions," both in their colonies and at home, in often subtle but important ways. (For an innovative account of how the nineteenth-century colonial experience in Jamaica influenced British self-constructions both on the island and in Britain, see Hall 2002.) Since the middle of the twentieth century the globalization of culture has greatly increased not only in terms of its spread over the surface of the world but also in terms of the depth to which it has influenced the populations of other societies.

Four factors account for this sudden change of pace (Robertson 1992; Hopper 2007). The first is the spread of mass literacy throughout the world, which resulted from the new nations of the postcolonial era investing vast sums and human energy in their educational systems, the structure and content of which were largely influenced by Western models. The second is the rise of mass communication, beginning with the radio and later TV and the cinema but greatly accelerating since the 1990s, with the emergence and spread of the internet. The third is the growth of global organizations, both private and public, such as international nongovernmental organizations, multinational corporations, the United Nations, the World Bank, the International Monetary Fund, and the large number of regional agencies, themselves often modeled on and directly influenced and promoted by their counterparts on the global scene. One group of scholars sees the result as a world polity with an overarching global culture (see Meyer 1987; Boli and Thomas 1997). The fourth is the revolution in long-distance transportation, which has resulted not only in the mass migration of peoples around the world but also in the emergence of an entirely new kind of global, or more properly, subglobal system involving transnational communities or regional cosmoses in which people live in more than one society, with their loyalties and cultural experiences transcending national boundaries (Levitt 2001). One of the most remarkable of these emerging regional cosmoses is the West Atlantic system, encompassing the eastern seaboard of North America and the circum-Caribbean societies of Central America and the islands (Patterson 1987).

Global Popular Musical Culture

I choose to focus on popular music because it is in this area of the globalization process that the strongest claims of homogenization have been made. The classic statement of this view was given by the musicologist Alan Lomax (1968), who lamented the presumed passing of the great local cultures of the world under the impact of American popular culture, which, he feared, would lead to global rootlessness and alienation as the peoples of the earth all sank into the desolate gloom of the great global "cultural grey-out." For all his important musicological insights, Lomax was wrong in this prediction. To the contrary, Western and American cultural influence has generated enormous cultural production, in some cases amounting to near-hypercreativity, in the popular musical cultures of the world.

It must be wondered where the popular misconception of the homogenizing effect of the Western musical impact came from. One source is the propagandistic reaction of traditional cultural gatekeepers in Third World societies, whose monopoly and influence have been threatened by the Western cultural impact. That impact, in generating new cultural forms, invariably stimulates the emergence of new and competing cultural agents and managers. To monopolize the cultural resources of a country involves exercising enormous power, not to mention controlling large economic resources. What usually upsets traditional cultural gatekeepers about the Western impact on their mass cultures is not so much the content of Western culture—because it is invariably transformed—as the choice it immediately offers to the mass consumers of culture. Cultural hegemony, the "manufacture of consent," as Antonio Gramsci (1971), Steven Lukes (2005), and Herman and Chomsky (1988) have persuasively shown, is a major basis of elite control, as important as raw coercion and economic power. To the degree that there is radical change in the cultural production of the lower classes, to that degree the hegemonic symbiosis developed over the centuries between elite patronage and folk culture is disrupted, with consequences that can often have unintended political consequences. As the musicologist Wayne Marshall notes, comparing reggae with hip-hop: "As a form of rebellion against a Eurocentric status quo, reggae and hip-hop both partake in the networks, ideologies, and discourses of Anglo-American imperialism even as they fashion—in such sensuous forms as to find sympathetic ears nearly everywhere—new ways for subjects in postcolonial circumstances to struggle against (and make use of) the asymmetrical forces of global exchange and geopolitics, to imagine and create alternative cartographies and communities, and to express a disavowal and critique of the very system we find ourselves, in various ways, shoring up and chanting down" (2007: 84).

Ironically, criticism of the cultural disruptions of globalization comes as often from cultural gatekeepers in the West itself, on both the right and the left. The more abstract of these complaints about the influence of Western and especially American global popular culture stem from elitist, postmodernist pessimism, of the sort that stimulates similar complaints about the stultifying effects of popular culture on the Western working class. The cultural critic Paul Willis (1990) has taken issue with these pretentious criticisms. He notes that people never simply passively absorb cultural messages. There is always what Willis calls symbolic work at play: "The incandescence is not simply a surface market quality. It produces, is driven by, and reproduces further forms and varieties for everyday symbolic work and creativity, some of which remain in the everyday and in common culture far longer than they do on the market." Critics of global popular culture have in mind a world of passive consumers, homogenized and manipulated into Marx's notorious sack of (Westernized) potatoes. It is nothing of the sort. As Paul Hopper properly observes: "People are not just at home passively waiting for cultural flows" (2007: 185). The semi- and non-literate masses of the Third World invariably react to Western cultural influence in a non-passive manner, reinterpreting what they receive in the context of their own cultures and experience. Either the Western cultural form is reinterpreted in light of traditional meanings, or Western meanings are adapted to traditional patterns. In any case, something new, although still local, emerges. As the musicologist Peter Manuel (1988) points out, not only do local cultures "adapt foreign elements in distinctly idiosyncratic ways that substantially alter their function, context and meaning," but even what appears to Western ears and perception to be a major intrusion may, in fact, be so shallow functionally to the native listener as to not even be perceived. This is true, for example, of the influence of American music on the thriving world of Indian pop culture (Manuel 1988: 20).

In their comparative analysis of eight cultures, Robinson, Buck, and Cuthbert (1991) have demonstrated that "world musical homogenization is not occurring." As they put it, "even though information-age economic forces are building an international consumership for centrally produced and distributed popular music, other factors are pulling in the opposite direction. They are encouraging not only what we call 'indigenization' of popular music forms and production but also new, eclectic combinations of world musical elements that contradict the continuing constraints of national boundaries and global capitalism." The term *glocalization,* popularized by Roland Robertson (1995), signifying "the simultaneity—the co-presence—of both universalizing and particularizing tendencies," largely captures this process. However, I wish to emphasize an additional point: The common notion that the globalization of culture, especially on the popular level, is a one-way process, from the Western metropolis to the passive and vulnerable periphery, is also false, although it is certainly true that the major diffusionary source of this culture is a single Western country: the United States.

The global cultural exchange process, then, has led not to homogenization, but to the revitalization and generation of new musical forms. Some of these forms remain local, providing greater choice and stimulus to the local culture. Examples of such revitalization include the modernization of the traditional Cameroonian makassi style with the introduction of the acoustic rhythm guitar; the development of the highlife music of Ghana, which fused traditional forms with jazz, rock, and Trinidadian calypso rhythms; and the vibrant local modernization of traditional Afro-Arab music in Kenya. Elsewhere, musical forms showing signs of Western impact have broken out of their provincial boundaries to become regional currency, as, for example, the Trinidadian- and American-pop-influenced kru-krio music of Sierra Leone, which swept West Africa and beyond during the 1960s and 1970s; the Brazilian samba; the pan-American salsa; merengue of Dominican origin; the originally Cuban nueva trova, which became a radical pan-Latin form, stimulating the even more radical and pan-Latin nueva cancion; and the Colombian cumbia, which has become an important part of the music of the Tex-Mex regional cosmos. And there are those musical forms that experience their fifteen minutes of fame as the latest fad in the "world music" scene: the Argentinean tango, the Algerian rai, the Zairian soukous, and the Brazilian bossa nova.

Out of Jamaica

One of the most globally successful cultural creations of a less economically developed people is Jamaican reggae music, which strikingly illustrates the complexities of global cultural interaction. The creation of the Jamaican working classes and lumpenproletariat, reggae emerged in the late 1950s from a variety of influences, especially that of southern black Americans (Chang and Chen 1998; Bradley 2001; Stolzoff 2000). Jamaica has always had a rich musical tradition, originating mainly in the music of West Africa brought over by the slaves, but also influenced in its lyrical and melodic lines by British, especially Celtic, popular music of the late eighteenth and nineteenth centuries (Jekyll [1907] 2005). At the turn of the twentieth century, a popular secular form, mento, ideal for dancing, emerged. Similar to the Trinidadian calypso in its topical and satirical lyrics but thoroughly distinctive in its instrumental ensemble of banjo, acoustic guitar, bamboo flute, and other homemade instruments such as the rumba box and saxophone, mento had established itself as the primary traditional popular music of the island by the 1920s (Lewin 2000: 103–142; Neely 2007; Chang and Chen 1998: 10–18).

It is a remarkable though rarely noticed fact that even before the emergence of reggae, mento had had a profound impact on popular music in America. The very first LP album in the history of American music—or any music, for that matter—to sell more than a million copies was *Calypso,* by the Jamaican-raised musician Harry Belafonte (Fopelson 1991: 45). The record, in spite of its title, was a collection not of Trinidadian music but mostly of Jamaican folk songs and mento-style ballads composed by Irving Burgie. Burgie claimed authorship of all the songs, including the very popular "Day-O" (which would later be the title of Burgie's autobiography) and "Emanuel Road," both of which originated in late-nineteenth-century rural Jamaica (Jekyll [1907] 2005; Garnice 2018; Lewin 2000: 80–81). As in all diffusionary processes, the songs were presented in a manner that Americans could appreciate, thanks to Burgie's musical talents (Burgie 2007: 185–219). Belafonte was not the only singer to cash in on the popularity of Jamaican folk music during the 1950s. "Day-O," in particular, which became Belafonte's signature song (although the actual title was "The Banana Boat Song"), was successfully recorded by several popular artists such as the Tarriers, who in 1956 combined it with another very old Jamaican song, "Hill and Gulley Ride," to produce their biggest hit, even outselling Belafonte's. This led to a flood of successful recordings of the song by other artists—Shirley Bassey (in Britain), the Fontane Sisters, Frank Barry, and Jimmie Rodgers, to name a few. Thus, the process of cultural exchange between Jamaica and America began with musical movement from Jamaica to the continent, an important element in starting America's folk music wave of the 1950s and 1960s.

By the late 1950s, however, young working-class Jamaicans yearned for something more than mento. The popular ballads by mainly white North American singers being offered for a limited period each day by the local radio station, called ZQI, left them cold. What they did like were the rhythm-and-blues records being brought back by farm laborers returning from cutting cane in Florida and other migrants from parts of America where black music prevailed. Their preferences were almost exclusively songs by black Americans: Louis Jordan, Wynonie Harris, Bill "Mr. Honky Tonk" Doggett, Professor Longhair, Lloyd Price, and the perennial favorite Fats Domino (Bradley 2001: 15). Jordan was by far the most popular, said Clancy Eccles, an early, socially conscious star of the new music, in an interview with me and my research assistant: "His music was accepted deep down in the soul of the masses" (Eccles, interview with the author, July 18, 1969). Aspiring young Jamaican singers—including the teenage Bob Marley, Peter Tosh, Bob Andy, and numerous others—began singing imitations of American soul songs at the many talent parades that preceded weekend triple bill movies (nearly all C-grade Westerns, the source of Marley's international hit "I Shot the Sheriff") at working-class cinemas. These imitations were, at first, ghastly renditions of the original article. At this point—the late 1950s—Jamaica would seem to have had the worst of all possible worlds. A delightful indigenous musical tradition, mento, had been sidelined though not really abandoned, and in its place the island found its middle class swooning over syrupy white American ballads while its manual laborers sang imitations of African American music rendered in strange local versions of American accents.

What happened next demonstrates the complexity of the interaction between local and foreign influences that generate the global culture (White 1998; Marshall 2007: chap. 3). First of all, the imitations were so odd that they were almost unwittingly original. Furthermore, Jamaicans instinctively brought their own local musical cadences and rhythms to bear on the tunes being imitated. This coincided with an infusion of the neo-African music of the early Rastafarian and Afro-Jamaican cults. Both the movement and the accompanying rhythm of these religious cults were secularized in a manner similar to the crossover from gospel to soul music among African Americans (see Lewin

2000: 189–253). It is not by accident that the most important singer of the 1960s for Jamaican audiences was Frederick "Toots" Hibbert, who began singing as a boy in his father's revivalist church and was the first to abandon the imitation of American accents in favor of the native creole in his singing (on the revivalist religious influence, see White 1998: 18; Bilby 1995: 169–172). In his interview with us, Eccles emphasized the contribution of the Afro-Jamaican religious cults Pocomania and Kumina: "Poco is a African way of worship with a drumbeat, and you can feel it sometimes and it make you holler; and that deep Kumina sound, that is one thing no white man can do" (Eccles interview). Another reggae great we interviewed, John Holt, agreed that Pocomania was important but thought that its influence was more on the dance that accompanied the ska (Holt, interview with the author, July 2019), with which I am inclined to agree, the basic ska movement being almost identical to the motion of Pocomania devotees as they "labor" toward spirit possession.

Another important influence was jazz swing music, brought in by several of the formally trained musicians of the time such as Don Drummond and Sunny Bradshaw. From these syncretisms emerged the first phase of what was to become reggae, the ska.

At the time—the late 1950s and early 1960s—the vast majority of working-class Jamaicans were still too poor to buy record players or expensive imported records. This led to the formation of the "sound system," a record-playing system outfitted with enormous bass speakers, which the owners rented out, along with their record collections and themselves in the role of disc jockey (see Stolzoff 2000: 41–64; Bradley 2001: 22–62). They called themselves colorful names such as Tom the Great Sebastian, King Edwards, Lord Koos, and Sir Nick. The more successful owners of these systems at first competed with each other in finding the hottest singles from America, the sources of which they kept secret by scratching off the labels. Eventually they made the critical move toward producing local versions of these American hits sung by Jamaican artists. This in turn led to Jamaicans producing their own original songs in recording studios established by local entrepreneurs to meet the demand. The leaders of this innovation, the sound system owners Duke Reid, Clement Dodd, and Prince Buster, were, as Bradley notes, the most important figures in determining reggae's development (2001: 27).

Thus was born the Jamaican recording industry, which rapidly evolved into one of the most prolific sites for the production of 45 RPM discs in the world. It is remarkable that working-class Jamaicans not only maintained control over the technological aspects of the emerging music but would become world-class innovators over the "processes of creating, capturing, balancing, mixing and mastering musical sound" (Hitchins 2014: 3). As the music caught on, wealthy Jamaicans quickly saw its commercial possibilities and began to provide important services as agents, managers, and organized record sellers. The most successful of these was the white Jamaican Chris Blackwell, a scion of the planter class, who later, in Britain, founded Island Records and became the manager of Bob Marley. A white Jamaican of Lebanese descent, the politician and later prime minister Edward Seaga, actively promoted a bourgeois nationalist version of the budding music form, at home and abroad, out of genuine interest (a social anthropology graduate from Harvard, he had studied the folk music and religions of the island) and as an astute way of promoting his political career, since his constituency was based in the West Kingston ghettos. However, like many middle-class Jamaicans, he favored the folk forms of Jamaican music as the more "authentic" version of Jamaican culture, encouraging what Stolzoff has called "a 'museumizing' of cultural forms rooted in the past" (2000: 74–75; see also Thomas 2004: 65–70).

At about the same time that these developments were taking place, the Rastafarian religion, originally a millenarian back-to-Africa movement that was the religious component of the reaction to Western influence, was taking hold among the Jamaican proletariat of the Kingston shanties. The music, spiritualism, and radical racial ideology of the religion—a religious form of negritude, exemplifying Jean-Paul Sartre's "anti-racist racism"—greatly appealed to the very people developing the music, and it was not long before the two merged, with Rastafarian burru drums and "ridims" as well as its theology shaping the rhythm and giving substance and ideological content to many of the singers, most famously Bob Marley (Record 1998; Steffens 1998). The lyrics, however, covered a wide range of themes: social commentary including "rude boy" defiance and warnings about being too rude, comments on the cost of living, and politics, as well as love songs and social satires. Many were simply examples of what Stranger Cole, in an interview, described as the "throw word song," in which common phrases were worked into the lyrics, sometimes as the song's hook, such as "nothing try (nothing done)," "who are you that I should be mindful of," and "mama look deh—see the hypocrites them a go on deh" (Cole, interview with the author, July 24, 1969). Cole claimed that "Mama Look Deh," which he sang with the Reggae Boys, was his first big reggae hit, although there is no record of it being copyrighted to him. He denied that the song was a satirical reference to Prime Minister Hugh Shearer, saying with a sly smile: "I wasn't referring to anybody special, seeing that it was a Jamaican throw word." Socially and politically conscious singers had to be careful with their lyrics during the conservative reign of the Jamaica Labour Party, in spite of the fact that one of its leaders, Edward Seaga, claimed to be a great patron of "real" Jamaican folk music. Cole's caution was well founded, since one of his songs, "When I Get My Freedom," was banned from the local radio. As he explained:

> The way I am thinking that tune, I am thinking my freedom from poorness, not thinking it any way. My freedom from not living good and want to live good. They put it to mean I am saying things against the government, and at no time I ever make a song that fight against the government, because I know that a song like that could not play on the radio and I always wanted my song to go over as much, so I make it for the radio station to play it. (Cole interview)

The music swiftly went through several changes, first from ska to rocksteady, a more structured slow-tempo music, strongly influenced by Motown soul music, which many Jamaicans look back to with great fondness, that only lasted from about 1966 to 1968. It was replaced by what became known as reggae, a faster-paced form initiated by the Beltones, Larry Marshall, and Toots Hibbert (who first used the name of the genre, spelled "reggay," in a recording), its most distinctive innovations being a return to the strong mento-like emphasis on the offbeat, and the use of the shuffle organ using "a bubbling, brisk-paced keyboard style that allowed former pianists to show off the electric organs that were by now studio staples" (Bradley 2001: 198–205).

Reggae swiftly caught on, greatly enabled by the growth of the local record industry (most notably Clement "Sir Coxsone"

Dodd's Studio One; see Hitchins 2014); the development of local radio, which finally began to take the music of the working class seriously; and the rise of cultural nationalism among both political parties and the urban bourgeoisie. Several unusually brilliant talents gained fame in the late 1960s and early 1970s. In addition to Hibbert were Jimmy Cliff, Desmond Dekker, Peter Tosh, Dennis Brown, Marcia Griffiths, Burning Spear, Lee "Scratch" Perry (also one of the music's great technical innovators), and the most famous of all, Bob Marley, whose enormous showmanship and songwriting ability were important in internationalizing the music.

One other factor was equally important in explaining the rapid spread of reggae and its eventual emergence as a global musical form. This was the large-scale migration of working-class Jamaicans. The first such movement was to Britain, where Jamaicans effectively transformed what had previously been an all-white country into a multiracial society. By 1964, a thinly Anglicized version of ska known as blue beat was already in vogue (Patterson 1966). In 1969 a song by Desmond Dekker from the previous year, "Israelites," became the first reggae track to make it to number one on the British hit parade as well as the first to crack the top ten in the United States. Almost no one outside of Jamaica understood Dekker's Jamaican lyrics and therefore hadn't the slightest clue that they had been inspired by the Rastafarian theological view of black Jamaicans as the "true" Israelites suffering Babylonian exile in Jamaica and yearning for the day they would return to Zion. By the mid-1970s Jamaican music had been completely embraced by white British youth, who by then viewed it as an integral part of their culture (Davis and Simon [1979] 1992; Partridge 2010). From its British base, it would spread rapidly throughout continental Europe and north and sub-Saharan Africa.

The artist who most embodied the international spread of the music was, of course, Bob Marley, whose status as a global icon of popular music is truly phenomenal. Few were surprised when *Time* magazine in the last month of 1999 named *Exodus,* an album he recorded with the Wailers, the best of the century, writing that "Every song is a classic, from the messages of love to the anthems of revolution. But more than that, the album is a political and cultural nexus, drawing inspiration from the Third World and then giving voice to it the world over." This judgment persists: As the *New York Times* noted in 2018: "His music has achieved steady, far-reaching popularity that has lasted for decades. According to Nielsen, Marley's songs have been streamed more than 1.7 billion times in the United States alone, and his fame permeates deep into emerging markets like Africa and India." The remarkable feature of Marley's lyrics is that they remained deeply rooted in his Jamaican rural and working-class background and identity, a classic instance of the universalization of the particular that is the hallmark of great art. This, however, was not enough for the restlessly demanding Jamaican music audience.

Jamaica's astonishing global musical influence did not end with Marley. Indeed, as Marley gained fame on the international scene, local musicians began to react against the very global success of his music. As Bradley observes, it is a "colossal irony" that at the height of his international fame Marley had almost no influence on what was happening at the grassroots level in the Kingston studios and in the dancehall scene (2001: 397). The fear was that reggae had fallen too much under the control of foreign and elite Jamaican managers (most notably Blackwell, whose British-based Island Record company had become a powerhouse of popular music) who, in order to extend its appeal, had used foreign backup musicians and highly technical

Western pop arrangements beyond the reach of local, largely self-taught musicians (for a highly critical appraisal of this global "crossover," see Alleyne 1998).

Taking the music back was the work of the sound system artists. The sound system had, of course, been there from the beginning of the modern phase of Jamaican music. However, starting in the mid-1970s its artists initiated two radical evolutions from what had emerged since the late 1940s, one purely musical and the other mainly performative. The sound system disc jockeys, out of a desire to give a "live" quality to the performance of their systems, started to deliberately play around with the records as they were being played. They voiced over the reggae records with their own rhythmic commentary or "toasts," improving their "riddim" as they understood it, either through grunts and screams or through an accompanying screed that might be biting social and political commentary or self-promotion when it wasn't sheer exuberant nonsense. This was rapidly to become a distinctive feature of reggae. The disc jockey would also "play" the turntable, stopping and pushing the record as it turned on the platter in order to induce strange new sounds. This, too, was later to become an essential part of the music, except that the strange noises were to be made through the manipulation of sophisticated studio electronics. What emerged from these experimentations was another distinctive musical form, dub. Veal has compared the dub mixer to an "action painter of sound": "Operating upon a continuously unfolding 'canvas' of drum and bass, the engineer throws up a brief snatch of piano, a few seconds of organ, a bit of guitar, and a dash of singing, modulating and blending the 'colors' (frequencies) through the use of reverb, equalization, and other sound processing" (2007: 77–78).

Dub from its inception was intimately linked to the electronics of the recording industry and, as the linguist Hubert Devonish

(1998) argues in a fascinating commentary, its major "discovery" was to recognize—and to exploit before anyone else—the fact that electronics made possible an entirely new mode of communicating speech, in much the same way that printing had done for writing centuries earlier. The dub artist does not have to make sense verbally—to many of them, that was an early twentieth-century concern—he (very occasionally, she) communicates on the mixing deck to produce a kind of "aural fireworks" (Veal 2007: 78) in which sound, body, feeling, and movement create clashing meanings of ribald ecstasy. This musical innovation of dub is what has had the most profound influence on global music, as several writers have now documented in great detail (Marshall 2007; Veal 2007; Cooper 2012; Partridge 2010; Sullivan 2014). In all these respects dub was a radical departure from the global crossover sounds of classic or roots reggae, and Marley himself was honest in his view of the matter. As he told Dick Hebdige, "Me love dub, but I and I don't get involved with it too much. Dub means right and tight, the perfect groove. When Wailers say dub this one, dis mean we gonna play it right and tight" (1987: 82).

Another related innovation, with which Marley and the Wailers were even less involved, came in reaction to the Marleyan globalization of what is sometimes called "roots reggae" (a serious misnomer, since previous and later versions of the music were even rootsier). This is what came to be called dancehall (somewhat confusingly, since the music had been closely linked to dancing in halls from the beginning, especially after the emergence of the sound system during the late 1950s). The term, however, did signal that Jamaican popular music was not only being brought back to Jamaica, but was intended to serve what was the primary function of all African and neo-African music, namely dance and, more generally, movement of all kinds, whether it be the movement of digging a yam hole, laboring up to spirit possession by the gods and the ancestors, or playing a ring tune. Sad to say, this is what the music of Marley had underplayed, a loss reinforced by the very genius of his melodic lyricism. One is inclined to listen to Marley the way one listens to Schubert's lieder, to move seamlessly (as I do, anyway) between "Three Little Birds" and "Das Abendrot," both great men's songs of praise to the calming power of nature. But where was the urge to dance? To black lower-class Jamaicans, that was an abomination.

Indeed, it drove them to violence. There was a sad and terrible moment of transition one night in Jamaica when the masses rejected the classic reggae of Bob Marley and violently expressed their embrace of the "renewed" dancehall. At a concert in 1990 Bunny Wailer, an original founder and sole survivor of Bob Marley and the Wailers, was pelted with glass bottles when he overstayed his time, the audience having lost patience in its wait for the promised clash between two of the new stars of dancehall (Hope 2006: 114–117). Although the incident left the nation in a daze of cultural shock and disbelief for several days— Wailer being by then a revered national icon—it marked the culmination of a major cultural turn, or rather return, one so extreme that Bilby (1995: 177) considers it odd that dancehall continues to be referred to by the generic term "reggae." It was a rejection not only of classic cosmopolitan reggae but also of its mellow, crossover lyricism and Rastafarian ideology. Replacing it was a reclamation not simply of the local but of the blackest, folksiest, and most lumpenproletarian aspects of Jamaican culture. It was also a deliberate embrace of all that was considered nastiest, baddest, most ragamuffin, illiterate, indeed anti-literate in that tradition—a celebration of guns, drugs, and violence, of Dionysian sexuality and in-your-face obscenity, and of misogyny and homophobia (Stolzoff 2000: 99–106). Where Marley's reggae celebrated a millenarian vision of an African future, dancehall culture celebrated a bawdy, neo-African Jamaican past intertwined with its ghetto present. Above all, it was a complete surrender to the passions of the body, the most "vulgar body," in which the "primary function of the DJ's art is to ram dancehall and cork party" (that is, exercise Afro-Jamaican verbal skill; see Cooper [1993] 1995: 136) in the service of massive all-consuming dance. Indeed—and this is a point brilliantly made by Carolyn Cooper but too often missed by musicologists—outside of its context and role of driving dancers to the point of erotic delirium, dancehall lyrics are nearly meaningless, their rude orality, "submerged in a wash of sound," absorbed by the body rather than the ear, penetrating every crevice like "noises in the blood" (Cooper [1993] 1995: 136–173). There is a deeply sociological dimension to dancehall culture. Dancehall is a performative venue that incites the most aural and carnal assault on the traditional inequities of class, color, language, gender, and social mores in Jamaican society. It is not so much an expression of outrage at these inequities—that was already found in the socially conscious lyrics of the 1960s and 1970s—but an indulgence in all that was most outrageous to bourgeois Jamaicans (see Cooper 1993 [1995]: chap. 8; Stolzoff 2000: 6–12; Hope 2006: chaps. 3–4).

In spite of the relentless localism and deliberate antiglobalism of dancehall, both it and its twin, dub, have attracted and deeply influenced global popular music. The most important instance of this is the role of the music in the formation and evolution of American rap music. Up to the 1970s Jamaican music generally had little influence on African Americans; the mento influence via Belafonte was almost entirely confined to white Americans. The same held for the early waves of the music from ska to roots reggae. When I spent a summer in New York in the early 1960s at the height of the ska movement, I was surprised to learn that blacks in Bedford-Stuyvesant had no interest in it even though it was being blasted from Jamaican-themed shops in neighboring Crown Heights, where my folks lived. Indeed, when I asked fellow Jamaicans why this was so, they told me that black Americans were contemptuously dismissing ska as "jungle music."

All this was to change in the 1970s. By then a new generation of Jamaicans were arriving in New York in great numbers, the result of the radical change brought about by the Immigration and Nationality Act of 1965. This generation differed from the earlier groups of Jamaicans who had settled in New York, most having arrived prior to the passage of the racist Immigration Act of 1924. The descendants of that earlier group had been moderately successful and had settled into petit-bourgeois ethnic enclaves around the city. The post-1965 arrivals came from the working and lower classes and, partly out of necessity, settled among the poorer neighborhoods of black Americans. They brought with them the emergent sound system dance and all the new and exciting dub innovations as well as the tough and violent ways of the Kingston "yardies" (Marshall 2007: 222). Their black American neighbors were suddenly hearing and seeing something they liked. A hotbed of hybridity emerged, especially in the South Bronx, and this constituted the roots of the revolutionary pop genre of rap. Several of the major innovators of rap were of Jamaican or Jamaican-influenced West Indian background, most notably DJ Kool Herc (Clive Campbell), who built on the Jamaican DJ techniques of boastful toasting and turntabling in which the most percussive parts of the record are isolated, as well as Grandmaster Flash (John Saddler), a Barbadian greatly influenced by Herc, who perfected the technique of scratching and produced the first successful rap record, "The Message," with his group the Furious Five. That record was in the first group of fifty chosen by the Library of Congress to be added to its National Recording Registry in 2002.

Rap's evolution was a truly hybrid process. As Wayne Marshall has expertly demonstrated, both musical traditions have evolved in mutual engagement with each other: "The interplay between hip-hop and reggae has been a rather consistent, crucial feature in the development of both genres as well as in the musically-mediated processes of racialization, Americanization, and Caribbeanization that have animated cultural politics and informed social formations and subject formation from New York to Kingston, Miami to London and beyond. Somewhat suddenly, Jamaica—a nation increasingly constituted as much by its diasporic citizenry as those living on the island—seemed not to lie at the margins so much as at the center of global culture" (Marshall 2007: 31–32; Marshall 2015).

But Jamaica's global musical influence is not exerted solely through its ongoing hybridization with rap. It has also directly influenced other musical traditions in Europe, Africa, Asia, and Latin America both through acceptance of the music in its pure form (exemplified by hugely attended festivals all over Europe) and through its hybridic stimulation of other "glocal" traditions: reggaeton throughout Latin America (Rivera, Marshall, and Hernandez 2009); punk and other reggae-pop fusion genres in England by artists such as UB40, Steel Pulse, and the Police; mbaqanga in South Africa; Pinoy in the Philippines, and Japanese reggae. Indeed, there is not a corner of the globe in which the music is not heard either in its original form or in syncretic transformations (Cooper 2012). Interestingly, the music's influence is not confined to its latest phase. Earlier versions of reggae such as its birth phase, ska, have passionate followers who continue to play it even though Jamaicans themselves largely view it as a relic of their musical past.

Perhaps the most remarkable aspect of this global influence is the fact that dancehall, in spite of its aggressive localism, has nonetheless attracted devout followers from all over the world, so much so that there is now a thriving "ghetto" branch of the country's tourist industry catering to young visitors from Europe and Asia who spurn the island's beaches in favor of makeshift B&Bs close to the dancehall action. There can be few more confounding sights in popular culture than that of the small Japanese dancehall queen known as Junko beating the Jamaicans at their own game by winning the annual dancehall competition in the heart of the Kingston slums.[1]

Conclusion

This brief account of reggae has, I hope, demonstrated the vitality of globalization as a generative cultural force and, at the same time, the silliness of the elitist argument that we are headed toward some numbing global homogenization. While there is much to criticize in the sexism, homophobia, slackness, obscenity, and violence of dancehall, it is ironic that reggae at its best, as a subaltern critique of the popular culture industry, is actually in line with Adorno's more highbrow critique of it, addressing "the commodification, fetishization and standardization of its products, together with the authoritarian submissiveness, irrationality, conformity, ego-weakness and dependency behaviour of its recipients" (Witkin 2003: 3). Reggae, and especially dub's deconstructive use of electronics, is the very antithesis of commodification, fetishization, and standardization. Classic rude boy reggae, Marley's Rastafarianism, and dancehall's outrageous rootsiness are the ultimate rejection of submissiveness, conformity, ego weakness, and dependency. And the repeated reinventions of reggae, like those of rap at its most innovative, are exemplars of constant wariness and struggles against (albeit only partially achieved) corporate control.

This dialectic of the foreign and the local, I should make clear, succeeds mainly in the domain of popular culture when under the control of the subaltern classes. At the elite-led macroeconomic levels of Caribbean and other postcolonial societies it is, in the main, an entirely different story. For a long time, the dominant theory of development held that the path to economic growth lay in the assimilation not only of the economy and technology of the West but also of its consumer and extreme individualist values, in short, modernization (Sklair 2002: 164–207). In this assimilation of Western consumerism, a large number of developing societies, most notably those of the Caribbean, were extremely successful. But it was a success that established the basis of economic failure. The imitative modernization of values, far from promoting development, grossly undermined it. When the middle classes learned to consume and to valorize like the West, especially America, before they could produce like the West, they effectively short-circuited the institutional and economic foundations of change, increasingly spending more than they were able to produce, accumulating ever greater burdens of debt that culminated in economic catastrophes in Puerto Rico and Jamaica, both of which can boast of being among the most modern bourgeois cultures outside of the advanced world. When we closely examine the successful cases of transition to economic prosperity among formerly poor countries—Korea, China, and Japan—what we find is a process of entrepreneurial glocalization at the national economic, institutional, and political levels similar to what the masses have achieved at the popular cultural level; we also find that mass consumption and modernization followed, rather than preceded, the glocal transformation of their economies. If they wish to succeed, the elites of the Caribbean could do worse than to follow, in the economic and technical domains, the glocal creativity of their own underprivileged masses. At the very least they could heed Bob Marley's warning: "Don't let them change you / Or rearrange you / We've got a mind of our own."

III

The Failures of Policy
and Politicians

7

Why Do Policies to Help the Poor So Often Fail?

A Jamaican Case Study

Plus ça change, plus c'est la même chose. Alphonse Karr's oft-quoted phrase is largely apt in reference to policies aimed at improving the lot of the poor in developing countries. When the UN, in 2000, declared a set of eight Millennium Development Goals for economic development, the focus was squarely on the eradication of poverty and hunger and the promotion of childhood education, health, and female empowerment. The field of applied economic development is likewise now increasingly dominated by a microeconomic emphasis on the reduction of poverty, including that of the ultra-poor, through small changes aimed at goals similar to the UN's, distinguished mainly by the use of randomized experiments to ascertain what works (Banerjee and Duflo 2011).

This approach marks a radical shift from the neoliberal macroeconomic emphasis on economic growth during the 1980s and 1990s, championed by the World Bank and the International Monetary Fund (IMF), which often did not properly heed the failure of such programs to make a serious dent on the lives of the poor. However, there had been a nearly identical change of course at the end of the period between the late 1940s and the early 1970s. Development in the 1950s and 1960s was focused on grand five-year plans intellectually supported by macroeconomic theories that pursued GDP growth, which was assumed to trickle down to the poor but rarely did. To the contrary, growth was often associated with increased poverty, rising unemployment, and the massive expansion of urban slums. In the late 1960s and early 1970s, in reaction to these failures, there arose the "basic needs approach" among many applied economists and policy developers, which gave more emphasis "to the poor and destitute than to other economic groups ... to immediate consumption than to investment for the distant future, to the detailed composition of consumption, in terms of specific quantities and specific tools and services, than to overall income" (Overseas Development Institute 1978). By 1976, when the approach was formally enacted at the World Development Conference held under the auspices of the International Labour Organization (ILO), it had won wide favor among many in the development field.

I was an early and enthusiastic adopter of this approach and applied it in several of my roles as special advisor for social policy and development to Prime Minister Michael Manley, who needed little prodding from me to recognize its merits. Indeed, I was directed by him to implement a program along these lines in his own constituency of South Central Kingston. This chapter is an evaluation of that effort. It is also a case study in the serious problem of institutional efficacy in Jamaica. The administrators of the program were quick to grasp the declarative knowledge of urban upgrading but failed badly in its implementation due to a conjunction of conflicting goals, political cynicism, unrealistic aspirations, conflicting professional interests, a failure to take the expressed preferences of the targeted poor seriously, and more generally a failure of leadership, including my own.

What are the basic social needs in Third World societies? What role can the private sector play in meeting them? Can private enterprise ever hope to make a profit in such endeavors? And is there a role for foreign companies or nongovernmental organizations (NGOs) in meeting these needs?

The first question was implicitly answered by the major shift of emphasis in development thinking during the early 1970s toward the so-called basic human needs approach. But there is no easy response to the other questions, largely because there is so little concrete experience to rely on. In this chapter I draw on my own experiences in a typical Third World society, Jamaica, during the 1970s, when there was an unusually strong commitment to the basic needs approach under the democratic socialist regime of Prime Minister Michael Manley. Based on this experience I will illustrate the formidable sociocultural problems associated with efforts to address basic human needs among the poorest elements of Third World populations. Some of these problems probably have a counterpart among the poorest groups in developed societies as well. These problems may be summarized as a profound sociocultural mismatch and conflict of interest between the needy and those attempting to help them. The mismatch is acute where public-sector personnel are the change agents and even greater when local entrepreneurs with a free enterprise orientation are involved. Foreign entrepreneurs, with far less awareness of local realities, are faced with problems of sociocultural accommodation that would seem to be even more formidable.

The Basic Social Needs Approach

An unusual consensus emerged in the early 1970s among specialists in economic development. They increasingly agreed that a policy aimed directly and immediately at the problems of absolute poverty was essential, not only as a painfully obvious end in itself but as a means of achieving overall growth in national product. Until the early 1970s the conventional wisdom among development specialists was that Third World countries should concentrate on increasing their gross national product before attempting to directly tackle the problems of distribution and social welfare. The pie was simply too small to provide resources for redistribution or for social programs, such as health, education, and housing, without diverting capital needed for growth. Planners were urged to concentrate on capital accumulation to increase the aggregate rate of growth. With increased wealth would come either a trickling down of the benefits of development or the opportunity for meaningful redistribution of the increased national wealth (ILO 1977; Tinbergen 1976).

The early 1970s saw a drastic departure from this approach for many reasons. The most obvious was the clear failure of earlier strategies to make a dent in the welfare of the mass of people in Third World countries, even when there were impressive rates of aggregate growth. Unemployment remained high, absolute poverty continued at unacceptable levels, and in most cases relative poverty increased rather than decreased with increased growth rates (World Bank 1980; Chenery 1979; Young, Bussink, and Hasan 1980).[1] Recognition of the failure of the traditional approach, reflected, for example, in a UN report in 1971 (United Nations 1971a), was accompanied by a new conception of basic needs in the development process (ILO 1977;

Hicks 1979; Streeten 1979).[2] While structural economic change was still recognized as necessary, it came to be realized that improvement of the human condition of the poorest segments of the population would contribute both directly and indirectly to accelerated socioeconomic development. A healthy, better-educated population with a sense of belonging to the larger society would be more productive. Specifically, the basic needs approach called for a direct assault on problems of nutrition (especially childhood nutrition), education (especially primary literacy and day care facilities, and preschool education for the poor), family planning, health facilities, and housing and care for the elderly.

This emphasis entailed new programs and implementation techniques. First, there was a shift in focus from the aggregate population to targeted population groups; the neediest groups were now clearly specified, and the success of any given program was measured in terms of its impact on the welfare of those groups. Second, and closely related, was the partial shift of focus from the nation and regions to specific communities—for example, a particular village or cluster of villages, rather than the rural poor in general, a particular slum community rather than all urban slums, and so on.

Thus the basic needs strategy saw a reinvigoration of the community development approach and, at the same time, attention to improvement of the individual.[3] Several elements underlay this strategy. One was that people are more motivated to engage in new productive activities if their immediate neighbors are also involved and if they see tangible benefits for themselves and their community. Second was self-help: The best way to improve the conditions of the poor was to help them to help themselves. Third, local resources that go untapped in traditional macroeconomic planning could now be mobilized for the common good.

In particular, the so-called informal economy, which provided the livelihood for most of the Third World poor (and still does), could now be integrated into formal planning and change. Finally, broader community participation was seen as a key factor in any successful program (Cohen and Uphoff 1980; Goldsmith and Blustain 1980; Patterson 1977).

Where the United Nations, with its strong input from Third World planners, led the way, the World Bank eventually followed. The World Bank had been the major institutional purveyor of the traditional macroeconomic aggregative approach to planning, so its acceptance of the basic needs approach meant that the latter had achieved, if not dominance, at least respectability in development circles. To be sure, the World Bank still insisted on traditional growth strategies and saw what it called the "human development" approach as complementary. It also cautioned that such programs must be carefully chosen and efficiently carried out. Human resource development, it wrote, was "an end as well as a means of economic progress," which integrates the traditional approach with a concern for "increasing employment, meeting basic needs, reducing inequalities in income and wealth, raising the productivity of the poor" (World Bank 1980: 32, 96–97). One important aspect of the basic needs approach was the complementarity and mutual reinforcement of the different components: "Health, nutrition, education and fertility all affect each other." Thus, to be effective, these programs had to be applied simultaneously within a community.

In an important paper, the social anthropologist M. G. Smith (1983) identified other factors that had to be kept in mind in designing a basic needs program. The first was that social needs were culturally determined and required social legitimacy gained through participation of the intended beneficiaries within the community. Second, the basic needs approach focused on individuals and families and should not be confused with the provision of social goods such as prisons, courts, and other institutions designed to meet the needs of society at large. And, third, the needs of individuals within the community "vary with categories and conditions of persons," such as sex, age, and state of employment.

Failures of Economic "Development" in Jamaica

When the People's National Party won office in 1972, it inherited a socioeconomic situation that was almost a textbook case of the failures of traditional postwar strategies of development. During the 1960s the conservative Jamaica Labour Party did all the "right things" in terms of conventional neoclassical doctrine. It planned carefully, invested heavily in an import-substitution, light industry program, and encouraged foreign investment in its booming bauxite and tourist industries. It also achieved the predicted success, measured in conventional economic terms; the rate of growth of gross domestic product in real terms between independence (1962) and 1970 was 4.5 percent per year. With a rate of population growth of 1.6 percent per year, per capita output grew at a rate of almost 3 percent. Investment between 1961 and 1967 was a striking 20 percent of gross domestic expenditure, rising to 31 percent in 1969. This was financed by external loans and local savings, which together amounted to a savings rate of 17 percent during the decade (World Bank 1971; Girvan 1971; Jefferson 1972).

In spite of this impressive record of growth, there was clear evidence of serious social and economic problems. On the economic front the largest failing was in agriculture, where an increase of only 1.5 percent per year in the value of agricultural output from 1963 to 1969 meant a decline in real output, increased dependence on foreign sources of basic foods, and rising rural unemployment and underemployment (Beckford 1972). A second major problem was overall unemployment. Including the estimated effects of underemployment, the national figure for unemployment was put at between 25 percent and 33 percent of the available labor force.

Most serious of all was the island's third major problem: massive overurbanization (discussed at greater length in Chapter 3). The urban population, which was 22.4 percent in 1943, was projected to rise to over 50 percent by the early 1980s; 63 percent of this urban population lived in the Kingston Metropolitan Area in 1970, the vast majority in low-income areas varying from dilapidated working-class districts to horrendous shantytowns and squatter settlements. A 1973 study estimated that over 70 percent of the Kingston population lived in households with an annual income below the poverty level (Patterson 1973). The problems were not confined to the poor, because the entire urban population faced the consequences of these deplorable social situations in terms of an unusually high and growing crime rate, exacerbated by the alienation and desperation bred of poverty.

When the People's National Party gained office in 1972 it immediately recognized this urban crisis as one of its major problems. As with previous governments, the standard reaction was to institute slum-clearance strategies. However, by the early 1970s it was already well established, through experience in both the Third World and advanced societies, that such plans could only benefit a tiny, favored minority of the most prosperous workers who, despite government subsidies, were the only ones able to qualify financially for new housing. Except for these favored few, slum clearance merely worsened the already dismal condition of the abject poor by destroying and dispersing the communities on which they relied for mutual aid. Since the number of units in the new housing plans rarely exceeded 10 percent of units destroyed to make way for them, the rents that the poorest paid rose such that they were less able to compete for the available units. Because the rents in the newer units occupied by the better off were already subsidized by taxes, the poorest were indirectly forced to support the more fortunate. Finally, slum-clearance programs, by concentrating on housing structures, neglected the other major problems of the slums stemming from lack of participation in the money economy.

The slum-clearance approach was too ingrained, however, to be easily abandoned for alternate strategies. When I was appointed special advisor to the prime minister in 1972, I lobbied strongly for a different approach to the problems of the urban slums and, with the prime minister's support, the Cabinet agreed to an urban upgrading program on a pilot basis in one area of the low-income neighborhoods in south central Kingston. The first step in this program was a socioeconomic survey of the proposed project area, the main goals of which were to generate a detailed assessment of the socioeconomic condition of the area and to get the residents' views on the basic needs approach in general, as well as on the specific program we had in mind for the area. The results are described in the next section.

The Project Area

Southside was one of Kingston's worst slum areas, notorious throughout the city for its political violence, gang warfare, and high crime rate. The project area occupied a total of 71 acres with a population of 5,732. It was an extremely youthful population, the mean age being twenty years—eighteen years for men, twenty-two for women. Over 45 percent were under fifteen years of age and 50 percent under twenty. Over 70 percent of all households lived in single-room dwellings, while 19 percent lived in two-room apartments. A detailed physical survey of 402 of the 521 residential buildings in the area revealed that 169 needed minor repairs, 79 needed moderate repairs, 23 needed major repairs, and 131 were irredeemable and should be demolished. Over one-third of all households lived in dwellings with four or more people per room. Forty-three percent of households were headed by women and 44 percent by men.

A striking feature of the area was that the larger the household, the smaller the mean individual and household income. The combined mean weekly income was only $16.22 in Jamaican dollars. Approximately 78 percent of all individuals lived in households where the head was unemployed. Only 40 percent of the population over fifteen were employed, and only 30 percent were working for wages. Over 33 percent of the unemployed were seeking a job, and 12 percent had taken themselves out of the labor market. In the 20–24 age group, the unemployment rate was 49 percent. The proportion of the self-employed increased with increasing age. Of the surveyed population, men had an average of seven years of schooling, women eight years. Years of schooling only slightly influenced a person's employment status, more so for men than for women. Apart from the overall record of depressed social conditions, another general finding was that women bore the major burden of poverty. Since they also were the chief providers for children growing up in the area, it was evident that the situation was even worse for the children than the already dismal figures suggested.

The Program

The pilot program I designed for south central Kingston began in the summer of 1975 and continued until the end of 1980. The major goals of the program were:

- To improve the physical condition of life;
- To improve the general level of social welfare;
- To improve the sense of community in the area through self-help and local leadership;
- To generate special employment and training; and
- To construct and demonstrate a model urban strategy for other low-income areas in Kingston and other urban areas of Jamaica.

The pilot program was based on three main strategies: rehabilitation of the physical environment, provision of social services, and reduction of unemployment.

Rehabilitation of the Physical Environment

The first objective of the program was upgrading the entire environment, rehabilitation and new construction being simply one component. The plan was to proceed in three phases.

Phase 1 involved rehabilitating buildings requiring minor and moderate repairs, along with improving environmental sanitation services in the entire area. Phase 2 was scheduled to begin with the construction of a transition center where residents of buildings requiring major repairs could stay while their dwellings were being repaired. Phase 3 involved the construction of a second transition center, which together with the first would house residents of buildings that had to be demolished. New low-cost units would then be built in situ to replace the demolished units. It was strongly emphasized that the intention was not to build new units that were in any way comparable to those in a typical housing plan. Households of four or five people would still occupy a single room, if that was all they could afford, but the room would be secure and impenetrable to intruders, with walls and ceilings not likely to fall on children (several of whom had been killed by falling walls) and floors that were not breeding grounds for roaches, rats, scorpions, and other pests. It was agreed by all concerned that this was the fairest way to proceed, entailing the minimum of displacement while improving the living conditions of the maximum number of people. It was easy to demonstrate from the income data that, even with subsidies of over 50 percent, fewer than 10 percent of the residents of the area could afford a unit in a traditional housing scheme. The survey also made it clear that the new approach was favored by the overwhelming majority of the residents of the area.

Provision of Social Services

The project was to provide certain services (many of which had been indicated by the socioeconomic survey) for the residents. These were located in the Community Service Center that housed the administrative offices of the project and an information and service center, which provided, for example, legal aid; poor relief; small loans to operate in the informal sector; assistance in procuring help from the public sector; a demonstration day care center, with satellite centers throughout the area; a basic school for up to one hundred children; adult literacy classes; a community council of elected block leaders to ensure community participation in the project's activities; a public library; and cultural activities, such as dancehall and drama classes and a brass band for the area's youth. (Many of the musicians in the rapidly growing reggae music culture had picked up rudimentary music skills playing in brass bands.) The project also established a separate day care center in another part of the area and jointly sponsored a health clinic with the Ministry of Health, and a geriatric center to cater to the large number of destitute elderly residents. The clinic, located behind the community center, was designed to provide comprehensive clinical services, dental care, nutritional and public health services, and family planning and health care demonstration services.

Reduction of Unemployment

The third major objective of the project was to improve the desperate unemployment situation. The rehabilitation and construction activities of the project provided some immediate relief, but this was temporary. Increased employment was to be generated in three ways. First, small capital loans of up to JA$50 were made to hawkers and others in the informal sector. Second, more substantial loans of up to JA$5,000 were made to local self-employed individuals, such as cabinetmakers, tailors, and shop owners who, with improved and expanded facilities and operations, would create additional jobs in the area.

The third and most ambitious effort involved the rehabilitation of an old garage as a small industries complex. The plan was to introduce between seven and twelve small firms, chosen on the basis of the available pool of underutilized skilled labor in the area and a feasibility study of the market. These firms included an aluminum casting works, a radiator repair shop, a mechanic shop, and a pottery operation, activities that could be found all over the shantytown areas of the city. The Small Industries Development Division of the Jamaica Industrial Development

Corporation agreed to provide technical and managerial help, and financial support was to be secured from the many government agencies already established for this purpose.

Financial Support for the Project

How was the program to be funded? When I originally developed the program, I won approval from the prime minister, in whose constituency it was physically located, and the minister of local government, in whose ministry the program was administratively placed, for two basic principles. First, the program would be self-supporting, as much as possible. Second, every effort would be made to engage the private sector where there were business opportunities.

Four types of funding would be involved. The first, direct government grants, would fund the administrative costs of the project as well as the community services. No tangible return was expected on these grants. In keeping with the basic needs philosophy, we considered such expenditures an investment in human resources, with returns of a public, long-term nature.

The second type of funding involved government aid for self-supporting activities. This aid took the form of loans to build the small industries complex (to be repaid on an interest-free basis from the rent paid by the small enterprises participating in the project); loans to small businesses and individuals working in the informal sector from government agencies that already existed for this purpose; and startup matching funds, provided by government in the form of mortgages to landlords participating in the rehabilitation scheme. It was anticipated that some landlords would refuse to participate, in which case the government would compulsorily rehabilitate them and charge the costs to them.

Another group of landlords, while willing to participate, were shown by the survey to be clearly incompetent to manage the rehabilitation loans. In such cases the project officer would rehabilitate with government funds and arrange for repayment from the incompetent landlords (mainly old and infirm people living on their own premises, often in conditions no better than their tenants). Finally, government funds would be used as direct subsidies for the transition centers until they were converted to permanent dwellings.

In the third and major source of the rehabilitation funds, we saw the greatest opportunities for the private sector—second mortgages to all landlord-owners in the area. A technical survey had specified the required repairs and costs, and mortgage funds were to be used only for the repairs approved by the project's housing officer. Finally, the landlord was free to make additional repairs with funds of his or her own. There were several incentives to the landlord. The most important was that at the time it was impossible to obtain second mortgages, or any kind of home improvement loan, through the normal commercial channels for any dwelling in the low-income areas of Kingston. Mortgage houses and banks considered the risks too great, at any rate of interest. A second incentive was the fact that the entire area was to be developed, increasing the locational value of the premises.

At the same time, the landlord had certain obligations. The objective of the program was to assist all the residents of the area, most of whom were tenants. The landlord would therefore have to negotiate with the project's housing officer the appropriate rent after the rehabilitation. This, as one would expect, proved to be the most sensitive and difficult part of the program. In some cases we anticipated no increase in rent, since the rent was already too high. The landlord would then have to bear the full cost of the rehabilitation. In other cases a modest increase in rent would be allowed, depending on the tenants' ability to pay. The survey, incidentally, had indicated that almost all the residents were willing to pay as much as 20 percent more rent if the improvements promised were actually undertaken. Thus we expected that the costs of rehabilitation would be borne jointly by landlords and tenants.

Landlords are, of course, businesspeople. Their role in the program constituted one important business opportunity to meet a basic need. But the principal involvement of the private sector was providing mortgage funds. With the project providing continuous monitoring and with funds guaranteed by the government, I expected that the risks would be sufficiently reduced such that private-sector financial institutions would no longer avoid the slums as a bad bet. In the summer of 1975 I approached several private institutions with my plan and received favorable responses from two of them. The chairman of the association of building societies (as Jamaican mortgage houses are called) put the idea to his board, which accepted it in principle. One of the building societies agreed to participate on an experimental basis, and the managing director, after negotiating with me and his board, made an informal commitment of half a million Jamaican dollars for the program. This was to have been confirmed later at a meeting of the full board.

The second source of private funding was the Workers Loan and Savings Bank. As its name implies, this bank was originally established to make funds available to working-class borrowers. However, it was run on strict commercial lines and over the years had become simply another commercial bank, no more involved with workers than its counterparts. With a democratic socialist government in power, the bank's departure from its original objective had become something of an embarrassment to its board. My proposal was therefore quickly embraced as a risk-free way of helping the poor. The bank immediately voted to set aside an initial quarter million Jamaican dollars of its mortgage funds for the project, one-half of which was made available immediately. The bank also offered to play another vital role in the project. The experience of the Ministry of Housing indicated that the risk of bad loans was much greater when government agencies directly disbursed and collected mortgage money. It was decided therefore that the disbursement of the rehabilitation loans and the collection of repayments would operate on a strict commercial basis. The project's housing officers would determine the upgrading to be done, its cost, and the qualified landlords. They would also monitor the work. Other than that, the whole transaction would be a private matter between the landlord and the bank. The bank, however, agreed not to apply the same stringent rules it used when dealing with other clients. It would, for example, run a credit check but drop a few of its usual criteria concerning levels and sources of income; it would not demand standard fire insurance, since no insurance company was prepared to insure against fire in the Kingston slums; and it would waive its customary 1 percent development fee.

Thus, between the Workers Bank and the Building Society, we thought we had secured a sufficient commitment of funds from the private sector to finance the first two phases of the rehabilitation. By the end of the summer of 1976 all seemed set for an innovative joint venture between government and the private sector in meeting some of the most pressing basic needs of this urban area. Events, alas, proved otherwise.

Evaluation of the Program

Three years after implementation, the Urban Upgrading Program had achieved only the first of its three major objectives: the delivery of improved social services. It failed in the generation of employment and the rehabilitation of the environment.

Provision of Social Services

All the social services offered were eagerly accepted by the residents of the area. Within a couple of years, forty-five infants were being provided care in the two day care units; over sixty preschool children were being educated in the basic school; there were 1,002 registered users of the library, 238 of them adults, 764 children. The clinic was completed in the third year and was immediately swamped with patients who would otherwise have gone unattended. The geriatric center was also enormously successful. It rescued several of its original members from a premature death; as the first such center on the island, possibly in the entire Caribbean, it served as a model for other projects. By the middle of the second year of operation, the project social workers had a caseload of forty-five people to whom they were offering a variety of services. These services included help to destitute or terminally ill people and to those in need of emergency loans or getting around red tape. Perhaps the project's greatest success was the reduction of crime, especially violent crime. In the early 1970s the area was notorious for its gang warfare and frequent political maimings and killings. The project staff was able to negotiate a formal truce between the warring gangs. It became possible for outsiders (including the author) to enter the area on a regular basis without risking their lives. So secure had the neighborhood become that in 1977, Rosalynn Carter, the wife of US president Jimmy Carter, visited the area with security precautions no more elevated than usual for visiting dignitaries. The few disappointments arose in areas where construction costs and standards set by the health coordinator conflicted with the other objectives of the program. In particular, the yard-type day care centers to be run by local women never materialized for this reason.

Increasing Employment Opportunities

The small-scale industrial project failed to get off the ground for three main reasons. First, the elaborate and expensive cluster of agencies that had long existed for this purpose proved to be significantly fraudulent. Though staffed with "experts" with economics or business degrees, these agencies did not have a single person capable of setting up a small business in a low-income area. The project staff eventually abandoned all efforts to mobilize existing agencies and instead secured funds to hire their own specialist in small-scale industrial development. No one on the island could be found with the right combination of managerial, community, organizing, and entrepreneurial skills. An attempt was made to attract former businesspeople with a proven record of running successful businesses. These entrepreneurs, however, were either afraid of entering the area or felt that the salaries were much too low for such demanding and "hazardous" work.

Rehabilitation of the Physical Environment

The failure of the rehabilitation program can be attributed to three kinds of problems—financial, political, and administrative. Analysis of this failure suggests several basic dilemmas that all programs aimed at meeting the basic needs of the poorest residents of urban areas face.

In regard to funding, our experience with the building societies was a great disappointment. After the initial expression of enthusiasm, the society assigned to assist the project lost interest. Instead of candidly stating so, their representatives delayed matters by demanding one concession after another from the government to guarantee the security of their investment, until they finally backed off after a demand for a new parliamentary law could not be met. Later I learned that the real reason for the loss of interest in the project was hostility to the government on the part of many of the board members of the building society, which intensified after the elections of 1976—a violent, partisan event in which the "socialists" won by a landslide. Almost no board of directors was prepared to become involved with a government that they regarded as "socialist" and hostile to their basic political and economic interests. (The Manley government designated itself as "democratic socialist," as its approach was modeled on the welfare states of Western Europe, especially that of the British Labour Party.) As it turned out, however, availability of funding was not the major problem. The Workers Bank continued to lend support. Furthermore, the Agency for International Development (AID) made a positive evaluation of the project and in record time I led a team on behalf of the government that negotiated a US$15 million loan for a national program. After three years, however, not even a fraction of the original small credit of $125,000 offered by the Workers Bank had been used, and less than ten yards had been rehabilitated.

To some extent the failure was due to the resistance of landlords. There were three classes of landlord: those living in their own residences in the area, those who lived in the area but on other premises, and absentee landlords. The first group, owner-occupants, was by far the largest. They were the ones most willing to cooperate. Their dwellings, however, were the ones with the least problems. Many in the second group were not interested, but substantial numbers did express an interest, although they had reservations concerning the rate of interest charged on the loans and the rents that could be recovered afterward. The absentee landlords presented the biggest problem. Many of them could not be found and, when they were, they were rarely interested. Unfortunately, the dwellings of these landlords were the ones in greatest disrepair.

Other problems also got in the way. Of these the biggest turned out to be the extraordinary difficulty of working out a negotiating procedure for the disbursement of the home improvement loans. Although everyone involved was mindful of the need to simplify the loan procedure, safeguards nonetheless were necessary. No matter how hard it tried, the bank simply could not go beyond a certain point in relaxing its creditworthiness criteria or the formality of the negotiating procedure. Nor, for that matter, could the project officer in charge of this aspect of the program, an experienced accountant with a strong commitment to the ideals of the program. After months of careful pruning, he and his staff handed me a procedure manual for processing loan applications that left me flabbergasted. Processing each loan required seventeen forms and a sequence of twenty-seven activities. As much as I would like to fault them for their punctiliousness, on reflection it is clear to me that circumstances made these complicated procedures necessary.

The urban poor in Jamaica (like similar groups in other parts of the world) live by their wits in a highly informal and unforgiving economic environment. This is a world in which trust simply does not exist. In the urban slums the trusting person, as even every preschooler will cheerfully acknowledge, is fair game for the "scuffler," who will seize any opportunity to get something for nothing. Thus we were faced with the first of the several dilemmas that all programs aimed at meeting the basic needs of the poorest members of urban areas must come to terms with.

Dilemma 1: The Delivery Crisis of the Extremely Poor. The poorer the urban population to which one wishes to deliver "self-help" services, the greater the security risks in delivering such services. The greater the security risks in delivering self-help services, the greater the administrative costs will be. Thus self-help services cannot be implemented in a cost-effective manner, for if necessary administrative precautions are not taken, the program will suffer losses through fraud or theft, but if adequate precautions are taken the services will cost too much.

Dilemma 2: The Lack of Interest on the Part of the Ablest. Very often, landlords who were the best able to participate, those with alternative sources of income, were precisely those who felt they were doing well on their own and thus had little interest in the development of the area. Either they were absentee owners, or they were interested in getting out. Thus many of them offered their properties for sale to the project, while declining the offer of a rehabilitation loan. My experience with these landlords led me to formulate this second dilemma of basic needs programs, namely: Those most able to participate are usually the least interested in participating.

Dilemma 3: The Inability of the Neediest to Participate. The tenants of the least cooperative landlords were usually the most desperately poor; with no marketable skills, they were essentially unemployable. Any direct assistance to them had to take the form of direct grants and subsidies. We could only involve them in the self-help rehabilitative scheme indirectly through their landlords and by helping better-off individuals in the area to increase employment opportunities, which would trickle down to the poorest. The third dilemma of the basic needs approach was suggested by this experience, the counterpart of the second dilemma stated above, namely: Those most in need of basic needs are the least able to participate directly in a basic needs program.

The political problems of the project came from two sources: outside the area (from the Ministry of Housing) and within the area. From the very start the minister of housing and his staff opposed the project despite, or perhaps because of, their strong political commitment to the poor. First, for the minister and his staff, helping the poor meant bringing their standard of living up to the level of the middle classes as quickly as possible. Even if this was impractical for the great mass of the poor, it should at least be held out as an ideal. The minister felt that any program, no matter how equitable compared to alternatives, that assumed that the poor would continue to live in slums was "an insult to the masses." He frequently referred to the program derisively as "Patterson's African-yard concept."

Second, the traditional slum clearance and housing plan approach offered political payoffs that few politicians could resist. There was patronage: not only massive building contracts to business supporters but also substantial employment for local supporters during the construction period. The negative political response of the many displaced people was diffused by their dispersion elsewhere in the city. At the same time, the new housing estate provided a golden opportunity to carefully select and concentrate the party faithful. It also allowed for closer monitoring of voting behavior. These advantages more than compensated for the negative votes of the disgruntled few who remained in the area. And a housing estate is also a more politically exploitable asset than a basic needs community development program.

Furthermore, the counterpart to the absence of trust among the very poor is their strong propensity to gamble. Since life offers so little, people are strongly motivated to place their hopes on a lucky break. It is the poorest who engage most in lotteries, as every astute politician knows. A housing plan has the same effect on the fortunes and legitimacy of politicians as a lottery winner from the poor has on the legitimacy and success of the lottery. Community-based basic needs programs have no such dramatic political payoffs. Indeed, their very emphasis on equity, on smaller marginal gains for all as opposed to major gains for a lucky few, gives them little political appeal. And politics, especially in Third World countries, not to mention democratic ones in the First World, is above all about drama. Hence, *Dilemma 4: The Incongruity between Solving the Needs of the Poor and Maintaining the Power of Political Leaders*. A depressing corollary is that the more democratic the polity, the greater that incongruity is.

Another political problem springs from one important segment of the population of low-income areas. The members of the community most willing and able to cooperate with the program were also those who were better off. Many of them simply wanted to leave the area. However, a few did want to stay and upgrade the community. These were the natural local leaders, whom we eagerly sought out and who just as eagerly sought us out. Invariably they turned out to be people already well locked into the political structure who saw the program as a way to expand their influence in the political process. But the local leadership had a different conception of basic needs than the developers of the program. Their aspirations were more those of the petit bourgeoisie. Their commitment to living in the area was conditioned on the implicit understanding that their leadership would be rewarded with a petit bourgeois lifestyle. This translated into a housing plan. Thus there was pressure to shift the focus of the program away from environmental and housing rehabilitation to the construction of new dwellings from the very people within the area on whom we were relying the most for support in achieving our objectives. (Indeed, the local leadership, ably assisted by a key member of the project staff, successfully lobbied the prime minister for a housing plan behind my back.) This is a good example of *Dilemma 5: The Incompatibility of the Goals of Local Leaders and of Basic Needs Programs.* Those residents best able to provide leadership in achieving the objectives of the basic needs program—and outwardly most committed to it—are the very same people who are likely to emphasize goals that, if they do not undermine the program's objectives, at least entail a drastic shift in its priorities.

In addition we faced three important administrative problems. The first was the difficulty of getting qualified personnel to work in the area. The second was the failure to find a first-rate director of the project. The position demanded two different kinds of skills: the ability to manage a multi-million-dollar budget and coordinate many different activities, on the one hand, and the social skills of a first-rate community organizer, on the other. These rarely go together. The problem was compounded by the unrealistic pay scales imposed by the government's personnel office and the great difficulty of redefining job descriptions. The result was high turnover for this most important position.

The third major administrative problem was what can only be described as the subversive role of technical experts from the private sector. What we learned, quite simply, was that if you hire an architect-planner you get an architect-planner, no matter what his rhetoric, and that architect-planners, like other people, are inclined to do what they do best—in their case, designing and supervising the construction of buildings.[4] After the architect-planner joined the team, he rapidly broadened the scope of his activities. Many activities that should have been performed by the director or one of his officers were soon being performed by the architect-planner, all at exorbitant professional fees. Second, the construction aspects of the program quickly ran ahead of other developments that should have preceded them. The building to house the small-scale industrial program, for example, was well underway before the director of the project knew what industries it would house. Third, there were large cost overruns.

But the worst was yet to come. The planner quickly sensed the political pressures favoring a housing plan. At about that time, the downturn in the economy, reflected most dramatically in a slump in the private construction industry, meant that the architect-planner had a largely unemployed staff. He therefore had a powerful personal interest in mobilizing support for a housing plan, justifying it on the grounds that his technical survey showed that 131 units in the area were unfit for habitation and had to be demolished. To replace them, he designed a housing scheme of 168 two-bedroom units. His argument was utterly spurious. With the most generous subsidy these units were esti-mated to cost (in 1977 Jamaican dollars) $8,700 each, resulting in a monthly mortgage payment of approximately $41. Assuming that 25 percent of total household income went to housing, this meant that only families earning a total household income of $164 per month could afford these highly subsidized units. The socioeconomic survey of the area had shown, however, that only 3 percent of all households earned this income. This, incidentally, is typical of the proportion of low-income families capable of participating in slum-clearance housing plans and is one of the main reasons for preferring an urban upgrading program. So it was that I learned the sixth and final dilemma besetting any basic needs program.

Dilemma 6: The Incompatibility between the Goals of Tech-nical Experts and of Basic Needs Programs. All such programs are caught on the horns of a technical dilemma. If they proceed without technical expertise they are likely to fail, because certain minimum levels of engineering, architectural, and other skills are required in even the most basic programs (for example, improving drainage and sanitation; providing running water even at the modest level of a standpipe in each yard; increasing the number of public latrines and baths; demolishing and replacing dangerous buildings). But the moment that professionals are employed, they tend to reorient programs toward traditional modern-sector thinking with its physical and capital-intensive biases. In so doing they will be abetted by interest groups, within and outside the target area, best served by traditional modernization programs. The propensity for subversion is further enhanced by the inexperience and political weakness of many of those who direct projects. Thus, unless basic needs programs are directed by forceful, well-paid directors with strong political backing, the original objectives will almost certainly be subverted by the technical experts.[5]

The Private Sector and Basic Needs

This case study of urban upgrading in Kingston illustrates the enormous difficulties that any attempts to meet the basic needs of the poorest sectors of a Third World society are likely to encounter. Even with a democratic socialist government strongly committed to a basic needs approach, the political and administrative leadership faces complex cultural and economic problems. There is a profound lack of congruence between the political and social interests of leadership and those whose problems it attempts to alleviate.

I have demonstrated, also, how serious the problem of what M. G. Smith (1983) calls "social recognition and legitimacy" can be. It was assumed by a socialist minister of housing, himself elected from an urban slum community in another part of the city, that the most urgent housing need of his constituents was a modern two-bedroom unit. My surveys and ethnographic studies, and anthropological field studies by others, indicated that this level of housing improvement was not given high priority by the urban poor, for the very sensible reason that they considered it wildly unrealistic and attempts to achieve it highly disruptive. Yet the minister of housing, like those before and after him with quite different ideological persuasions, persisted in the pursuit of wasteful and inequitable slum-clearance policies.

Tragically, these housing schemes imposed on low-income areas turned out to be the major source of rapidly rising violence in the island. Securing a unit in one of them became the most desired payoff for political work and support of various kinds by local residents in the highly clientelistic political system. This greatly increased the cost of one's patron's party losing an election. When this happened the new government's member of parliament and constituency political aides immediately sought to evict tenants and apartment owners supporting the losing party and to replace them with their own supporters. Anticipating this, current tenants and owners armed themselves and resorted to violence to ensure that their patron and his party won the election and, in the event that they did not, to prepare for the open warfare that inevitably ensued after the election. Housing plans, especially those in the low-income areas of Kinston, rapidly transformed into what became known as armed "garrison" communities, a major factor in Jamaica's descent into chronic violence.

This case study also points to the even greater problems of the private business sector in meeting the needs of low-income areas. Businesses cannot make a profit where potential customers have little or no income. Over a third of the poor in most Third World countries are in this situation. It could be argued that businesspeople can deliver services more efficiently than government, and that profits potentially exist in the difference between the cost to government and the lower cost to business. Experience leads me to doubt this. Where it was successful—in the mobilization and delivery of existing government services—the project staff was actually highly efficient, and it is very unlikely that a private concern could have performed such tasks more efficiently. Nor—and this is the crucial issue— is it likely the private sector would be interested in such ventures. The work involved is complex and often risky and entails a great deal of human interaction that cannot be assigned a cost. And the returns are often difficult, if not impossible, to quantify in monetary terms and therefore cannot be rewarded objectively. However, it was my hope that there was a role for business in the financing services required by the project. I still think that the private sector can participate in financing such projects, but only if it is understood that the funding must be guaranteed by government and supplemented by public subsidies. My experience shows that a private company alone cannot take on such risks. The security and administrative costs are simply too great.

Perhaps the most important point is that most of the problems faced by the Kingston project were not peculiar to the public sector. Exactly the same problems would have been faced by private businesspeople—the difficulty of securing competent staff, the status problem of working in the slums, the political pressures to subvert project goals from both inside and outside the area, and, most critical of all, the fact that those most in need are the weakest source of political support for the goals of the program.

The private sector may have a role in one area: the construction of buildings. Governments, especially Third World governments, should have as little as possible to do with the provision of new housing stock. Building should be left entirely to the private sector, and government should intervene only through the provision of subsidies, where necessary. Housing, like education, employment, and other needs, means different things to different people. To the extent that the private sector can construct modern housing more efficiently than the public sector, it can participate in providing basic needs. But whose needs? We have seen that even with enormous subsidies new housing is well beyond the reach of all but 5 percent or less of the residents of the poor areas of Kingston, and I suspect that the same is true of low-income areas all over the undeveloped world. The question then is not simply what the basic needs are and who can best provide them, but for whom are they being furnished?

When I speak of businesspeople, I mean those from the area. It should be obvious that multinational firms and NGOs face the same problems (but greatly magnified), as do local firms. The most important factors accounting for the success or failure of basic needs programs are political will or commitment and acumen. Next is a thorough understanding of the cultural patterns, needs, anxieties, hostilities, and vulnerabilities specific to the populations targeted for improvement. One cannot expect representatives of foreign firms or even the most well-meaning NGOs to have these skills and knowledge.

In fact, it is precisely the things that multinationals are good at providing that a basic needs program is least likely to need—namely, capital-intensive technologies and products. For example, over the years that I served as a consultant for the Jamaican government, I examined numerous so-called breakthroughs in low-cost housing for the poor in the Third World. In every case the "breakthrough" turned out to be impractical, expensive, and culturally inappropriate and, even if transferable, would become a heavy drain on already desperately low foreign exchange reserves.

I do not oppose the participation of multinational firms or NGOs in the development of Third World countries. With adequate knowledge, supervision, sensitivity to local needs on the part of foreign personnel, flexibility for the host country to renegotiate contracts, and other safeguards cited by the United Nations (United Nations 1978: chaps. 4 and 5), it is possible for multinational firms to participate constructively in the development of the more advanced sectors of a Third World economy. A case in point was the success of the Rockefeller-sponsored public health program that resulted in the remarkable rise in life expectancy in the middle of the twentieth century in Jamaica. Alas, this was not the case with the urban upgrading project.

Why Policies Fail: Institutional Incompetence and Bad Politics

The failure of the urban upgrading project in Kingston is a good example, at the ground level, of why nations fail: "not the ignorance of politicians but the incentives and constraints they face from political and economic institutions in their societies" (Acemoglu and Robinson 2012: 67). To rephrase slightly, not ignorance of good policies but flawed and inappropriate institutions, or, where the appropriate institutions exist, as they often do in Jamaica, institutional incompetence and bad politics. The urban upgrading approach to the problem of urban slum communities is a well-conceived program with numerous successful applications around the world (World Bank 2001). Our application was carefully thought out and was based on thorough research and planning that incorporated the participation of local leaders and a survey of the views of members of the community. When asked which they would prefer—a shot at an apartment in a new housing plan or an upgraded community—the overwhelming majority chose the latter.

The institutions needed to launch the program were already in place. There were many departments of the Ministry of Housing and the Ministry of Local Government, staffed by numerous employees with the requisite paper qualifications, dedicated to improving the condition of the urban poor. There was the institution of the Worker's Bank. There was the Small Industries Development Division of the Jamaica Industrial Development Corporation. And there was the Urban Development Corporation, an ambitious public sector organization "charged with preparing, developing and implementing plans for urban development, urban renewal and rural modernization, in collaboration with other agencies." We were given the authority to draw on all these institutions. But while they existed organizationally and were comfortably quartered, with well paid and "qualified" staff, they were of little help to us. Teams of officers from the various departments I contacted would come to the area, walk around, earnestly discuss the plan and their potential contribution, then leave for their offices, where a report would be written simply repeating what they had heard from us, in addition to a few boilerplate platitudes and promises to follow up, never to be heard from again. The Urban Development Corporation, seemingly the most appropriate institution for our project, made it clear very early that they did not do this sort of thing, in spite of their mission statement.

The most serious problem, however, was the lack of political will. The Kingston urban upgrading project did not work primarily because the politicians involved did not want it to work or were pressured by alternate demands and constraints to make decisions detrimental to the project. The minister of housing wanted the project to fail even though he had promised the prime minister that his ministry would do everything to assist us. He wanted failure partly because of his misguided—and cynical—commitment to the "socialist" ideal of a two-bedroom unit for every family in the slums, which was good for his stump speeches, but mostly because the typical slum-clearance housing plans were a political gold mine, a way of locking in the votes of the party faithful and of displacing nonsupporters as well as the mass of politically indifferent community residents. The prime minister, originally all in with the program, gave in to pressure from local leaders and political henchmen who viewed a housing plan as the best way to generate jobs in his constituency during a period of depressed economic conditions and public contestation with the IMF and as a way of rewarding aides in preparation for the upcoming political election.

Like the nation at large, then, the urban upgrading project failed because available institutions did not work due to the country's chronic "implementation deficit" (Bertelsmann Stiftung 2016) and because of contradictory political aims and decisions.

8

Sad about Manley

Portrait of a Flawed Charisma

When Rachel Manley asked me to write the foreword to *Slip-stream: A Daughter Remembers,* her memoir of her father, Michael, I was finally able to break, briefly, the mental block I previously had in writing about him. Rachel's exquisitely crafted memoir, written with unsparing candor, allowed me to reflect openly about, and to pass my own judgment on, the flawed, confounding mentor, advisee, hero, and statesman who had so greatly influenced my own life and early work.

At the most particular level, *Slipstream* is a deeply personal account of one daughter's intricate relationship with a complex and emotionally elusive father. At the most general, it is an impassioned exploration of loss and emotional betrayal, of the search for anchorage and meaning in personal relations, and of forgiveness and reconciliation, feelings we all experience at some time by simply being human. But the ultimate value of the memoir lies somewhere between these two planes of knowing. The book answers one of the more perplexing questions haunting a troubled nation: Who was Michael Manley?

Jamaica and the world knew him as the island's charismatic fourth prime minister, the son of a revered national hero and founding father and of a renowned mother who inspired the nation's first generation of notable artists and writers. They knew him as the fiery orator who tried to refashion Jamaica's unjust postcolonial economy and society into a democratic socialist mold, who helped to liberate the previously denigrated subaltern culture of the black masses, who irked the American giant with his radical foreign policy, most notably his friendship with Fidel Castro, and who, in spite of his small land, marched "boastily" onto the world stage as a leader of the Socialist International, spokesman for the dispossessed of the Third World, defender of antiracist and anticolonial movements, and advocate of a brave new world economic order.

To his fellow Jamaicans who lived through these changes, he was the most loved and feared, cherished and reviled, cursed and worshipped, forgiven and unforgiven figure in the history of his nation. He came to power in 1972 promising radical change, insisting with the rod and passion of Joshua that "better *must* come" for the downtrodden masses, especially those in the unspeakable slums and shanties of Kingston. Change came, indeed, but when he was turned out of office eight years later, the economy had shrunk and lay in shambles, vast numbers of the nation's middle classes and badly needed professionals had fled, Jamaica had emerged as one of the world's most violent places, and political and social divisions festered. And yet, the nation remained obsessed. For all their impoverishment, many among the downtrodden still venerated him. In his own constituency, where I had worked for several years in one of my capacities as his advisor, one plaintive sign said it all: "Wi love you Michael but wi hungry" (see the excellent recent biography of Manley [Smith 2016, esp. 255–290]).

But who exactly was this towering figure? When the fire of the 1970s smoldered—it never cooled—it dawned on many of us that the man we all either loved or hated (or both), about whom we remained so obsessed, we hardly knew. This became clear to me when every effort I made to write about him during the 1980s, in response to the solicitations of numerous editors, failed, even though I had known him from my student days at the University of the West Indies and was for eight years his special advisor for social policy and development. I once asked one of his former ministers, Carlyle Dunkley, a friend I had known from high school, a man who had spent a great deal of personal time with Manley, what he was really like. Beyond the usual platitudes—"good man," "love him people, you know," "really care about you"—he was tongue-tied.

* * *

In Rachel Manley's memoir, we are led behind the walls he built around his very private self by a remarkably perceptive daughter searching for the man she likens to a "lone city, a single culture with its own province," as he lay dying. Her grief, her unyielding love, all that she has found and all that finally came to her during his painful final months, are made ours, through the gift of her lyrical, poignant prose.

As with so many larger-than-life figures, Manley was a web of contradictions. He was generous and caring and "believed the best of everyone"—I still treasure a warmly appreciative letter he took the time from his busy schedule to write me after reading my last novel—but on his terms, and always from a distance, shunning situations that made demands on his feelings, including even the simple familial exchanges of Christmas. This spellbinding orator was "painfully shy"—had actually overcome an early stutter and made his first public speech at twenty-six—and never fully at ease in intimate gatherings but became refulgent before a large audience, devouring their devotion even as they basked in the glow of his charisma. He loved the People, the Workers, the Op-

pressed, as well as the intellectual, rhetorical, and personal challenges of democratic rule and contestation. But he hated retail
politics, the nitty-gritty of constituency work, recoiling from the
emotional demands of his often boisterous constituents as an invasion of his privacy. He was upright and incorruptible in public
life but unscrupulous and dishonest in his intimate relations and
"could be ruthless about departures," a trait the author claims he
shared with other members of his family.

His regime is credited with the rise of Afro-Jamaican culture,
its vibrant popular music, dance, and religions, and with the assertion of black pride. But we learn from his daughter that Manley
remained firmly ensconced in the tastes and personal habits of the
elite Anglo-Jamaican culture in which he was brought up, that
her father "had spent his adult life representing a world with
which he shared very little social intimacy." In the land of reggae
he was a lover of classical music; he rejected the island's spicy
cuisine for the bland British dishes of his English mother; in the
home of dancehall he did not care much for dance and, when he
did, preferred the cha-cha-cha. The few close friends he had were
almost all from his own light-skinned, privileged caste, an inbred
pampered set brought up by retinues of fawning black servants.
On the occasions I saw him relaxing with them I was at a loss as
to what he saw in them (see also Smith 2016: 105–109).

Manley adored his mother, a formidable presence who was
still imposing in her seventies when I first met and spoke at length
with her at a small dinner party. He cared in his own way for his
daughters and was a firm believer in women's rights, Jamaica's
first office of women's affairs appearing during his administra-
tions. Nonetheless his intimate relations with women were dis-
graceful; he was as undisciplined, unfaithful, and hurtful in them
as he was disciplined, trustworthy, and caring in his nonintimate
and formal relations. "My father kept falling in love and into

bed," Rachel writes plaintively, "and was a bit too in need of immediate gratification." As a politician, it was Manley's good fortune that the sexually promiscuous and conjugally challenged nation he ruled adored him for his carnal recklessness. However, it
was a deep source of anguish not only for the women he slept
with and left, married, and divorced but, as Rachel repeatedly
shares with us in some of the memoir's most sensitive and reso-
nant passages, for her and the other daughters he enchanted and
emotionally neglected. Manley's greatest personal tragedy was
the fact that the two occasions on which he appeared ready to
commit himself to a loving relationship were cut short by death,
that of his third wife and his own. It was only his impending
death, chronicled here in agonizing detail, that brought him finally to the full realization of the love he could have given and
of what he had missed and nearly abject remorse for the grief he
had caused and, in his own words, the need to "heal the hurts . . .
to build bridges, if only one could. To have time."

I have often wondered what his compulsive womanizing was
all about and, at last, we begin to understand. Manley's relations
with women were a vital clue to the nature of his political behavior. We learn that he needed desperately to be loved and to be
in love but found it hard to love and nearly impossible to commit
himself emotionally. When Rachel tells us that "he'd enter a
woman's unsuspecting world and astonish it with the possibilities
engendered by his enthusiasm," we think, even before she makes
the connection, of his dashing entry into Jamaican politics, a
transition that was also her "deepest trough," reviving her chronic
fear of abandonment. "Of all the mistresses of his heart," she
writes, "I would discover that Jamaica was the most powerful."
In one of the work's most discerning passages, she elaborates:
"The island was living his personality. His restlessness, his rapture, his rash impetuousness—his causes and carings, his sudden

concepts—seemed to be no different from the nation's." Manley's mother, Edna, whose intensely complicated relationship with her son was surely implicated in all this, observed of his growing passion for his third wife, Barbara—the one I was certain, after a quiet evening I once spent with them, he might have truly committed himself to, had she lived—that "he falls in love so colossally." That is as apt a description as any of his leadership style and its consequences for the country he led.

It was a colossal period in Jamaica's tragic history: colossal in its changes, its socioeconomic and political passions, its failures and, yes, its successes. It is often said that the Manley regime failed badly in social and economic terms but succeeded in transforming the island's pernicious neocolonial culture. That is far too tidy a description of what really happened. For if, on the one hand, it failed in its economic policies, it is also the case that the turmoil it engendered and the flight of the traditional white, Asian, and light-skinned elite unlocked their stranglehold of centuries on the nation's wealth and opened entrepreneurial doors for the black businesspeople who stayed. The immediate postcolonial arrangement, promoted by the conservative Jamaica Labour Party that Manley had dislodged, in which blacks moved up in politics and the civil service but remained largely excluded from the nation's economic heights, was shattered for good. Today, Jamaica leads the racially mixed societies of the Caribbean and Latin America in the proportion and growth of black people leading major corporations. The opening also paved the way for female business leaders. And whatever the problems, it was the first time that the peasantry was given an even break with his government's severe restriction on imported food (for a fine study of the democratic socialist period, see Stephens and Stephens 1986).

On the other hand, while the policies of his regime broke the shackles on the Afro-Jamaican culture of the masses, they also unleashed centuries of pent-up rage, culminating in a culture of violence and nihilism that has earned the country the unenviable status of having one of the highest homicide rates in the world. Unclothed with the violence, also, were seamier aspects of its mass culture that its own heralders defiantly call "ragamuffin," chief among which are the island's now notorious misogyny, relational slackness, paternal irresponsibility, and homophobia. Manley can hardly be held solely responsible for this—the evidence suggests that the internal and external forces opposed to him were more at fault. Indeed, he was appalled by these developments and tried hard to put the lid back on, both with his "gun court" and other drastic security measures as well as the symbolic waving of his "rod of correction" and the threat of placing the island under "heavy manners," hardly persuasive from a man whose intimate life was so undisciplined.

But it was all too late to halt the social descent, as were attempts to undo the economic tailspin into which the country had fallen. When he returned to office in the late 1980s Manley abandoned his earlier socialist policies and shifted sharply to the center, embracing many of the open market and free enterprise economic prescriptions that he had castigated in his first term of office, a change paralleled in his personal life with his discovery of the joys of stable marriage to his fifth wife, snatched from a former close friend. But that also was too late, his declining health forcing him to retire in midterm. Time caught up with his changing economic and political vision as it did with his personal life and wishes. There is a strange detachment in one of his last observations about the island he had, for better and for worse, so completely transformed: "Sad about Jamaica, its insurmountable problems." He could have been talking about himself and his unfulfilled promises and relationships.

Epilogue

Jamaica confounds—that much should be evident by now. A little island of less than three million people should not be punching so much above its weight. And yet it does, above the belt and, often, below it, in its terrible failures and its remarkable achievements. Jamaicans are all too aware—and proud—of this. As one informant told the anthropologist Deborah Thomas: "If I had to use words to describe Jamaican culture, I would say, it's big. We do everything in a big, loud attention-getting way" (2004: 1–2). In this book I have tried to show how and why this state of affairs came about.

The institutional sociologist Peter Evans once asked: "What kinds of circumstances increase the determinative weight of prior institutional legacies?" (2006: 48). I have addressed this question for an island where the institutional weight of history is dense and pervasive. What I wrote decades ago (Patterson 1967) has been largely confirmed by subsequent scholarship: that slave society on the island came close to a Hobbesian state of nature in the immorality, brutality, and venality of its enslavers and the unremitting hell on earth for its slave population, who suffered a kind of slow-motion genocide over a century and a half. A team of distinguished economic historians recently concluded that late-eighteenth-century Jamaica was the most unequal society in the world and that "Jamaican slaves lived at the bare edge of subsistence even in good times. Slaves were worked excessively hard, and lived short lives" (Burnard, Panza, and Williamson 2017).

The post-emancipation history of the island perpetuated much of this monstrous heritage of slavery: the highly extractive and inefficient nature of its economy; the extreme inequalities in income and wealth, especially in land ownership; the racial and cultural contempt for the black peasantry and working classes, who were burdened with heavy taxes and starvation-level wages; the nefarious skin-color values of all strata, but especially the colored middle class; the deep, justifiable distrust of all authority figures among workers and the constant unsuccessful struggle for more land by the peasants and repeated revolts by the working class; and the fragile nature of familial and gender relations among the non-peasant lower and working classes. In addition there was, and remains, the continued use of violence at all levels of the society as a primary means of control: by the state, in its use of the cat-o'-nine-tails and hard labor for petty offenses; by teachers, who were officially armed with thick leather straps that they used liberally on their students; by parents, in the disciplining or "murderation" of their children (Yvonne Brown 2010); by men, in their often compensatory patriarchal dealing with women, on an island that currently has the highest rate of female homicide victims in the world; and by employers, in their contemptuous and exploitative treatment of workers, their ingrained conviction of the inherent laziness of blacks, and their liberal use of the compliant colonial police force and courts.[1]

With independence Jamaica declared its official motto to be "Out of many, one people." According to the island's national plan, the motto "perfectly defines and provides insight into our culture" (Planning Institute of Jamaica 2009: 90). This is the view of the dominant ruling group, and it is a misleading one. Culturally, economically, and socially there are really three Jamaicas: the multicolored hegemonic elite, the basal Afro-Jamaican neopeasantry and working class, and the alienated lumpenproletariat on the margins of both in the rural canefield shanties and smoldering "dead-yards" of the urban slums (Thomson 2011).

Today, the hegemonic elite consists of professional bourgeois blacks, mixed-race "brownings" (the non-elite name for them), and a sprinkling of economically dominant whites, brownish Chinese and Jews, and Middle Easterners, all of whom have far more in common economically, culturally, politically, and socially than the skin tones and marital preferences that superficially, if obsessively, distinguish them. Predominantly urban and residentially segregated, this stratum lives an island version of British culture, increasingly influenced by American lifestyles and aspirations (Austin-Broos 1984; Carnegie 2014). Since independence, the political realm has been increasingly taken over by black and brown leaders originating mainly from the more prosperous small farmers and the professional lower middle class who, beginning in the late 1980s, have pushed hard to penetrate the commercial sector (Robotham 2000). At its lower edges are the more prosperous unionized and highly skilled blue-collar workers and low- to mid-level professionals. This elite is, indeed, the most diverse in the Caribbean, but the national motto is really a description of themselves and their utopian vision of "tamed blackness" projected onto the entire population, 85 percent of whom are of unmixed West African ancestry, with a more complex vision of what Deborah Thomas calls "modern blackness" (Thomas 2004: 1–15).

The basal peasantry (and its offspring, the stable small- to mid-sized farmers and rural artisanal classes) has been in decline since independence and was hit hard by the neoliberal structural adjustment policies of the 1980s and 1990s (Weis 2006). Nonetheless it still constitutes a critical sector of the society. Some 45 percent of Jamaicans live in rural areas, and over 85 percent of them live on small farms; even those who do not earn their living from farming are strongly influenced by the still vibrant Afro-Jamaican peasant culture. Although, in formal economic terms, agriculture now contributes only 8 percent of GDP, it is the single largest employer of labor, employing about a fifth of the workforce, and there is reason to believe that the GDP measure substantially underestimates the real contribution of the peasant and small farming sector, especially in light of Jamaica's large informal economy (FAO 2014: 6). The influence of the peasant and broader rural culture, as we saw in Chapter 3, also extends to the cities, a substantial proportion of whose population originated in and maintain connections with the rural areas. Although declining, it is still an important source of the island's cultural creativity, although not in the romanticized manner fashioned by middle-class nationalists (Thomas 2004: 4–6, 65–67, 176–183). It is not an accident that Bob Marley, like Usain Bolt, grew up in the deep, peasant heartland of the island, his universally loved lyrics and melodies rooted as much in the spirituality and folk wisdom of rural Nine Miles as in the lower-class urban culture of Trench Town to which he migrated in his teens.

The large and growing mass of the urban lower classes who live in the vast spreading slums of its cities constitutes the third exposed rail of Jamaican society. Chronically unemployed, with over a third of its youth either completely disconnected from work and school or experiencing unemployment (over 40 percent for youth), living in rickety shacks, or bullet-pocked tenement-garrisons, this group evinces a despair and anger that is "the most glaring evidence of post-colonial socio-economic failures" (Patterson 1964; see also Moser and Holland 1997). This group has been exploited and prodded to violence by earlier generations of postcolonial politicians, "protected" by criminal dons who fill the governmental vacuum left by the state, and hounded by corrupt and incompetent police who kill them with impunity. A culture of primal honor and gangsterism has consequently emerged among them that, tragically, is most often turned inward in chronic violence over turf or against the most vulnerable—women, the elderly, children, and members of the LGBT community. Nonetheless, however "demeaned," the urban poor are culturally "empowered" (Gray 2004). The more pacific among them have greatly contributed to the creation of a potent international religion, Rastafarianism, that influenced the broader culture both directly and indirectly through its influence on roots reggae (Chevannes 1995). The more militant among them have created a dancehall culture that has become "a key cultural matrix and social institution" in the island, "a way to deal with the racism, poverty, and exploitation of living in an oppressive postcolonial society" (Stolzoff 2000: 7).

The misdirection, until very recently, and stagnation of the postcolonial economic system I have attributed primarily to the failure of Jamaica's older generation of leaders to overcome the distorted institutional inheritance of colonial rule. This institutional heritage made them especially vulnerable to the negative aspects of the neoliberal, structural adjustment policies conditionally required by Washington at some time in nearly all Caribbean societies after the 1980s. These neoliberal policies have done little to promote growth and exacerbated already existing social harms, but they are hardly the cause of Jamaica's problems, any more than they generated Barbados's successes and those of the other high-income Caribbean economies that were equally exposed to the liberalizing dictates of the global economy. Thus the sources of the island's catastrophic debt burden, at one time the highest in the world at 147 percent of GDP, are largely endogenous, as noted in Chapter 1. My work supports the critique of what Acemoglu and Robinson call the "ignorance hypothesis" of economic development, the view that what is primarily required for successful change is the knowledge of good policies (2012: 67–68). Before any such policies can take effect, leaders must "break out of the institutional patterns condemning them to poverty" and misrule. Jamaica's economic stagnation has resulted mainly from the failure to break out of these inherited patterns, as surely as its successes have followed from unshackling from them.

I have argued that while the British institutional structures brought to the island were superficially similar to those of Barbados and other islands, all but a small elite were excluded from meaningful participation in them. Quite apart from the lack of experience in governance among the decolonizing elite, the model of political rule presented by the colonial regime augured poorly for independence. There were, to be sure, several people of great integrity among those leading the country to independence, such as the revered founding father Norman Washington Manley, but for too many the path toward tribal politics and self-interested disregard for the common good was already rooted in the bourgeois-led decolonizing movement that co-opted the last great revolt for social justice on the part of the Jamaican masses during the 1930s (Munroe 1972; Post 1978: chaps. 7, 11, 12).

The same problem of exclusion from meaningful management roles holds for most of the other important institutions from the colonial era: the civil service, the police force, and what there was of an educational system. The conclusions of a thorough evaluation of the Jamaican civil service soon after independence hold true for all the other inherited institutions: "Jamaican civil servants continue to accept the British colonial model. The significance of this fact can only be understood when it is appreciated that the British did not allow local Colonial civil servants to take real decisions. Real decision-making was conducted outside the system" (Mills and Robertson 1974: 327). Much the same holds for the police force, where British colonial officers ruled as far down the ranks as inspector and even sergeant. The experience of my own father, who joined the force in the 1920s, was typical. An intelligent, hard-working man, proud that he was among the first of the "natives" to make detective, he was never promoted beyond the rank of lance corporal. When, in frustration, he helped lead the movement to unionize the force, he was summarily fired. Years of protracted legal struggle to win a meager pension left him disillusioned and alcoholic, resulting in a long separation from my mother. The incompetence of the island's present police force, a major factor in the failure to control crime (Harriott 2000: 41–71), can be traced straight back to the leadership vacuum inherited from the colonial past with the withdrawal of the British officers. This is in stark contrast to Barbados, where, as we saw in Chapter 1, from early in the post-emancipation era blacks replaced working-class whites in the force, their descendants gradually moving up the ranks, resulting in the inheritance of a well-functioning police institution upon independence that today solves the great majority of homicides, compared with the Jamaican force's dismal record.

Of all the institutional legacies derived from the colonial era, none has been more damaging than the paucity of resources and lack of institutional leadership and competence in the educational system, generally considered the most important for economic growth (Engerman, Mariscal, and Sokoloff 2009: 93). The colonial ruling class never relented in its view that education merely created spoiled workers, and "the social relations and organization of the classroom continued to replicate the social relations between planters and field-workers" (Jeffrey 1980: 179–80). High schools were largely restricted to the brown and white elites with a small sprinkling of scholarship blacks.

Although postcolonial Jamaican governments have attempted to change the educational system, with a major thrust toward free secondary education during the democratic-socialist period of the 1970s, the effort has largely failed. The colonial pattern of a dual educational system has persisted in a new form. A small number of students now receive, largely at taxpayer expense, a first-rate education at a limited number of secondary schools and at the high-ranking University of the West Indies, the great majority of whose graduates migrate soon after graduation, Jamaica having one of the highest rates of tertiary brain drain in the world. At the same time, education at the pre-primary, primary, and secondary levels has floundered. A high proportion of high school students either drop out or graduate with marginal literacy; either outcome makes them simply unqualified for the modern economy. The World Bank recently reported, "Children in Jamaica can expect to complete 11.7 years of pre-primary, primary and secondary school by age 18. However, when years of schooling are adjusted for quality of learning, this is only equivalent to 7.2 years: a learning gap of 4.5 years" (World Bank 2018). Some 70 percent of the labor force has no formal training, and 20 percent is functionally illiterate (Planning Institute of Jamaica 2009: 65). The Jamaican sociologist Don Robotham, in his recent assessment of the crisis in the nation's high schools, notes the dire implications for its students: "a lifetime of hardship and disappointment; a mass of alienated young people ... an economy able to generate only low-paying jobs, if any at all" (2018).

If Jamaica is ever to get out of its economic stall, it must solve its educational problem. One critical change to this end, as I proposed in Chapter 2, has to be a re-prioritization of where it allocates its resources and a fundamental re-thinking of the aims of education. I completely disagree with the position taken in the nation's Vision 2030 national plan that "the benefits to the country from investments in tertiary education far outweigh the costs and justify continued budgetary support to the institutions" (Planning Institute of Jamaica 2009: 63). The Planning Institute offers no support for this assertion, and it seems to make no sense in light of the report's own documentation of the poor performance of the sub-tertiary levels, the severe shortage of resources at these levels, the high loss of tertiary graduates to other countries, and the fact that the nation's universities "are not sufficiently responsive to the demands of the labor market" (Planning Institute of Jamaica 2009: 62–63). Some of the disproportionate sums spent on tertiary education must be shifted to the lower sectors. Furthermore, while there should be some grammar schools at the secondary level for academically talented students, the system has to reorganize and greatly expand its vocational and technical training system. The one successful element of the educational system is the HEART Trust/NTA (Human Employment and Resource Training Trust/National Training Agency), which provides vocational and technical training to unemployed and unattached youth in its own institutions, in on-the-job and community-based training at over a hundred centers (HEART Trust–National Training Agency 2009). Not only should this program be expanded, but there should be greater integration and expansion of technical and vocational training within the formal primary and secondary sectors of the educational system.

As usual, Jamaicans are fully aware of what needs to be done, as the national strategy proposed in the Vision 2030 plan makes clear (Planning Institute of Jamaica 2009: 67–76). It is in the implementation of these institutional changes that the nation falters. Thus, in 2018, nearly a decade after the publication of the 2030 Vision plan, the Ministry of Education was still promising to increase vocational and technical training (Williams 2018). One encouraging recent development is that the country's capable prime minister, Andrew Holness, has considerable experience working in education, including a stint as minister of education. In addition, the influential minister of finance, Nigel Clarke, was formerly chairman of the successful HEART Trust program. They are both fully aware of the problems and have the political capacity to make real changes, assuming that they have the political will and support to do so.

In the face of all this are the island's successes. First, there is Jamaica's impressive demographic transition to a high life expectancy. The nation's life expectancy now stands at seventy-six years and is still increasing, placing it near the top third of nations, higher than Hungary and many Western Hemisphere countries. It has achieved this level in spite of the high rate of preventable causes of death such as violence (the fifth cause of mortality). More impressively, the nation's health transition, from that of a low stationary life expectancy at birth of about thirty-six years in the early 1920s to the threshold life expectancy of seventy years in 1977, took only about fifty years, which is one of the fastest transitions ever documented (Riley 2005: 21–22). Most impressive of all, a great deal of this change took place between 1925 and 1940, before the availability of modern antibiotics or the wide availability of doctors or any improvement in standard of living. It was, instead, the result of the successful institutionalization of a public health campaign initiated by the Rockefeller Foundation. The colonial authorities had initially been skeptical of the entire campaign, informing the American public health NGO that they were wasting their time because Jamaican blacks were a "willful and disobedient" people too ignorant to appreciate what was in their own interest.

However, James Riley's research demonstrates that the most important factor explaining this health revolution was the cooperation, participation, and resilience of the Jamaican people, who energetically engaged once they realized that it was to their own benefit:

> Among the people the British regarded as willful and disobedient, the essential steps were taken by self-reliant Jamaicans, who decided to become better informed about hygiene and health and to have their children learn about these things, who agreed to build latrines with locally available materials, and who cooperated with the new public health authorities and modified their own behavior in many ways. (2005: 131)

One basic principle that informed the campaign was a blend of top-down and bottom-up leadership, a clear departure from the prevailing pattern of top-down colonial paternalism. Another important reason for the success of the program was that it was a classic case of participants learning by doing. As the economist Kenneth Arrow pointed out: "Learning is the product of experience. Learning can only take place through the attempt to solve a problem and therefore only takes place during activity" (1962: 155). The leadership of the public health movement mobilized a large number of modestly educated black Jamaicans—low-level clerks, parochial workers, agricultural field officers, pupil-teachers, practical nurses, small farmers—to educate the masses. By this means, they learned by doing public health management and eventually placed themselves in a position to lead and educate others to work toward better health on their own. There is much that Jamaican leaders can learn from this isolated, ground-level success from the late colonial past. Writing recently on institutional learning and change, a group of development researchers (Watts et al. 2003) at a Dutch research center laid out a framework for successful development practice that includes the following: the importance of partnership and grassroots participation; the interaction of top-down and bottom-up learning; the expansion of the role of teacher and supervisor to those of facilitator and coach; a re-conception of desired outcomes from rigidly defined objectives to a focus on processes and capabilities; the treatment of failure as a valued learning opportunity; and a conceptualization of change in evolutionary and adaptive, rather than prescriptive and predetermined, terms. We find, in one form or another, similar principles at play in Jamaica's other successes.

The global triumph of Jamaica's athletes, as I pointed out in Chapter 4, is a clear case of institutional learning, innovation, and adaptation and not, as some are inclined to think, a lucky streak of talented individuals. It is the result of a virtuous cycle of top-down and bottom-up institution building, of learning by doing, of coaching and facilitating with mutual respect between coach and athlete, of scaling out and up to the national level of Champs, a unique institution in the history of modern athletics. The commercial side of this institution, the island's track and field clubs, are stellar cases of institutional entrepreneurs learning through the adoption, adaptation, and implementation of American scholastic and commercial athletic practices.

Similar factors underlie Jamaica's global success in its music industry, one of the island's most "remarkable contributions to our planet's cultural repertoire" (Bilby 1995: 123). Jamaica's musical success was initiated by, and was largely the product of, a bottom-up movement, as I explained in Chapter 5. It is significant that this is also true of the more technical, production side of the island's music industry. The creation of an internationally competitive music industry in Jamaica with its own distinctive, globally influential "recording model" required a complex mix of technical, creative, economic, and cultural processes, and, as Ray Hitchins (2014) has definitively shown, involved bottom-up and some top-down interactions between individuals of different classes, colors, and ethnicities commanding different musical, audio engineering, and management skills and access to funds. The remarkable thing about the development of the music is that working-class Jamaicans never lost control of its production at home, even in its most technical and organizationally demanding aspects. It is an outstanding instance of learning by doing and of adoption, adaptation, and evolutionary change, culminating in the dominant music studios of reggae greats such as Clement "Sir Coxsone" Dodd, Duke Reid, Lee "Scratch" Perry, King Edwards, and others. As I noted in Chapter 5, on the one occasion in which it appeared that they would lose control of their music with the internationalization of Bob Marley and others by Chris Blackwell's Island Records company, there was a vigorous re-assertion of local musical and technical control, "a celebration of the local" through the summary rejection of Marley's roots reggae—epitomized in the tragic stoning of Bunny Wailer—and its rapid replacement, for better or worse, with the dancehall genre (Stolzoff 2000: 97–103).

Another of the island's globally competitive achievements is its press freedom and robust civic culture. Once again punching far above its weight, it has recently been ranked sixth of 180 countries in the world in press freedom, above the United Kingdom, most of Western Europe, the United States, and Canada (Reporters without Borders 2018). One striking exception to the extractive institutional structures and racial exclusiveness of the colonial era was the newspaper the *Gleaner,* established by two Jewish half-brothers in 1834, some seventeen years before the *New York Times.* (Jews at that time were viewed as outsiders by the white elite, not having gained full civil liberties until 1826, the same year as the free colored group.) In spite of its conservative slant and its century-long virtual monopoly—many Jamaicans came to use the term *Gleaner* as a generic for all newspapers—the *Gleaner* trained generations of mainly self-educated journalists and in 1951 took the historic step of elevating a black journalist, Theodore Sealy, as its editor, in contrast to the virtual lockout of the majority population from managerial positions at that time (diG 2019). As a child my vocabulary greatly expanded by my daily practice of reading the *Gleaner* to my mother while she sewed; my first published work, a short story written in my mid-teens, appeared in *The Star* (the evening tabloid edition of the *Gleaner*), much to the horror of my prudish headmaster.[2] The *Gleaner,* along with its first-rate national competitor, the left-leaning *Jamaica Observer*, and several local papers, plus many radio stations and cable outlets, are cornerstones of the island's lively civic culture. In Chapter 2, I argued that in spite of the violent nature of its clientelistic, tribal politics, Jamaica remains a genuine democracy, its people deeply committed to freedom and democratic governance, thanks to its free press and advanced civil society.

One of the island's many paradoxes is that, in spite of its horrendous crime rate, it has a large, growing, and highly competitive tourist industry, with over 4 million people visiting the island in 2018. The tourist industry is the country's second largest employer, and it accounts for 47 percent of its foreign exchange. For all the criticisms leveled at it, some justified (Dunn and Dunn 2002), the tourist industry is one of Jamaica's major economic successes. Its overall economic impact has been estimated at 19.5 percent of total GDP, exceeding all other sectors (Oxford Economics 2012: 11; Fernandez-Stark and Bamber 2018). The growth of this industry stems from the reinvention of the all-inclusive model of tourism by two exceptional local entrepreneurs: Abe Issa and Gordon Stewart. They could not have done it without the bottom-up engagement of their employees, whose friendliness and hospitality emerge in every survey as key factors in the attraction of the all-inclusive hotels. These resorts, which provide all services to visitors for one price (and obviate the need for tourists to ever leave the grounds), effectively solve what might otherwise have been a fatal problem for the industry—the island's high crime rate. Compared with the other Caribbean countries, the industry retains a much higher percentage of its earnings (70 percent vs. 30 percent for the region), and it has the highest percent of local ownership and management. But there are problems. The industry poses a serious environmental threat, seen in the massive degradation of the island's coral life and coastal mangrove forests and wetlands, the main culprits of late being a chain of foreign hoteliers who violate environmental laws and building codes by means of bribing and intimidating incompetent and corrupt public officials (Salmon 2008; Matsangou 2018).

The industry has also been criticized for the limited degree of linkage with the rest of the local economy, especially the agricultural sector, most of the food consumed by tourists being imported. The hotel industry, however, can hardly be blamed for this failure. Hoteliers aren't farmers or manufacturers. It is, in fact, a huge missed opportunity on the part of the commercial and landowning classes, abetted by irrational government agricultural policies that persist in subsidizing the failing plantation system. Sixty percent of the nation's farmland is owned by 4 percent of families, and the land is left either idle or in the declining plantation crops of sugar and bananas. There may, however, be some hope. The Canadian rural sociologist Tony Weis has proposed that "historic possibilities could be opening for Jamaica's peasants" and for efficient small and mid-sized farmers, since the collapse of the island's plantation system may open up these lands to them. With an imaginative land reform program, Weis speculates, "lies the potential for a more economically viable, socially equitable, and ecologically rational agricultural landscape, dignified labour absorption (with pressing and broad social implications, including poverty reduction and decreased rural-urban migration), and enhanced food security" (2006: 62). Weis has elsewhere (2004) made an excellent case for a reconsideration of land reform and the promotion of a diversified farming system as foundational strategies for the island's economic recovery and progress. In an impassioned speech, Peter Phillips, leader of the opposition and initiator of the new wave of smart and effective politics, declared that a massive land reform program will be a major plank of his government when it returns to power (Henry 2018). He might consider starting the reform even sooner, in a bipartisan effort with the present government, inspired by the closing line of the poem "Dream" by Jamaican poet Lorna Goodison: "Only the bush promises healing" (1992: 42).

Epilogue

A New Start?

Many may doubt if such agricultural reforms, as well as other reforms in the broader economy, will ever be possible. However, in this little island of endless surprises are some encouraging signs of hope. In recent years a new generation of young, able, and principled leaders has been replacing the postcolonial politicians and business leaders who have made such a mess of the island's development. They include, in particular, its former and current ministers of finance, Peter Phillips and Nigel Clarke (a Rhodes Scholar with a PhD in mathematics from Oxford); its young, accomplished prime minister, Andrew Holness; and many executives in the private sector with a newfound sense of the common good (Hamilton 2017). Both Holness and Clarke are in their forties and, like most members of the cabinet, belong to the generation of leaders born after independence. Over the past six years they have achieved what was considered nearly impossible in global financial circles: substantially reducing the island's national debt from a catastrophic 147 percent of GDP to a manageable and declining 96 percent. They did this without any international bailout or reneging on debts, keeping both the IMF and World Bank at bay while reducing both unemployment and poverty, expanding infrastructure, implementing tax policy reforms, improving the investment climate, and producing a modest return to growth after decades of stagnation (see Clarke 2019; Collister 2019). As the IMF points out: "Jamaica is entering its sixth year of economic reform. Through ongoing fiscal consolidation and active debt management, the public debt-to-GDP ratio is on a firm downward path. Macroeconomic stability is entrenched: inflation is well-anchored, the current account deficit has been reduced, foreign exchange reserves are being rebuilt, and supply-side reforms are improving the business environment" (2018b). In 2015 Bloomberg declared the island's little stock exchange the best-performing in the world (Fieser 2015). Jamaica is now rated the best place to do business in the Caribbean and among the five best in the world to start a business (*Forbes* 2019; *Global Banking and Finance Review* 2018). An important element of this striking turnaround was the revival and extension of the once-moribund social partnership program, originally adopted from Barbados, into a vigorous oversight committee in which all stakeholders—government (including the two major political parties), business, labor, the media, and academia—participate and closely monitor and communicate to the public the often painful economic reforms. It is arguably one of the most remarkable examples anywhere in the world of civil society engagement in national crisis management and development.

This is a badly needed new start for Jamaica, illustrating once again that it is "not better advice or better understanding of how the economy work[s]" that explains economic success but better politics from leaders capable of breaking from the institutional tentacles of the past (Acemoglu and Robinson 2012: 68). Nonetheless, there is still a great deal to be done and undone, and the downside risks are high, including those from natural disasters that are on the increase due to climate change (Selvaraju et al. 2013).[3] It is questionable whether the hungry, angry, and violent urban poor are willing to give them the time they need; in spite of these remarkable recent improvements, crime rates continue to rise. However, they could take heart and find hope in the long-suffering rural half of the population, the vibrant source of so much of the island's successes, by keeping in mind one of the most famous of their many wise proverbs, which, in defiance of all that they have suffered, still steadfastly avers: *Time langa dan rope.*[4]

Notes

1. Why Has Jamaica Trailed Barbados on the Path to Sustained Growth?

1. I use my own tables and figures to highlight the contrast, in part because they are more up to date, but also because they utilize the recent refinement of the Real GDP variable by the Penn World Tables group, which greatly improves cross-national economic comparisons over time. See Feenstra, Inklaar, and Timmer 2013.

2. There were twelve hurricanes in Barbados between 1851 and 2010, compared with twenty-five in Jamaica; seven of these were severe category 3–5 storms in Jamaica, compared with three in Barbados (see Caribbean Hurricane Network 2011; Chenoweth 2003; Schwartz 2015).

3. Contributing to this lower sex ratio is the still-unexplained fact that the sex ratio at birth for African ancestry persons is lower than that of whites and Asians. Thus the mere fact that the Barbadian slave population was reproducing would generate this surplus of women. Compounding this is the fact that infant girls have higher survival rates than males, especially under stressful or deprived conditions such as slavery (see Kiple 1984: 48–49; Kaba 2008).

4. In British Honduras (later Belize), where land was abundant, the ruling elite was nonetheless able to exercise extreme control through state-enforced, monopolistic control of the land and a system of debt

bondage. As Bolland himself concedes, however, British Honduras was an unusual case and labor was controlled "through a combination of techniques and circumstances unique to Belize" (Bolland 1981: 606).

5. As late as 1951–1955 the infant mortality rate for Barbados was nearly twice that of Jamaica's (132.8 per 1000 compared with Jamaica's 69.1). Jamaica's rapidly declining infant mortality, especially after the early 1930s, was long a demographic mystery that was largely solved by the historical demographer James Riley (2005), whose findings I briefly return to in Chapter 4.

6. "Most people know their civil responsibilities, the role of the Government, what it does and what it should do. They know when the Government is pursuing the overall good of the people, and that the action or inaction of an individual, section or public authority directly affects the well-being of the whole society" (Fashoyin 2001: 60).

7. Among the worst offenders are countries such as Liberia, Andorra, Liechtenstein, the Marshall Islands, Monaco, Bahrain, the Cook Islands, Vanuatu, Antigua, and Dominica (Rose and Spiegel 2007: 1311). For a complete list of OFC jurisdictions identified by the IMF and the Financial Stability Forum, see Zoromé 2007: 23, table 10.

8. In addition to my urban upgrading program, described in Chapter 7, I also designed and helped to implement a basic food program that brought essential consumer items to the urban and rural poor, a domestic water supply program that brought standpipe and potable water to the urban neighborhoods, and a nationwide community development program that tried to counter the growing atomization of the rural areas.

9. Barbados for a long time dominated the West Indian team, especially during the team's heyday of world dominance from the mid-1970s to the early 1990s. Barbados has unusual representation among the greatest cricketers in history.

10. There is one major exception to this sorry record of institutional incompetence. The Jamaican public health sector has had stunning successes since the early 1930s, resulting in life expectancy levels that have placed the island among those of the advanced countries. Significantly, the best explanation of this paradox is that it has little to do with the formal medical institutions and more to the mass dissemination of basic health information by a few public health officials, vigorous sanitary inspectors, and primary school teachers, combined with the tradition of Jamaicans "fending for themselves" (Riley 2005). See also Chapter 4.

11. The IMF estimated that the island's manufacturing sector operated at 50–60 percent of its capacity, its electricity industry at an abysmal 43.2 percent.

2. Why Is Democratic Jamaica So Violent?

1. The political scientist Steve Chan (1984) has argued that contradictory findings can be explained by different analytic choices. For example, the democratic peace thesis is contradicted if we include colonial and imperial wars and those of the past but is supported if we do not. It is not clear to me why we should do so, and recent American foreign excursions flatly contradict this attempt to rescue the thesis.

2. Disclosure: I was a founding member of the New World intellectual group at the University of the West Indies to which Rodney belonged and had studied the Rastafarian group years before he became involved with it; indeed, my first book, a novel, was based on this study. I was not involved with Rodney's attempt to radicalize the Rastafarians, although I did participate in the demonstrations against his deportation.

3. Another perverse effect of successful interdiction of international drugs onshore was a sudden collapse of the fish market and rapid rise in the price of fish in the island due to the fact that the international drug traders, now effectively policed by the Americans and their Jamaican trainees, instead of dropping loads of cocaine from light aircraft in the island's interior, began to drop their loads in the sea, which were then picked up by boats equipped with newly available GPS technology. These boats were operated by former Jamaican fishermen who eagerly abandoned their legal occupation for the vastly more profitable task of recovering bags of cocaine floating in the Caribbean.

3. Were Female Workers Preferred in Jamaica's Early Economic Development?

1. The terms *supply-driven* and *demand-driven* were proposed by James Scoville (1988), who links the factors determining the supply of labor from the traditional sector to employment opportunities in the "modern sector," as well as other factors such as the man/land ratio and the dependency ratio.

2. The "informal economy" concept gained currency during the 1970s and early 1980s but was sharply questioned with the swing back to neoclassical modes of thinking about development during the 1980s (see Sethuraman 1981; for a balanced assessment in light of neoclassical criticisms, see Stewart 1989).

3. This paradoxical pattern was detected early by the "New World" group of economists at the University of the West Indies (see, for example, Brewster 1972).

4. For a detailed analysis of the different kinds of low-income areas and settlements in the Kingston Metropolitan Area, see Patterson 1973: chap. 3.

5. On race, color, and class prejudices during the late colonial period, which carried over to the early postcolonial period, see Henriques 1953: chap. 3. Colonial color-class discrimination and prejudice changed significantly during and after the 1970s, especially due to the socioeconomic turbulence of the Manley democratic socialist regime when large numbers of people from the light-skinned, white, and Chinese bourgeoisie and managerial class fled the island, creating openings for the darker-complexioned middle and lower middle classes who remained. Manley's cultural policies, arguably the most successful aspect of the regime, also radically altered class and color attitudes, especially with the rise and legitimation of the Rastafarian and reggae culture of the urban lumpenproletariat and lower working classes who initially strongly supported the democratic socialist regime. What terrified the fleeing elite even more than threats to their income and status was the sight of their sons and daughters beginning to grow their hair in dreadlocks. Color prejudice persists nonetheless, though in more subtle ways, and remains a source of grievance among the black poor (Brown 1979; Gray 2004: 67–68, 97, 147–148, 310–316). A complicating factor is the growing use of skin-bleaching cream among dark-skinned lower- and lower-middle-class women (Brown-Glaude 2013).

4. Why Are Jamaicans the Fastest Runners in the World?

1. In 2008 the Nigerian relay team was awarded the gold medal in the 4×400 meter relay only after the International Olympic Committee stripped the American winners of the prize following one of its members' confession to using performance enhancing drugs.

2. White was my homeroom teacher and history master throughout my high school years and coached me after school, free of cost, in British and West Indian history on the veranda of his East Kingston family home with the same selfless dedication that he showed in training the school's top athletes.

3. Manley made an important contribution to athletics even as a lawyer. In 1941 a twenty-one-year-old civil servant and rising athlete accidentally shot a colleague at the office while playing around with the cashier's gun, which had been thought to be unloaded. Facing a charge of manslaughter and long imprisonment that could have ended his athletic career, the young clerk was brilliantly defended by Manley, free of charge. The clerk was given a sentence of only two years probation and allowed to continue with his athletic training. The young athlete was Arthur Wint, who went on to become Jamaica's first Olympic gold winner and its most iconic athlete (Wint 2012: 25–29).

4. The Jamaican diet has begun to change with modernization and the growing influence of American fast foods, although this deleterious development is disproportionately affecting the nation's middle classes, who can better afford these empty calories (Virtue 2012; Henry, Caines, and Eyre 2015). Peasant and working-class Jamaicans in rural areas from which most of the high-performing athletes come still consume a strikingly healthy diet. One of the most popular national dishes, "rice and peas," which is rice and beans cooked down with coconut milk and served with stewed chicken or ackee and saltfish, is a nutritious and well-balanced meal. Jamaicans, especially those in the country, also eat an enormous amount of fruit. Growing up in the (then) small country town of May Pen, during the summer holidays I would often daily eat three or four mangoes, a dozen guineps, an orange, a banana, and an otaheiti apple, which together cost only a few pennies. While there was the occasional malnourished child in the overcrowded elementary school I attended, almost all were healthy and well exercised from the long walk, or run, to and from school. I do not recall ever having an obese classmate. This has changed with the coming of fast foods.

5. Sadly, this remarkable system of self-reliant community development began to decline from governmental neglect during the 1960s. By the time I studied it during the 1970s for the government of Michael Manley, it was in an advanced state of decline (see Patterson 1977).

6. Contrary to what the Hofstede Insight group thinks, a liking for "in-groups" is not inconsistent with extreme individualism, as studies

of gang behavior demonstrate. For example, Jankowski discusses the "defiant individualism" of urban gang members (1991, chaps. 1–2).

7. A famous Brazilian soccer coach, hired by the Jamaican government to train the island's national team, finally gave up in exasperation and went back home after failing to make progress with the Jamaican players he considered as good as any he had trained in Brazil. He just couldn't get the Jamaicans to coordinate or pass in time.

8. Barbados, meanwhile, as well as the other eastern Caribbean colonies, was doing the same thing with cricket.

5. Why Did Jamaicans Riot at a Cricket Match against England?

1. The first draft of this chapter was written in 1968 soon after I recovered from inhaling tear gas while caught up in the riot at the cricket match, which I had attended.

2. The idea of a symbol standing for itself was the subject of a book by the anthropologist Roy Wagner entitled *Symbols That Stand for Themselves,* first published by the University of Chicago Press in 1989. Wagner, in all likelihood, independently arrived at the idea. Nonetheless, it first appeared in this essay, which was originally published in 1968.

6. Why Does Globalization Not Produce Cultural Homogenization?

1. See the incredible Junko performing her winning dance in 2003 at https://www.youtube.com/watch?v=JX8ptm8diNo.

7. Why Do Policies to Help the Poor So Often Fail?

1. For a thorough documentation of these failures, see World Bank 1980. For a general analysis from the neoclassical viewpoint, see Chenery 1979: chap. 11. And for a good case study of a country that experienced high growth without significant change in its level of poverty, see Young, Bussink, and Hasan 1980: esp. 3–9, chaps. 4, 5, and 8.

2. Attempts by econometricians to measure the effects of basic needs programs on national income are conceptually spurious, methodologically flawed, and socially irrelevant, especially when such needs are interpreted from the demand side. For a typical collection of such approaches, see Kassalow 1968. As Benjamin Higgins bluntly put it, "as long as the sole guide to benefits is social demand, the whole question of costs becomes irrelevant. The implication of the social demand approach is that the demand must be met, whatever the costs. And when one comes right down to it, there is no reason to suppose that the electorate, or the general public is less able to judge costs than it is to judge benefits" (1971: 54).

3. The track record of community development programs is hardly an impressive one. For a good critical appraisal of this approach and the essential prerequisites for success, see United Nations 1971b. For an assessment of the policy issues for both urban squatter settlements and rural areas, see United Nations 1970.

4. On this problem, see United Nations 1973. An important finding of these five case studies from around the world was that "some level of technical know-how must be present before self-help housing or mutual aid housing can be given a better than average chance for success" (iv).

5. For an excellent comparative study of several similar programs at about this same period that strongly emphasizes the role of power and the problems of internal subversion, see Ness 1970.

Epilogue

1. Incredibly, the last lashing of a prisoner in Jamaica took place in 1997 before he was released after serving his four-year term, and a court last ordered the penalty in 2004, forty-two years after independence. The law was abolished only in 2013 under pressure from the UN Human Rights Committee. In 1935 there were 350 whippings by the state authorities in Jamaica, about normal for the late colonial period.

2. Written at the height of the first wave of mass migration of Jamaicans to Britain in the mid-1950s, this story featured a teenage migrant girl trafficked into prostitution in England. The headmaster of my Anglican grammar school threatened to expel me for writing and publishing such a thing in the island's "scandal sheet," as he called it. The expulsion threat was withdrawn only after my profuse apologies. Nonetheless I was promptly kicked off the school chapel's choir.

3. The FAO report opens with the following dire warning: "Climate change is likely to have adverse effects on the agriculture sector in Jamaica. Increase in the intensity and frequency of climate-related natural hazards, escalating rainfall variability, droughts and floods combined with fragile ecosystems and coastal zones, and agriculture-dependent livelihoods all contribute to Jamaica's overall vulnerability to climate change." It adds that Jamaica's Vision 2030 highlights these vulnerabilities as a threat to sustainable development, and provides the framework within which corrective and preventive actions should be undertaken." (Selvaraju et al. 2013: v) It is to be hoped that this will not be another case of institutional availability and declarative knowledge with little procedural capacity and the usual 'implementation deficit.'

4. "Time is longer than rope."

Works Cited

Acemoglu, Daron. 1995. "Reward Structures and the Allocation of Talent." *European Economic Review* 39 (1): 17–33.

Acemoglu, D., S. Johnson, and J. A. Robinson. 2001. "The Colonial Origins of Comparative Development: An Empirical Investigation." *American Economic Review* 91 (5): 1369–1401.

Acemoglu, D., S. Johnson, and J. A. Robinson. 2005. "The Rise of Europe: Atlantic Trade, Institutional Change, and Economic Growth." *American Economic Review* 45 (3): 546–579.

Acemoglu, Daron, and James Robinson. 2012. *Why Nations Fail.* New York: Crown.

Adorno, T. 1990. "On Popular Music." In *On Record: Rock, Pop, and the Written Word,* ed. S. Frith and A. Goodwin, trans. George Simpson, 301–314. New York: Pantheon.

Ahiram, E. 1964. "Income Distribution in Jamaica, 1958." *Social and Economic Studies* 13 (3): 333–359.

Alda, Erik. 2011. *Violence in the City: Understanding and Supporting Community Responses to Urban Violence.* Washington, DC: World Bank.

Alleyne, Mike. 1998. "'Babylon Makes the Rules': The Politics of Reggae Crossover." *Social and Economic Studies* 47 (1): 65–77.

Allum, Felia, and Renate Siebert, eds. 2008. *Organised Crime and the Challenge to Democracy.* Abingdon, UK: Routledge.

Amnesty International. 2006. "Jamaica: Sexual Violence against Women and Girls in Jamaica: 'Just a Little Sex.'" June 21. www .amnesty.org/en/documents/AMR38/002/2006/en/.

Anderson, David M., and David Killingray. 1991. *Policing the Empire: Government Authority and Control, 1830–1940.* Manchester, UK: Manchester University Press.

Anderson, Myrdene, and Cara Richards. 2004. "Introduction: The Careless Feeding of Violence in Culture." In *Cultural Shaping of Violence: Victimization, Escalation, Response,* ed. Myrdene Anderson, 1–8. West Lafayette, IN: Purdue University Press.

Anderson, Patricia. 1987. "Informal Market or Modern Labour Market? Towards a Synthesis." *Social and Economic Studies* 36 (3): 149–176.

Anderson, P., and M. Witter. 1994. "Crisis, Adjustment, and Social Change: A Case Study of Jamaica." In Le Franc, *Consequences of Structural Adjustment,* 1–55.

Arrow, Kenneth. 1962. "The Economic Implications of Learning by Doing." *Review of Economic Studies* 29 (3): 155–173.

Arscott-Mills, Sharon. 2001. "Intimate Partner Violence in Jamaica: A Descriptive Study of Women Who Access the Services of the Women's Crisis Centre in Kingston." *Violence against Women* 7 (11): 1284–1302.

Arthur, Owen. 2000. "Economic Policy Options in the Twenty-first Century." In *Contending with Destiny: The Caribbean in the Twenty-First Century,* ed. Kenneth Hall and Denis Benn. Kingston, Jamaica: Ian Randle.

Arthur, Owen. 2015. "The Social Partnership: Making the Decisive Difference." Keynote address at the Second Annual Retreat of the National Partnership Council of Jamaica, Kingston, Jamaica, July 16. Jamaica Information Service News.

Asemota, H. 2010. "Jamaican Yams, Athletic Ability and Exploitability." In *Jamaican Gold: Jamaican Sprinters,* ed. R. Irving and V. Charlton, 36–46. Kingston, Jamaica: University of the West Indies Press.

Asprey, David. 2002. "Barbadians in the Peruvian Amazon 1910." Genealogy.com forum. September 12. https://www.genealogy.com /forum/regional/countries/topics/barbados/1202/.

Austin, Dennis. 1994. *Democracy and Violence in India and Sri Lanka.* London: Pinter.

Austin-Broos, Diane. 1984. *Urban Life in Kingston, Jamaica: The Culture and Class Ideology of Two Neighborhoods.* Philadelphia: Gordon and Breach Science Publishers.

Works Cited

Austin-Broos, Diane. 1997. *Jamaica Genesis: Religion and the Politics of Moral Orders.* Chicago: University of Chicago Press.

Bakan, Abigail. 1990. *Ideology and Class Conflict in Jamaica: The Politics of Rebellion.* Montreal: McGill-Queen's University Press.

Banerjee, A., and E. Duflo. 2011. *Poor Economics: A Radical Rethinking of the Way to Fight Global Poverty.* New York: Public Affairs.

Barro, Robert J. 1997. *Determinants of Economic Growth.* Cambridge, MA: MIT Press.

Baumgartner, J., et al. 2009. "The Influence of Early Sexual Debut and Sexual Violence on Adolescent Pregnancy: A Matched Case-Control Study in Jamaica." *International Perspectives on Sexual and Reproductive Health* 35 (1): 21–38.

Beck, S. 2012. "Survival of the Fastest: Why Descendants of Slaves Will Take the Medals in the London 2012 Sprint Finals." *Daily Mail,* July 1.

Beckford, George. 1972. *Persistent Poverty: Underdevelopment in Plantation Economies of the Third World.* New York: Oxford University Press.

Beckford, George, and Michael Witter. 1982. *Small Garden Bitter Weed: The Political Economy of Struggle and Change in Jamaica.* Westport, CT: Lawrence Hill and Co.

Beckles, Hilary. 1984. *Black Rebellion in Barbados: The Struggle against Slavery, 1627–1838.* Bridgetown, Barbados: Antilles Publications.

Beckles, Hilary. 1989. *Natural Rebels: A Short History of Enslaved Women in Barbados.* New Brunswick, NJ: Rutgers University Press.

Beckles, Hilary. 1990. *A History of Barbados.* New York: Cambridge University Press.

Beckles, Hilary. 1993. "White Women and Slavery in the Caribbean." *History Workshop Journal* 36 (1): 66–82.

Beckles, Hilary. 2003. *Great House Rules: Landless Emancipation and Workers' Protest in Barbados, 1838–1938.* Kingston, Jamaica: Ian Randle.

Beissinger, Mark R. 2008. "A New Look at Ethnicity and Democratization." *Journal of Democracy* 19 (3): 85–97.

Bennett, Richard. 1991. "Development and Crime: A Cross-National, Time-Series Analysis of Competing Models." *Sociological Quarterly* 32 (3): 343–363.

Bertelsmann Stiftung. 2016. "BTI 2016: Jamaica Country Report." Gütersloh, Germany: Bertelsmann Stiftung.

Bertram, Arnold. 2012. "The Beginning of Organised Athletics in Jamaica." *Gleaner,* February 19.

Bertram, Arnold. 2013. *The Making of a Sprinting Superpower: Jamaica on the Track*. Kingston, Jamaica: Arnold Bertram.

Besson, Jean. 2002. *Martha Brae's Two Histories: European Expansion and Caribbean Culture-Building in Jamaica*. Chapel Hill: University of North Carolina Press.

Bilby, Kenneth. 1995. "Jamaica." In Manuel with Bilby and Largey, *Caribbean Currents: Caribbean Music from Rumba to Reggae*, 143–182.

Blake, Damion. 2012. "Garrisons: Empires of the Dons." *Gleaner,* February 27.

Blake, Damion. 2013. "Shadowing the State: Violent Control and the Social Power of Jamaican Garrison Dons." *Journal of Ethnographic and Qualitative Research* 8 (1): 56–75.

Bloom, David, and Jeffrey Sachs. 1998. "Geography, Demography, and Economic Growth in Africa." *Brookings Papers on Economic Activity* (2): 207–273.

Bobea, Lilian. 2011. "Democratizing Violence: The Case of the Dominican Republic." Applied Research Center, Florida International University. https://digitalcommons.fiu.edu/whemsac/34/.

Boli, John, and George M. Thomas. 1997. "World Culture in the World Polity: A Century of International Non-Governmental Organization." *American Sociological Review* 62 (2): 171–190.

Bolland, Nigel. 1981. "Systems of Domination after Slavery: The Control of Land and Labor in the British West Indies after 1938." *Comparative Studies in Society and History* 23 (4): 591–619.

Bosch, Andrew N., Brian R. Goslin, Timothy D. Noakes, and Steven C. Dennis. 1990. "Physiological Differences between Black and White Runners during a Treadmill Marathon." *European Journal of Applied Physiology and Occupational Physiology* 61 (1): 68–72.

Boserup, Ester. 1970. *Woman's Role in Economic Development*. London: George Allen and Unwin.

Bourdieu, Pierre. 1990. *The Logic of Practice*. Cambridge, MA: Polity Press.

Bradley, L. 2001. *This Is Reggae Music: The Story of Jamaica's Music.* New York: Grove Press.

Brei, Michael. 2013. "Offshore Financial Centers in the Caribbean: An Overview." Working Paper 2013–40, University of Paris West. https://ssrn.com/abstract=2392316.

Brewster, Havelock R. 1972. "The Analysis of the Growth of Employment/Unemployment in the Caribbean." In U.S. Department of Labor, *Manpower: Promoting Employment and Reducing Poverty,* 64–71. Washington, DC: International Manpower Institute.

Brinton, Mary, and Victor Nee. 2002. *The New Institutionalism in Sociology.* Stanford, CA: Stanford University Press.

Bromley, Ray, and Chris Gerry. 1979. *Casual Work and Poverty in Third World Cities.* Somerset, NJ: John Wiley and Sons.

Brooks, M. 2014. "Why Are Jamaicans So Good at Running?" *Guardian,* July 21.

Brown, Adlith. 1981. "Economic Policy and the IMF in Jamaica." *Social and Economic Studies* 30 (4): 1–51.

Brown, Aggrey. 1979. *Color, Class, and Politics in Jamaica.* New Brunswick, NJ: Transaction.

Brown, J., and S. Johnson. 2008. "Childrearing and Child Participation in Jamaican Families." *International Journal of Early Years Education* 16 (1): 31–40.

Brown, O. 2016. "Jamaica Uphold Siege Mentality as Nesta Carter Revelations Cast Shadow over Sprint Success." *Daily Telegraph,* June 16.

Brown, Vincent. 2010. *The Reaper's Garden: Death and Power in the World of Atlantic Slavery.* Cambridge, MA: Harvard University Press.

Brown, Yvonne S. 2010. *Dead Woman Pickney: A Memoir of Childhood in Jamaica.* Waterloo, Ontario: Wilfrid Laurier University Press.

Brown-Glaude, Winnifred. 2013. "Don't Hate Me 'Cause I'm Pretty: Race, Gender, and the Bleached Body in Jamaica." *Social and Economic Studies* 62 (1/2): 53–78.

Bryan, Patrick. (1991) 2000. *The Jamaican People, 1880–1902.* London: Macmillan Caribbean. Repr. Kingston, Jamaica: University of the West Indies Press.

Buckley, Roger N. 1979. *Slaves in Red Coats: The British West India Regiments, 1795–1815.* New Haven: Yale University Press.

Bureau of Gender Affairs. 2016. "Draft of National Strategic Action Plan to Eliminate Gender-Based Violence in Jamaica (2016–2026)." Government of Jamaica, December 6. http://americalatinagenera .org/newsite/includes/fichas/politica/JAMAICA.pdf.

Burgie, Irving. 2007. *Day–O!!!: The Autobiography of Irving Burgie.* Bloomington, IN: Xlibris.

Burnard, T. 2001. "'Prodigious Riches': The Wealth of Jamaica before the American Revolution." *Economic History Review* 56 (3): 506–524.

Burnard, T. 2002. "Not a Place for Whites? Demographic Failure and Settlement in Comparative Context: Jamaica, 1655–1780." In *Jamaica in Slavery and Freedom: History, Heritage, and Culture,* ed. Kathleen E. Monteith and Glen Richards, 73–114. Kingston, Jamaica: University of the West Indies Press.

Burnard, Trevor. 2004. *Mastery, Tyranny, and Desire: Thomas Thistlewood and His Slaves in the Anglo-Jamaican World.* Chapel Hill: University of North Carolina Press.

Burnard, Trevor, Laura Panza, and Jeffrey Williamson. 2017. "Sugar and Slaves: Wealth, Poverty, and Inequality in Colonial Jamaica." *Vox: CEPR Policy Portal,* December 6. https://voxeu.org/article /wealth-poverty-and-inequality-colonial-jamaica.

Butler, Mary K. 1995. *The Economics of Emancipation: Jamaica and Barbados, 1823–1843.* Chapel Hill: University of North Carolina Press.

Campbell, Mavis. 1976. *The Dynamics of Change in a Slave Society: A Socio-Political History of the Free Coloreds of Jamaica, 1800–1865.* Rutherford, NJ: Associated University Presses.

Caplan, Lionel. 1995. *Warrior Gentlemen: "Gurkhas" in the Western Imagination.* Providence, RI: Berghahn Books.

Capoccia, Giovanni. 2015. "Critical Junctures and Institutional Change." In *Advances in Comparative-Historical Analysis,* ed. James Mahoney and Kathleen Thelen, 147–179. New York: Cambridge University Press.

Caribbean Hurricane Network. 2011. "Climatology of Caribbean Hurricanes." http://stormcarib.com/climatology/freq.htm.

Caribbean Leadership Project. 2013. "Spotlight on Barbados' Social Partnership." News post, Caribbean Leadership Project, University of the West Indies, Barbados, March 27. https://www .caribbeanleadership.org/news_publisher/news/view/spotlight-on -barbados-social-partnership.

CariCRIS. 2019. "CariCRIS Has Raised Its Local Currency Rating for the Government of Barbados." Press release, Caribbean Information and Credit Rating Services, January 14.

Carnegie, Charles. 2014. "The Loss of the Verandah: Kingston's Constricted Postcolonial Geographies." *Social and Economic Studies* 63 (2): 59–86.

Carrington, S., H. Fraser, J. Gilmore, and A. Forde. 2003. *A–Z of Barbados Heritage.* Oxford: Macmillan Caribbean.

Carter, Gercine. 2013. "Sir Courtney Reflects." Nation News, Barbados, April 28. http://www.nationnews.com/nationnews/news/44819/sir-courtney-reflects.

Carter, Kenneth L. 1997. *Why Workers Won't Work: The Worker in a Developing Economy: A Case Study of Jamaica.* Oxford: Macmillan Education.

Cavallar, Georg. 2001. "Kantian Perspectives on Democratic Peace: Alternatives to Doyle." *Review of International Studies* 27 (2): 229–248.

Census of the Colony of Barbados, 9th April, 1946. Bridgetown, Barbados: The Colonial Secretary, 1950.

Chamberlain, Mary. 2010. *Empire and Nation-Building in the Caribbean: Barbados, 1937–66.* Manchester, UK: Manchester University Press.

Chamlin, Mitchell, and John Cochran. 2005. "Ascribed Economic Inequality and Homicide among Modern Societies: Toward the Development of a Cross-National Theory." *Homicide Studies* 9 (1): 3–29.

Chamlin, Mitchell, and John Cochran. 2006. "Economic Inequality, Legitimacy, and Cross-National Homicide Rates." *Homicide Studies* 10 (4): 231–252.

Chan, Steve. 1984. "Mirror, Mirror on the Wall . . . : Are the Freer Countries More Pacific?" *Journal of Conflict Resolution* 28 (4): 617–648.

Chang, Ha-Joon. 2006. "Understanding the Relationship between Institutions and Economic Development: Some Key Theoretical Issues." WIDER Working Paper 5/2006, United Nations University. www.wider.unu.edu/publication/understanding-relationship-between-institutions-and-economic-development.

Chang, Kevin, and Wayne Chen. 1998. *Reggae Routes: The Story of Jamaican Music.* Kingston, Jamaica: Ian Randle.

Charles, A. A. 2011. "Representations of Homosexuality in Jamaica." *Social and Economic Studies* 60 (1): 3–29.

Charles-Soverall, Wayne, and Jamal Khan. 2004. "Social Partnership: New Public Management Practice in Barbados." *African Journal of Public Administration and Management (AJPAM)* 15 (1): 22–36.

Chatterjee, I., and R. Ray. 2009. "Crime, Corruption, and Institutions." Discussion paper 20/09, Department of Economics, Monash University, Clayton, Australia. www.monash.edu/__data/assets/pdf_file/0011/925490/crime,_corruption_and_institutions.pdf.

Chenery, Hollis. 1979. *Structural Change and Development Policy.* New York: Oxford University Press.

Chenoweth, Michael. 2003. "The 18th-Century Climate of Jamaica Derived from the Journals of Thomas Thistlewood, 1750–1786." *Transactions of the American Philosophical Society* 93 (2).

Chevannes, Barry. 1994. *Rastafari: Roots and Ideology.* Syracuse, NY: Syracuse University Press.

Chevannes, Barry. 1995. "The Origin of the Dreadlocks." In *Rastafari and Other African-Caribbean Worldviews,* ed. Barry Chevannes. London: Macmillan.

Chevannes, Barry. 2000. "Those Two Jamaicas: The Problem of Social Integration." In *Contending with Destiny: The Caribbean in the Twenty-First Century,* ed. Kenneth Hall and Denis Benn, 179–184. Kingston, Jamaica: Ian Randle.

Clarke, Edith. 1957. *My Mother Who Fathered Me: A Study of the Families in Three Selected Communities of Jamaica.* London: Allen and Unwin.

Clarke, Nigel. 2019. "Lessons from Jamaica for Small Countries with Big Debts." *Financial Times,* February 19.

Clayton, A. 2012. "A New Approach: National Security Policy for Jamaica 2012." Prepared for the Ministry of National Security and Cabinet Office, Jamaica. http://bunting.org.jm/wp-content/uploads/prsantation/NATIONAL-SECURITY-POLICY-for-JAMAICA-2012.pdf.

Cohen, John M., and Norman T. Uphoff. 1980. "Participation's Place in Rural Development: Seeking Clarity through Specificity." *World Development Report* 8 (3): 213–235.

Collister, K. 2019. "Clarke Points to Improvements in Jamaica's Economy." *Jamaica Observer,* February 15.

Cooper, C. (1993) 1995. *Noises in the Blood: Orality, Gender, and the "Vulgar" Body of Jamaican Popular Culture.* Oxford: Macmillan Caribbean. Repr. Durham, NC: Duke University Press.

Cooper, C. 2004. *Sound Clash: Jamaican Dancehall Culture at Large.* New York: Palgrave Macmillan.

Cooper, C., ed. 2012. *Global Reggae.* Mona, Jamaica: University of the West Indies Press.

Couacaud, Leo. 2012. "The Effects of Industrialisation on Gender and Cultural Change in Jamaica." *Social and Economic Studies* 61 (4): 1–36.

Council of Europe. 2014. *White Paper on Transnational Organized Crime.* Strasbourg, France.

Covert Action Publications. 1980. "Destabilization in the Caribbean." *Covert Action Information Bulletin* 10, August–September. https://www.cia.gov/library/readingroom/docs/CIA-RDP90 -00845R000100190003-4.pdf.

Craton, Michael. 1982. *Testing the Chains: Resistance to Slavery in the British West Indies.* Ithaca, NY: Cornell University Press.

Craton, Michael, and James Walvin. 1970. *Jamaican Plantation: The History of Worthy Park, 1670–1970.* Toronto: University of Toronto Press.

Cumper, G. 1954a. "Labor Supply and Demand in the Jamaica Sugar Industry, 1830–1950." *Social and Economic Studies* 2 (4): 37–86.

Cumper, G. 1954b. "A Modern Jamaican Sugar Estate." *Social and Economic Studies* 3 (2): 119–160.

Cumper, G. 1958. "The Jamaican Family: Village and Estate." *Social and Economic Studies* 7 (1): 76–108.

Curtin, Philip. 1968. *Two Jamaicas: The Role of Ideas in a Tropical Colony.* New York: Praeger.

Dahl, Robert A. 1971. *Polyarchy: Participation and Opposition.* New Haven: Yale University Press.

Daley J., K. Matthews, and K. Whitfield. 2008. "Too-Big-to-Fail: Bank Failure and Banking Policy in Jamaica." *Journal of International Financial Markets, Institutions and Money* 18 (3): 290–303.

Dann, Graham. 1984. *The Quality of Life in Barbados.* London: Macmillan.

Works Cited

Davis, Stephen, and D. Simon. (1979) 1992. *Reggae Bloodlines: In Search of the Music and Culture of Jamaica.* Oxford: Heinemann Educational. Repr. New York: Da Capo.

Dawes, A. 2016. "Why Are Jamaicans So Fast?" *Gleaner,* August 31.

Dawson, Andrew. 2013. "The Social Determinants of the Rule of Law: A Comparison of Jamaica and Barbados." *World Development* 45: 314–324.

de Man, A., and G. Blais. 1982. "Relationship between Preference for a Type of Sport and Two Aspects of Personality: Social Alienation and Self-esteem." *Perceptual and Motor Skills* 54 (1): 11–14.

Dessing, M. 2002. "Labor Supply, the Family, and Poverty: The S-Shaped Labor Supply Curve." *Journal of Economic Behavior and Organization* 49 (4): 433–458.

Devonish, Hubert. 1998. "Electronic Orature: The Deejay's Discovery." *Social and Economic Studies* 47 (1): 33–53.

Diamond, Larry, and Marc F. Plattner, eds. 1994. *Nationalism, Ethnic Conflict, and Democracy.* Baltimore: Johns Hopkins University Press.

diG. 2019. "The Story of the Gleaner Company." diG Jamaica. http://digjamaica.com/m/our-past/historical-eras/gleaner/.

Douglas, Mary. 1986. *How Institutions Think.* Syracuse, NY: Syracuse University Press.

Downes, Andrew. 2001. *Economic Growth in a Small Developing Country: The Case of Barbados.* Bridgetown, Barbados: Sir Arthur Lewis Institute of Social and Economic Studies.

Doyle, Michael. 1983a. "Kant, Liberal Legacies, and Foreign Affairs, Part 1." *Philosophy and Public Affairs* 12 (3): 205–235.

Doyle, Michael. 1983b. "Kant, Liberal Legacies, and Foreign Affairs, Part 2." *Philosophy and Public Affairs* 12 (4): 323–353.

Doyle, Michelle, and Anthony Johnson. 1999. "Does Offshore Business Mean Onshore Economic Gains?" Presentation at the Annual Review Seminar, Research Department, Central Bank of Barbados, July 27–30. http://www.centralbank.org.bb/Portals/0/Files/WP1999-07.PDF.

Dreher, Axel, and Stefanie Walter. 2010. "Does the IMF Help or Hurt? The Effect of IMF Programs on the Likelihood and Outcome of Currency Crises." *World Development* 38 (1): 1–18.

Dubois, Laurent. 2005. *Avengers of the New World: The Story of the Haitian Revolution.* Cambridge, MA: Belknap Press of Harvard University Press.

Dubois, Laurent. 2012. *Haiti: The Aftershocks of History.* New York: Metropolitan Books.

Du Bois, W. E. B. 2007. *Black Reconstruction in America: An Essay toward a History of the Part Which Black Folk Played in the Attempt to Reconstruct Democracy in America, 1860–1880.* New York: Oxford University Press.

Dunn, Hopeton, and Leith Dunn. 2002. "Tourism and Popular Perceptions: Mapping Jamaican Attitudes." *Social and Economic Studies* 51 (1): 25–45.

Durand, J. D. 1975. *The Labor Force in Economic Development: A Comparison of International Census Data, 1946–1966.* Princeton, NJ: Princeton University Press.

Economist. 2000. "Phoney Democracies." June 22.

Eggleston, E., J. Jackson, and K. Hardee. 1999. "Sexual Attitudes and Behavior among Young Adolescents in Jamaica." *International Family Planning Perspectives* 25 (2): 78–84.

Eighth Census of Jamaica and Its Dependencies, 1943. Kingston, Jamaica: Central Bureau of Statistics, Jamaica, 1945.

Eisner, Gisela. 1961. *Jamaica, 1830–1930: A Study in Economic Growth.* Manchester, UK: Manchester University Press.

Eldemire, Summer. 2018. "How Phone Scamming Has Fueled a State of Emergency in Jamaica's Tourist Capital." *Intercept,* October 18. https://theintercept.com/2018/10/16/jamaica-phone-scamming-state-of-emergency/.

Ellis, A. B. 1885. *History of the First West India Regiment.* London: Chapman and Hall.

Ellis, H. 1991. *Identifying Crime Correlates in a Developing Society: A Study of Socio-Economic and Socio-Demographic Contributions to Crime in Jamaica, 1950–1984.* New York: Peter Lang.

Engerman, Stanley L. 2007. *Slavery, Emancipation, and Freedom: Comparative Perspectives.* Baton Rouge: Louisiana State University Press.

Engerman, Stanley, Elisa Mariscal, and Kenneth Sokoloff. 2009. "The Evolution of Schooling in the Americas, 1800–1925." In *Human Capital and Institutions: A Long-Run View,* ed. David Eltis, Frank Lewis, and Kenneth Sokoloff, 93–142. Cambridge: Cambridge University Press.

Engerman, S., and K. Sokoloff. 1991. "Factor Endowments, Institutions, and Differential Paths of Growth among New World Economies." In

How Latin America Fell Behind, ed. Stephen Haber, 260–304. Stanford, CA: Stanford University Press.

Engerman, S., and K. Sokoloff. 2002. "Factor Endowments, Inequality, and Paths of Development among New World Economies." *Economica* 3 (1): 41–109.

Engerman, S., and K. Sokoloff. 2008. "Debating the Role of Institutions in Political and Economic Development: Theory, History, and Findings." *Annual Review of Political Science* 11 (1): 119–135.

Enloe, Cynthia. 1980. *Ethnic Soldiers: State Security in Divided Societies.* London: Penguin.

Entine, Jon. 2001. *Taboo: Why Black Athletes Dominate Sports and Why We're Afraid to Talk about It.* New York: Public Affairs.

EPOC. n.d. "What Is EPOC?" Economic Programme Oversight Committee, Jamaica. http://epocjamaica.com/about/, accessed May 16, 2019.

EPOC. 2019. "Update on 3-Year IMF Precautionary Stand-By Arrangement (PSBA)." Communiqué no. 23, Economic Programme Oversight Committee, Jamaica, February. http://epocjamaica.com /communiques/february-2019-update-on-3-year-imf-precautionary -stand-by-arrangement-psba/.

Epstein, David. 2013. *The Sports Gene: Inside the Science of Extraordinary Athletic Performance.* New York: Current, Penguin.

Ermakoff, Ivan. 2008. *Ruling Oneself Out: A Theory of Collective Abdications.* Durham, NC: Duke University Press.

Eubank, William, and Leonard Weinberg. 1994. "Does Democracy Encourage Terrorism?" *Terrorism and Political Violence* 6 (4): 417–435.

Eubank, William, and Leonard Weinberg. 1998. "Terrorism and Democracy: What Recent Events Disclose." *Terrorism and Political Violence* 10 (1): 108–118.

Evans, H. 1989. "Perspectives on the Socialisation of the Working-Class Jamaican Child." *Social and Economic Studies* 38 (3): 177–203.

Evans, Peter. 2005. "The Challenges of the 'Institutional Turn': New Interdisciplinary Opportunities in Development Theory." In *The Economic Sociology of Capitalism,* ed. Victor Nee and Richard Swedberg, 90–116. Princeton: Princeton University Press.

Evans, Peter. 2006. "Extending the 'Institutional' Turn: Property, Politics and Development Trajectories." In *Institutional Change and Economic Development,* ed. Ha-Joon Chang, 35–52. New York: United Nations University Press.

Eyerman, Joe. 1998. "Terrorism and Democratic States: Soft Targets or Accessible Systems." *International Interactions* 24 (2): 417–435.

Fahim, Kareem. 2010. "Jamaica Strains to Fill Void Left by Gang Bosses." *New York Times,* May 31.

Fajnzylber, Pablo, Daniel Lederman, and Norman Loayza. 2002. "Inequality and Violent Crime." *Journal of Law and Economics* 45 (1): 1–40.

Fanon, Frantz. 1961. *The Wretched of the Earth.* New York: Grove Press.

FAO. 2014. *Jamaica: Review of Agricultural Sector Support and Taxation.* Rome: Food and Agriculture Organization, United Nations.

FAO. 2015. *AQUASTAT Country Profile: Jamaica.* Rome: Food and Agriculture Organization, United Nations.

Fashoyin, Tayo. 2001. "Barbados: Fostering Economic Development through Social Partnership." Working Paper, International Labour Organization, Geneva. www.ilo.org/public/libdoc/ilo/2001/101B09 _340_engl.pdf.

Feenstra, Robert, R. Inklaar, and M. Timmer. 2013. "The Next Generation of the Penn World Table." *American Economic Review* 105 (10): 3150–3182.

Fernandez-Stark, Karina, and Penny Bamber. 2018. "Jamaica in the Tourism Global Value Chain." Duke Global Value Chain Center, Duke University, April. https://gvcc.duke.edu/wp-content/uploads /2018_04_26_Tourism-GVC_Jamaica_public.pdf.

Fieser, Ezra. 2015. "It's Jamaica Jammin': Jamaica's Tiny Stock Market Conquers World in 2015." Bloomberg, December 23.

Figueroa, J. P., et al. 2008. "A Comprehensive Response to the HIV/AIDS Epidemic in Jamaica: A Review of the Past 20 Years." *West Indian Medical Journal* 57 (6): 562–576.

Figueroa, Mark, and Amanda Sives. 2003. "Garrison Politics and Criminality in Jamaica: Does the 1997 Election Represent a Turning Point?" In *Understanding Crime in Jamaica,* ed. A. Harriott, 63–88. Kingston, Jamaica: University of the West Indies Press.

Finley, M. I. 1960. "Was Greek Civilization Based on Slave Labor?" In *Slavery in Classical Antiquity,* ed. M. I. Finley, 141–154. Cambridge: Heffer.

Fish, M. Steven, and Matthew Kroenig. 2006. "Diversity, Conflict, and Democracy: Some Evidence from Eurasia and East Europe." *Democratization* 13 (5): 828–842.

Fogel, Robert, and Stanley Engerman. 1974. *Time of the Cross: The Economics of American Slavery.* New York: Norton.

Foner, Eric. 1983. *Nothing but Freedom.* Baton Rouge: Louisiana State University Press.

Foner, Nancy. 1973. *Status and Power in Rural Jamaica.* New York: Teachers College Press.

Fopelson, G. 1991. *Harry Belafonte.* Los Angeles: Holloway House.

Forbes. 2019. "Best Countries for Business: 2018 Ranking." www .forbes.com/best-countries-for-business/list/#tab:overall.

Forster, Jens, and Nira Liberman. 2007. "Knowledge Activation." In *Social Psychology: Handbook of Basic Principles,* ed. Arie W. Kruglanski and E. Tory Higgins, 2nd ed. New York: Guilford Press.

Fox, Sean, and Kristian Hoelscher. 2012. "Political Order, Development, and Social Violence." *Journal of Peace Research* 49 (3): 431–444.

Francis, A., and K. T. Campbell. 2001. "A Supply Function for Violent Crime in Jamaica 1970–1999." Mona, Jamaica: University of West Indies. Published 2002, *Caribbean Journal of Criminology and Social Psychology* 7 (1–2): 89–114.

Francis, A., A. Harriott, G. Gibbison, and C. Kirton. 2009. *Crime and Development: The Jamaican Experience.* Mona, Jamaica: Sir Arthur Lewis Institute of Social and Economic Studies, University of the West Indies.

Francis, Sybil. 1969. "The Evolution of Community Development in Jamaica (1937–1962)." *Caribbean Quarterly* 15 (2/3): 40–58.

Frank, Lenny. 2007. *Hegemony and Counter-Hegemony.* St. Petersburg, FL: Red and Black.

Franklyn, D. 2009. *Sprinting into History: Jamaica and the 2008 Olympic Games.* Kingston, Jamaica: W. F. Barnes.

Fredrickson, George. 1982. *White Supremacy: A Comparative Study of American and South African History.* New York: Oxford University Press.

Freedom House. 2007. "Country Reports: Jamaica." *Freedom in the World 2007,* 406–409. Lanham, MD: Rowman and Littlefield.

Freedom House. 2016. "Country Reports: Jamaica." *Freedom in the World 2015,* 339–342. Lanham, MD: Rowman and Littlefield.

Freedom House. 2018. "Country Reports: Jamaica." *Freedom in the World 2017,* 267–268. Lanham, MD: Rowman and Littlefield.

Garnice, M. 2018. "What Is Mento Music?" *Mento Music,* Jamusica website, January 17. www.mentomusic.com/WhatIsMento.htm.

Gatehouse, Mike. 2012. "The Putumayo Atrocities." Latin America Bureau, London, October 25. https://lab.org.uk/the-putumayo -atrocities/.

Gaviria, Alejandro, and Carmen Pagés. 2002. "Patterns of Crime Victimization in Latin American Cities." *Journal of Development Economics* 67 (1): 181–203.

Gayle, H. 2009. "Young Boys Learning to Fear, Hate or Harm: A Recipe for Sustaining Tribal Political Violence in Jamaica's Garrisons." *IDS Bulletin* 40 (1): 53–62.

Gerring, J., P. Bond, W. T. Barndt, and C. Moreno. 2005. "Democracy and Economic Growth: A Historical Perspective." *World Politics* 57 (3): 323–364.

Gerry, C., ed. 1979. *Casual Work and Poverty in the Third World.* New York: John Wiley.

Gibney, James. 2014. "Panama Voters Should Thank George H. W. Bush." *Bloomberg View,* May 5.

Gilbert, K., and S. Sookram. 2010. "The Socio-Economic Determinants of Violent Crime in Jamaica." Unpublished manuscript. www .semanticscholar.org/paper/The-Socio-economic-Determinants-of -Violent-Crime-in-Gilbert-Sookram/7d73e2771206276aea06c7c49 5c636ca78a04ecd.

Gilley, Bruce. 2006. "The Meaning and Measure of State Legitimacy: Results for 72 Countries." *European Journal of Political Research* 45 (3): 499–525.

Girvan, Norman. 1971. *Foreign Capital and Economic Development in Jamaica.* Kingston, Jamaica: Institute of Social and Economic Research.

Girvan, Norman. 1989. "Comment." In *Development in Suspense: Selected Papers and Proceedings of the First Conference of Caribbean Economists,* ed. Norman Girvan and George Beckford, 314–320. Kingston, Jamaica: Friedrich Ebert Foundation.

Girvan, Norman, ed. 1993. *Working Together for Development: D. T. M. Girvan on Cooperatives and Community Development 1939–1968.* Kingston: Institute of Jamaica.

Gittings, Paul. 2012. "Lightning Bolts: Why Do All the Top Sprinters Come from Jamaica?" CNN, Jun 21. http://edition.cnn.com/2012/06/21/sport/olympics-jamaica-sprinting-heroes-bolt/index.html.

Glaeser, Edward L., Rafael La Porta, Florencio Lopez-de-Silanes, and Andrei Shleifer. 2004. "Do Institutions Cause Growth?" NBER Working Paper 10568, National Bureau of Economic Research, Cambridge, MA.

Glaeser, Edward L., and Bruce Sacerdote. 1999. "Why Is There More Crime in Cities?" *Journal of Political Economy* 107 (S6): S225–S258.

Gleaner. 2015. "Youth Ministry Not Ready to Ban Corporal Punishment." May 11.

Global Banking and Finance Review. 2018. "Ranked: 12 Best Economies to Start a Business in 2018." July 16. www.globalbankingandfinance.com/ranked12-best-economies-to-start-a-business-2018/.

Gmelch, George, and Sharon B. Gmelch. 1997. *The Parish behind God's Back: The Changing Culture of Rural Barbados.* Prospect Heights, IL: Waveland Press.

Goldin, C. 1990. *Understanding the Gender Gap: An Economic History of American Women.* New York: Oxford University Press.

Goldsmith, Arthur A., and Harvey S. Blustain. 1980. *Local Organization and Participation in Integrated Rural Development in Jamaica.* Ithaca, NY: Rural Development Committee, Center for International Studies, Cornell University.

Goodison, Lorna. 1992. *Selected Poems.* Ann Arbor: University of Michigan Press.

Gordon, D. 1987. "The Sexual Division of Labor and Intergenerational Mobility in Jamaica." In *Research in Social Stratification and Mobility,* vol. 6, ed. R. V. Robinson. Greenwich, CT: JAI Press.

Gordon, D. 1996. "Women, Work, and Social Mobility in Post-War Jamaica." In Hart, *Women and the Sexual Division of Labor in the Caribbean,* 72–86.

Gordon D., P. Anderson, and D. Robotham. 1997. "Jamaica: Urbanization during the Years of Crisis." In *The Urban Caribbean: Transition to the New Global Economy,* ed. Alejandro Portes, Carlos Dore-Cabral, and Patricia Landolt, 190–223. Baltimore: Johns Hopkins University Press.

Gordon, Leo-Rey. 2008. "An Empirical Investigation of the Relationship between Offshore Center and Banking System Performance in the Caribbean." Financial Stability Department, Bank of Jamaica. www.academia.edu/1625856/.

Gordon, Shirley. 1998. *Our Cause for His Glory: Christianization and Emancipation in Jamaica.* Kingston, Jamaica: University of the West Indies Press.

Gould, D., K. Dieffenbach, and A. Moffett. 2002. "Psychological Characteristics and Their Development in Olympic Champions." *Journal of Applied Sport Psychology* 14: 172–204.

Gramsci, A. 1971. *Selections from the Prison Notebooks of Antonio Gramsci.* Trans. Q. Hoare and G. N. Smith. New York: International Publishers.

Grantham-McGregor, S., J. Landmann, and P. Desai. 1983. "Childrearing in Poor Urban Jamaica." *Child Care, Health, and Development* 9: 57–71.

Gray, Obika. 1991. *Radicalism and Social Change in Jamaica, 1960–1972.* Knoxville: University of Tennessee Press.

Gray, Obika. 2004. *Demeaned but Empowered: The Social Power of the Urban Poor in Jamaica.* Kingston, Jamaica: University of the West Indies Press.

Green, William A. 1976. *British Emancipation: The Sugar Colonies and the Great Experiment, 1830–1865.* Oxford: Oxford University Press.

Greenfield, Sidney. 1966. *English Rustics in Black Skin.* New Haven: College and University Press.

Greenfield, Sidney. 1983. "Barbadians in the Brazilian Amazon." *Luso-Brazilian Review* 20 (1): 44–64.

Grillo, Ioan. 2014. "Jamaican Organized Crime after the Fall of Dudus Coke." *CTC Sentinel* 7 (1). Combating Terrorism Center, West Point, New York. www.ctc.usma.edu/posts/jamaican -organized-crime-after-the-fall-of-dudus-coke.

Grix, Jonathan, and Fiona Carmichael. 2012. "Why Do Governments Invest in Elite Sport? A Polemic." *International Journal of Sport Policy and Politics* 4 (1): 73–90.

Gunst, Laurie. 1995. *Born Fi' Dead: A Journey through the Posse Underworld.* New York: Henry Holt.

Hall, C. 2002. *Civilising Subjects: Metropole and Colony in the English Imagination, 1830–1867.* Chicago: University of Chicago Press.

Hall, Douglas. 1959. *Free Jamaica: 1838–1865.* New Haven: Yale University Press.

Hall, Douglas. 1978. "The Flight from the Estates Reconsidered: The British West Indies, 1838–42." *Journal of Caribbean History* 10–11: 7–24.

Hamilton, Kirk-Anthony. 2017. "Jamaica's Business Pioneers Renew the Island's Spirit for Global Success." *Huffington Post*, June 9.

Hansmann, H. B., and J. M. Quigley. 1982. "Population Heterogeneity and the Sociogenesis of Homicide." *Social Forces* 61 (1): 206–224.

Hardman, D. 2014. "Road Running Is All the Rage in Jamaica." *Guardian*, January 22.

Harriott, Anthony. 2000. *Police and Crime Control in Jamaica: Problems of Reforming Ex-Colonial Constabularies.* Cave Hill, Barbados: University of the West Indies Press.

Harriott, A. 2003. "The Jamaican Crime Problem: New Developments and New Challenges for Public Policy." In *Understanding Crime in Jamaica: New Challenges for Public Policy,* ed. A. Harriott, 1–13. Mona, Jamaica: University of the West Indies Press.

Harriott, A. 2008. *Organized Crime and Politics in Jamaica: Breaking the Nexus.* Kingston, Jamaica: Canoe Press.

Harriott, Anthony, and Marlyn Jones. 2016. *Crime and Violence in Jamaica.* IDB Series on Crime and Violence in the Caribbean. Kingston, Jamaica: Inter-American Development Bank.

Hart, Keith, ed. 1996. *Women and the Sexual Division of Labour in the Caribbean.* Mona, Jamaica: Canoe Press of the University of the West Indies.

Hart, Mrs. Ernest. 1900. "The West Indies: General." In *The British Empire Series: British America.* London: Kegan Paul, Trench, Tribner and Co.

Hayek, Friedrich A. 1960. *The Constitution of Liberty.* Chicago: University of Chicago Press.

HEART Trust–National Training Agency. 2009. "Unattached Youth in Jamaica." Planning and Project Development Division, December. www.mona.uwi.edu/cop/sites/default/files/Unattached%20youth_0 .pdf.

Hebdige, Dick. 1987. *Cut 'n' Mix: Culture, Identity and Caribbean Music.* London: Routledge.

Hegre, H., T. Ellingsen, S. Gates, and N. P. Gleditsch. 2001. "Toward a Democratic Civil Peace: Democracy, Political Change, and Civil War, 1816–1992." *American Political Science Review* 96 (1): 33–48.

Helliwell, John, Richard Layard, and Jeffrey Sachs, eds. 2012. *World Happiness Report*. New York: Earth Institute, Columbia University.

Henke, Holger. 1999. "Jamaica's Decision to Pursue a Neoliberal Development Strategy: Realignments in the State-Business-Class Triangle." *Latin American Perspectives* 26 (5): 7–33.

Henriques, Fernando. 1953. *Family and Colour in Jamaica*. London: Eyre and Spottiswoode.

Henry, Balford. 2018. "Opposition Leader Eyes Massive Land Reform for Economic Growth." *Jamaica Observer*, March 16.

Henry, F. J., D. Caines, S. Eyre. 2015. "Healthy Eating in Jamaica: The Cost Factor." *West Indian Medical Journal* 64 (3): 181–185.

Henry, Peter Blair. 2013. *Turnaround: Third World Lessons for First World Growth*. New York: Basic Books.

Henry, Peter B., and Conrad Miller. 2009. "Institutions vs. Policies: A Tale of Two Islands." *American Economic Review* 99 (2): 261–267.

Herman, Edward, and Noam Chomsky. 1988. *Manufacturing Consent: The Political Economy of the Mass Media*. New York: Pantheon Books.

Heuman, Gad. 1981. *Between Black and White: Race, Politics, and the Free Coloreds in Jamaica, 1792–1865*. New York: Praeger.

Heuman, Gad. 1994. *"The Killing Time": The Morant Bay Rebellion in Jamaica*. Knoxville: University of Tennessee Press.

Hibbert, Sybil. 2013. "Jamaica's First Treason/Felony Trial Featuring the Rev Claudius Henry." *Jamaica Observer*, December 10.

Hickling, F. W., and G. Walcott. 2013. "A View of Personality Disorder from the Colonial Periphery." *West Indian Medical Journal* 62 (5): 383–388.

Hicks, Norman. 1979. "Growth versus Basic Needs: Is There a Trade-off?" *World Development Report* 7 (11/12): 985–994.

Higgins, Benjamin. 1971. "Planning Allocations for Social Development." *International Social Development Review* (November): 47–55.

Higman, B. W. 1976. *Slave Population and Economy in Jamaica*. Cambridge: Cambridge University Press.

Higman, B. W. 1984. *Slave Populations of the British Caribbean, 1807–1834*. Baltimore: Johns Hopkins University Press.

Hitchins, Ray. 2014. *Vibe Merchants: The Sound Creators of Jamaican Popular Music*. London: Routledge.

Hofstede Insights. 2019. "What about Jamaica?" Helsinki, Finland. www.hofstede-insights.com/country/jamaica/.

Holt, Thomas. 1992. *The Problem of Freedom: Race, Labor, and Politics in Jamaica and Britain, 1832–1938*. Baltimore: Johns Hopkins University Press.

Holt, Thomas. 2000. "The Essence of Contract: The Articulation of Race, Gender, and Political Economy in British Emancipation Policy, 1838–1866." In *Beyond Slavery: Explorations of Race, Labor, and Citizenship in Postemancipation Societies,* ed. F. Cooper, T. C. Holt, and R. J. Scott, 33–60. Chapel Hill: University of North Carolina Press.

Hope, Donna P. 2006. *Inna di Dancehall: Popular Culture and Politics of Identity in Jamaica.* Mona, Jamaica: University of the West Indies Press.

Hopper, Paul. 2007. *Understanding Cultural Globalization.* Cambridge, MA: Polity Press.

Howard, M. 1989. *Dependence and Development in Barbados, 1945–1985.* Bridgetown, Barbados: Caribbean Research and Publications.

Hsieh, Ching-Chi, and M. D. Pugh. 1993. "Poverty, Income Inequality, and Violent Crime: A Meta-Analysis of Recent Aggregate Data Studies." *Criminal Justice Review* 18 (2): 182–202.

Hunja, Robert. 2015. "Here Are 10 Ways to Fight Corruption." World Bank, December 8. worldbank.org/governance/here-are-10-ways -fight-corruption.

Hussmanns, Ralf, Farhad Mehran, and Vijay Verma. 1990. *Surveys of Economically Active Population, Employment, Unemployment and Underemployment: An ILO Manual of Concepts and Methods.* Geneva: International Labour Office.

Hutchinson, M. K., L. S. Jemmott, E. B. Wood, H. Hewitt, E. Kahwa, N. Waldron, and B. Bonaparte. 2007. "Culture-Specific Factors Contributing to HIV Risk among Jamaican Adolescents." *Journal of the Association of Nurses in AIDS Care* 18 (2): 35–47.

Hutton, Clinton. 2009. "The Revival Table: Feasting with the Ancestors and Spirits." *Jamaica Journal* 32 (1–2): 18–31.

ILO (International Labour Office). 1977. *Meeting Basic Needs: Strategies for Eradicating Mass Poverty and Unemployment.* World Employment Conference. Geneva: ILO.

ILO (International Labour Office). 1983. *Bulletin of Labour Statistics.* Geneva: ILO.

ILO (International Labour Office). 2011. *Estimates and Projections of the Economically Active Population: 1990–2020: Methodological Descriptions.* Geneva: ILO.

ILO (International Labour Office). 2014. *World of Work Report 2014: Developing with Jobs.* Geneva: ILO.

ILO (International Labour Office). 2015. *Key Indicators of the Labor Market,* 9th ed. Geneva: ILO.

IMF (International Monetary Fund). 2005. *Eastern Caribbean Currency Union: Selected Issues.* www.imf.org/en/Publications/CR/Issues/2016/12/31/Eastern-Caribbean-Currency-Union-Selected-Issues-18520.

IMF (International Monetary Fund). 2014a. *Barbados: Staff Report for the 2013 Article IV Consultation.* Country Report 14/52, February. Washington, DC: IMF.

IMF (International Monetary Fund). 2014b. *Jamaica.* Country Report 14/85, March. Washington, DC: IMF.

IMF (International Monetary Fund). 2018a. "IMF Concludes Visit to Jamaica." December 7. www.imf.org/en/News/Articles/2018/12/07/pr18459-imf-staff-concludes-visit-to-jamaica.

IMF (International Monetary Fund). 2018b. "Jamaica: 2018 Article IV Consultation." April 16. www.imf.org/en/Publications/CR/Issues/2018/04/16/Jamaica-2018-Article-IV-Consultation-Third-Review-Under-the-Stand-By-Arrangement-and-Request-45801.

IMF (International Monetary Fund). 2019. "IMF Reaches Staff Level Agreement on the First Review of Barbados' Economic Program under the Extended Fund Facility." Press release 19/172, IMF.

Ince, B. A. 2012. *Black Meteors: The Caribbean in International Track and Field.* Kingston, Jamaica: Ian Randle.

International Finance Corporation. 2011. "Public-Private Partnership Stories. Jamaica: Air Jamaica." Washington, DC: World Bank Group. www.ifc.org/wps/wcm/connect/4ceb7d00498391e08654d6336b93d75f/PPPStories_Jamaica_AirJamaica.pdf?MOD=AJPERES.

Irving, Rachel. 2010. "Charting the Ancestry of Elite Jamaican and US Sprinters." In *Jamaican Gold: Jamaican Sprinters,* ed. R. Irving and V. Charlton, 5–10. Kingston, Jamaica: University of the West Indies Press.

Irving, Rachael, and Vilma Charlton. 2010. "Why Jamaica Rules in Sprinting: University Research Explores the Reasons." In *Jamaican Gold: Jamaican Sprinters,* ed. R. Irving and V. Charlton, 1–4. Kingston, Jamaica: University of the West Indies Press.

Irving, Rachael, Vilma Charlton, Errol Morrison, Aldeam Facey, and Oral Buchanan. 2013. "Demographic Characteristics of World Class Jamaican Sprinters." *Scientific World Journal* 2013 (3), article 670217.

Ishida, K., P. Stupp, and O. McDonald. 2011. "Prevalence and Correlates of Sexual Risk Behavior among Jamaican Adolescents." *International Perspectives on Sexual and Reproductive Health* 37 (1): 6–15.

Jaitman, L., ed. 2017. *The Costs of Crime and Violence: New Evidence and Insights in Latin America and the Caribbean.* Washington, DC: Inter-American Development Bank.

Jamaica Constabulary Force. 2011. *Three-Year Anti-Gang Strategic Plan.*

James, C. L. R. 1963. *Beyond a Boundary.* London: Hutchinson.

Jankowski, Martin. 1991. *Islands in the Street: Gangs and American Urban Society.* Berkeley: University of California Press.

Jefferson, Owen. 1972. *The Post-War Economic Development of Jamaica.* Kingston, Jamaica: Institute of Social and Economic Research.

Jefferson, T. 1787. "Extract from Thomas Jefferson to William S. Smith." Jefferson quotes, Monticello website. http://tjrs.monticello .org/letter/100.

Jeffrey, Duncan. 1980. *Education, Economy and Class in Colonial Jamaica: 1700–1944.* MA thesis, McMaster University.

Jekyll, W. (1907) 2005. *Jamaican Song and Story.* London: D. Nutt. Repr. Mineola, NY: Dover.

Jones, Cecily. 2007. *Engendering Whiteness: White Women and Colonialism in Barbados and North Carolina, 1627–1865.* Manchester, UK: Manchester University Press.

Kaba, Amadu J. 2008. "Sex Ratio at Birth and Racial Differences: Why Do Black Women Give Birth to More Females than Non-Black Women?" *African Journal of Reproductive Health* 12 (3): 139–150.

Kant, I. (1795) 1986. "Toward Perpetual Peace: A Philosophical Sketch." In *Toward Perpetual Peace and Other Writings on Politics, Peace and History,* 67–109. New Haven: Yale University Press.

Kassalow, Everett M., ed. 1968. *The Role of Social Security in Economic Development.* Washington, DC: U.S. Department of Health, Education and Welfare.

Keagy, Thomas. 1972. "The Poor Whites of Barbados." *Revista de historia de América* 73/74: 9–52.

Keane, John. 2004. *Violence and Democracy.* Cambridge: Cambridge University Press.

Kerr, M. 1963. *Personality and Conflict in Jamaica.* London: Collins.

King, Damien, and Anita Kiddoe. 2010. "Achieving Fiscal Sustainability in Jamaica: The JDX and Beyond." Kingston, Jamaica: Caribbean Policy Research Institute.

King, Ruby. n.d. "Education in the British Caribbean: The Legacy of the Nineteenth Century." http://www.educoas.org/Portal/bdigital /contenido/interamer/BkIACD/Interamer/Interamerhtml/Millerhtml /mil_king.htm.

Kiple, Kenneth F. 1984. *The Caribbean Slave: A Biological History.* Cambridge: Cambridge University Press.

Kirkpatrick, Colin, and David Tennant. 2002. "Responding to Financial Crisis: The Case of Jamaica." *World Development* 30 (11): 1933–1950.

Kleck, G., and D. Jackson. 2016. "What Kind of Joblessness Affects Crime? A National Case-Control Study of Serious Property Crime." *Journal of Quantitative Criminology* 32 (4): 489–513.

Klein, Herbert, and Stanley L. Engerman. 1978. "Fertility Differentials between Slaves in the United States and the British West Indies: A Note on Lactation Practices and Their Possible Implications." *William and Mary Quarterly* 3 (35): 357–374.

Knowles, William H. 1956. "Social Consequences of Economic Change in Jamaica." *Annals of the American Academy of Political and Social Science* 305: 134–144.

Knox, A. J. G. 1977. "Opportunities and Opposition: The Rise of Jamaica's Black Peasantry and the Nature of Planter Resistance." *Caribbean Review of Sociology and Anthropology* 14 (4): 381–395.

Kohli, Atul. 1999. "Where Do High-Growth Political Economies Come From? The Japanese Lineage of Korea's 'Developmental State.'" In *The Developmental State,* ed. Meredith Woo-Cumings, 93–136. Ithaca: Cornell University Press.

Kolodko, Grzegorz W. 2006. "Institutions, Policies and Economic Development." UNU-WIDER Research Paper 2006/21, United Nations University. www.wider.unu.edu/publications/working -papers/research-papers/2006/en_GB/rp2006-21.

Krahn, H., T. Hartnagel, and J. Gartrell. 1986. "Income Inequality and Homicide Rates: Cross-National Data and Criminological Theories." *Criminology* 24 (2): 269–294.

Krugman, P. 1991. "History and Industry Location: The Case of the Manufacturing Belt." *American Economic Review* 81 (2): 80–83.

Lacey, Terry. 1977. *Violence and Politics in Jamaica, 1960–1970.* Manchester, UK: Manchester University Press.

LaFree, Gary, and Andromachi Tseloni. 2006. "Democracy and Crime: A Multilevel Analysis of Homicide Trends in 44 Countries, 1950–2000." *Annals of the American Academy of Political and Social Science* 605: 26–49.

Lambert, David. 2005. *White Creole Culture, Politics, and Identity during the Age of Abolition.* New York: Cambridge University Press.

Layne, Anthony. 1979. "Race, Class and Development in Barbados." *Caribbean Quarterly* 25 (1/2): 40–51.

Lazarus-Black, M. 2008. "Vanishing Complainants: The Place of Violence in Family, Gender, Work, and Law." *Caribbean Studies* 36 (1): 25–51.

Lee, Matthew. 2001. "Population Growth, Economic Inequality, and Homicide." *Deviant Behavior* 22 (6): 491–516.

Le Franc, Elsie, ed. 1994. *Consequences of Structural Adjustment: A Review of the Jamaican Experience.* Kingston, Jamaica: Canoe Press.

Le Franc, Elsie. 1996. "Petty Trading and Labour Mobility: Higglers in the Kingston Metropolitan Area." In Hart, *Women and the Sexual Division of Labour in the Caribbean,* 103–138.

Le Franc, E., M. Samms-Vaughan, I. Hambleton, K. Fox, and D. Brown. 2008. "Interpersonal Violence in Three Caribbean Countries: Barbados, Jamaica, and Trinidad and Tobago." *Pan-American Journal of Public Health* 24 (6): 409–421.

Letts, Richard. 2003. "The Effects of Globalisation on Music in Five Contrasting Countries: Australia, Germany, Nigeria, the Philippines, and Uruguay." International Music Council, UNESCO, Paris. October. www.imc-cim.org/mmap/pdf/int-dl-finrep-brief-e.pdf.

Levi, Darrell. 1989. *Michael Manley: The Making of a Leader.* Kingston, Jamaica: Heinemann.

Le Vine, Victor T. 2000. "Violence and the Paradox of Democratic Renewal: A Preliminary Assessment." *Terrorism and Political Violence* 12 (3–4): 261–292.

Levitsky, Steven, and Maria Murillo. 2009. "Variation in Institutional Strength." *Annual Review of Political Science* 12: 115–133.

Levitt, K. 1996. "From De-Colonialisation to Neo-Liberalism: What Have We Learned about Development?" In *The Critical Tradition of Caribbean Political Economy: The Legacy of George Beckford,* ed. K. P. Levitt and M. Witter. Kingston, Jamaica: Ian Randle.

Levitt, Peggy. 2001. *The Transnational Villagers.* Berkeley: University of California Press.

Levy, H. 1995. "Jamaica Welfare, Growth and Decline." *Social and Economic Studies* 44 (2/3): 349–357.

Levy, J. S. 2013. "Interstate War and Peace." In *Handbook of International Relations,* ed. W. Carlesnaes, T. Risse, and B. A. Simmons, 2nd ed., 581–606. Los Angeles: Sage.

Lewin, Olive. 2000. *Rock It Come Over: The Folk Music of Jamaica.* Kingston, Jamaica: University of the West Indies Press.

Lewis, W. Arthur. 1960. *The Theory of Economic Growth.* London: Allen and Unwin.

Ligon, Richard. (1657) 2011. *A True and Exact History of the Island of Barbados.* Indianapolis: Hackett.

Lijphart A. 1977. *Democracy in Plural Societies: A Comparative Exploration.* New Haven: Yale University Press.

Lin, Ming-Jen. 2007. "Does Democracy Increase Crime? The Evidence from International Data." *Journal of Comparative Economics* 35 (3): 467–483.

Lipton, M. 1977. *Why Poor People Stay Poor: Urban Bias in World Development.* Cambridge, MA: Harvard University Press.

Lizardo, Omar. 2010. "Culture and Stratification." In *Handbook of Cultural Sociology,* ed. John Hall, Laura Grindstaff, and Ming-Cheng Lo, 305–315. New York: Routledge.

Lomax, A. 1968. *Folk Song Style and Culture.* Washington, DC: American Association for the Advancement of Science.

Long, Anton V. 1956. *Jamaica and the New Order: 1927–1947.* Mona, Jamaica: Institute of Social and Economic Research.

Look Lai, Walton. 2004. *Indentured Labor, Caribbean Sugar: Chinese and Indian Migrants to the British West Indies, 1838–1918.* Baltimore: Johns Hopkins University Press.

Lowenthal, David. 1957. "The Population of Barbados." *Social and Economic Studies* 6 (4): 445–501.

Lowenthal, David. 1978. *West Indian Societies.* New York: Oxford University Press.

Lukes, S. 2005. *Power: A Radical View.* New York: Palgrave.

Mackey, Wade. 2004. "Violent Crimes and the Loss of Fathers: Beyond the Long Run." In *The Cultural Shaping of Violence: Victimization, Escalation, Response,* ed. Myrdene Anderson, 67–81. West Lafayette, IN: Purdue University Press.

MacMillan, W. M. 1936. *Warning from the West Indies.* Harmondsworth, UK: Penguin.

Mangan J. 1998. *The Games Ethic and Imperialism: Aspects of the Diffusion of an Ideal.* London: Frank Cass.

Manley, M. 1987. *Up the Down Escalator: Development and the International Economy: A Jamaican Case Study.* London: Andre Deutsch.

Manley, Rachel. 2000. *Slipstream: A Daughter Remembers.* Toronto: Key Porter Books.

Mansfield, Edward, and Jack Snyder. 2007. *Electing to Fight: Why Emerging Democracies Go to War.* Cambridge, MA: MIT Press.

Mantzavinos, C. 2001. *Individuals, Institutions, and Markets.* New York: Cambridge University Press.

Mantzavinos, C., and D. North. 2004. "Learning, Institutions, and Economic Performance." *Perspectives on Politics* 2 (1): 75–84.

Manuel, P. 1988. *Popular Music of the Non-Western World.* New York: Oxford University Press.

Manuel, Peter, with Kenneth Bilby and Michael Largey. 1995. *Caribbean Currents: Caribbean Music from Rumba to Reggae.* Philadelphia: Temple University Press.

Manwaring, Max. 2007. "A Contemporary Challenge to State Sovereignty: Gangs and Other Illicit Transnational Criminal Organization in Central America, El Salvador." US Army War College, Carlisle, Pennsylvania. https://ssi.armywarcollege.edu /pdffiles/PUB837.pdf.

Marsala, Vincent. 1967. "Sir John Peter Grant, Governor of Jamaica, 1866–1874: An Administrative History." PhD dissertation, Louisiana State University.

Marshall, W. 2007. "Routes, Rap, Reggae: Hearing the Histories of Hip-Hop and Reggae Together." PhD dissertation, University of Wisconsin.

Marshall, W. 2015. "Hip-Hop's Irrepressible Refashionability: Phases in the Cultural Production of Black Youth." In *The Cultural*

Matrix: Understanding Black Youth, ed. O. Patterson and E. Fosse. Cambridge, MA: Harvard University Press.

Marshall, Woodville. 1993. "Peasant Development in the West Indies since 1838." In *Caribbean Freedom,* ed. Hilary Beckles and Verene Shepherd. Kingston, Jamaica: Ian Randle.

Matsangou, Elizabeth. 2018. "The Precarious Balancing Act Facing Jamaica." *World Finance,* London, October 22. https://www .worldfinance.com/strategy/the-precarious-balancing-act-facing -jamaica.

Mau, James A. 1968. *Social Change and Images of the Future: A Study of the Pursuit of Progress in Jamaica.* Cambridge, MA: Schenkman.

Maunder, F. W. 1962. *Employment in an Underdeveloped Area: Survey of Kingston, Jamaica.* New Haven: Yale University Press.

Mayhew, Marriott. 1968. "The Marriott Mayhew Report, 1933." In *Reports and Repercussions in West Indian Education, 1835–1933,* ed. Shirley Gordon. London: Ginn.

McEvoy, Claire, and Gergely Hideg. 2017. "Global Violent Deaths 2017: Time to Decide." Report, Small Arms Survey, Geneva, December.

McRae, Donald. 2010. "Cradle of Champions Where Jamaican Sprinters Earn Their Spurs." *Guardian,* April 1.

Meeks, Brian. 2000. *Narratives of Rebellion: Jamaica, Trinidad, and the Caribbean.* Kingston, Jamaica: University of the West Indies Press.

Meier, Gerald M., ed. 1989. *Leading Issues in Economic Development.* New York: Oxford University Press.

Menard, Russell R. 2006. *Sweet Negotiations: Sugar, Slavery, and Plantation Agriculture in Early Barbados.* Charlottesville: University of Virginia Press.

Messner, S. 1980. "Income Inequality and Murder Rates: Some Cross-National Findings." *Comparative Social Research* 3: 185–198.

Meyer, John W. 1987. "The World Polity and the Authority of the Nation-State." In *Institutional Structure: Constituting State, Society, and the Individual,* ed. G. M. Thomas, J. W. Meyer, F. O. Ramirez, and J. Boli, 41–70. Beverly Hills, CA: Sage.

Meyer, John W., and Brian Rowan. 1977. "Institutionalized Organizations: Formal Structure as Myth and Ceremony." *American Journal of Sociology* 83 (2): 340–363.

Michnik, Adam. 1998. "An Anatomy of Dictatorship." *Index on Censorship* 27 (1): 17–24.

Mills, G., and P. Robertson. 1974. "The Attitudes and Behavior of the Senior Civil Service in Jamaica." *Social and Economic Studies* 23 (2): 311–343.

Ministry of Labour. 2018. "Social Partnership." Government of Barbados. https://labour.gov.bb/social-partnership/.

Ministry of National Security. 2017. "Five-Pillar Strategy for Crime Prevention and Citizen Security." Government of Jamaica. https://mns.gov.jm/content/five-pillar-strategy-crime-prevention-and-citizen-security.

Minkov, M. 2009. "Risk-Taking Reproductive Competition Explains National Murder Rates Better than Socioeconomic Inequality." *Cross-Cultural Research* 43 (1): 3–29.

Minto-Coy, Indianna D. 2011. "Social Partnership and Development: Implications for the Caribbean." Caribbean Paper No. 12, Centre for International Governance Innovation, Waterloo, Canada.

Mintz, Sidney. 1961. "The Question of Caribbean Peasantries: A Comment." *Caribbean Studies* 1: 31–34.

Mintz, Sidney. 1974. "The Origins of Reconstituted Peasantries." In *Caribbean Transformations.* Baltimore: Johns Hopkins University Press.

Mintz, Sidney. 1979. "The Rural Proletariat and the Problem of Rural Proletarian Consciousness." In *Peasants and Proletarians: The Struggles of Third World Workers,* ed. Robin Cohen, Peter C. W. Gutkind, and Phyllis Brazier. London: Hutchinson.

Mintz, Sidney. 1987. "The Historical Sociology of Jamaican Villages." In *AfroCaribbean Villages in a Historical Perspective,* ed. Charles V. Carnegie, 1–19. Kingston, Jamaica: Jamaica Publications.

Mintz, Sidney, and Douglas Hall. 1960. "The Origins of the Jamaican Internal Marketing System." In *Papers in Caribbean Anthropology,* ed. Sidney Mintz. New Haven: Yale University Publications in Anthropology, 57.

Moore, Brian L., and Michele Johnson. 2002. "Celebrating Christmas in Jamaica, 1865–1920: From Creole Carnival to 'Civilized' Convention." In *Jamaica in Slavery and Freedom: History, Heritage, and Culture,* ed. Kathleen E. Monteith and Glen Richards, 144–178. Kingston, Jamaica: University of the West Indies Press.

Moore, R. 2015. *The Bolt Supremacy: Inside Jamaica's Sprint Factory.* London: Yellow Jersey Press.

Morgan, Edmund. 1975. *American Slavery, American Freedom: The Ordeal of Colonial Virginia.* New York: Norton.

Morrison, E., and P. Cooper. 2006. "Some Bio-Medical Mechanisms in Athletic Prowess." *West Indian Medical Journal* 55 (3): 205–209.

Moser, Caroline, and Jeremy Holland. 1997. "Urban Poverty and Violence in Jamaica." Report 16309, World Bank, Washington, DC.

Mottley, Mia. 2018. "Prime Minister Mia Mottley Addresses Barbados Following a 2nd Session with the Social Partnership." *Bajan Reporter,* June 4.

Mousseau, M. 2009. "The Social Market Roots of Democratic Peace." *International Security* 33 (4): 52–86.

Mousseau, Michael, and Yuhand Shi. 1999. "A Test for Reverse Causality in the Democratic Peace Relationship." *Journal for Peace Research* 36 (6): 639–663.

Munroe, Trevor. 1972. *The Politics of Constitutional Decolonization in Jamaica.* Mona, Jamaica: Institute of Social and Economic Research, University of the West Indies.

Murad, A. 2016. "Usain Bolt and Why Jamaican Sprinters Are So Fast." *Financial Times,* August 15.

Neapolitan, Jerome. 2003. "Explaining Variation in Crime Victimization across Nations and within Nations." *International Criminal Justice Review* 13 (1): 76–89.

Neely, Daniel. 2007. "Calling All Singers, Musicians, and Speechmakers: Mento Aesthetics and Jamaica's Early Recording Industry." *Caribbean Quarterly* 53 (4): 1–15.

Ness, Gayl D. 1970. "Planning and Implementation: Paradoxes in Rural Development." In *The Sociology of Economic Development,* ed. Gayl D. Ness. New York: Harper and Row.

Nettleford, Rex. 1972. *Mirror, Mirror: Identity, Race, and Protest in Jamaica.* Kingston, Jamaica: William Collins and Sangster.

Neumayer, E. 2003. "Good Policy Can Lower Violent Crime: Evidence from a Cross-National Panel of Homicide Rates, 1980–1997." *Journal of Peace Research* 40 (6): 619–640.

New Economics Foundation. 2016. *Happy Planet Index.* London.

Newman, Margaret, and Elsie Le Franc. 1994. "The Small-Farm Sub-Sector: Is There Life after Structural Adjustment?" In Le Franc, *Consequences of Structural Adjustment.*

Newman, Simon. 2013. *A New World of Labor: The Development of Plantation Slavery in the British Atlantic.* Philadelphia: University of Pennsylvania Press.

Newton, Melanie. 2008. *The Children of Africa in the Colonies: Free People of Color in Barbados in the Age of Emancipation.* Baton Rouge: Louisiana State University Press.

Nisbett, R. E., and D. Cohen. 1996. *Culture of Honor: The Psychology of Violence in the South.* Boulder, CO: Westview Press.

North, Douglass C. 1990. *Institutions, Institutional Change, and Economic Performance.* Cambridge: Cambridge University Press.

Olson, Mancur. 1965. *The Logic of Collective Action: Public Goods and the Theory of Groups.* Cambridge, MA: Harvard University Press.

Overseas Development Institute. 1978. Briefing Paper No. 5, ODI, London, December. https://www.odi.org/sites/odi.org.uk/files/odi -assets/publications-opinion-files/6616.pdf.

Owen, John M. 1994. "Give Democratic Peace a Chance? How Liberalism Produces Democratic Peace." *International Security* 19 (2): 87–125.

Oxford Economics. 2012. *Travel and Tourism as a Driver of Economic Development in Jamaica.* March. www.caribbean hotelandtourism.com/downloads/TEOxford-TravelTourism Jamaica032112.pdf.

Papaioannou, Elias, and Gregorios Siourounis. 2007. "Democratization and Growth." Working Paper 07-13, Centre for Economic Development and Institutions, Brunel University, West London.

Parkins, C. P. 2010. "Push and Pull Factors of Migration." *American Review of Political Economy* 8 (2): 6–24.

Partridge, C. 2010. *Dub Inna Babylon: Understanding the Evolution and Significance of Dub Reggae in Jamaica and Britain from King Tubby to Post-Punk.* Sheffield, UK: Equinox.

Paton, Diana. 2004. *No Bond but the Law: Punishment, Race, and Gender in Jamaican State Formation, 1780–1870.* Durham, NC: Duke University Press.

Patterson, O. 1964. *The Children of Sisyphus.* London: Hutchinson.

Patterson, O. 1966. "The Dance Invasion of Britain: On the Cultural Diffusion of Jamaican Popular Arts." *New Society,* 207.

Patterson, O. 1967. *The Sociology of Slavery: Jamaica, 1655–1834.* London: McGibbon and Kee.

Patterson, O. 1970. "Slavery and Slave Revolts: A Socio-Historical Analysis of the First Maroon War, Jamaica 1655–1740." *Social and Economic Studies* 19 (3): 289–325.

Patterson, O. 1973. *The Condition of the Low Income Population in the Kingston Metropolitan Area.* Kingston, Jamaica: Office of the Prime Minister.

Patterson, O. 1975. "Context and Choice in Ethnic Allegiance: A Theoretical Framework and Caribbean Case Study." In *Ethnicity: Theory and Experience,* ed. Nathan Glazer and Daniel P. Moynihan. Cambridge, MA: Harvard University Press.

Patterson, O. 1977. *Community Councils in Jamaica: A Critical Appraisal.* Kingston, Jamaica: Office of the Prime Minister.

Patterson, O. 1982. "Persistence, Continuity, and Change in the Jamaican Working Class Family." *Journal of Family History* 7 (2): 135–161.

Patterson, O. 1987. "The Emerging West Atlantic System: Migration, Culture and Underdevelopment in the U.S. and Caribbean." In *Population in an Interacting World,* ed. William Alonso. Cambridge, MA: Harvard University Press.

Patterson, Orlando. 1991. *Freedom: Freedom in the Making of Western Culture.* New York: Basic Books.

Patterson, O. 2003–2004. "Ethnicity and Caribbean Development in Hemispheric Perspective: Eleventh Dr. Williams Lecture Delivered in 1993." In *The Faces of Man: Dr. Eric Williams Memorial Lectures.* Port of Spain, Trinidad: Central Bank of Trinidad and Tobago.

Patterson, O. 2014. "Making Sense of Culture." *Annual Review of Sociology* 40 (1): 1–30.

Patterson, O. 2015. "The Social and Cultural Matrix of Black Youth." In *The Cultural Matrix: Understanding Black Youth,* ed. Orlando Patterson with Ethan Fosse, 45–135. Cambridge, MA: Harvard University Press.

Permanent Mission of Jamaica to the UN. 2017. "10-Year Action Plan to Eliminate Gender-Based Violence Launched." www.un.int/jamaica/news/10-year-action-plan-eliminate-gender-based-violence-launched.

Pfau, Wade. 2006. "Predicting the Medal Wins at the 2006 Winter Olympics: An Econometrics Approach." *Korean Economic Review* 22 (2): 233–247.

Pitsiladis, Y., R. Irving, V. Charlton, and R. Scott. 2010. "'White' Men Can't Run: Where Is the Scientific Evidence?" In *The Anthropology of Sport and Human Movement: A Biocultural Perspective*, ed. R. Sands and L. Sands, 243–262. New York: Lexington Books.

Planning Institute of Jamaica. 2009. *Vision 2030 Jamaica National Development Plan*. www.vision2030.gov.jm/National -Development-Plan.

Planning Research and Development Unit. 2000. *Historical Developments of Education in Barbados*. Bridgetown, Barbados: Ministry of Education.

Portes, A., and R. Rumbaut. 1990. *Immigrant America*. Berkeley: University of California Press.

Post, Ken. 1978. *Arise Ye Starvelings: The Jamaican Labor Rebellion of 1938 and Its Aftermath*. The Hague: Martinus Nijhoff.

Post, Ken. 1981. *Strike the Iron: A Colony at War, Jamaica 1939–1945*. The Hague: Humanities Press.

Pridemore, William. 2011. "A Reassessment of the Inequality-Homicide Relationship in Cross-National Studies." *British Journal of Criminology* 51 (5): 739–772.

Przeworski, A., M. E. Alvarez, J. A. Cheibub, and F. Limongi. 2000. *Democracy and Development: Political Institutions and Well-Being in the World, 1950–1990*. Cambridge: Cambridge University Press.

Rabushka, Alvin, and Kenneth Shepsle. 1972. *Politics in Plural Societies: A Theory of Democratic Instability*. Columbus, OH: Merrill.

Ragatz, L. J. 1931. "Absentee Landlordism in the British Caribbean, 1750–1833." *Agricultural History* 5 (1): 7–26.

Ragatz, L. J. 1963. *The Fall of the Planter Class in the British Caribbean, 1763–1833*. New York: Octagon.

Rapoport, David, and Leonard Weinberg, eds. 2012. *The Democratic Experience and Political Violence*. New York: Routledge.

Ray, James Lee. 1998. "Does Democracy Cause Peace?" *Annual Review of Political Science* 1 (1): 27–46.

Reckord, Mary. 1968. "The Jamaican Slave Rebellion of 1831." *Past and Present* 40 (3): 108–125.

Record, Verena. 1998. "From Burru Drums to Reggae Ridims: The Evolution of Rasta Music." In *Chanting Down Babylon: The*

Rastafari Reader, ed. N. S. Murrell, W. D. Spencer, and A. S. McFarlane, 231–252. Philadelphia: Temple University Press.

Reddy, Sheshalatha. 2017. *British Empire and the Literature of Rebellion: Revolting Bodies, Laboring Subjects.* Cham, Switzerland: Palgrave Macmillan.

Reiche, Danyel. 2016. *Success and Failure of Countries at the Olympics.* New York: Routledge.

Reiter, Dan. 2018. "Is Democracy a Cause of Peace?" *Oxford Encyclopedia of Empirical International Relations Theory.* Oxford: Oxford University Press.

Reporters without Borders. 2018. "World Press Freedom Index, 2018." https://rsf.org/en/ranking/2018.

Richardson, Bonham. 1985. *Panama Money in Barbados, 1900–1920.* Knoxville: University of Tennessee Press.

Richardson, Bonham. 1997. *Economy and Environment in the Caribbean: Barbados and the Windwards in the Late 1800s.* Gainesville: University of Florida Press.

Riley, James. 2005. *Poverty and Life Expectancy: The Jamaica Paradox.* New York: Cambridge University Press.

Ritzer, G., and M. Ryan. 2002. "The Globalization of Nothing." *Social Thought and Research* 25 (1/2): 51–81.

Rivera, R., W. Marshall, and D. Hernandez. 2009. *Reggaeton.* Durham, NC: Duke University Press.

Roberts, G. W. 1955. "Emigration from Barbados." *Social and Economic Studies* 4 (3): 245–288.

Roberts, G. W. 1957. *The Population of Jamaica.* Cambridge: Cambridge University Press.

Robertson, R. 1992. *Globalization: Social Theory and Global Culture.* London: Sage.

Robertson, R. 1995. "Glocalization: Time-Space and Homogeneity-Heterogeneity." In *Global Modernities,* ed. M. Featherstone, S. Lash, and R. Robertson, 25–44. London: Sage.

Robinson, Corey. 2018. "Despair in Denham Town: ZOSO Peace Dream Becomes Bloody Nightmare for Residents after Police and Soldiers Pull Out." *Gleaner,* April 22.

Robinson, D., E. Buck, and M. Cuthbert. 1991. *Music at the Margins: Popular Music and Global Cultural Diversity.* Newbury Park, CA: Sage.

Robinson, P. 2009. *Jamaican Athletics: A Model for 2012 and the World.* London: BlackAmber.

Robotham, Don. 1981. "The Notorious Riot: The Socio-Economic and Political Base of Paul Bogle's Revolt." Working Paper 28, Institute of Social and Economic Research, Mona, Jamaica.

Robotham, Don. 2000. "Blackening the Jamaican Nation: The Travails of a Black Bourgeoisie in a Globalized World." *Identities: Global Studies in Culture and Power* 7 (1): 1–37.

Robotham, Don. 2018. "Crisis in High School Education." *Sunday Gleaner*, April 8.

Rodriguez, Junius. 2006. *Encyclopedia of Slave Resistance and Rebellion*. Westport, CT: Greenwood Press.

Rodrik, Dani, Arvind Subramanian, and Francesco Trebbi. 2004. "Institutions Rule: The Primacy of Institutions over Geography and Integration in Economic Development." *Journal of Economic Growth* 9 (2): 131–165.

Roediger, David. 2007. *The Wages of Whiteness: Race and the Making of the American Working Class*. New York: Verso.

Rose, Andre K., and Mark Spiegel. 2007. "Offshore Financial Centres: Parasites or Symbionts?" *Economic Journal* 117 (523): 1310–1335.

Rummel, R. J. 1983. "Libertarianism and International Violence." *Journal of Conflict Resolution* 27 (1): 27–71.

Russett, B., and J. Oneal. 2001. *Triangulating Peace: Democracy, Interdependence, and International Organizations*. New York: Norton.

Salmon, L. 2008. "The Second Spanish Conquest of Jamaica." *Daily Gleaner*, September 8.

Samms-Vaughan, M. E., S. Williams, and J. Brown. 2005. "Disciplinary Practices among Parents of Six Year Olds in Jamaica." *Journal of the Children's Issues Coalition* 1: 58–70.

Samuda, P. M., R. A. Cook, C. M. Cook, and F. Henry. 1998. "Identifying Foods Commonly Consumed by the Jamaican Population: The Focus Group Approach." *International Journal of Food Sciences and Nutrition* 49 (1): 79–86.

Sandiford, Keith A. 1998. *Cricket Nurseries of Colonial Barbados*. Kingston, Jamaica: University of the West Indies Press.

Santiago, C. 1992. *Labor in the Puerto Rican Economy*. New York: Praeger.

Satchell, Veront. 1990. *From Plots to Plantations: Land Transactions in Jamaica, 1866–1900*. Mona, Jamaica: Institute of Social and Economic Research.

Schipke, Alfred. 2011. "Offshore Financial Centers (OFCs): Opportunities and Challenges for the Caribbean." Presentation at the Conference on Economic Growth, Development and Macroeconomic Policy (sponsored by University of the West Indies, Central Bank of Barbados and IMF), Bridgetown, Barbados, January 27–28.

Schmid, Alex. 1992. "Terrorism and Democracy." *Terrorism and Political Violence* 4 (4): 14–25.

Schuler, Monica. 1980. *Alas, Alas, Kongo: A Social History of Indentured African Immigration into Jamaica, 1841–1865.* Baltimore: Johns Hopkins University Press.

Schwartz, Stuart B. 2015. *A Sea of Storms: A History of Hurricanes in the Greater Caribbean from Columbus to Katrina.* Princeton: Princeton University Press.

Scott, James C. 1985. *Weapons of the Weak: Everyday Forms of Peasant Resistance.* New Haven: Yale University Press.

Scott, R., et al. 2010. "*ACTN3* and *ACE* Genotypes in Elite Jamaican and US Sprinters." *Medicine and Science in Sports and Exercise* 42 (1): 107–112.

Scoville, J. 1988. "Hewers of Wood and Drawers of Water: Incomes and Employment in the Traditional Unskilled Sector." *World Development* 16 (2): 305–316.

Selvaraju, R., P. Trapido, N. Santos, M. Lacasa, and A. Hayman. 2013. *Climate Change and Agriculture in Jamaica.* Rome: Food and Agriculture Organization of the UN.

Semmel, Bernard. 1962. *The Governor Eyre Controversy.* London: McGibbon and Kee.

Sethuraman, S. V., ed. 1981. *The Urban Informal Sector in Developing Countries.* Geneva: ILO.

Sheller, Mimi. 2001. *Democracy after Slavery: Black Publics and Peasant Radicalism in Haiti and Jamaica.* Gainesville: University Press of Florida.

Sheppard, Jill. 1977. *The "Redlegs" of Barbados: Their Origins and History.* Millwood, NY: KTO Press.

Sheridan, Richard. 1985. *Doctors and Slaves: A Medical and Demographic History of Slavery in the British West Indies, 1680–1834.* New York: Cambridge University Press.

Sheridan, Richard. 1995. "Strategies of Slave Subsistence: The Jamaican Case Reconsidered." In *From Chattel Slaves to Wage Slaves,* ed. Mary Turner. Bloomington: Indiana University Press.

Sives, Amanda. 2010. *Elections, Violence and the Democratic Process in Jamaica: 1944–2007*. Kingston, Jamaica: Ian Randle.

Sklair, L. 2002. *Globalization: Capitalism and Its Alternatives*. New York: Oxford University Press.

Small, Mario, David Harding, and Michele Lamont. 2010. "Reconsidering Culture and Poverty." *Annals of the American Academy of Political and Social Science* 629 (1): 6–27.

Small, Melvin, and David Singer. 1976. "The War-Proneness of Democratic Regimes, 1816–1965." *Jerusalem Journal of International Relations* 1 (4): 50–69.

Smith, D. E., and Gail Mosby. 2003. "Jamaican Child-Rearing Practices: The Role of Corporal Punishment." *Adolescence* 38 (150): 369–381.

Smith, Eliot R. 1994. "Procedural Knowledge and Processing Strategies in Social Cognition." In *Handbook of Social Cognition,* vol. 1: *Basic Processes,* ed. Robert S. Wyer Jr. and Thomas K. Srull, 99–152. Hillsdale, NJ: Lawrence Erlbaum Associates.

Smith, Godfrey. 2016. *Michael Manley: The Biography.* Kingston, Jamaica: Ian Randle.

Smith, M. G. 1971. *West Indian Family Structure.* Seattle: University of Washington Press.

Smith, M. G. 1983. "The Study of Needs and Provisions for Social Assistance." Unpublished manuscript. Department of Anthropology, Yale University, New Haven, CT.

Snyder, Jack L. 2000. *From Voting to Violence: Democratization and Nationalist Conflict.* New York: Norton.

Social Development Commission. 1974. "Community Development in Jamaica." *Community Development Journal* 9 (1): 40–42.

Solis, Luis G., and Francisco R. Aravena, eds. 2009. *Organized Crime in Latin America and the Caribbean: Summary of Articles.* San José, Costa Rica: FLACSO.

Standing, G. 1981a. *Labour Force Participation and Development.* Geneva: International Labor Office.

Standing, G. 1981b. *Unemployment and Female Labour: A Study of Labour Supply in Kingston, Jamaica.* New York: St. Martin's Press.

Steffens, Roger. 1998. "Bob Marley: Rasta Warrior." In *Chanting Down Babylon: The Rastafari Reader,* ed. N. S. Murrell, W. D. Spencer, and A. S. McFarlane, 253–265. Philadelphia: Temple University Press.

Stephens, Evelyne Huber, and John D. Stephens. 1986. *Democratic Socialism in Jamaica: The Political Movement and Social Transformation in Dependent Capitalism.* Princeton: Princeton University Press.

Stewart, F. 1989. "Summary of Discussions and Suggestions for Future Research." In *Fighting Urban Unemployment in Developing Countries,* ed. B. Salome. Paris: OECD.

Stiglitz, Joseph. 2019. "Progressive Capitalism Is Not an Oxymoron." *New York Times,* April 21.

Stolzoff, Norman. 2000. *Wake the Town, Tell the People.* Durham, NC: Duke University Press.

Stone, C. 1973. *Class, Race, and Political Behavior in Urban Jamaica.* Mona, Jamaica: Institute of Social and Economic Research.

Stone, C. 1983. *Democracy and Clientelism in Jamaica 1983.* New Brunswick, NJ: Transaction.

Stone, C. 1986. *Class, State, and Democracy in Jamaica.* New York: Praeger.

Stone, C. 1992. "Values, Norms, and Personality Development in Jamaica." Unpublished manuscript, March 23. http://gtuwi.tripod.com/stonearticle.htm.

Straw, K. H. 1953. "Some Preliminary Results of a Survey of Income and Consumption Patterns in a Sample of Households in Barbados." *Social and Economic Studies* 1 (4): 5–40.

Streeten, P. 1973. "A Critique of Concepts of Employment and Unemployment." In *Third World Employment: Problems and Strategy,* ed. Richard Jolly et al. Harmondsworth, UK: Penguin.

Streeten, P. 1979. "Basic Needs: Premises and Promises." *Journal of Policy Modeling* 1: 136–146.

Sturge, Joseph, and Thomas Harvey. 1838. *The West Indies in 1837.* London: Hamilton, Adams.

Sullivan, P. 2014. *Remixology: Tracing the Dub Diaspora.* London: Reaktion Books.

Tam, H. 2011. "U-shaped Female Labor Participation with Economic Development: Some Panel Data Evidence." *Economic Letters* 110 (2): 140–142.

Thomas, Clive Y. 1988. *The Poor and the Powerless: Economic Policy and Change in the Caribbean.* New York: Monthly Review Press.

Thomas, Damani, and Prudence Serju. 2009. "Explaining Jamaica's Growth Puzzle: A Comparative Growth Accounting Exercise with Other Caribbean Countries." *Business, Finance, and Economics in Emerging Economies* 4 (1): 39–72.

Thomas, Deborah A. 2004. *Modern Blackness: Nationalism, Globalization, and the Politics of Culture in Jamaica.* Durham, NC: Duke
University Press.

Thomas, Deborah. 2011. *Exceptional Violence: Embodied Citizenship in Transnational Jamaica.* Durham, NC: Duke University
Press.

Thomson, Ian. 2011. *The Dead Yard: A Story of Modern Jamaica.*
New York: Nation Books.

Thorne, Alfred P. 1955. "Size, Structure, and Growth of the Economy
of Jamaica." *Social and Economic Studies* (4 supp.): 1–112.

Tinbergen, Jan, coord. 1976. *Reshaping the International Order.*
Rome: Club of Rome.

Tinker, Keith L. 2011. *The Migration of Peoples from the Caribbean
to the Bahamas.* Gainesville: University Press of Florida.

Transparency International. 2013. "Holding Politicians to Account:
Asset Declarations." www.transparency.org/news/feature/holding
_politicians_to_account_asset_declarations.

Transparency International. 2016. "How to Stop Corruption: 5 Key
Ingredients." www.transparency.org/news/feature/how_to_stop
_corruption_5_key_ingredients.

Tsai, Ming-Chang. 2001. "Dependency, the State, and Class in
Neoliberal Transition of Taiwan." *Third World Quarterly* 22:
359–379.

Turner, Mary. 1995. "Chattel Slaves into Wage Slaves: A Jamaican
Case Study." In *From Chattel Slaves to Wage Slaves,* ed. Mary
Turner. Bloomington: Indiana University Press.

United Nations. 1970. *International Social Development Review.*
No. 2. New York: Department of Economic and Social Affairs,
United Nations.

United Nations. 1971a. *International Social Development Review.*
No. 3. New York: Department of Economic and Social Affairs,
United Nations.

United Nations. 1971b. *Popular Participation in Development:
Emerging Trends in Community Development.* ST/SOA/106. New
York: United Nations.

United Nations. 1973. *Self-Help Practices in Housing: Selected Case
Studies.* ST/ECA/183. New York: United Nations.

United Nations. 1978. *Transnational Corporations in World Development: A Re-Examination.* New York: UN Economic and Social
Council.

United Nations. 2014. *Human Development Report: 2013.* New York: UNDP.

UNODC (United Nations Office on Drugs and Crime). 2011. *Global Study of Homicide: Trends, Contexts, Data 2011.* Vienna: UNODC.

UNODC (United Nations Office on Drugs and Crime). 2014a. *Global Status Report on Violence Prevention, 2014.* Geneva: WHO Publications.

UNODC (United Nations Office on Drugs and Crime). 2014b. *World Drug Report.* Vienna: UN Publications.

UNODC (United Nations Office on Drugs and Crime) and World Bank. 2007. *Crime, Violence, and Development: Trends, Costs, and Policy Options in the Caribbean.* Washington, DC: World Bank.

U.S. Department of Labor. 1972. *Manpower: Promoting Employment and Reducing Poverty: The Caribbean.* Washington, DC: International Manpower Institute.

Van den Berghe, Pierre. 1972. *Race and Racism.* New York: John Wiley and Sons.

Veal, Michael. 2007. *Dub: Soundscapes and Shattered Songs in Jamaican Reggae.* Middletown, CT: Wesleyan University Press.

Vickery, Kenneth. 1974 "'Herrenvolk' Democracy and Egalitarianism in South Africa and the U.S. South." *Comparative Studies in Society and History* 16 (3): 309–328.

Virtue, E. 2012. "High Calorie Diet Killing Jamaicans: Obesity Soars as Consumers Gulp Down Fast Foods." *Gleaner,* December 16.

Wacquant, Loïc. 2016. "A Concise Genealogy and Anatomy of Habitus." *Sociological Review* 64 (1): 64–72.

Wagner, Roy. 1989. *Symbols That Stand for Themselves.* Chicago: University of Chicago Press.

Ward, E., D. Brown, and A. Butchart. 2009. "Results of an Exercise to Estimate the Costs of Interpersonal Violence in Jamaica." *West Indian Medical Journal* 58 (5): 447–451.

Ward, Michael D., and Kristian S. Gleditsch. 1998. "Democratizing for Peace." *American Political Science Review* 92 (1): 51–61.

Warner-Lewis, Maureen. 2002. "The Character of African-Jamaican Culture." In *Jamaica in Slavery and Freedom: History, Heritage, and Culture,* ed. Kathleen E. Monteith and Glen Richards, 89–114. Kingston, Jamaica: University of the West Indies Press.

Waszak Geary, Cynthia, et al. 2006. "Sexual Violence and Reproductive Health among Young People in Three Communities in Jamaica." *Journal of Interpersonal Violence* 21 (11): 1512–1533.

Watson, Hilbourne. 2000. "Global Neo-liberalism, the Third Technological Revolution, and Global 2000: A Perspective on Issues Affecting the Caribbean on the Eve of the Twenty-first Century." In *Contending with Destiny: The Caribbean in the Twenty-First Century,* ed. Kenneth Hall and Denis Benn, 382–446. Kingston, Jamaica: Ian Randle.

Watson, Karl. 1979. *The Civilised Island, Barbados: A Social History, 1750–1816.* Bridgetown, Barbados: Graphic Printers.

Watts, David. 1987. *The West Indies: Patterns of Development, Culture, and Environmental Change since 1492.* Cambridge: Cambridge University Press.

Watts, J., R. Mackay, D. Horton, A. Hall, B. Douthwaite, R. Chambers, and A. Acosta. 2003. "Institutional Learning and Change: An Introduction." ISNAR Discussion Paper 03-10, International Service for National Agricultural Research, The Hague, October. www.researchgate.net/publication/253441670_Institutional _Learning_and_Change_An Introduction.

Wedderburn, Maxine, Deborah Bourne, Veronica Samuels-Dixon, and Nadia Robinson. 2011. "Study of Female Sex Workers, Client Types and Risk Behavior in the Sex Work Industry in Jamaica."Population Services International/Caribbean, September. www.psi.org/wp-content/uploads/drupal/sites/default/files /publication_files/Report%20-%20Jamaica,%20FSW_0.pdf.

Weede, Erich. 1984. "Democracy and War Involvement." *Journal of Conflict Resolution* 28 (4): 649–664.

Weeks, J. 1973. "Does Employment Matter?" In *Third World Employment: Problems and Strategy,* ed. Richard Jolly et al. Harmondsworth, UK: Penguin.

Weis, Tony. 2004. "(Re-)Making the Case for Land Reform in Jamaica." *Social and Economic Studies* 53 (1): 35–72.

Weis, Tony. 2005. "A Precarious Balance: Neoliberalism, Crisis Management, and the Social Implosion in Jamaica." *Capital and Class* 29 (1): 115–147.

Weis, Tony. 2006. "The Rise, Fall, and Future of the Jamaican Peasantry." *Journal of Peasant Studies* 33 (1): 61–88.

West, Cornel. 2002. *Prophesy Deliverance: An Afro-American Revolutionary Christianity.* Louisville, KY: Westminster John Knox Press.

White, G. 1998. "The Evolution of Jamaican Music. Pt. 1. 'Proto Ska' to Ska." *Social and Economic Studies* 47 (1): 5–19.

Wignall, Mark. 2012. "Are Jamaicans Happy for the Wrong Reasons?" *Jamaica Observer,* June 21.

Williams, J., and V. Krane. 2001. "Psychological Characteristics of Peak Performance." In *Applied Sport Psychology: Personal Growth to Peak Performance,* ed. J. Williams, 37–147. Mountain View, CA: Mayfield.

Williams, Kareen. 2011. *The Evolution of Political Violence in Jamaica, 1940–1980.* PhD dissertation, Columbia University.

Williams, Raymond. 1977. *Marxism and Literature.* Oxford: Oxford University Press.

Williams, Rochelle. 2018. "Education Ministry to Increase Promotion of TVET in Secondary Schools." Jamaica Information Service News. https://jis.gov.jm/education-ministry-to-increase-promotion-of-tvet-in-secondary-schools/.

Willis, P. 1990. *Common Culture.* Boulder, CO: Westview.

Wint, V. 2012. *The Longer Run: A Daughter's Story of Arthur Wint.* Kingston: Ian Randle.

Witkin, R. 2003. *Adorno on Popular Culture.* London: Routledge.

Wolfe, David A. 1993. *Wolfe Report of the National Task Force on Crime.* https://informationja.files.wordpress.com/2012/06/wolfe-report-19931.pdf.

World Bank. 1971. *Current Economic Position and Prospects of Jamaica.* Vol. 1. Central America and the Caribbean Series. Washington, DC: World Bank.

World Bank. 1980. *World Development Report, 1980.* New York: Oxford University Press.

World Bank. 1994. *Report on the World Social Situation.* New York: Oxford University Press.

World Bank. 2001. *What Is Urban Upgrading? Reference for Administrators, Policy-makers, and Decision-makers.* Washington, DC: World Bank.

World Bank. 2004. *The Road to Sustained Growth in Jamaica.* Washington, DC: World Bank.

World Bank. 2014. *Country Partnership Strategy for Jamaica for the Period FY2014–2017.* Report 85158-JM. Washington, DC: Caribbean Country Management Unit. http://documents.worldbank.org/curated/en/2010/02/12.

World Bank. 2015a. *Jamaica Country Report.* Washington, DC: World Bank.

World Bank. 2015b. *Barbados Country Profile*. Washington, DC: World Bank.

World Bank. 2016. "Labor Force Participation Rate, Total (% of total Population Age 15+) (Modeled ILO Estimate)." http://data .worldbank.org/indicator/SL.TLF.CACT.ZS.

World Bank. 2018. "Human Capital Index: Country Briefs and Data: Jamaica." www.worldbank.org/en/publication/human -capital#Data.

Wyatt-Brown, Bertram. 1986. *Honor and Violence in the Old South.* New York: Oxford University Press.

Young, Kevin, William Bussink, and Parvez Hasan. 1980. *Malaysia: Growth and Equity in a Multiracial Society.* Baltimore: Johns Hopkins University Press.

Zoromé, Ahmed. 2007. "The Concept of Offshore Financial Centers: In Search of an Operational Definition." IMF Working Paper 07/87, International Monetary Fund, Washington, DC.

Acknowledgments

I learned much about Jamaica's current dilemmas, achievements, and prospects from my many conversations with friends and colleagues from the island, especially Noel Lyon, Grace Ann McDonnough-Lyon, Nigel Clarke, Rupika Delgoda, Eleanor Brown, and Chris Berry. Peter Phillips enlightened me about the complexities of violence, drug interdiction, and crime control in Jamaica, especially during a lengthy discussion at his home when he was the minister for national security.

I have been thinking, researching, and teaching about Jamaica and the broader Caribbean all my adult life. The foundation of these ideas goes back to my undergraduate days as a member of the first class of social science students at what was then the University College of the West Indies (now the University of the West Indies). It is no exaggeration to say that most of us in that class were obsessed with the past, present, and future development of the West Indies. Among those with whom I was most intellectually involved and who shaped my emerging thoughts were Norman Girvan and Walter Rodney. Norman was my graduate student flatmate for several years in London and later a colleague at the University of the West Indies. Walter was a fellow Chancellor Hall resident who helped in the preparation of my first sociological study—an ethnography of undergraduate life in Chancellor Hall—and was later a colleague at the University of the West Indies before being banned from Jamaica and, not long after, assassinated in Guyana. Soon after arriving in London, Norman, Walter, and I were summoned to the apartment of the great West Indian scholar and revolutionary C. L. R. James, where, every Friday evening for several months, we engaged in deep conversations on Marxism and its relevance to the understanding of underdevelopment in general, and in the Caribbean in particular. I learned an immense amount both from those conversations and from James's writings, especially for my studies on slavery, underdevelopment, and the culturally protean game of cricket. In addition, George Beckford and Lloyd Best, colleagues at the University of the West Indies and cofounders of the New World group of Caribbean social scientists, were important influences in my developing thoughts on the region. M. G. Smith, my main mentor at the University of the West Indies, was the person who first put the idea in my head that my destiny was to be a professional sociologist. He introduced me both to the study of sociology and to its applications to Jamaica and to West Indian societies more broadly. I was fortunate to have other undergraduate mentors who strongly disagreed with him, and with each other, in the study of the Caribbean—among them Raymond Smith, Lloyd Braithwaite, and George Roberts, from whom I learned about the many ways of approaching the study of the region as well as the art of constructive disagreement.

For feedback and encouragement on Chapter 1, I wish to thank Stanley Engerman and Daron Acemoglu. Burak Eskici provided useful preliminary research for an early version of the chapter. I have benefited from years of collaboration and teaching with Ethan Fosse, especially for work on the problem of violence and democracy, which contributed to the writing of Chapter 2. I have had numerous productive conversations on the difficult problem of how the past, especially slavery and colonialism, influences the present with Chris Muller, who cofounded the workshop in History, Culture, and Society with me when he was a graduate student at Harvard, and Zach Wehrwein, who now administers the workshop as well as my course on the Caribbean at Harvard.

Chapters 1 and 2 benefited greatly from the feedback I received at the workshops, seminars, and conferences where I presented them, especially the History, Culture, and Society Workshop at Harvard, the Comparative Research Workshop of Yale's Sociology Department, the 2014 annual conference of the Caribbean Studies Association, and the fiftieth anniversary commemoration of the transition of the University of the West Indies from a college of London University.

Several chapters in the book are based on my research and policy work for the government of Jamaica during my tenure as special advisor for social policy and development to Prime Minister Michael Manley. I owe him a debt of gratitude for encouraging me to leave my faculty position at the London School of Economics in order to help rebuild our country from the remains of the colonial past, for the opportunity he gave me to research and help change the lives of the urban poor, and for the many stimulating conversations we had together, in which his incisive comments on my reports, policy work, and ideas always led to improvements. A photograph from the Jamaican *Daily Gleaner* of "comrade leader" standing next to me as he introduced my urban upgrading project to his constituency holds pride of place in my collection of images from that period. Another prime minister, Portia Simpson, spoke candidly with me for the better part of an afternoon at Vale Royal, the elegant former residence of the colonial secretary and prime minister, on the problems of governing so difficult a place as Jamaica, especially as a woman in an island of patriarchal men. This was at a difficult time during her prime ministership, when she refused to meet with the press or with most prying scholars. So, thank you "Sista P"; I, and the readers of the 2007 column I wrote for the op-ed page of the *New York Times,* learned much from that interview. Rachel Manley's witty and perceptive observations on her famous family, and on the social and political intricacies of late colonial and decolonizing Jamaica, were also invaluable. Our public conversation in 2004 at the Celeste Auditorium of the New York Public

Library about her father and his times led me to think in novel ways about our little island. The final chapter of this work is due entirely to her, for, as I explained in the Introduction, I was able to write about Michael Manley only by way of my reflection on her deeply moving account of his last days.

Since I began my examination of Jamaica through the medium of the novel, *The Children of Sisyphus* being a literary prelude to my historical and sociological studies of the island, it was important for me to keep my connections to this domain. Another set of friends, Valerie Facey, her late husband, Maurice, and her daughter, the distinguished sculptor Laura Facey, along with the late Annabella and Peter Proudlock, have kept me involved with the rich artistic life of our country, for which I am truly grateful.

The comments of the two reviewers of the manuscript were extremely valuable, as were those of Andrew Kinney, my editor at Harvard University Press; Louise Robbins, manuscript editor; and Martin Schneider, copyeditor.

I am deeply grateful for the love, support, patience, and encouragement I have received over the years from my wife, Anita, as well as my three daughters, Kaia, Barbara, and Rhiannon—especially Kaia, who is just beginning to discover her Jamaican roots.

Three chapters first appeared in slightly different form in previous publications. Chapter 5 was published as "The Ritual of Cricket," *Jamaica Journal* 3 (1969): 22–25. Chapter 7 was published as "The Realities of Intervention in Alienated Cultures: A Jamaican Case Study," in Harvey Brooks, Lance Liebman, and Corinne Schelling, eds., *Public-Private Partnership: New Opportunities for Meeting Social Needs* (Cambridge, MA: Published for the American Academy of Arts and Sciences by Ballinger Publishing Company, 1984), chap. 6. Chapter 8 appeared as the foreword to Rachel Manley, *Slipstream: A Daughter Remembers* (Westland, MI: Dzanc Books, 2013).

Index

The letter *f* following a page number denotes a figure; the letter *t* denotes a table.

Franklyn, Delano, 233
Fraser, Shelly-Ann, 214, 235
Freedom House, 122
free press, 81, 123, 131, 333–334
free trade, 47, 48

Gambia, 76
gangs. *See* organized crime;
 violence
gay men, violence against, 165
GDP per capita, 29, 30*f*, 33*f*, 91,
 96–97, 108, 339n1. *See also*
 debt-to-GDP ratio; economic
 development
gender: education and, 70–72;
 employment and, 7–8, 188–202,
 208–210; population differences,
 42; violence against women, 153,
 157–160, 166–167. *See also*
 women
Gender Inequality Index, 72, 210
genetic theories on athleticism,
 214–218
genocide, 5, 322
geocultural theory on athleticism,
 229–230
geography of Barbados and
 Jamaica, 38–42, 111, 229–230
Germany, 53
Ghana, 76, 215, 260
Girvan, Norman, 118, 119, 229,
 231–232
Gleaner, 334
Global Banking and Finance, 3
globalization, 12–13, 257–260
glocalization: of music, 12–13,
 275, 277–278; as term, 12, 260

Goodison, Lorna, 336
Gordon, Derek, 190
Gordon, George William, 53
Gordon, Leo-Rey, 92
Gramsci, Antonio, 258
Grandmaster Flash, 274
Grant, John Peter, 55–56
Gray, Obika, 124, 144, 206, 207,
 325
Greenfield, Sidney, 71, 77, 78
Griffiths, Marcia, 268
Guatemala, 135, 170
"Gurkha syndrome," 74
Guyana, 50, 146

habitus, 155–156
Haiti, 53, 54, 146, 170
happiness, 4
Happy Planet Index, 4
Hardman, Dean, 237–238
Harris, Wynonie, 263
hawkers, 198, 199*t*, 201–202, 208,
 209, 293
health system. *See* public health
 system
HEART Trust/NTA, 329–330
Hebdige, Dick, 271
Hegre, H., 131–132
Henry, Peter, 6, 22, 28–38,
 101
Henry, Ronald, 133
herbal tonics, 235–236
Hibbert, Frederick "Toots," 12,
 264, 267
Higgins, Benjamin, 345n2
higglers, 198, 199*t*, 201–202, 208,
 209, 293

women: abuse of, 153, 157–160,
166–167, 325; businesses lead by,
319; color prejudice and, 342n5;
Manley's treatment of, 317–319;
as plantation slaves, 42; in
postcolonial labor force, 7–8,
171–173; slavery and sex ratio of,
43, 339n3; in urban populations,
188–191; white women on
Barbados, 44–45. *See also* gender
Workers Bank, 300
World Bank: on basic needs
approach, 286; on crime and
inequality, 139, 142, 144, 159;
on drug trade, 149; on education, 36*f*, 108–109; on governance, 33, 34*f*, 84; on Jamaican
economy, 3, 32, 33*f*, 178, 179;
on transparency, 164–165
World Happiness Report (2012), 4
Wretched of the Earth, The
(Fanon), 243

Zaire, 261
Zambia, 112
Zimbabwe, 112